D1997882

STRAIGHT THROUGH *from* LONDON

Rowley Taylor was born near Otahuhu, New Zealand, in 1931 and spent his school years in Whangarei and the Hutt Valley. He now lives in Nelson. An early interest in the outdoors and wildlife led to holiday employment with the Department of Scientific & Industrial Research (DSIR) in Wellington. In 1950 he joined the permanent staff of DSIR, and remained with them for the next 41 years – at first as a technical trainee and eventually as a scientist – studying the ecology and conservation of New Zealand's fauna and flora. This work took him throughout the country and on numerous expeditions to outlying islands and to Antarctica.

For 18 years he was a member of the Outlying Islands Reserves Committee which advised the Department of Lands & Survey on management and research issues concerning the Antipodes, Bounties and other remote island reserves. After retiring from Government service in 1991, he has continued similar work as a contractor or volunteer in New Zealand, Canada and Alaska – and has been a lecturer and guide on cruise ships to the subantarctic islands and Antarctica.

Rowley has authored over 80 research papers, but this is his first book.

C.N.Worsley

STRAIGHT THROUGH *from* LONDON

THE ANTIPODES AND BOUNTY ISLANDS, NEW ZEALAND

Rowley Taylor

To Pat (Patricia May Taylor, 1936–2005)
your inspiration, help and encouragement were crucial

First published in 2006 by Heritage Expeditions New Zealand Ltd.
P.O. Box 7218
53B Montreal Street
Christchurch
New Zealand

www.heritage-expeditions.com

Designed and typeset by Egan-Reid Ltd
www.eganreid.co.nz
Printed in China

ISBN 0-473-10650-7

A catalogue record for this book is available
from the National Library of New Zealand

Contents

Cover: Calm after the storm. Antipodes Island, 11 March 1969.

Frontispiece: A vice-regal party, including Lord and Lady Ranfurly, ashore at the Antipodes Islands, January 1902. Watercolour by Charles N. Worsley. (*Alexander Turnbull Library, Wellington, New Zealand D-022–013*)

List of Maps and Tables

MAPS

TABLES

Neither man nor beast could exist on the Bounty's, and had I known their nature, I would not have deemed it necessary to visit them.

– Henry Armstrong, 1868.

The Antipodes Islands have no harbours, very little or no soil, very little extent of country, and absolutely no history.

– Robert Carrick, 1892.

It was difficult as we stood away not to believe we were leaving friends [the penguins] ashore, not to flutter a farewell to this vast sea-going population, something of whose life we had for one portion of one day beheld. Then slowly the Bounty Island Group became a thing of the past. At length save in memory the group was gone, yet wonderful still it is to reflect on the modes of life that know no change.

– H. Guthrie-Smith, 1936.

Alas! that there should not have been days, weeks, months to be spent when there were only hours; moreover had I given the whole, every moment of this precious day to the Albatross I should not have tasted the happiness of the little parakeets, so fearless, so lovely in their loneliness, so contented with their simple fare of grass and stitchwort – I should have seen nothing of the Nellies – their rookeries represented by only two or three late straggling birds quite able to fly – or the pipits – or the penguins. Oh! if only on the Antipodes Islands I could but have recovered days sad in the loneliness of cities, wasted in futilities, squandered in the daily ineptitudes of life.

– H. Guthrie-Smith, 1936.

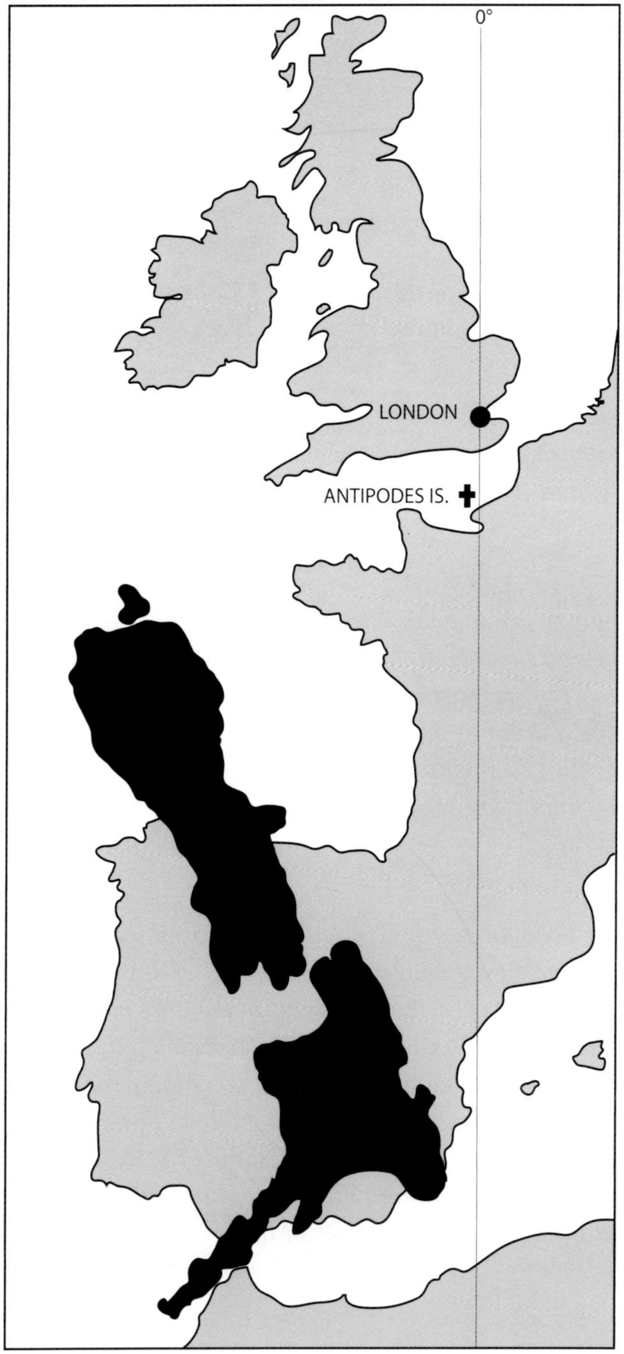

Antipodes.

Antipodes

The word "antipodes" is of Greek derivation (*anti*, opposed to; *podes*, feet), from the concept of people on opposite sides of the earth walking feet to feet. Any two places are antipodal when a straight line from one to the other passes through the centre of the globe. Such places will be distant from each other by 180 degrees of longitude, and one will be as many degrees to the north of the equator as the other is to the south. Noon at one is midnight at the other, and mid-winter at one corresponds with mid-summer at the other.

The Antipodes Islands are not exactly antipodal to London, but no other land is closer in this respect. The islands' true antipodes is a spot in the middle of the English Channel approximately halfway between Brighton and Le Havre. Knowing this, their discoverer in 1800, Captain Waterhouse, carefully named them Penantipode (*pen* being from the Latin *paene*, almost). However, within 10 years the name Antipodes Islands was in common use by sealers and Sydney merchants.

Preface

My first practical introduction to New Zealand's outlying islands was in March 1954. As a young technician with the then Animal Ecology Section of the Department of Scientific and Industrial Research (DSIR), I was invited (at 20 hours' notice) to voyage south with zoologists Dick Dell and Peter Bull on a three-man Dominion Museum/DSIR expedition. We were taken to the Auckland Islands by the coaster *Holmlea* – on a mission to Macquarie Island – and picked up four days later on the vessel's return north.

Our party's first landfall was in the dark, through surf, on to Sandy Bay beach, Enderby Island. The lively reception given by the resident sea lions as we carried our gear to the castaway boat shed remains well imprinted in my memory; as also are first recollections of the wild, deserted nature of the islands. The shed, built in 1888, was full of history. There was the old boat itself and various sealing and whaling artefacts – unfortunately all long since purloined and lost. This short trip kindled an intense and now longstanding interest in the history, ecology and conservation of these remote and most isolated parts of New Zealand.

Much has been published on the history of the Auckland and Campbell Islands, but very little about the Antipodes and Bounties. The desire to redress the balance arose in 1969, during the University of Canterbury Antipodes Island expedition. We were camped next to the old castaway depot with its interior covered with the names of ships, seafarers and dates going back to 1886; it still contained castaway provisions, and when exploring the island we discovered 19th-century sealers' huts and ancient caches of penguin skins.

Then and later, on both the Antipodes and Bounty Islands, I was involved in population surveys of New Zealand fur seals that required research into earlier numbers. All this provided the necessary stimulus. Subsequent searching-out and assembling of information, published and unpublished, revealed that the two island groups had rich, but little-known, histories.

This book is the result. It deals with the history of the islands from the discovery of the Bounty Islands by Captain Bligh of HMS *Bounty* in 1788, to the year 2000 – the bicentenary of the first sighting of Antipodes Island by Captain Waterhouse of HMS *Reliance*. The narrative relates the islands' discovery; exploitation by sealers; shipwrecks; the establishment of castaway depots; patrols by Government steamers; attempts to promote pastoral farming; and visits by naval ships, fishing vessels, scientists, government officials and tourist expeditions.

Despite a human contact spanning over 200 years, the islands, their plants and animals remain in a remarkably natural state. Fur seal populations, once harvested to the brink of extinction, are now recovering on both island groups. Fortunately, the vegetation of the Antipodes has never been modified by fire or grazing animals, despite attempts in the 1890s to lease these islands for pastoral purposes. With a flourishing wildlife and several species of endemic plants, birds and invertebrates, the islands are truly unique, and today are totally protected.

Unlike at the Auckland Islands, which were once known as a "graveyard of sailing ships", there have been no recorded shipwrecks at the Bounty Islands and only three at the Antipodes – the three-masted barque *Spirit of the Dawn* in 1893, the four-masted barque *Président Félix Faure* in 1908, and the sailing research vessel *Totorore* in 1999. Considering the islands' early sealing history, their position on the favoured sailing route from the Indian Ocean and Australia around Cape Horn, and the occasional finding of unidentified wreckage, it is likely that others occurred. During fog or darkness, sailing ships could have been driven onto the rock-bound shores and sunk without trace. Discussing the Antipodes Islands in 1893, Captain Fairchild of the Government steamer *Hinemoa* thought it was "fairly certain that vessels were lost there of which nothing was ever heard", with their disappearance being

The wreck of the French barque *Président Félix Faure* at Antipodes Islands, 1908.

blamed on striking an iceberg or catching on fire. He concluded: "The only thing is for captains to give these islands as wide a berth as possible." Readers may agree that the survivors of the first two wrecks could be considered fortunate to have got ashore. There were no survivors from the *Totorore*.

For over half a century, I have been privileged to visit all of New Zealand's outlying islands from the Kermadecs to Campbell Island – as well as Macquarie Island and Antarctica – on numerous scientific and tourist expeditions. My most vivid memories of these trips are not so much of the work done but of people and their interactions with the often harsh environment. Unfortunately, much history can only be retrieved from official reports and documents where the recorded details often cloak a fuller and more exciting story. I have often felt frustrated by this while writing the present account, and owe a debt to those that have shared their reminiscences with me. The following helped considerably with recollections, advice, documents, and illustrations:

Jacinda Amey; Alan Baker; Sandy Bartle; Kerry Barton; Alex Black; Brian Bell; Grainger Brown; Jeremy Carroll; Martin Cawthorn; Sean Cooper; Andy

Cox; Lloyd Davis; Elliot Dawson; Paul Dingwall; Graeme Elliott; Pamela Fingleton; Jane Forsyth; Henk Haazen; Robert Headland; Brian Hooker; John Hollins; Woody Horning; Norm Judd; Alan Knowles; Mary LeCroy; John Ling; Pete McClelland; Colin Meurk; John Newton; Baden Norris; Andy O'Grady; Rhys Richards; Tom Ritchie; Chris Robertson; Margaret Rooney; Rodney, Shirley, Aaron and Nathan Russ; Chris Sale; Lance Shaw; Wendy Shaw; Leif Skog; Mickey Squires; Rob Stanley; Graeme Taylor; Alan Tennyson; John Thomson; Ian Turnbull; Kath Walker; John Warham; Murray Williams; and Peter Wilson. I am grateful to them all – and especially to Kath Walker and Graeme Elliott, who provided so much detail regarding the last 10 years of the islands' history.

I also wish to record my thanks to all those who have previously written, preserved, compiled, and archived material on the Antipodes and Bounty Islands. Unfortunately for those interested in researching the early maritime history of New Zealand, most Marine Department files and records dated prior to 1911 were destroyed, or severely damaged, in a 1952 fire in the Hope Gibbons Building, Wellington.

While researching this book I have been greatly assisted by the collections and staff at the Rakiura Museum, Stewart Island; New Zealand Department of Conservation, Invercargill; Hocken Library, Dunedin; McNab New Zealand Collection, Dunedin Public Libraries; Canterbury Museum, Christchurch; University of Canterbury, Christchurch; Archives New Zealand, Dunedin and Wellington; Alexander Turnbull Library and National Library, Wellington; Museum of Wellington City and Sea; New Zealand Ship and Marine Society, Wellington; Museum of New Zealand/Te Papa Tongarewa, Wellington; New Zealand Geographic Board, Wellington; Nelson Public Library; Nelson Museum; Auckland War Memorial Museum Library; Pacific Manuscripts Bureau, Canberra; State Library of Tasmania, Hobart; American Museum of Natural History, New York; G.W. Blunt Library, Mystic Seaport Museum, USA; United States Coast Guard, Washington; National Archives, Washington; National Maritime Museum, Greenwich; Public Record Office, London; United Kingdom Hydrographic Office, Taunton; Liverpool Museum and William Brown Library; and the Merseyside Maritime Museum.

I owe a debt to the following people who read through one or more of the chapters and made many helpful comments: Elliot Dawson, Graeme Elliott, Rhys Richards, Rodney Russ, Kath Walker, Murray Williams and John Yaldwyn. Nevertheless, errors and opinions remain mine.

I especially wish to thank Pat Taylor, my wife, for her continual support. After decades of looking after home and family while I was away, she at last discovered for herself the charm of the subantarctic during a cruise on *Pacific Ruby* in 1992–93. Subsequently, Pat accompanied me on many visits to archives, museums and libraries, helped search old files and newspapers, read and criticised each bit of the text as it was written, and gave lots of ongoing encouragement and advice.

Finally, sincere thanks are due to the New Zealand History Research Trust Fund, Ministry of Culture and Heritage, for generous financial assistance and support.

The title *Straight Through from London* was originally used by the *New Zealand Listener* for an interview with Dr R.A. (later Sir Robert) Falla published in December 1950.

CHAPTER ONE

Introduction

The Antipodes Islands and the Bounty Islands are the most easterly of New Zealand's subantarctic islands. They lie 220 kilometres apart and over 800 kilometres east-south-east of the port of Bluff, Southland, and about 450 and 220 kilometres respectively south-west of the Chatham Islands. The two groups rise from the Bounty Platform, an extension of the relatively shallow sub-marine Campbell Plateau to the south-east of New Zealand. Over 80 million years ago, before the south-west Pacific Ocean formed by a process of continental drift, this plateau – along with the rest of New Zealand, Antarctica and Australia – was part of the super-continent of Gondwanaland. Basement rocks beneath the plateau include granite, schist and greywacke.

The Antipodes and Bounty Islands, together with their widely scattered neighbours – Campbell Island, the Auckland Islands and the Snares – are sovereign territories of New Zealand, and are economically important in defining the limits of New Zealand's Exclusive Economic Zone. The Antipodes and Bounties have no harbours and landing is often difficult. They are remote and, except for fur seals, possess no exploitable resources – so have remained the least visited of New Zealand's outlying islands, even in modern times.

Because of the outstanding value of their relatively undisturbed ecosystems, the Antipodes and Bounty Islands were declared Reserves for the Preservation of Fauna and Flora in 1961. Later, they were reclassified as Nature Reserves under the Reserves Act 1977;[1] and in 1986, they and their foreshores down to the mean low-tide mark were accorded National Reserve status. As with all other New Zealand subantarctic islands, this dual status gives the Bounties and Antipodes the highest level of protection available under New Zealand law.

As nature reserves, the islands cannot be visited unless a landing permit has been granted by the Department of Conservation (DOC). All physical contact is otherwise prohibited, and this includes mooring a boat to the shore. No plants or animals may be taken or introduced without a permit. As National Reserves, the status of the islands cannot be revoked or changed except by an Act of Parliament. Other legislation safeguarding the islands' ecosystems includes the Wildlife Act 1953 and the Marine Mammals Protection Act 1978, which absolutely protect indigenous wildlife and apply to both the land and territorial waters.

Equally importantly, New Zealand's subantarctic islands were inscribed on the World Heritage List in 1998 as natural areas of "outstanding universal value". New Zealand, as a signatory of the World Heritage Convention, has thus pledged to ensure their continued protection and conservation for future generations.[2]

ANTIPODES ISLANDS

The Antipodes Island Group is made up of a main island, six smaller islands up to one kilometre offshore, and numerous sea stacks and rocks. All are steep-sided. The total area of the islands is 2097 hectares. Antipodes Island (2025 ha) measures about seven kilometres by five kilometres, and its highest point on the summit of Mount Galloway is 366 metres above sea level. The only other island of any size is Bollons (50 ha).

The Antipodes are entirely volcanic and geologically are by far the youngest of New Zealand's subantarctic islands. The main island was formed during several volcanic periods. The oldest volcanic flows, ash and breccias (some containing fragments of basement granite and sedimentary rocks) have been dated at up to five million years old. After erosion took place,

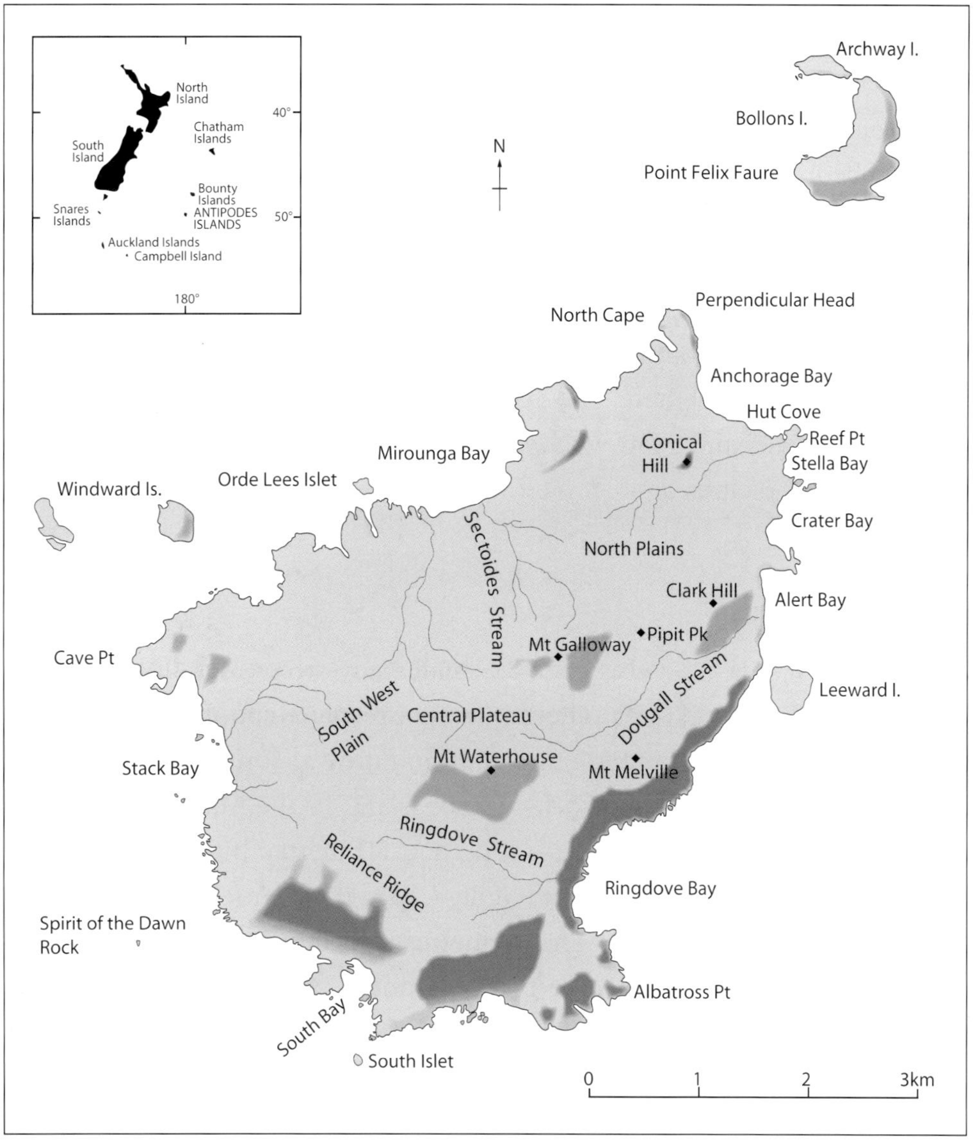

Antipodes Island Group.

these were overlain by further volcanics – the contact being marked by a layer of old beach boulders. In turn, these rocks were covered by more ash and lava flows sloping into the centre of the island. Smaller volcanic centres of similar rocks form Windward, Leeward, and Bollons and Archway Islands. The last period of volcanism formed a central cone, represented by Mounts Waterhouse and Galloway, as well as columnar basalt flows at Anchorage and Crater Bays. These rocks are as young as half a million years.[3]

The coasts consist mainly of sea cliffs up to 160 metres high which are indented by narrow coves and spectacular sea caves. Boulder beaches are few, and scattered at the heads of small sheltered bays and coves. Often they are inaccessible except from the sea. Streams are entrenched in gullies, down to bedrock, and small waterfalls are common around the coast. Much of the main island is a high undulating plateau surrounding the central peaks. There are no lakes, only a few small ponds and swamps. Nearly all the land is covered by a deep layer of spongy peat, formed over thousands of years from slowly decomposing plant material, under the influence of high humidity and a cool climate. The vegetation is mainly tussock grasses, ferns, herbaceous plants and a few woody shrubs. Chapter 20 deals with the fauna and flora of the islands.

BOUNTY ISLANDS

The Bounty Islands are a cluster of 22 small spray-swept rocky islands, with a total area of 135 hectares. The entire group spans about 4.5 kilometres from east to west and three kilometres from north to south, and includes a number of partly submerged rocks. Depot Island in the Main Group is the largest island (roughly 700 metres long and 50 metres high), whereas the much smaller islands of Funnel and Molly Cap in the Centre and East Groups are the highest – at 73 metres and 70 metres respectively.

All these islets are of coarse biotite granite, with some finer-grained variations, and are the eroded remnants of a ridge of buckled and uplifted basement rock. They provide a rare example of the ancient basement that lies beneath the Campbell Plateau. Now worn smooth near sea level and fractured in angular blocks higher up, the granite of the islands has been dated at around 190 million years old. Three younger basaltic dikes have also been found cutting across several of the islands.[4]

All shores at the Bounties are steep, and no beaches of any sort exist. In summer the islands are thick with breeding seabirds, and above the spray zone a surface layer of polished guano covers the rocks, making them very slippery underfoot when wet. This thin guano crust is essentially of the mineral struvite, and has been formed by precipitation and crystallisation of excreta within the protected micro-enviroment of tiny crevices and pits on the rock surface.[5]

There is no true soil, but hollows become filled with organic mud derived

Bounty Islands.

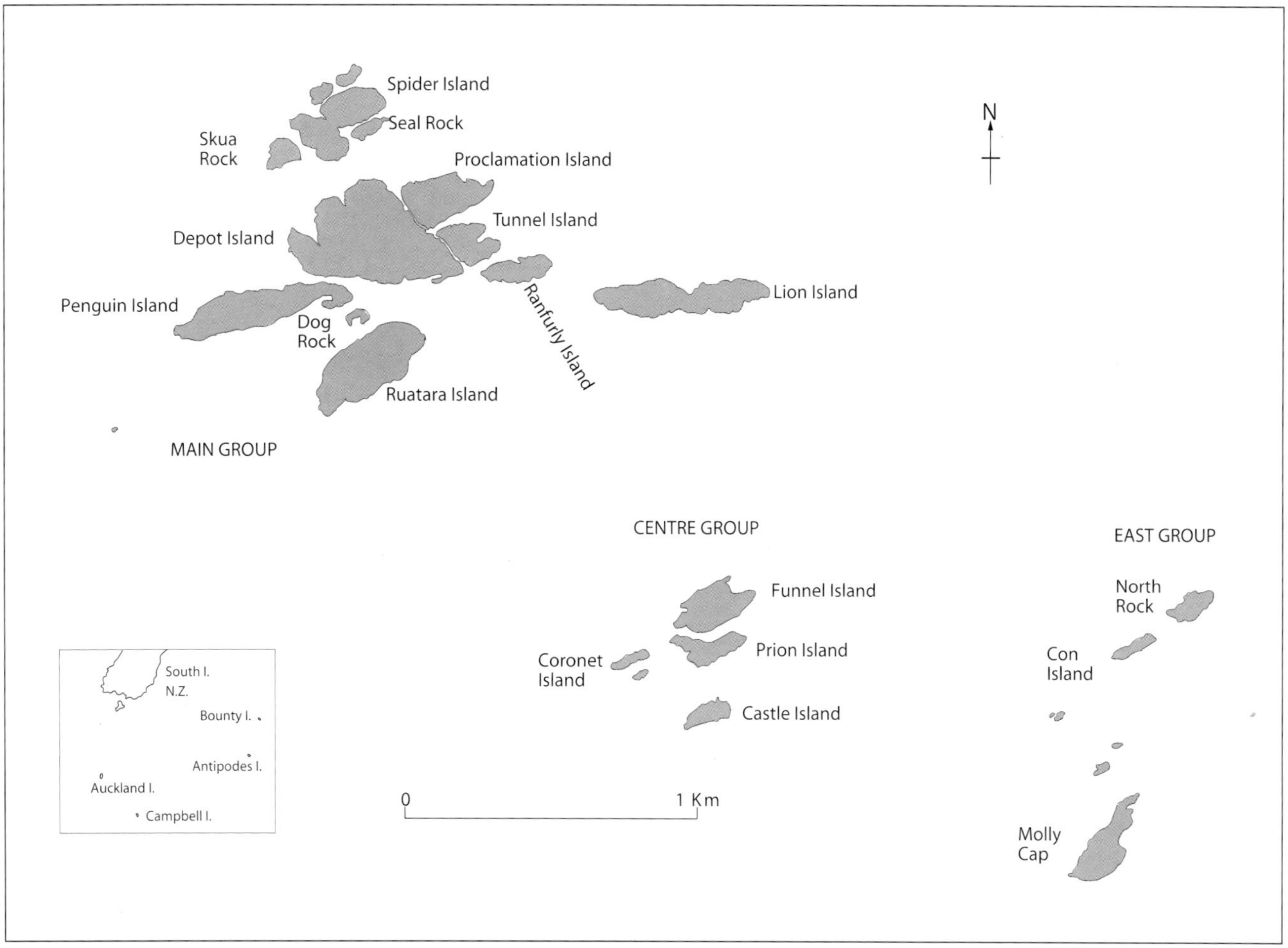

from dead birds, moulted feathers, bird guano and regurgitated food, seal dung, seaweed and freshwater algae. Vascular plants are limited to a few specimens of one species (*Lepidium oleraceum*) on the two highest islands.[6] Other land vegetation comprises lichens and algae. In summer immense numbers of seabirds and fur seals arrive to breed, and these secure all their food from the sea.

THE SURROUNDING SEAS

The Antipodes Islands lie close to the Subantarctic Front and between two other oceanographic features – the Subtropical Front (or Convergence) near the Chatham Islands, and the Polar Front near Macquarie Island. Each of these three fronts mark steep hydrological gradients between relatively warm, salty waters to the north and cooler, less saline waters to the south. In these latitudes strong prevailing winds drive the surface waters eastwards, at a rate equal to about two per cent of wind speed. The Bounty Islands are located to the south of the Subtropical Front where the warm, saline water of the East Cape Current meets the cooler, less saline waters of the West Wind Drift.

Infra-red measurements by satellite of sea-surface temperatures around New Zealand's five subantarctic island groups show January and August monthly mean values as follows: Campbell Island (9°C, 5.5°C), Auckland Islands (11°C, 7.5°C), Antipodes Island (11°C, 6.5°C), Bounty Islands (13°C, 8°C) and Snares Islands (12°C, 9°C). Winter water temperatures at the Antipodes are colder than at the much more southerly Auckland Islands because, from about 170° W longitude, the West Wind Drift drives the Subantarctic Front northwards around the eastern side of the Campbell Plateau.

At the Antipodes Islands the tidal range is somewhat less than one metre, and the entire coastline is exposed to ocean swells. On some steep headlands the wave impact is too great for kelp to grow. Narrow tidal platforms occur along parts of the eastern coastline, and in some bays the seafloor slopes at 5–10° out to about 300 metres offshore. Here there are thick, subtidal forests of massive bull-kelp *Durvillaea antarctica* and, further out, small beds of the

South coast of Antipodes from Reliance Ridge.

bladder kelp *Macrocystis pyrifera*. The coastline of the Bounties is everywhere exposed to heavy seas. Underwater, the slopes are very steep and rough, with ledges and overhangs. In some narrow channels there is a "sandy" seafloor composed of shells and the bones of seals and birds.[7]

CLIMATE

Although the Antipodes Islands are approximately antipodal to London, the climates of the two places are vastly different, for the Antipodes and Bounties are in the persistent westerly wind belt of the "Roaring Forties" and surrounded by the cold Southern Ocean. The climate of both groups is characterised by strong westerly winds; frequent cloud, fog, rain and drizzle; cool temperatures with little annual or daily variation; and high humidity (usually above 70 per cent). Over 80 per cent of the winds have a westerly component, with north-westerlies being the most common.

Air temperatures at Reef Point, Antipodes Island, are typically between 2° and 7°C (recorded range 0–11°C) in June; and between 7° and 13° (recorded range 2–18°C) in February. Temperatures on the Central Plateau are about 3° cooler. At both islands, hail can fall in any month, and snow has frequently been recorded at Antipodes Island between May and November.

Visitors to the Antipodes have often noted the apparent "dryness" of the peat compared to that on other southern islands, suggesting a lower rainfall. However, accurate precipitation records have been made there for only a few months over widely scattered years – and never at the Bounty Islands. The average annual rainfall at the Chatham and Macquarie Islands is about 900 mm, and at Campbell about 1400 mm. As rainfall at the Antipodes seems to be fairly evenly spread with a slight autumn maximum – as at the other islands mentioned – the available records suggest a total of around 650 mm falling on about 280 days of the year. Rainfall and rain days at the Bounty Islands should be less, due to the islands' low profile and hence minimum interference with frontal weather systems.[8]

CHAPTER TWO

Discovery

HMS *BOUNTY*

There is an interesting historical connection between Tahiti in the lush tropical Pacific and the discovery of the spray-swept, desolate Bounty Islands. Breadfruit is the fruit of *Artocarpus altilis*, a tree native to the Pacific region. The large starchy fruit is melon-sized and was once a staple item in the diet of South Sea islanders. The famous navigator and privateer William Dampier had first described its merits in 1688, but it was largely brought to the notice of the outside world following Captain James Cook's three voyages of exploration in the Pacific Ocean (1768–71, 1772–75, and 1776–79).[1]

Both Cook and Sir Joseph Banks, who had visited Tahiti with Cook in 1769, were of the opinion that it might be successfully cultivated in the West Indian colonies – and recommended its transplantation there. It was not long before London merchants and planters with interests in these colonies made

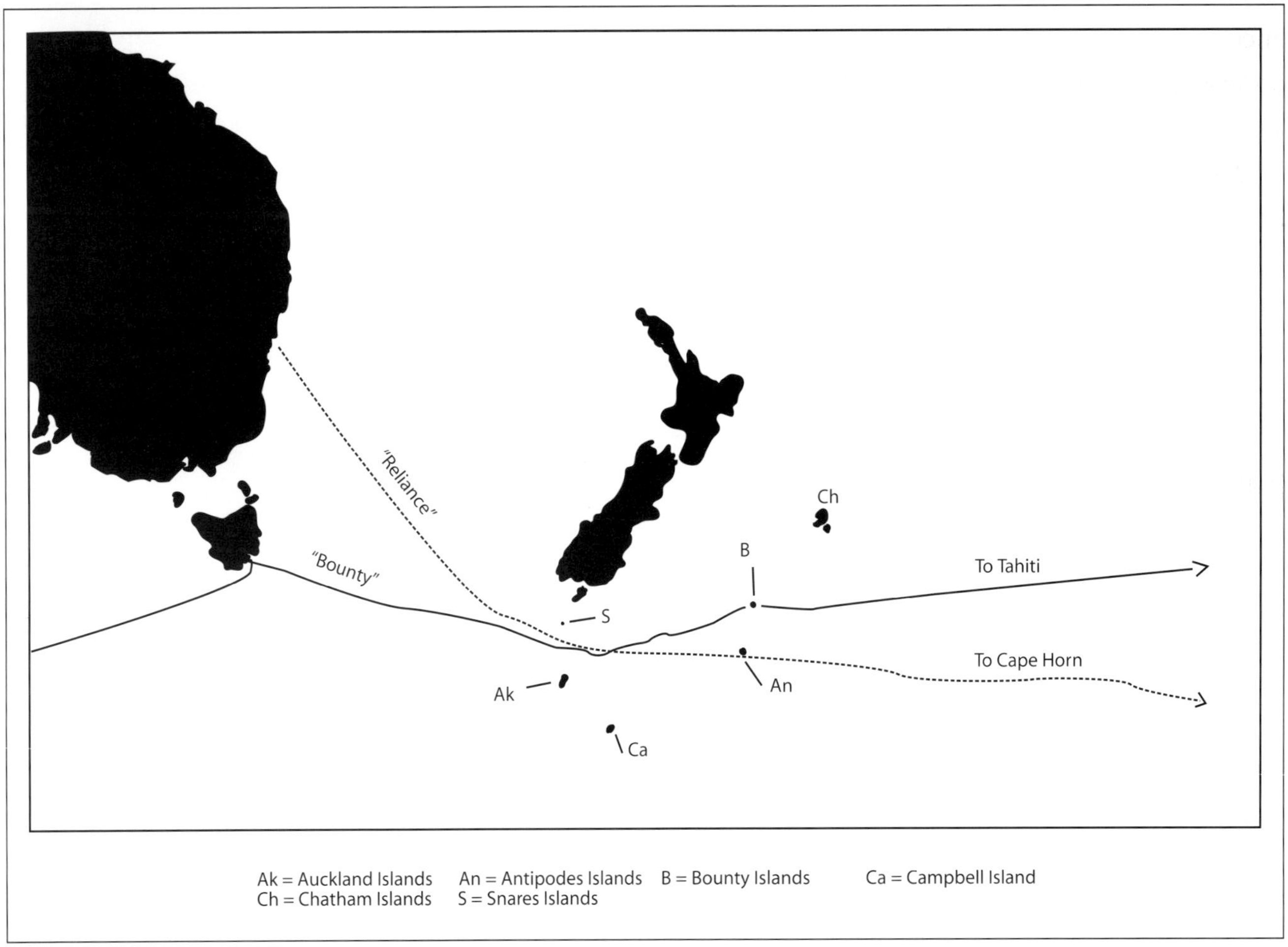

The sailing tracks of HMS *Bounty* in 1788, and HMS *Reliance* in 1800.

representations to King George III for breadfruit trees to be introduced to the British Caribbean to help feed the slave population. The King agreed, so in 1787, the British Government sent HMS *Bounty* commanded by Lieutenant William Bligh to Tahiti, to collect as many breadfruit trees as possible and convey them to the West Indies (Bligh had previously served four years in the *Resolution* as sailing master under Captain Cook). After failing to round Cape Horn, due to the lateness of the season and contrary winds, the *Bounty* sailed via the Cape of Good Hope and St. Paul Island for Van Diemen's Land (Tasmania). After re-provisioning with wood and water at Captain Cook's old anchorage in Adventure Bay, Bruny Island, Bligh "steered towards the ESE", and in mid-September 1788 passed to the south of New Zealand expecting to encounter constant westerly winds. At dawn on 19 September 1788 the crew observed a cluster of small rocky islands about four leagues off the port bow. Thus the Bounty Islands were discovered.[2]

Later, after the *Bounty* had left Tahiti loaded with over one thousand breadfruit plants, the famous mutiny on the *Bounty* occurred. Bligh and 18 of his crew were set adrift in a small boat in the central Pacific Ocean. After many hardships Bligh ultimately reached England, and was once again commissioned to transplant the breadfruit trees. This was successfully accomplished in the years 1792–93.[3]

Regarding the first ever sighting of the Bounty Islands, Lieutenant Bligh's journal for 19 September 1788 records:

> At day-light, we discovered a cluster of small rocky islands, bearing east by north four leagues distant from us. We had seen no birds, or anything to indicate the nearness of land, except patches of rock-weed, for which the vicinity of New Zealand sufficiently accounted. The wind being NE prevented our near approach to these isles; so that we were not less than three leagues distant in passing to the southward of them. The weather was too thick to see distinctly: their extent was only 3½ miles from east to west, and about half a league from north to south: their number, including the smaller ones, was thirteen. I could not observe any verdure on any of them: there were white spots like patches of snow; but, as Captain Cook, in describing the land of New Zealand, near South Cape, says, in many places there are patches of white marble, it is probable that what we saw might be of the same kind as what he had observed. The westernmost of these islands is the largest; they are of sufficient height to be seen at the distance of seven leagues from the ship's deck. When the easternmost bore north, I tried for soundings, being then 10 miles distant from the nearest of them, and found bottom at 75 fathoms, a fine white sand: and again at noon, having run six leagues more to the ESE, we had soundings at 104 fathoms, a fine brimstone-coloured sand. The latitude of these islands is 47° 44′ S; their longitude 179° 7′ E, which is about 145 leagues to the east of the Traps, near the south end of New Zealand. Variation of the compass here

Facing page: Part of "Map of the Antarctic and Sub-Antarctic Regions" published in 1909. Showing the reported positions of the mythical Emerald Island, Royal Company Islands, and the Nimrod Group. The position of the equally imaginary Dougherty or Keates Island, given as 59° S, 120° W, was about halfway between the Antipodes and Cape Horn. South is at the top of the map. (*Philosophical Institute of Canterbury.*)

> 17° E. While in sight of the islands, we saw some penguins, and a white kind of gull with a forked tail. Captain Cook's track, in 1773, was near this spot, but he did not see the islands: he saw seals and penguins hereabouts, but considered New Zealand to be the nearest land. I have named them after the ship, the Bounty Isles.[4]

The group comprises 20 small islands as well as some rocks in three distinct clusters (Main, Centre and East). Many islands in the Main Group are very close together, so it is not surprising that Bligh was unable to count them all when passing "three leagues" to the south. The islands cover about 4.5 kilometres from east to west and the highest point is 73 metres above sea level. Bligh was right about the lack of any vegetation. The "white spots like patches of snow" were not marble, as Bligh supposed, since the islands are composed entirely of granite. Rather, he was seeing light reflected from a surface of hard polished guano. In summer, several hundred thousand seabirds breed there, but they would have been away for the winter at the time of the *Bounty*'s visit. Bligh was a renowned navigator but he was using a cut-price experimental chronometer (K2) with known defects.[5] Nevertheless, his assigned position for the islands varied from modern readings by only one minute of latitude and four minutes of longitude.

It seems that after Bligh's visit, the islands were not sighted again for 16 years. It has been claimed that the British frigate HMS *Pandora* "touched at the islands on her quest for the fugitive mutineers".[6] However, this is wrong. Captain Edward Edwards did not follow Bligh's track. After rounding Cape Horn he arrived at Tahiti in March 1791, and later searched various islands of the Central Pacific before the *Pandora* was wrecked on the Great Barrier Reef in August the same year.

HMS *RELIANCE*

The little sloop of war had seen better days. Only a year before the 90ft-long vessel had been condemned as unseaworthy by the Royal Navy, and laid up in Port Jackson, in the 12-year-old colony of New South Wales. Now having

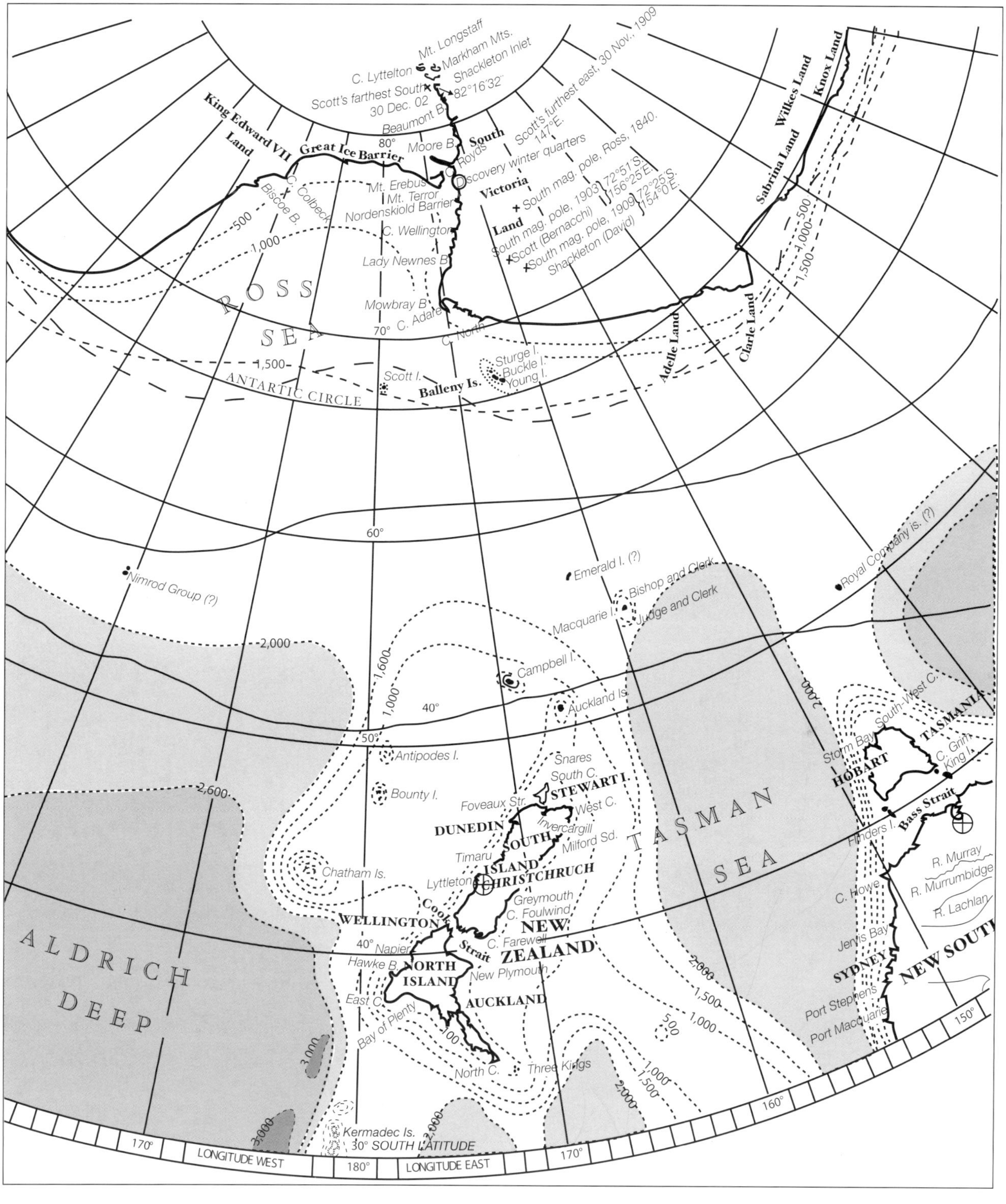

C. Lyttelton
Mt. Longstaff
Markham Mts.
Shackleton Inlet
82°16'32'
Scott's farthest South
30 Dec. 02
Beaumont B.
Scott's furthest east, 30 Nov., 1909
147°E.
Wilkes Land
Knox Land
King Edward VII Land
Great Ice Barrier
80°
Moore B.
C. Royds
South
Victoria
Land
Discovery winter quarters
South mag. pole, Ross, 1840.
Sabrina Land
Mt. Erebus
Mt. Terror
Nordenskiold Barrier
C. Colbeck
Biscoe B.
500
1,000
1,500
C. Wellington
South mag. pole, 1903 72°51'S. 156°25'E.
Scott (Bernacchi)
South mag. pole, 1909 72°25'S. 154°0'E.
Shackleton (David)
Lady Newnes B.
ROSS SEA
Mowbray B.
C. Adare
70°
C. North
Adelle Land
Clarie Land
Sturge I.
Buckle I.
Young I.
Scott I.
Balleny Is.
ANTARTIC CIRCLE
60°
Emerald I. (?)
Nimrod Group (?)
Bishop and Clerk
Judge and Clerk
Macquarie I.
Royal Company Is. (?)
2,000
1,600
Campbell I.
Auckland Is.
40°
50°
Antipodes I.
Bounty I.
Snares
South C.
STEWART I.
Foveaux Str.
West C.
DUNEDIN
Invercargill
SOUTH ISLAND
Milford Sd.
Timaru
CHRISTCHURCH
Lyttleton
Chatham Is.
Greymouth
C. Foulwind
WELLINGTON
Cook Strait
NEW ZEALAND
C. Farewell
Napier
Hawke B.
NORTH ISLAND
New Plymouth
East C.
AUCKLAND
Bay of Plenty
North C.
Three Kings
2,600
3,000
ALDRICH DEEP
Kermadec Is.
30° SOUTH LATITUDE
TASMAN SEA
South-West C.
Storm Bay
TASMANIA
HOBART
C. Grim
King I.
Bass Strait
Flinders I.
R. Murray
R. Murrumbidgee
R. Lachlan
C. Howe
Jervis Bay
SYDNEY
NEW SOUTH
Port Stephens
Port Macquarie
150°
160°
170°
180°
LONGITUDE WEST
LONGITUDE EAST

been re-caulked and re-masted at Sydney Cove, she was on her way home to Portsmouth while still fit to face the long ocean voyage around Cape Horn.[7] His Majesty's Ship *Reliance* was 23 days out, south-east of New Zealand, and being battered by rough seas and strong westerly gales. Captain Henry Waterhouse reckoned there were still over 1350 leagues of empty ocean to the Horn, but at two hours after midnight on 26 March 1800, those on watch were the first to see Antipodes Island.[8]

A casual glance at a map of the South Pacific could suggest that the *Reliance* was well off-course, but in the days of sail, ships leaving Australia for Europe followed the Great Circle Route – the fastest line of travel. At first steering south of New Zealand to pick up the strong, predictable westerly winds of the Roaring Forties and Furious Fifties, they were then driven westward towards South America or around Cape Horn. These patterns of winds and shipping had also led to the chance finding, 12 years earlier, of the Bounty Islands – the first of New Zealand's subantarctic islands to be discovered.

OUTPOSTS IN THE SOUTHERN OCEAN

From New Zealand the Southern Ocean stretches eastwards over 7000 km towards Cape Horn, and southwards almost 3000 km to Antarctica. In this vast tract of ocean below 40° S and north of the pack ice there are only seven small island groups. All are within 900 km of New Zealand and, except for the Chatham Islands, all lie to the south of the subtropical convergence and were uninhabited when discovered by early European navigators.

Four of these groups were encountered by chance by British Royal Navy ships in transit across the South Pacific bound for Cape Horn, the Society Islands or North America. A passing British whaler was the first to see the Auckland Islands. Campbell and Macquarie were the last two islands to be discovered during a search by an Australian vessel for new sealing grounds. Notable dates are:

1–5 December 1773. Captain James Cook during his second voyage of exploration in HMS *Resolution* passes about 90 km to the east of the Bounty Islands and 110 km south east of the Antipodes Islands on his southward probe towards Antarctica.

19 September 1788. Lieutenant William Bligh in HMS *Bounty* discovers the Bounty Islands on his way from Tasmania to the Society Islands.

23 November 1791. Commander George Vancouver in HMS *Discovery* bound from Dusky Sound to Tahiti discovers the Snares Islands. Later that day the islands are sighted independently from the armed tender HMS *Chatham* and named Knight's Islands.

29 November 1791. Lieutenant William Broughton in HMS *Chatham* sights the Chatham Islands, lands and encounters the Moriori inhabitants.

26 March 1800. Captain Henry Waterhouse in HMS *Reliance* discovers the Antipodes Islands while en route from Sydney to Cape Horn.

18 August 1806. Captain Abraham Bristow in the whaler *Ocean* returning to England from Tasmania discovers the Auckland Islands and names them Lord Auckland's Islands.

Early January 1810. Captain Frederick Hasselburg in the sealing brig *Perseverance* discovers Campbell Island and names it after his employers, Campbell & Co. of Sydney.

11 July 1810. Hasselburg in the *Perseverance* discovers Macquarie Island, and names it after the Governor of New South Wales.

From time to time during the 19th century, ships traversing this stretch of the Southern Ocean claimed to have discovered other islands. Those that made it onto early published charts included the Royal Company Islands, the Nimrod Group, Dougherty Island and Emerald Island. Despite dogged searches by sealers desperate for profitable new grounds, no further trace of these mythical islands was ever found. The most likely explanation is that all were icebergs.

The sloop was tracking a general course taking it over 100 nautical miles south of the known position of the Bounty Islands when, through darkness and squally weather, land was unexpectedly sighted only two miles off the lee beam. The episode was recorded in the ship's log:

> March 1800. Wednesday 26. Wind West. Course S 88° E. Distance [travelled in last 24 hours] 131. Latd. in South 49° 51′ Longd. in East 180° 5′. Strong gales and squally, handed the Fore Topsail. A.M. at 2 discovered land on our lee beam about 2 miles distant, hauled to the wind and stood off, at daybreak wore and stood in for the land, which proved to be a desolate, mountainous, and barren Island, scarce any verdure to be seen upon it, at 6 running along the eastern coast of the Island, at 8 bore up and stood on our course the eastern extremity of the land – SbW to SWbW, distant from a small Island at the NE end of the large one, 3 miles, at 9 the small Island bore WbS distant 3 leagues.[9]

The group was charted during these manoeuvres, and the resulting sketch is surprisingly accurate. It shows most of the prominent coastal features of the southern, eastern and northern coasts, and includes five of the outlying islets – and the ship's track. This sketch map was "copied" (drawn in final form) by Midshipman Samuel Flinders, and is now in the National Maritime Museum, Greenwich.[10]

Captain Waterhouse named the larger island "Isle Penantipode" – "from its approach to the Antipodes of London". He reported that "there were seals

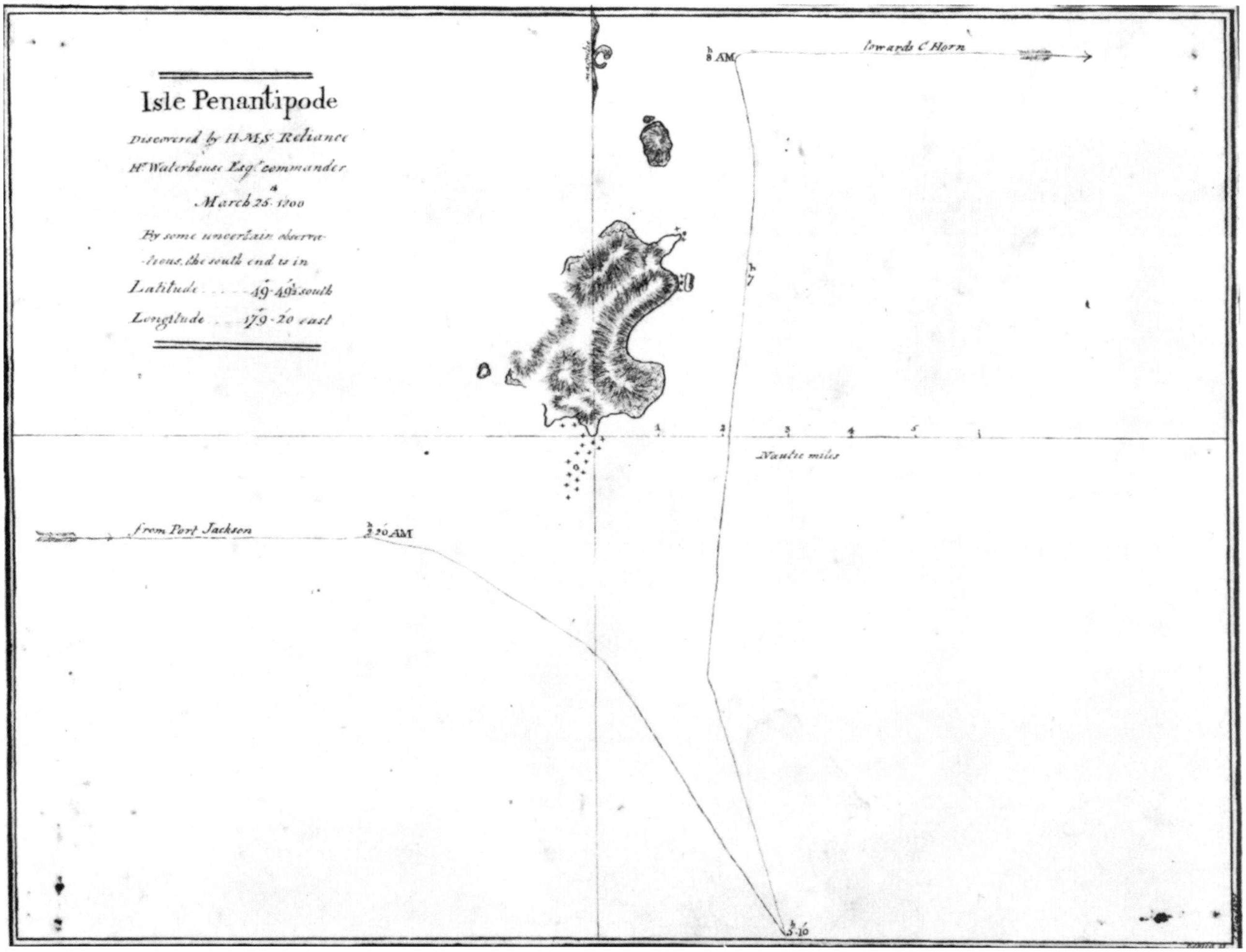

"Isle Penantipode" as charted on 25 March 1800 by HMS *Reliance*, Henry Waterhouse, Commander. (*National Maritime Museum, Greenwich, C 1714.*)

on it, and it did not appear quite so large as Norfolk Island". He calculated the position of the south end of the main island as 49° 49′ 30″ S and 179° 20′ E, but noted that as the nearest of the double altitudes by which the ship's position was determined (as entered in the ship's log, see above) was nearly four hours after leaving the island:

> the latitude ought not to be depended on nearer than 5′ to 10′. The error of the chronometer being uncertain at the time, no correction was applied to the longitude, which may very probably be within half a degree, or much nearer.[11]

The Antipodes Islands comprise Antipodes Island (Waterhouse's

"Penantipode"), six nearby smaller islands, and numerous inshore stacks and rocks. The second "small island" noted by Waterhouse as being "at the NE end of the large one" would have been Bollons Island. As we have seen, the main island consists of an elevated plateau with hills reaching about 400 metres above sea level. The vegetation above the towering cliffs and rocky shores is predominantly tussock and fern. No doubt, as seen by the crew of the *Reliance* through rain and spray, and in the early morning light, it appeared particularly barren and forlorn. Obviously, Captain Waterhouse was well aware of possible inaccuracies in his charted position. In the event, his calculated latitude was out by 8′ and his longitude by 33′ – more or less within the limits of accuracy he suggested.

CHAPTER THREE

The Early Sealers

George Bass was the surgeon on HMS *Reliance* for most of its five-year (1795–1800) tour of duty in the New South Wales. With Mathew Flinders he carried out several explorations of the south-eastern Australian coastline, and discovered Bass strait in 1797–98. Bass was much more than a Royal Navy surgeon. He was also an expert navigator and seaman, while at heart remaining an explorer and adventurer. Flinders described him as "a man whose ardour for discovery was not to be repressed by any obstacles nor deterred by any danger".[1]

Bass left Port Jackson in May 1799, having been granted sick leave by the navy. After only a few months in London, he again left for Sydney in December 1800 as "Supercargo and managing owner" aboard the *Venus*, a brig of 142 tons commanded by his trading partner Charles Bishop. Captain Bishop was an experienced British mariner who had pioneered the Bass Strait sealing trade in 1798 with the brig *Nautilus*.

By November 1802 the two partners had completed a profitable voyage to New Zealand and the South Sea islands, under contract to the supply-starved colony. This amazing venture involved 14 days in Dusky Sound, Fiordland, cutting timber to make casks and reclaiming unwrought ballast iron from the wreck of Captain Brampton's old ship *Endeavour*.

The *Venus*'s blacksmith converted the iron into axes, and on arriving at Tahiti these and other goods were traded for pork. Over 120,000 pounds of pork was salted and packed into the casks made at Dusky Sound, and into others supplied by the New South Wales Governor. They also called at the Sandwich Islands (Hawaii) and obtained a quantity of "very fine salt". On the ship's return to Sydney, the Government purchased most of the pork at 6d per pound, and 30,034 pounds of salt at "three half-pence a pound", to the satisfaction of both Bass and the Governor.

In January 1803, Bass applied to Governor King to lease or be granted exclusive privileges to the south part of New Zealand including the Bounty Isles and the Penantipodes. Bass wrote:

> From the dearness of animal food in this country, and the little prospect there is of its price being reduced by killing the live stock for many years yet to come, I have been induced to make some consideration upon the chance of lessening the vast sums expended annually by the Government, in sending out hither supplies of beef and pork for the rations of the convicts . . . I have every proof short of actual experiment, that fish may be caught in abundance near the South part of the South Island of New Zealand, or at the neighbouring islands. And that a large quantity might be supplied annually to the Public Stores. Government aiding me in this project, I will make the experiment. The aid I ask the Government is an exclusive privilege or lease of the South Part of New Zealand, or that South of Dusky Bay, drawing the line in the same parallel of latitude across to the East side of the Island, as also of the Bounty Isles, Penantipode Isle, and the Snares, all being English discoveries, together with ten leagues of sea around their coasts. The lease to continue for seven years yet to come; renewal to twenty-one years, if the fishery within the first seven, is judged likely to succeed.[2]

In conclusion, Bass wrote:

> If I can draw up food from the sea in places which are lying useless to the world, I surely am entitled to make an exclusive property of the fruits of my ingenuity, as much as the man who obtains Letters Patent for a corkscrew or a cake of blacking.

This vast scheme which involved sealing, fishing and trading was no doubt inspired by his experiences in Dusky Sound in December 1801 and his inside knowledge of the Bounty, Snares and Penantipodes Islands – all discovered by Royal Navy ships. Sealing was very much part of Bass's plans and he had already written to his London agent enquiring into prices likely to be realised in London for sealskins and oil, the sealskin trade having recently shifted to there from China. It is probable that the supplying of fish to the New South Wales Government was included in the proposal to justify the request for a monopoly to this vast area.

Robert McNab in his classic history *Murihiku* presumed that Bass was aboard HMS *Reliance* in March 1800, on its return voyage to England, when the Penantipodes and their fur seals were discovered.[3] In fact we know now that Bass had been granted leave for sickness and had left for England, by way of China, on 29 May 1799. However, later in London, Bass would often meet Captain Waterhouse and Flinders – who had returned in the *Reliance* – and learn of the discovery of the island and the seals seen upon it. Bass married Waterhouse's sister and both the Captain and his father were investors in the trading venture of the *Venus*.

The fisheries proposal was considered favourably by Governor King, who agreed to buy as much fish as the settlement could use, but would not commit the Government to leasing the vast area asked for without first consulting the authorities in London. However, Bass was given conditional approval, and in subsequent correspondence he appeared convinced that the concessions were to be granted following his return from an imminent trading voyage. Some details of his immediate plans were outlined in a letter to Captain Waterhouse in England on 5 January 1803:

> I shall go to Dusky Bay again this voyage for the purpose of picking up two anchors and breaking the iron fastenings out of an old Indiaman that lies there deserted, with the intention of selling the former to the Spaniards, and of working up the other to purchase pork in the Islands. Of the iron we took out last voyage, converted by our smith into axes, we made a good thing. Now we shall be prepared for breaking her up.

On 2 February 1803, Bass again wrote to Waterhouse:

> In a few hours I will sail again on another pork voyage, but it combines circumstances of different nature also. From this place [Port Jackson] I go to New Zealand to pick up something more from the wreck of the old Endeavour in Dusky Bay, then visit some of the islands lying south of it in search of seals and fish. The former, should they be found, are intended to furnish a cargo to England immediately on my return from this trip. The fish are to answer a proposal I have made to Government to establish a fishery on condition of receiving an exclusive privilege of the south part of New Zealand and of its neighbouring isles, which privilege is at once to be granted to me. The fishery is not to be set in motion till after my return to old England . . . all depends upon the success of the voyage I am now upon. In the course of it I intend to visit the coast of Chili in search of provisions for the use of His Brit. Majesty's colony.

The *Venus* sailed for Dusky and the southern islands on 5 February 1803. From that day, nothing certain has been heard of Bass, the ship or of any of the other 24 people on board. This marked the end of his great southern fishery scheme, but within a few years the Sydney sealers made the coasts of southern New Zealand and the Snares, Bounty and Antipodes islands, which Bass planned to exploit, one of the world's greatest sealing grounds.

Did the *Venus* reach Dusky Sound? Possibly – the two anchors are gone and there is no record of anyone else removing them. However, over 12 tons of iron ballast remained at the *Endeavour* wreck in 1805, most of which was removed that year by the *Governor King*. When Captain John Fairchild salvaged parts off the wreck in 1878, he recorded that her bow was in only five feet of water. There were no anchors – but still "some pieces of cast iron amongst the ballast".[4]

Perhaps, as speculated by McNab, George Bass "skirted the southern part of the colony, to perfect his knowledge of the coastline of his intended monopoly, and following it along, he could not escape passing through what is now known as Foveaux Strait". And then, perhaps, Bass and the crew of the *Venus* may have sailed on to become the first people to land and harvest seals from the Antipodes and Bounty Islands. We shall never know.

THE FIRST RECORDED SEALING ON THE ANTIPODES

We have seen that George Bass knew of Captain Waterhouse's discovery of Penantipodes Island and its seals when he returned to Sydney from England on 28 August 1801. No doubt at first he kept this knowledge pretty much to himself, but in developing plans for his southern fishery he would have taken other Sydney merchants, notably the astute trader and ex-convict Simeon Lord, into his confidence. Whatever happened, it is certain that others in Sydney knew of the Penantipodes and their seals by January 1803, before Bass and the *Venus* sailed on their final voyage.

Popular history has it that the first people ashore on Antipodes Island were a 12-strong sealing gang from the American ship *Union* left there by Captain Isaac Pendleton in about June 1804. Many sources also say that Pendleton rediscovered Antipodes Island without knowledge of Captain Waterhouse's observations, but both these claims are incorrect.

Pendleton had sailed the 99-ton Brig *Union* from New York to Australia in 1803. He carried carpenters and shipbuilding tools and materials, and an unusually large crew of 38 men. Sixteen of the crew, under the command of Owen F. Smith, landed at Kangaroo Island on the South Australian coast, where they built a 35-ton schooner, the *Independence*. Meanwhile, the *Union* was sealing at Kangaroo Island and in Bass Strait, and arrived in Sydney on 6 January 1804 with a cargo of 5000 sealskins.[5]

COMMON FALLACIES

Major errors concerning the history of sealing at the Antipodes Islands have been regularly recycled for well over 100 years. Examples are:

The first sealers ashore. The most popular fallacy concerns Captain Isaac Pendleton of the American brig *Union*, who is said to have independently rediscovered the Antipodes and landed the first sealers there in June 1804. This error dates from Captain Edmund Fanning's *Voyages* published in 1833. Although Pendleton did indeed plan to visit the Antipodes, which he had heard of through Sydney traders, neither he nor the *Union* ever got closer to New Zealand's subantarctic islands than Bass Strait. In 1804, Pendleton was killed by natives at Tonga and the *Union* was wrecked with the loss of all hands at Fiji. The first sealers ashore at the Antipodes were three gangs landed from the schooner *Independence* in February 1805.

Record take of sealskins. There is an often-quoted report by A.W. Scott published in 1873, based on information furnished by an old Sydney sealer named Morris, "that in two years (1814 and 1815) no less than 400,000 skins were obtained from Pennantipod, or Antipodes Islands, alone". This information was next repeated in Sherrin's *The Handbook of the Fishes of New Zealand* published in 1886. In fact, the greatest tallies of skins from the Antipodes were in the years 1806–07 when around 280,000 were obtained. The total haul of sealskins from the Antipodes for all years up to 1880 was about 330,000. By 1814–1815, fur seal populations were badly depleted on all the islands to the south of New Zealand, and about 4000 skins in a voyage were considered a good haul.

100,000 rotten sealskins sold as manure. There is a well-known story that in the years 1814 and 1815 the ship *Pegasus* took home from the Antipodes 100,000 imperfectly cured skins, and that "on her arrival in London the skins, having heated during the voyage, had to be dug out of the hold, and were sold as manure — a sad and reckless waste of life". This claim also dates from A.W. Scott's book. It is completely erroneous — the date, the number of skins and the name of the ship do not fit the facts. The *Pegasus* did not visit the Antipodes. On her final voyage from Sydney in 1809, she arrived in London with 10,400 fur seal skins, which sold on a depressed market for about 3s 5d each. However, Scott may have been confusing an incident involving the whaler *Alexander* in 1806–1807. During a long voyage to England, whale oil seeped from casks and damaged sealskins in the hold. The total number of skins lost is uncertain, but the Sydney merchant Simeon Lord had a shipment of 14,000 on board. He was later paid insurance — £492 6s 0d "compensation for skins thrown overboard" and £700 11s 5d for "damaged" skins.

The *Union*'s owners, Fanning and Company, had previously had commercial dealings with Lord, and when the ship arrived in Sydney its cargo of skins was disposed of through that merchant. The *Union* next sailed on 12 January under charter to Governor King with passengers and cargo for Norfolk Island. Also carried was cargo and illicit liquor on behalf of Lord. On 28 April the vessel left Sydney, once again sealing at Bass Strait and Kangaroo Island. From there, she returned to Sydney on 29 June with 12,000 sealskins. The skins were again left in Lord's store. The *Independence* arrived in Sydney from Kangaroo Island three days later on 1 July.

By this time Simeon Lord and Pendleton were in a close business relationship. The most likely scenario is that Lord then told Pendleton of Penantipodes Island and its seals, and his plans to exploit them. Sharing knowledge of the Penantipodes through some sort of deal was to Lord's advantage, as his scheme – inherited from Bass – needed a relatively large vessel to transport sealers, stores and skins to and from the Antipodes.

On 16 July 1804, articles of agreement were signed between Simeon Lord, Captain Pendleton and John Boston as joint owners of the *Independence* of the one part, and Isaiah Townsend, master of the schooner *Independence*, O.F. Smith, master of the sealing gangs on shore, John Voce, Chief Officer, and 18 others, of the other part. The latter were to take the *Independence* "to such islands, parts and places to the southward or elsewhere" – a destination that revealed little of their intentions – and to exert their utmost endeavours to procure sealskins or oils for a period of 18 calendar months, or if it should be found necessary, for two years. Under the articles of agreement Townsend and Smith were each to get six per cent (a 16th "lay" or share) of all property obtained. Voce agreed to a 50th lay. Other signatories included several "sealmen" on 70th or 80th and eight others on 125th lays.[6]

THE SEALING LIFE

The early sealers lived an extremely harsh and hazardous life for scant reward. Many were marooned for years with only a few months' provisions on cold, spray-swept, subantarctic islands. Sometimes they built huts of stones, scrub and tussock, but for those on the Bounty Islands, seals and seabirds ultimately became their only source of shelter, food, fuel, bedding and clothing. Many drowned or died from accidents on shore; most suffered from injury, exposure and starvation. At least on the Antipodes and Bounty Islands, sealers did not face the fear of being killed and eaten by Maori — a fate that befell some of their contemporaries on the main islands of New Zealand.

Basic sealing gear consisted of wooden clubs, lances, knives, sharpening stones, ropes, "pegging wood" for spreading out skins, and salt for curing them. Just how fur seal skins were harvested was described by a veteran American sealer named Phelps in 1871: "We killed them with clubs. A single blow across the nose is sufficient to bring down the largest, when they are finished with the touch of a knife under the flipper; the knife is then passed round the head and flippers, and the skin being slit from head to tail, in front, it is taken off with much ease. When taken to our rendezvous, the skins are beamed with a currier's knife, and stretched out on the ground in proper shape to dry, fourteen pegs being put in each skin."

Some sealers preferred to kill with a lance rather than a club. Charles Heaphy vividly described an incident involving ship-based sealers at the Chatham Islands in 1843, where both methods were used:

> Lowered boats, with salt and three days provisions; captain's boat to take the weather side of the Keys and ours the lee side . . . 11 p.m. . . . pulled to windward on a bearing; captain's boat taking the lead, as it had to weather the reefs to take the seals, if there be any, in the rear. Pulled on with muffled oars until near daybreak, when smoothing water indicated the approach of the reefs, though as yet they were not discernible . . . Suddenly the headsman makes a sign for "oars", and they are laid in noiselessly, the bow-oarsman previously ascertaining the depth of the water . . . the grapnel is dropped over the bow at such a distance that the boat shall not touch, and taking our clubs and lances, we wade, waist deep in the water, to the rocks. It is not yet sufficiently light to discern whether there be any seals, but we think we can hear them grunting. It is very cold; blowing from the south right into us, with no shelter but a shelf of rock, and even smoking prohibited.
>
> In half an hour . . . we hear noise from the opposite side of the reefs. It is the captain's party startling the seals. We get to the top . . . quickly . . . and right in front of us, almost as thick as a drove of sheep, but each taking its own way, come the seals. Striking, spearing, right and left! Some of the seals making, like pigs, between one's legs, with here a tumble and a roll. The captain and his party are following them closely, and by the time the last has reached the water, sixty-seven seals are lying dead or stunned on the reef. A couple of hands are now set to get breakfast ready, and

> to look for sea-birds' eggs, while the remainder of the two crews commence skinning. There are no means here of "trying out" or melting down the blubber, and that is abandoned.

As fur seal numbers dropped, iron pots were used on shore for "trying out" the blubber, and wooden casks for storing the seal oil, but this was never practised at the Antipodes — and only in the 1880s at the Bounty Islands. The boats used from a sealing vessel were short, handy whaleboats — but some shore parties were equipped with larger boats capable of safely holding up to one-and-a-half tons of skins. Ship's boats were usually left with the gangs at the Antipodes, but often the sea was too rough for their use. At the Bounties it was impossible to keep boats ashore safely.

Like whalers, sealers were paid in shares (called "lays") of the catch of their ship or gang, minus expenses, landed safely at their home port. The men were contracted to the ship owners by "articles of agreement" for the proposed length of the voyage — usually up to two years. An ordinary sealer was often on an 80th lay, but some with extra responsibilities could negotiate more. An overseer in charge of a gang was commonly on a 25th, whereas a ship's boy could be on as little as a 180th. It was usual for the sealers' lays, in total, to equal about 35 per cent of the total catch.

However, the lay of skins was not a share of the profits and was seldom given as a cash payment. In theory, if a sealer had an 80th lay on a catch of 1050 skins then he was entitled to 13 skins to sell or keep at the end of the voyage. By then, sealers were almost always in debt to their employers for alcohol and goods supplied at inflated prices. They usually had little choice but to sell their smallholding of skins to their masters for whatever was offered — often less than 3s a skin. A substantial number received no cash in hand at the end of a voyage. D.R. Hainsworth records that in 1803, one Sydney sealer who shared in a catch of over 50,000 skins on an 80th lay for which he was offered £84 19s 6d, ran away still owing the ship's owner £1 2s 9d.

It has been asked why men chose to go sealing at all. First-timers could have been ignorant of the hardships involved, but many became veterans of the trade. Many enjoyed the independence, free from the demands and constraints of employers. Then again, perhaps it was the gambling instinct (akin to gold fever) of finding a new ground, taking a huge catch and making it rich. In 1823 the French sailor/naturalist Jules de Blosseville met and talked with several experienced Sydney sealing captains and crews, and later noted "how powerful must be the love of gain when it can induce men to support the fatigues and privations which fall to the lot of the seal fishers!" Sadly for the ordinary sealer, the dream of wealth was realised only by the ship owners and traders.

The agreement seems to have been that Pendleton would first sail the *Union* to Fiji, obtain sandalwood, and take it on to the lucrative China market.[7] Also en route he would make an illegal landing of rum at Norfolk Island. Only later would the *Union* be used to relieve the sealing gangs on the Antipodes, and bring back their haul of sealskins.

The great secrecy that surrounded Lord's plans has led to much confusion regarding the voyages of both the *Union* and the *Independence*. However, detailed historical research, pioneered by Dr John Cumpston and continued by Admiral John Ross, reveals much more of the true story – and the intrigue which accompanied the departure of the first sealers to the Antipodes Islands.

For some time Governor King had been concerned with foreigners, particularly Americans, becoming involved in the Port Jackson sealing trade to the detriment of British and colonial interests. He was also suspicious that Lord was planning to continue an illicit liquor trade. To obstruct any such plans, King promulgated a General Order on 11 August 1804. He directed that the clearance of foreign vessels for sealing voyages out of Port Jackson "within the limits of this Territory", which included southern New Zealand and the subantarctic islands, was "strictly forbidden". Further, he imposed a penalty of £50 for each offence, where masters of foreign vessels were found to have recruited residents of the colony for such work. King hoped to discourage the *Union* and the *Independence* departing on their voyages as planned, and also to stop the embarkation of the large sealing gang already engaged.[8]

On 28 August when the two vessels cleared Port Jackson, they appeared to be abiding by the Governor's order. Both were declared as "bound for China", and neither carried the sealing gang. The *Union* was manned by her usual complement of 22 men. Isaiah Townsend had taken over from Smith as captain of the *Independence*, which carried a total crew of eight.

Unknown to the New South Wales authorities, many of Lord's sealers had already left quietly in other vessels. One of these vessels appears to have been the *Contest* commanded by Joseph Oliphant. Others involved in the plan were the *Endeavour* which later transported some of the sealers including Owen F. Smith from Port Jackson to Bass Strait, and then the *Honduras Packet* which took them on to Stewart Island.

On departure "for China" both the *Union* and the *Independence* made for Norfolk Island where the rum was sold – much to the annoyance of Governor King when he heard of it later. Here Pendleton was able to recruit 11 men, probably for sealing. The *Union* then proceeded on its sandalwood venture, but on calling at Tonga those landing in one of the ship's boats, including Pendleton and John Boston, were all killed by the natives. The mate, Daniel Wright, sailed the *Union* back to Sydney where Governor King gave him permission to strengthen his crew with any Americans he could find in the town. After re-provisioning, the ship once more set out after sandalwood, only to be wrecked at Fiji with the loss of all hands. From Norfolk Island the *Independence* sailed south, no doubt carrying the additional 11 recruits, to meet up with the rest of Lord's sealing gang on the New Zealand coast.

While waiting at Stewart Island, Smith was searching for seals in a whaleboat when he discovered "a strait dividing the Southern Island [South Island] of New Zealand with the harbours of the Southern-most Island [Stewart Island]"

– which Captain James Cook had charted as one island. Smith drew the first map showing Fouveaux Strait.[9]

At Port Adventure, Stewart Island, Smith and the sealers from the *Honduras Packet* were transferred to the *Independence*. From there Townsend sailed for a pre-arranged rendezvous with the *Contest* in Dusky Sound. Probably the route was via the newly discovered "Smith's Strait". At Dusky Sound, apparently sometime in January 1805, command of the *Contest* was handed over to Jorgen Jorgenson. Oliphant and Voce and their respective gangs were then transferred to the little *Independence*. Only then did that vessel finally set off with the three sealing gangs for Antipodes Island – but because of the small size of the *Independence* they were obliged to leave two of their boats behind in Dusky Sound.[10] The *Contest* was under instructions to then investigate "Bligh's Islands" (the Bounty Islands) and the Chathams, but it developed leaks and returned direct to Sydney.[11]

Sometime in February 1805 the *Independence* landed the three sealing gangs, totalling about 31 men, under the command of Smith, Oliphant and Voce. Some of these sealers were to stay on the Antipodes for well over two years. They constructed rough huts with stones and tussocks. As recorded in their articles of agreement, their provisions consisted of a weekly ration of seven pounds of meat, mostly salt pork obtained at Norfolk Island, 10 pounds of flour or biscuit, one pound of sugar, "rice, ten bags for the voyage, tea or grain for coffee". The *Independence*, with a crew of six and still captained by Townsend, returned to Port Jackson on 23 April by way of Norfolk Island.

In January 1805, Lord had entered into a partnership with a prominent firm of Port Jackson shipbuilders and owners to create a new firm of Lord, Kable and Underwood. Lord now contracted with Captain Jonathon Paddock of another American vessel, the brig *Favorite*, to accompany the *Independence* back to the Antipodes to put fresh gangs ashore and collect skins. On 11 June both ships cleared Port Jackson, the *Favorite* bound, it was said, on a "whaling voyage", and the *Independence* carrying 18 men "for Canton". On 20 September the *Honduras Packet* sailed for London, but Lord had arranged for her to call at the Antipodes en route to land provisions, sealing gear and a new boat for Oliphant – and to load a cargo of skins.

Next, the *Governor King* cleared for "Bass Strait" in early November, but it was planned that her sealing gang would eventually go on to the Antipodes. She was followed in January 1806 by the whaler *Ceres* which also was to call at Antipodes Island on her way to London.

INTERNATIONAL CONFLICT AT THE ANTIPODES

Obviously it was Lord's plan to monopolise sealing at the Antipodes, and by disguising destinations he ensured that no word of the new sealing ground appeared in the press. However, there was no stopping talk within sealing circles. Within less than a month of the sailing of the *Favorite* and the *Independence*, Bass Strait sealer William Stewart entered into an agreement with John Palmer to undertake a voyage "for the purpose of sealing and oiling at a certain island called the Penantipodes". This was a different William Stewart from the one who charted Stewart Island, and after whom that island is named.[12]

On 29 July 1805, William Stewart left Port Jackson in the *Venus*. This was a small brig of 45 tons owned by Robert Campbell, a business partner of Palmer's. She first sailed to Norfolk Island for provisions, including salt pork, and then on a return voyage to the Bay of Islands on behalf of the New South Wales Government.

Sketch reconstructing a sealer's hut of stones, sticks, turfs and tussock grass. Based on the remains of structures found on the south coast of Antipodes Island.

The *Venus* arrived at the Antipodes Islands on about 20 November to find the *Favorite, Honduras Packet* and the *Independence* at anchor. On shore were the three sealing gangs led by Smith, Voce and Oliphant and also a new gang from the *Favorite*. All these ships and men owed allegiance to Simeon Lord and were in effective occupation. They were in no mood to share the riches of the Antipodes with rivals.

According to evidence given later before the Bench of Magistrates in Sydney, the crew of the *Venus* saw no one ashore on the day of their arrival. At Stewart's request, one of his officers, Owen Jones, raised the Union Jack and took possession of the island in the name of His Majesty the King of England. Next day, some of the resident gangs appeared and were very antagonistic to Stewart's attempt to land. Lord's sealers, though of mixed origins, were all from American ships, and Stewart was wary of American sealers following earlier competition and clashes with them in Bass Strait. During a heated confrontation Lord's sealers said they would pull down the British colours, and that any skins taken on the island by Stewart's men would be confiscated. However, the sealers from the *Venus* did not back off, and in the "affray" that followed Stewart received a slight injury to his head. Having flown over the Antipodes for the first time, the Union Jack was unceremoniously hauled down and tossed into the sea. Stewart and his companions were forced to retreat to their boat.[13]

Nevertheless, they were by no means beaten. Somehow, the *Venus* went on to land her sealing gang. It has been suggested that a compromise must have been reached with Lord's men, but it is more likely that the *Venus* simply left the main anchorage (at Anchorage Bay) and searched the coastline for somewhere else to land her gang. Nothing is recorded as to the disposition of the three gangs already on the island. Doubtless each was based on a different part of the coast, since there would have been many days when working boats was impossible, and the sealers would have found walking overland through the thick tussock tiring and time-consuming. From my knowledge of the island, and after considering such aspects as hauling up small boats, water supply, foot access for sealing along the shoreline, and relative ease of access overland to other parts of the island, I have selected the three most likely sites for early sealing camps. The first is near Anchorage Bay in the north – no doubt where the "affray" occurred – and the second is on the south coast with its small boat harbour of South Bay. Remains of early sealers' huts have been found at both of these sites. The third probable sealers' site is at the northern end of Alert Bay on the eastern coastline, where they would have been able to readily beach boats and access the higher parts of the island. If Lord's men were already occupying these three locations, William Stewart would have been obliged to look elsewhere.

SEALERS' HUTS AND OTHER RELICS

For many months, in 1805–07, at least 80 sealers lived on Antipodes Island. These men, marooned "without a ship at their back" were among the earliest European residents of New Zealand. They were preceded only by the sealing gang, under William Leith, left by the *Britannia* at Dusky Sound in 1792–93; and by Captain Brampton's party from the wrecked *Endeavour* who lived in the same Fiordland locality from 1795 to 1797.

Continuous settlement of the Antipodes ceased in 1810 after over-exploitation of the seal population, but during the following decades up until 1880, at least 10 other sealing gangs spent many months ashore. Today it is hard to imagine where and how these men lived, and only a few traces of their existence have been discovered on the island. The first record of relics of a sealing camp being found on Antipodes Island was on 4 November 1885, recorded by Captain W.J. Grey of the *Stella* who was searching for signs of the crew of the lost ship *North American*: "Landed in a nice little boat harbour on the NW side of the island. Here we found part of an old hut and fireplace. The hut had been blown down, but it did not look as if it had been long since people lived there." Since the hut and fireplace appeared of recent origin, they probably dated from a party off the sealer *Alert*, who had camped on the island four years earlier.

In March 1886, describing the building of the castaway depot near Reef Point, Captain Fairchild recorded in a letter to the Secretary of the Marine Department: "A peculiar incident happened whilst sinking the holes for the posts for the house. When down about 2ft. we unearthed a piece of an earthenware bowl . . . I also found some pieces of timber, which had been the remains of an old hut; but, as it was New Zealand wood, it had, no doubt, been a sealer's hut."

The deeply buried earthenware may have dated from the earliest sealers of 1805–06, or from William Stewart's gang who spent six or seven months here in 1825–26. In 1998 while excavating for a boardwalk, Kath Walker and Graeme Elliott found the remains of a very old glass bottle about 15 cm below the surface in this same vicinity. It is of a type free-blown between 1800 and 1810, and probably originally stored wine or spirits. The remains of the old hut found by Fairchild would have been the same as reported by Captain Grey only a few months before.

In a shallow cave on the cliffs of Anchorage Bay there is a cache of tightly rolled penguin skins dating from the sealing days. They were probably left there in 1880 when another 3500 penguin skins were loaded from the Antipodes onto the sealing schooner *Alert* by a gang who found no seals during a six-week stay ashore. These days, as when first discovered by the University of Canterbury expedition 1969, the skins are partially buried and preserved in penguin guano. The burnt remains of a few barrel staves were also located nearby.

In 1969, two stone structures thought possibly to be old sealers' fireplaces were found on the south-west coast of Antipodes Island by the University of Canterbury expedition. Because they lacked obvious chimneys their utility was uncertain; one suggestion was that they were parts of rock and tussock shelters built in 1893 by the survivors of the wreck of the *Spirit of the Dawn*. However, these castaways had no means of lighting a fire so would not have built fireplaces.

The connection between the fireplace-like structures and the early sealers was confirmed in 1978 by John Newton and members of the BAAS Expedition, when an additional and much more complete hut site was discovered nearby. This consists of a 3 m x 2.5 m pit dug about a metre deep into the toe of a bank, with built-up floor and earth walls around its lower end where there are entry points, or drainage channels, on each side. At the inner end there is a fireplace with a stone hearth at floor level extending 1 metre further into the bank. This fireplace is lined with blocks of stone and has a massive lintel stone (about 500 mm above the hearth) and a chimney of stacked stone blocks coming up through the bank. The chimney is partially collapsed at its upper end, but could once have extended over 2 metres above ground level. Along one side of the hut there is a raised area 1 metre wide — possibly a sleeping platform. Presumably the upper walls and roof (long since disappeared) were originally of poles, sticks and canvas brought ashore by the sealers, and tussocks and sealskins procured locally.

The hut was small, about 3 m x 4 m overall excluding the fireplace, and it is hard to imagine it accommodating more than four men. Considering the adjacent remains of at least two other similar structures and the building materials naturally available on the island, it is certain that these sealers found it easier to build many small huts rather than fewer large ones. That these huts belonged to the earliest sealers on the Antipodes (1805–1810) is suggested by an old earthenware bottle found close by in 1969. This artefact, now in the Canterbury Museum, has been identified as early 19th century.

Less than a kilometre north-west of the sealers huts an ancient fire-site, with charcoal and burnt penguin bones, was found under a rock overhang by geologists Jane Forsyth and Ian Turnbull in October 1990. The deposit was being eroded by storm waves and samples of charcoal and bones were collected but radiometric dating has yet to be done.

Many other archaeological finds related to the old sealing days await discovery on Antipodes Island.

Today, on the spray-swept Bounty Islands no traces of the early sealers remain. How they existed for months at a time on these barren rocks can only be imagined, perhaps aided by insights from the following two finds, over 50 years apart. In 1831, John Biscoe recorded a visit ashore by some of his men: "They found on landing on one of the rocks a hut, the roof of which was formed of the skins and wings of birds, a baking dish, a water cask, a bottle half filled with oil, some pieces of firewood, and an Irish (provision) cask & other things which clearly proved that Europeans had been recently there."

In 1886, when describing the erection of the first castaway depot on the islands, Captain Fairchild wrote: "Near where we built the house we found the remains of an old hut and some firewood; and, as it was New Zealand wood, it was probably left there by a party of sealers . . . who, to my knowledge, visited the Bounty Islands about six years ago." This was a hut built by a gang from the Bluff schooner *Alert* who spent three months on the Bounty Islands in August–November 1880.

Ringdove Bay on the eastern coast would have been an unlikely choice. No doubt it then contained countless seals, but its southern half could only be worked by boat and the northern end was accessible overland from any camp above Alert Bay. Worse still, it was completely cut off on the landward side by high cliffs or very steep slopes – and there was no suitable campsite near sea level. All this suggests that William Stewart had no option other than to base his gang somewhere on the very exposed western coastline. If this was so, then he probably landed and set up camp either in Stack Bay or, less likely, in the deep bay in the lee of the Windward Islands. Here and along the adjacent shoreline his sealing gang would be able to operate in isolation from the other parties.

Stewart and his sealers were ashore and well advanced in landing their stores when a sudden gale forced the *Venus* to put to sea. During the storm, she was blown well off the island and her rudder was badly damaged. Although most of the gang's salt meat and some sealing gear was still on board, the mate decided to sail back to Port Jackson for repairs – leaving Stewart and his 15 or 16 men ashore without much of their clothing and personal belongings, and with short rations.[14] This episode further suggests that they had been landed on a very exposed part of the Antipodes coastline. The *Venus* arrived back at Port Jackson on 24 January 1806.

The *Favorite, Honduras Packet* and *Independence* seem to have left the island shortly after Stewart landed. The next vessel to reach the island was the *Governor King*, owned by Lord, Kable and Underwood, which had left Port Jackson on a sealing voyage in November. She landed more sealers, a boat and sealing gear, and then carried on "to search for another island". It seems that Oliphant and Voce appropriated the boat and sealing gear for their use. While the *Governor King* was away her gang, handicapped by the lack of boat and gear, obtained only about 100 skins.[15]

TROUBLE ON THE "WATERFRONT"

From early 1806 a number of ships called at the island to load sealskins under arrangement with Lord, Kable and Underwood. This led to a series of strange events, which at first appeared to be no more than little-minded squabbling among the sealers.

Captain Edward Edwards of the *Honduras Packet* understood that three men from each of the gangs under Smith, Voce and Oliphant would load his ship. However, Voce refused, saying that it was Smith's responsibility and that he had work to do elsewhere on the island. According to Edwards, the sealers used insufficient boats for the work and it was done "in a dilatory fashion". Others present later gave evidence of "neglect", "tardiness" and "disobedience of orders" on the part of the sealers. Although the *Honduras Packet* had room in her hold for 60,000 skins and there were sufficient skins on the island to have filled her, on 6 January she was forced to leave only partly loaded, and without offloading all of the provisions

Sealers' fireplace, one of three now known from the south coast of Antipodes Island. (*Rob Stanley.*)

intended for the men on the island. She arrived in London on 27 May carrying 34,338 skins,[16] but 7000 of these had been loaded in Sydney, and many others may perhaps have been obtained elsewhere before or after she called at the Antipodes.

There were similar problems when the *Governor King* returned to the Antipodes in February. This time both Smith and Voce refused to load sealskins, claiming a lack of written orders from Lord, Kable and Underwood, and also that the ship was infested by rats. The agreement required the skins to be delivered in good order at Sydney wharf fit for market, and the sealers argued that the rats would damage the skins. This ship left the island without loading, and with salt and provisions for Lord's sealers still on board. It is presumed that she re-embarked her own gang and their 100 skins. She was later lost at the Hunter River on her return voyage to Sydney, when 200 seal skins were listed as on board.[17]

Nothing has been recorded about loading problems with the *Ceres* when she reached the Antipodes soon afterwards. On arrival in England her cargo included 20,507 sealskins[18] – but at least 2000 of these were on board before the *Ceres* arrived at the island.

When the *Favorite* returned to the Antipodes later in February loading went smoothly, in contrast to the earlier difficulties and bickering. Smith, Voce and some of their sealers were soon aboard along with 60,000 sealskins. It was quite the largest cargo of sealskins ever taken from the southern sealing grounds. However, 25,060 skins belonging to these gangs were deliberately left on the island, and Smith had two of his sealers, Wild and Hoef, remained behind to look after them.

The *Favorite* arrived in Sydney on 10 March bringing news of the disappearance of the *Independence*. After leaving Antipodes Island in November the two vessels had parted company, the *Favorite* obviously to go sealing, since she carried the gang previously aboard the *Independence* – but there is no record of where she was working. The *Independence* with a total crew of seven was reportedly scouting for fresh sealing grounds which almost certainly included the Bounties – but she failed to keep her arranged rendezvous with the *Favorite*. Like countless mariners before and since, Isaiah Townsend and the remaining six of his crew had disappeared without trace somewhere in the Southern Ocean.

Five days after the *Favorite* returned to Sydney, Governor King sent a report to England complaining about the behaviour of certain Sydney residents, notably Simeon Lord:

> Some of whom, under cover of procuring seals and oil about the coasts of this colony, have by the agency of American vessels, and in defiance of Colonial Regulations on the subject, taken a number of people off the islands of Bass's Strait and carried them to a smaller group of islands being considerably without the limits of this Territory, where upwards of 80 people are on those islets, the largest is a bare rock and not six miles round, where seals resort in great numbers. In the course of two years upwards of 160,000 skins have been taken from those islands.

King was referring to the Penantipodes, as their position 49° 49′ S, 179° 20′ E was noted in the margin of the dispatch.[19]

Apart from William Stewart and his 15 men, who had been there about four months, the inhabitants of the island were all Lord's men, now under the overall direction of Joseph Oliphant. They included Oliphant, now with 24 sealers, plus Wild and Hoef from Smith's gang – all having been there just on one year; and the "fresh gangs" (totalling about 40 men) brought down by the *Independence*, *Favorite* and the *Governor King* between July and December 1805.

The Antipodes Islands would have reached their highest human population ever in the four months between November 1805 and February 1806, when approximately 86 sealers were ashore. The rush for sealskins meant that in the years 1805 and 1806 alone, the Antipodes were inhabited for well over 32,000 person/days – a greater total than all the years since combined.

On 26 March 1806, the *Star*, a 119-ton fully rigged ship recently purchased by Lord and under the command of Captain James Birnie, cleared Port Jackson to "fish off New Zealand". She called at the Antipodes about two months later to load skins and relieve one of Lord's gangs. Shipping records are silent on the number of skins loaded, but it was probably on this voyage that Oliphant and his 24-strong gang returned after having "been fortunate enough to catch 56,692 fur skins".[20] This conclusion is supported by Governor King's report quoted above that by then "upwards of 160,000 skins" had been taken on the Antipodes. Wild and Hoef still stayed behind on the island with a secret hoard of 25,000 skins which Smith had entrusted to their care. Stewart accepted a passage to Sydney on the *Star*, but his gang and the skins they had accumulated remained on the island.

There is no doubt that the sealers on the Antipodes were gravely short of food both before and after the *Star*'s visit. The *Venus* had departed without unloading all the supplies for Stewart's gang, and due to squabbles with Lord's sealers both the *Honduras Packet* and the *Governor King* had sailed without landing most of the provisions they had brought to the island. It is not recorded what provisions the *Star* delivered to Lord's sealers, but Wild later related that during their stay on the island "the only sustenance many had was the insides of seals and birds". Soon after the *Star*'s departure, the penguins would have left the island for the winter, and from then on

Wandering Albatross and small burrowing petrels would have been the main birds used for food. The fat of seals was the only fuel available.

The whaler *Aurora* (Captain Andrew Meryck) left Sydney on a sealing and whaling cruise on 30 June, giving her destination as "Penantipodes, Straits". It appears that "Straits" referred to Foveaux Strait. This may have been as far as she went, as there is no record of the *Aurora* calling at the Antipodes Islands which were then populated by about 60 men. She returned to Sydney on 1 October having collected only 500 sealskins and four tons of sperm oil.

William Stewart's 15 sealers were not to be relieved for another nine months, long after their articles of agreement had expired. On 9 February 1807, Campbell and Company's newly built 136-ton brig *Perseverance* cleared Sydney in ballast "for China", under command of Captain Frederick Lelhof and with Owen Jones as mate. Jones had sailed with Stewart when the *Venus*'s gang had been landed at the Antipodes, and many of the 18-strong crew were experienced sealers. It seems certain that the sealers carried on the *Perseverance* relieved the gang on the Antipodes and the ship then took a load of skins to China.[21] How many is not recorded, but judging by the numbers of seals obtained per man by other gangs it was probably of the order of 40,000. The *Perseverance* returned from Canton via Hobart with a cargo of merchandise on 5 May 1808.

THE GREAT SEALSKIN SCAM

In his *Voyages around the World*, published in 1833, Edmund Fanning states that Simeon Lord swindled his New York firm – Fanning and Company, the owners of the *Union* and *Independence* – out of their share of the proceeds of sealskins collected by those two vessels at Kangaroo and Antipodes Islands. He claims that following the loss of the *Union*:

> Mr Lord chartered a ship and proceeded with her to the Island of Antipodes. At this place, the officers and crew whom Captain Pendleton had left, had taken and cured rising of sixty thousand pure fur seal skins, a parcel of very

> superior quality: these, from information since obtained, were received on board Mr Lord's ship, who thence proceeded to Canton and disposed of his valuable cargo at good prices, the proceeds being invested in China goods, he accompanied to an eastern port in the United States: these were also sold, and Mr Lord off to Europe with the amount of the proceeds, before the agent for the owners of the *Union* was made acquainted with the transaction: thus unfortunately terminating the *Union*'s voyage, her owners never receiving either for the skins taken from South Antipodes, or for the fourteen thousand left by Captain P. in Mr Lord's charge at Sydney, one farthing.

Fanning's narrative of these events contains many major inaccuracies. These obvious errors led McNab to conclude that the details "scarcely bear out this story of the iniquity of the Sydney Merchant, Lord", and that "the idea of such a crime is opposed to the doctrine of probability". However, from what we now know, Fanning's allegations of large-scale fraud were close to the mark.

Later, during a rash of civil cases in the Sydney Court, evidence would emerge that Owen Smith, in collusion with Lord, had devised a plan to defraud Lord's partners. The 25,000 skins left on the island had been accumulated through deliberately short-loading the earlier vessels. Wild and Hoef admitted that Smith had arranged for them to remain on the island with the skins, and await the arrival of an unnamed "American ship". The plan was that the skins would then be shipped directly to China and sold, without Lord's partners being aware of their existence. After a careful study of the court records, Admiral Ross[22] concluded that it was an extraordinary conspiracy, remarkable not only for its complexity, but also for its magnitude. Simeon Lord was the major beneficiary. Owen Smith's share of the proceeds was to be the sum of $10,000 to be paid to him by Lord.

While at the Antipodes, William Stewart had learned something of Smith and Lord's scheme regarding the 25,000 skins left at the islands, and on his return to Sydney on 21 June 1805 he advised his partner John Palmer of the situation. The *Favorite* was then officially preparing for a voyage "direct to China" with 60,000 sealskins on board. Knowing that she was really going via the Antipodes, Palmer seems to have immediately entered into an arrangement with Lord's agent aboard the *Favorite*, Daniel Whitney, that almost half of the skins would be unloaded and swapped for those gathered on the Antipodes by Stewart and his men. Simeon Lord, the principal owner of the skins in the *Favorite*, must have been party to this additional deal. No doubt it was done to keep Palmer and Stewart quiet, and help ensure that his own partners, Kable and Underwood, remained unaware of the 25,000 skins still waiting for an "American ship" at the Antipodes.

When the *Favorite* cleared Port Jackson on 29 July 1806, records show that her cargo had been reduced to 32,000 skins and that Owen Smith was on board to take charge of Lord's interests. Of course nothing was said in Sydney about any proposed visit to the Antipodes, but when the *Favorite* eventually reached Canton she was carrying 87,000 skins – the balance of which obviously had been embarked at Antipodes Island. At Canton, the *Favorite*'s cargo was landed in three separate lots, apparently on behalf of different persons. One landing was of 32,000 skins, which appear to have been those with which the *Favorite* had been loaded when she left Port Jackson. Another landing was made of about 30,000 skins, evidently those collected by Stewart and his men. A third landing was of around 25,000 skins, almost certainly those which had been accumulated on the Antipodes by Owen Folger Smith and held there by Wild and Hoef.[23]

It is possible that after the loss of the *Union* and the *Independence*, both with all hands, Owen Smith was the only surviving member of the 38 men who originally sailed in the *Union* from New York. Such secrecy and complexity was involved in the various deals that it is not surprising that Edmund Fanning was confused as to the facts. However, there can be no doubt that Fanning and Co. were defrauded of the proceeds of skins collected by the *Union* and *Independence* – as were Kable and Underwood, Lord's partners in Sydney, in respect of the proceeds from 25,000 skins accumulated on Antipodes Island. Captain Paddock of the *Favorite* must also have been party to the dealings.

The *Favorite* eventually returned to the United States, almost certainly with Smith on board since he had earlier been refused permission to settle in Sydney and trade in association with Lord. For many years Foveaux Strait was called Favorite Strait on American charts, probably since that ship was the first to take news of the newly discovered strait to the United States. In July 1810, after an absence of five years, Owen F. Smith again appeared in New South Wales. He was in command of the American brig *Aurora* which he chartered out to Simeon Lord for one of the first sealing voyages to Campbell and Macquarie Islands. The *Favorite*'s papers filed at Nantucket on 27 November 1807 show that 87,080 fur seal skins were sold at Canton in January of that year.[24] Obed Macy, agent for the *Favorite*'s owners Paul Gardner Jr and Co, noted:

> Whitney and Paddock gave me an account of the skins obtained by the ship's crew, of which they were to draw their shares, valuing the skins at the price in Canton. After deducting customary charges the whole number of skins they furnished me with were 34,356 . . . valuing the skins at 80 cents each, which they said was the price in Canton, amounting to $27,484.

Meanwhile, under Captain John Wilkinson, the *Star* left Sydney again on 30 July 1806 to land fresh sealing gangs on the Antipodes. She then sailed to the Chatham Islands and then on to northern New Zealand for wood and water. At Whangaroa a local chief was keen for his son Te Ara, who had been given the name King George Kira, to get to England to see King George III. The young man was taken on board the *Star* at his father's request and "sailed with Captain Wilkinson to the seal fishery at the Penantipodes". While on board he was called by the name of "George". After a few months at sea, George was returned to his people at Whangaroa. The *Star* arrived back at Port Jackson on 30 December with 14,000 sealskins – probably all collected from the Antipodes.

TE ARA ("GEORGE"), THE FIRST MAORI TO VISIT THE ANTIPODES

Following his visit to the Antipodes Islands on the sealing vessel *Star* in 1806, George's continuing desire to learn of things European led to his serving on whaling ships and finally to his involvement in a major incident in New Zealand's early maritime history — the *Boyd* massacre.

In November 1809 the 600-ton ship *Boyd* had just completed a voyage for the British Government bringing a detachment of soldiers and convicts to New South Wales. She was then chartered to carry cargo and passengers to the Cape of Good Hope and London, and en route to call at northern New Zealand and collect spars. At that time, George and several other Maori were stranded in Sydney, so were taken on board to work their passage home as deck hands. Three days after the *Boyd* arrived in Whangaroa Harbour, the local Maori suddenly attacked, killed and ate most of the 70-odd crew and passengers, and set fire to the ship. Attacks on visiting trading and whaling ships were not uncommon in those days, but what made the *Boyd* incident unusual was the large number of Europeans, and in particular passengers, killed.

Reasons for Maori attacks on European ships varied widely. Often it was based on suspicions of strangers, or to obtain utu (revenge) for violations of Maori customs or other wrongs committed by visiting sailors. But always there was the over-riding desire to procure muskets, axes and iron objects. In a letter to the London paper *Courier* in 1817, Jorgen Jorgenson suggested the *Boyd* massacre was prompted by Maori suspicions concerning the fate of several of their young countrymen who had sailed aboard European ships and never returned. But this seems unlikely to have been the prime motive for the attack on the *Boyd*.

In 1814 at Whangaroa, George and his brother, Te Puhi, told the Reverend Samuel Marsden their version of what had happened on the *Boyd*'s final voyage from Sydney. George became sick and was unable to work: "He was severely punished, refused provisions and threatened to be thrown overboard, and many other indignities were offered to him even by the common sailors. He remonstrated with the master, begged him not to inflict corporal punishment upon him, saying that he was a chief in his own country which they would know on their arrival in New Zealand. He was told he was no chief, with many abusive terms which he mentioned and which are but too commonly used by British sailors."

This was a terrible indignity to a chief and demanded utu. When the *Boyd* arrived at Whangaroa in December 1809 and George showed his scars to the tribe, vengeance was swift. The captain and a party that had been lured ashore to inspect trees for spars were murdered. Later that night George, Te Puhi and their followers stormed the *Boyd*, and slaughtered most on board. The dead were taken ashore and eaten. About five sailors took to the rigging and remained there all night, only to be killed while attempting to escape in the morning. Four of those on board were spared from the massacre. One was a young cabin boy. The others, a woman with an infant child and a little girl, had remained in a cabin during the attack and were not found by the Maori until next morning.

George told Marsden that his father and five others were blown up in the *Boyd*. The old chief had got some muskets and gunpowder up on deck, and was trying a musket to see if it would strike, when "a spark caught the powder and set the *Boyd* on fire and killed all that were near".

When news of the massacre reached the Bay of Islands, three armed boats from the *City of Edinburgh* went to Whangaroa on 31 December and rescued the four survivors. Alexander Berry from that ship "brought away the two principal chiefs" (George and his brother) as prisoners, but they were later released since there was no opportunity to send them to Port Jackson for trial. As a result of information from these chiefs and their followers, the blame for directing the attack on the *Boyd* fell on Te Pahi, a chief from the Bay of Islands who was visiting Whangaroa at the time. Berry was unable to question Te Pahi as he had "taken to the bush".

Frederick Hasselburg, captain of the brig *Perseverance* and discoverer of Campbell and Macquarie Islands, was one of five masters of whaling vessels who joined to avenge the massacre on 26 March 1810. They landed with their crews on Te Pahi's island "and took the island by force of arms", searched in vain for other survivors of the *Boyd*, and recovered one of the *Boyd*'s longboats. Te Pahi was mortally wounded, his village destroyed and 60 Maori killed.

Unfortunately the whalers appear to have taken their revenge on the wrong man. It was later revealed that Te Pahi was in his canoe some distance from the ship when the attack occurred, and that he later tried unsuccessfully to save the sailors who were in the rigging. His major mistake was to have taken possession of the longboat and some other booty after the massacre was over. It seems unlikely that the confusion — which Marsden blamed on the similarity between the names of Te Pahi and that of George's brother Te Puhi — was accidental, especially since George spoke fluent English. It is much more likely that, in order to escape punishment, George deliberately laid the blame on Te Pahi and his warriors. Marsden's friend and travelling companion, J.L. Nicholas, was convinced that George — whom he described as "obnoxious" and to possess "a sneering impudence" — was the main leader in the attack on the *Boyd*. It is easy to imagine how the captain and crew of a convict transport ship, used to no arguments and stern discipline, could not tolerate his demeanour.

In January 1815, George told Samuel Marsden that he wanted to visit Port Jackson again, but was afraid that he might be hanged if he went there. However, as he now had some Europeans living at his settlement "they would be security for him and, if he should be hung, his people would hang the Europeans". A very forgiving Marsden assured him that he would not be punished, "because the captain of the *Boyd* had flogged him first". George then vowed that he would not be involved in killing and cannibalism again — "as he knew better now. At the same time he would not venture yet to Port Jackson, but his brother's daughter should go . . . and, if she was not hung, he would afterwards go himself".

On 6 February 1807, one of Lord's vessels, the snow *Commerce*, cleared Port Jackson for London and "to touch at the sealing islands to take in skins". However, when she arrived at the Antipodes early in March, some of the sealers refused to load their skins unless they themselves were returned to Sydney. Captain Birnie agreed to these demands, since Lord's gangs had all been on the island long beyond the period stated on their sealing articles and the ship was in need of repair. The *Commerce* returned to Port Jackson with a cargo of 39,000 skins on 9 April.[25]

The *Star* sailed from Sydney for England via "the fishery" on 29 March with 14,000 sealskins and arrived in London in February 1808 with 19,823. It seems most likely that the extra 5823 skins were loaded at the Antipodes.[26]

SEALING AT THE BOUNTIES

Following the failure of the *Contest* to reach the Bounty Islands, two American vessels, the ship *Perseverance* and the schooner *Pilgrim* under overall command of Captain Amasa Delano, are the first known to have visited them since their discovery. After confrontations with Sydney-based sealers at the Bass Strait Islands, these two vessels left on 24 October 1804 for the South-West Cape of New Zealand, as Stewart Island was then known. Delano sighted the Snares on 3 November and described them as "a cluster of seven craggy islands". A strong westerly wind did not allow for a close inspection, but he noted that "they did not appear to be capable of affording any thing except it might be a few seals", and that " if . . . seals are on these islands, it would be very difficult to obtain them".

On 7 November the two vessels made the Bounty Islands. Again there was "a strong gale from the westward, with a large sea, and by no means clear weather". In his book Delano describes the encounter:

> We made the islands about four or five leagues distant, and run down within about one mile of them. We discovered broken water close under our lee bow, and immediately luffed to the southward of it; but as we passed, it fairly broke, and convinced us that there was not water enough for our ship on it. The breakers lie about west south west from the body of Bounty Islands, and will not always show themselves. We saw several other breakers on the south and west side, lying off from the main group; but we were convinced that it is a very dangerous place for a ship to come near to . . . They [the islands] cannot afford any kind of vegetable production. We saw shags and gulls, and a few seals round them; and I believe they are all they afford . . . It would be very dangerous for a ship to fall in with these islands in the night, or in thick weather.[27]

Obviously, the apparent dangers and difficulties of working the Snares and Bounty Islands discouraged Captain Delano from putting sealers ashore or investigating them more closely. Indeed, his journal gave a poor report on sealing prospects at both islands. Apparently he was not aware of the existence of the Antipodes Islands, for the two American vessels then carried on across the South Pacific to rendezvous at the renowned sealing island of Massa Fuero off the coast of Chile.

The first recorded landing on the Bounty Islands was in the second half of 1807, by a sealing gang from the schooner *Brothers* under command of Oliver Russell. The vessel left Port Jackson on 11 June 1807 "for the fishery", landed the gang, sailed to Norfolk Island to re-provision, and then returned to the Bounty Islands. She reached Sydney, via Norfolk Island, in February 1808 "with a cargo of thirty eight thousand fine salted fur seal skins on board her, of the reputed value of thirty thousand pounds sterling and upwards".

The *Commerce* also called at the Bounty Islands in early December 1807 on her way to leave a sealing gang at the Auckland Islands. At the Bounties she would have found the sealers from the *Brothers* in residence, and did not stay long since she was at the Auckland Islands 13 days later.[28]

Soon after, possibly in February 1808, Captain Moody of the *Santa Anna* left a sealing gang of 10 Europeans, two Tahitians and two Maori on the Bounty Islands. They were put ashore with a limited amount of water, salt provisions and bread before the ship sailed back to New Zealand for potatoes and to Norfolk Island for pork. While the captain was ashore at Norfolk Island the *Santa Anna* was "blown off" the island for over 10 weeks.

In May the owners in Sydney received word from Moody, dated from Norfolk Island, that his sealers must now be in distress for want of provisions. To allay fears it was stated in the press that "the *Commerce* had sailed from Sydney on 6 February to relieve the gang and that by this time they would be provided for". But as we will see, this did not happen. The *Sydney Gazette* reported on 12 June: "Wednesday last, arrived *Santa Anna,* Captain Moody, from Norfolk Island, where she arrived back on the 19th ult., after an absence of two months and ten days, during which she was driven considerably to the northward, and encountered much bad weather".

The *Santa Anna*'s gang on the Bounties was visited and given relief of food and water by Captain S.R. Chace of the ship *King George.* She had sailed from Sydney on 27 August for a six-month whaling and sealing voyage in southern waters, and "there were seven to eight thousand skins and about 1800 gallons of oil on board" when she returned to port on 13 March 1809. By the time she arrived at the Bounty Islands the sealers from the *Santa Anna* "had been greatly distressed for more than three months for want of water and provisions", as there was no water on the island "except when a shower of rain happened to fall". The only food obtainable was "seals and sea-fowl". Two Europeans and one Tahitian died from the hardships experienced. It was not until 15 October 1808 that the *Santa Anna* sailed from Sydney for "the Sealing Isles; from whence she is to proceed to Great Britain". She called at the

Bounties and took on board the gang and their catch of 8000 skins.

Many versions of this story exist. All are based on the account written by Samuel Marsden[29] as related to him by the Maori chief Ruatara, who was one of the sealing gang, and on research of shipping records. From the dates given it appears that the *Santa Anna*'s gang must have been on the Bounties for about nine months (February-November 1808). Possibly the *King George* called twice to check on them, first "about five months after the *Santa Anna* had left" and later "a few weeks" before the *Santa Anna* returned. After uplifting the marooned gang the *Santa Anna* seems to have visited further southern islands before returning to the Bounty Islands in January 1809. She reached London on 13 July 1809.[30] Obviously the *Commerce* did not reach the Bounties to relieve the marooned gang as the Sydney press had claimed was her intention. She returned to Sydney on 10 July 1808 after a six-month voyage with about 3000 skins from the "sealing islands", most probably the Chatham or Auckland Islands.[31] It is clear that the fur seal populations of the southern islands were declining fast.

In May 1808 the English firm of Enderby and Company, "finding the price of seal skins very high", fitted out two small vessels, the *Swan* of 153 tons (James Lindsay, master) and the *Otter* of 169 tons (Thomas Hopper, master) for a two-year voyage to explore the Southern Ocean. Their primary mission was to locate the true position of Cape Circumcision – a land mass discovered in 1739 at 54° S latitude somewhere below Africa by the French explorer Bouvet de Lozier – and harvest any seals found there. After separating from the *Otter*, Lindsay in the *Swan* rediscovered Cape Circumcision on 7 October and found it was an island – now known as Bouvet Island – but thick pack-ice prevented a landing. The *Swan*, following her owners' instructions, then continued to the west to visit the Antipodes and Bounty Islands. She reached the Bounties in January 1809, from where Captain Lindsay despatched a letter to London, apparently by the *Santa Anna*, reporting his discoveries and lack of success in sealing. The *Otter*, apparently following a similar course, arrived in Sydney via the Bay of Islands on 16 March. Here she was reported as having had "no present success" with sealing or whaling since leaving England. She left again on 2 April "on a sealing voyage". Later she was reported from the Derwent, with her master apparently "deranged in his intellect", and finally reached London under Captain Jobling on 24 January 1911.[32]

There was a gang of sealers already ashore when Captain S. Chase in the *Pegasus* visited the Bounty Islands in July 1809. Chase reported to his owners: "We made the Bounty Islands, there being a gang of men on it, we made no stay there".[33] Possibly this gang could have been from the *Otter* or the *Swan*, but more probably were from the *Star*, which sailed from Sydney on 20 January 1809 and returned from the "sealing islands" on 31 August with 2000 skins.

CHAPTER FOUR

The End of the Sealing Bonanza

FINAL INTERNATIONAL HARVESTS

The 58-ton schooner *Antipode* was launched at Port Jackson on 29 August 1807 and the next day advertised for "about twenty able-bodied seamen and sealers". On her maiden voyage she seems to have positioned a sealing gang on Antipodes Island. Captain Scott then took the schooner prospecting for seals to the Chathams, where on 21 November he encountered the *Topaz* commanded by Mayhew Folger of Nantucket. The *Topaz* later called at the Antipodes on 17 December and found two sealing gangs ashore. One gang, obviously the one left there by the *Perseverance* in March 1807, told of having accumulated "only 4000" skins in four months, so Folger cruised on southward looking for the Auckland Islands.[1]

On her next voyage the *Antipode*, under Captain Birbeck, again placed sealers on the Antipodes and returned to Sydney on 22 March 1809 with 4000 skins, most of which were probably obtained at that island.

The *Antipode* left Sydney again in September 1809, commanded by William Stewart, carrying about 26 sealers. Of these, 20 seem to have been left at the Auckland Islands. While at the Antipodes one sealer, named Needham, was embarked and six landed to reinforce the gang already ashore.[2] This was the last sealing voyage of the *Antipode*, for in February 1810 she returned to Port Jackson "in distress" and "in a shattered and dismantled condition". How many skins were loaded at the Antipodes is nowhere recorded, but the haul must have been substantial (perhaps 1000 or more) to warrant the six extra sealers left there.

On 1 May 1810, Thomas Moore, an owner of the *Pegasus*, wrote to Captain Chase: "There are six men on the Penantipodes left by the *Antipode* schooner. You may . . . [word omitted, perhaps 'uplift'] if you want them, but if you should fall in with that island relieve them with some provisions as they have none." However, the *Pegasus* did not call at Antipodes on her way to England. Just who rescued the *Antipode*'s sealers is unknown, but possibly it was the schooner *Unity* which returned to Sydney on 15 August with 6000 sealskins. These were collected during a long sealing voyage reportedly "mostly about the islands on the coast of New Zealand, and in Foveaux's Straits" – but possibly also including the Chatham and other outlying islands.[3]

The decline in the trade was very sudden, caused not only by rapidly declining seal populations but also by the collapse of the world markets for skins. The Chinese had been flooded with millions of sealskins from South America and elsewhere, and in London too many skins arrived in 1809 on to a weak market due to an economic downturn. In addition, the British Government placed a crippling duty on imports of oil and skins from colonial merchants. Many Sydney traders working on borrowed money were soon bankrupt and unable to uplift their sealing gangs from the southern islands. In several cases it was some years before these gangs were relieved. Only the discovery of the new rich sealing grounds of Campbell and Macquarie Islands in 1810 enabled a few Sydney sealing merchants to survive. In turn, these new grounds were largely cleared of fur seals in a very few years.[4]

After 1810, there were not enough seals left at the Bounty or Antipodes Islands to make them prime targets for sealing vessels. However, they continued to be visited on occasion by speculative sealers calling at all or most of the southern islands during a voyage.

One such ship was the *Henry*, under Captain Robert Johnson, which between 1823 and 1826 made two profitable sealing cruises to the "south of New Zealand". It was reported that during the first voyage from the Auckland and adjoining islands she took no less than 13,000 skins, described by one American as being "as good fur-seal skins as ever were brought to the New York Market". The next year Johnson returned to the same waters. After visiting the Chathams, he was in 1825 "spoken" to at South Cape, Stewart Island. He then had 1700 prime sealskins on board. From Stewart Island the *Henry* was reported to have sailed to the south and east in search of new sealing grounds. She called at the Auckland Islands on the way, and returned to New York on 18 April 1826 with 3000 skins. It is highly probable that on one or both of these voyages Johnson would have visited the Bounty and Antipodes Islands.[5]

Sometime in the 1820s or 1830s, Jack Coffee (a sealer of Irish decent who later settled on the Chatham Islands) and two companions were put ashore on the Bounty Islands. Many years later, in1868, Coffee told Percy Smith that:

> Once he went to the Bounty Islands with a Whaleship and was left there with two companions to catch seals under a promise from the Captn that he would come back in a few months to fetch them. The ship went to the Thames, where it was taken by the Maoris and burnt. Coffee and his mates waited on, living on penguins' eggs, but mostly starving, with no water but what they could catch in the little crevasses of the rock, until some stranger ship took them off after they had given up all hope. Those islands are bare rock with no vegetation on them.[6]

Just what ships were involved is a mystery. There seems to be no record of Maori taking and burning a ship near Thames. It has been suggested that perhaps these sealers were left by the *Mercury* or *Haweis*.[7] The former was a London sperm whaler that set out from Sydney in 1824 on a joint sealing and whaling voyage but was captured and burnt at Whangaroa Harbour early in 1825; but there is obvious disagreement in the reported site of this ship's capture. For a similar reason, as we shall see, it is unlikely that it was the *Haweis.*

In June 1825, William Stewart returned to the southern sealing islands during an "unknown speculating trip" in the *Prince of Denmark.* He had a gang of experienced sealers aboard, and his first and second mates both had wide sealing experience. The vessel first sailed for the Bay of Islands, and then headed southwards on 5 July. After calling at Hicks Bay and Akaroa the *Prince of Denmark* is thought to have visited Port Pegasus. From here Stewart took the ship southwards, probably to the Auckland, Campbell and Macquarie islands, and then in search of new sealing islands "in very high latitudes".[8] It has been speculated that he was searching for the non-existent Nimrod Group, which along with the just as mythical Emerald Island and the Royal Company Islands all appeared on early charts. In these high southern latitudes they were delayed "by divers unforseen accidents and disasters and great stress of bad and boisterous weather". Somehow, William Rook, the elderly second mate who had been a crew member of the *Venus* in 1805, a sealing "overseer" on Macquarie Island from 1810–1812 and later a sealing captain[9], suffered seriously from frostbite. He lost the use of his limbs and died on the return voyage. He was buried on Antipodes Island.

GRAVES AT THE ANTIPODES

On 19 November 1880 the schooner *Alert* arrived at Bluff with a sealing party from the Antipodes who told the *Southland Times* of: "Having come across two graves on the island, dated 1825. The one having a headboard to the memory of Alexander Foster, chief officer of the Prince of Denmark, who was drowned making the boat harbor [sic] on the 24th December, and the other William Rook, seaman on the same vessel, aged 67 years."

The headboard was rediscovered in 1888 by Mr Bethune, the second engineer of the Government steamer *Stella.* William Dougall, a passenger who accompanied Bethune ashore, records that the piece of totara board was found on a "almost precipitous ledge of rock and tussock" above their landing place. This was clearly at Stella Bay, as Dougall took a photograph of "a natural archway here which is at the entrance of the boat harbour, and also shows the grave". As "far as decipherable", the inscription on the board read: "To the M —— Foster, chief officer of the Schr. Prince of Denmark, who was unfortunately drown —— ke the Boat Arbour —— 14th day of December in the —— 1825."

A fellow passenger, Andreas Reischek, gave a slightly different interpretation, recording the message as: "To the memory of W. Foster, chief officer of the schooner 'Prince of Denmark', who was unfortunately drowned in the Boat Harbour, December 17, 1825".

Apart from the month and year of Alexander Foster's death, December 1825, all three records differ slightly. Probably Dougall's is the most precise as regards actual wording and spelling, but the date of 24th December as read by the crew of the *Alert* could be correct, as the headboard had possibly deteriorated in the following eight years. Robert McNab incorrectly argued that the date on the board must have been 1826 not 1825, but much more is now known of the *Prince of Denmark*'s voyages. One of Dougall's photographs illustrates the gravesite and shows a short post and a board lying on the ground. The post and headboard have long disappeared but the site is still easily recognisable.

Presumably William Rook is buried in the same locality. He was Second Mate of the *Prince of Denmark*, not a "seaman", as deciphered from the headboard on his grave in 1880. This marker was probably then in very poor condition, and has not been seen since. No grave relating to George Allen, who was drowned along with Foster, has been recorded. It is possible that his body was not recovered from the sea.

Stewart then left a sealing gang at the Antipodes under the charge of the first mate, Alexander Foster, and the carpenter, George Allen, before the *Prince of Denmark* sailed for the Bay of Islands. Port Jackson was reached on 18 December. The net result of the seven-month voyage was only 258 fur seal and 77 sea-lion skins. Obviously, most of these skins would have come from other islands.[10]

The *Prince of Denmark* next cleared Port Jackson on 18 January 1826. She first visited the Bay of Islands and embarked sawyers and colonists for Port Pegasus. Sometime during May she sailed from Stewart Island to re-embark her sealing gang. On arrival at the Antipodes it was found that the first mate and the carpenter had been drowned, the boats wrecked and a disappointing number of seals caught.[11] The meagre catch suggests that few fur seals were then visiting the islands, although the loss of the boats and two men may have restricted the sealing. The ship then went on to the Chatham Islands in an apparent attempt to increase the tally. There they encountered extremely bad weather, and short of provisions the *Prince of Denmark* returned to Sydney, via Port Pegasus, on 8 September. As a sealing venture Stewart's latest foray to the Antipodes was a failure. The total harvest for the voyage was only 460 sealskins and one-and-a-half tons of flax[12], amounting in value "to the sum of two hundred and seventy-one pounds three shillings and twopence".[13]

About March 1826, following two to three months' sealing at the Auckland Islands and three weeks at Stewart Island, the schooner *Sally* from Hobart went to the Antipodes and Bounty Islands, "but left from bad weather". Through rough weather they appear not to have encountered Stewart's gang at the Antipodes, so probably did not land there or at the Bounty Islands. In total only 460 sealskins and 12 hundredweight of flax were obtained during this cruise of over seven months – which included the Auckland Islands, Stewart Island, Antipodes, Bounties, Chatham Islands, Cook Strait, Taranaki (Sugar Loaves and Gannet Island), Cape Foulwind, Foveaux Strait, and south-east Otago.[14]

In late November 1828 the *Haweis* landed 10 sealers at the Antipodes and two at the Bounty Islands, before sailing for the North Island on a trading voyage. At Whakatane she was temporarily captured and looted, delaying her return to pick up the two gangs by several months.[15] After returning to the Bounties and Antipodes, she reached Sydney with 340 skins in June 1829.

On 9 and 10 January 1830, Captain Isaac Percival in the Boston brig *Rob Roy* took 21 prime sealskins and seven pups from the Bounty Islands under perfect conditions described in the ship's log as "clear weather" and "light airs and calms". Nevertheless, once the brig was underway a boat "which was stove yesterday at the Bountys" had to be mended. The *Rob Roy* arrived at the Antipodes on 12 January and landed a sealing gang of eight men under Mr Whitmarsh. They were left ashore with gear and a boat for over two weeks while the ship sailed for New Zealand. On the *Rob Roy*'s return, on 29 January, it was found that three of the sealing party had deserted – taking with them cooking pots and other gear. Percival recorded in the log:

> At 4 AM jibed ship at 5 made the land bareing E by S Dis[tance] about 20 miles At 8 close in with the landing place Mr Thare went on shore with the larg[e] boat to assift Mr Whitmarsh in feching things on board At 10 came on board with all these things. Deserted from the crew landed at this place Richard James, John French and Abraham Farerewell They stole some cook things. Sent Mr Whitmarsh on shore to find the same. Did not.
>
> Saturday January the 30 – 1830 . . . Mr Whitmarsh returned on board without men or cook things they not being to be found took in boat and made all sail to the westward the midel of the island bareing S by E from which we take our departer.

From the Antipodes the *Rob Roy* visited the Auckland Islands and the main islands of New Zealand. On the early morning of 19 March the brig returned to the Antipodes Islands in squally weather to pick up the missing men. The ship's journal records:

> Ran down the south part of the island At 7 the capt[ain] went on shore and took off the Stuart [steward] John French and Farewell At 9 took in the boat and made sail on a wind to the southward for Nimrods Group for the forth time At noon the Antipodes bore W by N 15m Dis[tance].

No sealskins are mentioned in the journal either during January or when the deserters were taken back on board. Since elsewhere even very small numbers of sealskins were meticulously recorded, this suggests strongly that the sealers from the *Rob Roy* took none at all at the Antipodes, and that there were no longer any there.[16]

On 14 July 1831, the London whaling firm of Enderby sent out a whaling and sealing expedition to explore the high southern latitudes south of New Zealand. Two ships were involved, the brig *Tula*, of 148 tons, under John Biscoe, and the cutter *Lively*, of 49 tons, under George Avery. After calling at Tasmania, the Bay of Islands and the Chathams, the expedition made for the Bounty Islands, which were sighted on 24 December. In his journal Biscoe records that the boats were sent ashore but:

> . . . returned having seen only 5 seal on one of the rocks which they could not approach on account of the swell, but they found on landing on one of the rocks a hut . . . & other things which clearly proved that Europeans had been recently there. The tops of the rocks were covered with penguins, gulls & other birds. The weather was now very clear and had any land been within 30 miles we must have seen it. I now determined to proceed directly to the southward.[17]

The hut and gear found could have been left by the gang from the Haweis who were landed in November 1828.[18] Biscoe claimed that the Bounty Islands were "erroneously laid down" on his chart and that their true position was 47° 49′ S, 178° 26′ E. However, modern charts show the centre of the group at 47° 45′ 30″ S, 179° 03′ E – much closer to Captain Bligh's original position (47° 44′ S, 179° 07′ E) than to Biscoe's "good observations". Nevertheless, the chart Biscoe was using was undoubtedly wrong. One such "Engraved chart of the World in two sheets", published by "Wm Heather, London" in 1828 incorrectly shows the Bounty Islands considerably further west than the "Penantipodes".

There are no known sealing visits to either the Antipodes or Bounties from 1831 until 1843, when the brigantine *Rodney* visited the Antipodes Islands.[19] Her crew also searched for seals at the Chathams, Traps, Snares and the Auckland Group. Their success or otherwise at the Antipodes is unrecorded, but on 2 May they took 67 fur seals from the Eastern Reef, Chatham Islands.[20]

On 7 April 1844 the New Bedford Whaler *Seine* (Captain J.S. Smith) "made the bountys . . . 48° 20 S . . . 179° 58 W". The log margin for that date contains a crude but recognisable silhouette of the group from the south.[21] In their search for whales, whaling vessels criss-crossed a patch of ocean often "steering by the wind". This meant that if the wind veered in direction the helmsman would alter course to keep the same set on the sails. The whalers, therefore, were not always sure of their position and found isolated islands very useful to check their navigation. Sketches of the land were often included in the log to aid future recognition.

Captain Nathaniel Middleton's whaler *Alert*, out of the port of New London, was at the Bounty Islands on 26 December 1845. Some of the crew landed in an unsuccessful attempt to "catch some fish and get penguin eggs". They must have had high hopes, for there were millions of penguins on shore. But, the Erect-crested Penguins of the Bounties and Antipodes lay during October and the last eggs would have hatched in mid-November. The log contains no mention of seals.

Apparently there were then quite a few whalers about – but few whales – for over the next two days Captain Middleton spoke to two other American whalers, the *Ontario* and the *Hellespont*. Although both of these ships were "4 months out", one had caught only four whales and the other three.[22]

On 13 February 1846, Captain John W. Norton, master of the New Bedford ship *Navy*, "made the island of Antipodes". At noon "the island bore E by N, 12 miles" – and here in the log is a tiny but recognisable silhouette of the island from the south-west. The group was still in view the following morning.[23] That same year, the Sydney-based whaling and trading brig *Lalla Rookh* visited the Bounty Islands, possibly looking for sealskins. While there, Captain Martyn made navigational observations suggesting that the correct latitude of the islands was 47° 55′ S.[24]

NEW ZEALAND ATTEMPTS CONSERVATION

There was no legal protection for seals in New Zealand waters until 1875, when regulations and annual closed seasons were first introduced under the Protection of Animals Amendment Act. The Seals Fisheries Protection Act of 1878 limited the hunting season from 1 June to 1 October each year, and also allowed for the season to be varied or closed for up to three years by Order-in Council. In 1880, a severely depressed New Zealand economy, and perhaps advance notice that the "seal fishery" was to be closed for at least three years from 1 November 1881, seems to have stimulated a minor rush of sealers to the southern islands. On 11 August the *Southland Daily News* reported:

> Sealing parties have been all the rage at the Port this season. At present there are fourteen parties now on the various sealing grounds comprising one hundred men and we hope success will attend those engaged in the undertaking. Should they be but moderately successful it will cause a considerable amount of the "needful" to be circulated in the place, which will be a great boon to the Bluff these hard times.

On 15 June 1880, Walter Henderson, a merchant of Bluff, and J.T. Thomson purchased the 45-ton schooner *Alert* for £595, and fitted her out for sealing. Under command of Captain Rattray she first sailed on 29 June and established two sealing parties on Campbell Island. On 9 August she left Bluff for the Bounty Islands with a third gang consisting of John Edwards (headman), James Spencer, William Newton, Henry Chasland, Tau Stroud, and Skerritt. This party was landed on Depot Island with their gear, stores, a trypot, firewood, as well as timber and other materials for a hut. There is no record of them having a boat. They found the schooner *William and Jane* already sealing at the islands. The *Alert* returned to Bluff on 28 August with 25 sealskins.[25]

SKINS AND OIL

Sealskins and seal oil were "among the very few natural productions" at first available for harvesting by the early settlers of New South Wales, and by 1802 the colony was actively encouraging the trade. Seals were relatively cheap to harvest and the rewards for the ship owners and merchants were good, especially when sealing was carried out by land-based gangs rather than directly from ships. The Bass Strait and South Australian seal colonies were soon over-exploited, and by 1803 Sydney-built schooners and sloops were regularly venturing across the Tasman Sea to leave gangs on the rich sealing grounds around southern New Zealand.

In the New Zealand region, the species targeted were New Zealand Fur Seal (*Arctocephalus forsteri*), Southern Elephant Seal (*Mirounga leonina*), and Hooker's Sea Lion (*Phocarctos hookeri*). Fur seals were the most sought-after species. They yielded valuable skins and some oil. Elephant Seals produced large amounts of useful oil, but their skins had little value. Sea lions, known as hair seals, produced a low-value skin (used for leather) as well as oil, and were harvested only as a last resort in the absence of the other species.

In the early days of the trade most fur seal skins were sent to China. However, although the Chinese would usually buy, they would seldom pay a good price. It seems that the Canton market was often flooded with skins from Siberia or the Pacific coasts of North and South America, and that it usually dealt in dried skins which were difficult to store and liable to attacks from "worm". Sometimes prices obtained fell to as low as 2s per skin.

Following the development of a technique enabling seal fur to be used to cover top hats, London was found to be a better market. Prices of over 10s each for salted skins were the norm, and large prime skins sometimes fetched 30s. The heyday of these prices lasted from

1805 to 1808. However, a glut of skins on the market, combined with a drastic slump in London commerce, saw the price drop to 4s in 1809. Then in 1810 the British placed a crippling duty on imported colonial skins and oil. This led to most Sydney merchants having to end sealing operations. Many became bankrupt. Those that survived in the sealing industry turned to Elephant Seal oil. For fascinating details of those times see works by John Cumpston, D.R. Hainsworth and Rhys Richards.

Throughout the 19th century there was a steady demand for animal oils for lighting, soap and paint manufacture, tanning, rust prevention and lubrication — and Elephant Seal oil was considered of good quality and little inferior to sperm oil. According to Captain Thomas Raine in 1822, it generally required three bulls or ten female Elephant Seals to yield a ton (about 1000 litres) of oil. In 1803, Southern Elephant Seal oil was selling on the London market at from £35 to £42 a ton, but prices fell during the imposition of heavy British import duties between 1810 and 1820. In 1819 a cargo of 500 tons taken to London on the Surry fetched only £16 10s 0d per ton, although by 1828 a price of £30 was being quoted. Elephant Seal oil from Macquarie Island was valued at £20 per ton in 1890.

Towards the end of the 19th century there was a trade in penguin skins, when for a short period of passing fashion they were harvested to be made into ladies' muffs, or hand warmers. As fur seals became scarce, sealers with time on their hands briefly turned their attention to items such as sea lion skins, seal oil, penguin skins and paua shells. In 1880–81, more than 15,000 penguin skins were collected from crested penguins, mainly from the Bounty, Antipodes and Snares Islands and sold to Walter Henderson, a merchant of Bluff. The top price obtained seems to have been 6d per penguin skin, 1s 6d per sea lion skin and 2s per gallon of seal oil. The supply obviously exceeded the demand. Henderson lost money on the transactions, and a cache of rolled penguin skins that was never worth collecting can still be found in a shallow cave above Anchorage Bay, Antipodes Island.

The *William and Jane*, chartered by Waddel and Co., had left Bluff on 25 July[26], and six days later reached the Bounty Islands. Here they were "exceedingly successful . . . one day's take consisting of 127 skins". The ship appears to have stayed at the Bounty Islands for over two weeks, for as we have seen they were there when the *Alert* arrived. Owing to deteriorating weather, Captain Burke then shaped a course for the Antipodes, which were reached on the 19 August. However, due to "very heavy W.S.W. weather" the ship had to stand off the island for several days. A party eventually sent ashore "soon returned with the news that seals were not to be found". The *William and Jane* then returned to the Bounty Islands where "a few more seals were captured". She left the Bounty Islands on 21 September, encountering heavy north-west to south-west winds en route to Bluff, which was reached on 1 October. According to the *Southland Times*, "very bad weather was experienced during the cruise, and in one gale the steering gear was carried away, necessitating the rudder being worked with the aid of ropes". It was also reported that all was well with the gang from the *Alert* when the *William and Jane* left the Bounty Islands. The total take for the two-month cruise consisted of 347 sealskins and 150 penguin skins.[27]

On 10 September the *Alert* again sailed from Bluff with a sealing gang for the Antipodes Islands. After a brief stop at Stewart Island, the Antipodes were sighted on 18 September. On the 20th the gang comprising Henry King (headsman), Jack Mee, Green, Hawero Moses, Finn, Johnson and Harper were landed along with their gear, stores, a boat, and timber and other material for a hut, which they built close to the site where the castaway depot now stands. At 8.30 on the morning of 21 September, Captain Rattray left for the Bounty Islands, which he reached two days later. After five days transporting Edwards and his sealers around other islands in the group, the *Alert* loaded 191 sealskins, 28 gallons of seal oil and 15 bags of feathers for return to Bluff.

On the return voyage the schooner encountered a strong south-west gale for two days, then the wind veered to the south-south-east and blew with terrific force. The *Alert* reached Bluff on 4 October.

Following an October trip to the sealing parties on the Auckland and Campbell Islands, she sailed again on 27 October via Stewart and Campbell Islands. After uplifting a sealing gang at Campbell she arrived at the Antipodes on 7 November. Here King's sealers had not seen "a sign of a seal upon the island" but near Reef Point they had discovered the graves of two sealers who had been buried there 55 years earlier. After loading 3500 penguin skins the *Alert* sailed for the Bounty Islands the same day.

She arrived at noon on 8 November and immediately shipped the sealers and their produce. This consisted of 57 sealskins, 2990 penguin skins, 50 gallons of seal oil and five bags of guano. She then sailed for Bluff with a fresh westerly wind which lasted until the 12th. The Nuggets were reached on the 16th and Bluff on 19 November.[28] The next day the *Southland Daily News* reported: "The *Alert* in this trip has brought back all the parties sent out by Messrs. Henderson and Thompson. They have only been moderately successful."

It has been incorrectly claimed that at about this time 3500 penguin skins were brought from the Antipodes by the cutter *Kent*.[29] However, the skins in question were those collected on the Antipodes by Henry King's gang and shipped back with that gang on the schooner *Alert*. Although King had previously commanded the *Kent* while sealing around Stewart Island, the little cutter never visited the Antipodes.[30]

When Henderson made up the accounts, John Edwards and his gang from the Bounty Islands received payment for 273 sealskins bought at 22s each, and for 2750 of the penguin skins at 6d each. Each man received one lay (or share) worth £35 9s 0d, with the exception of Skerritt, who received only a half-share. Three shares, amounting to £132 16s 6d, were retained as payment for the use of the Alert. Henry King and his party from Antipodes Island sold their 3500 penguin skins for £87 10s 0d. Each man received one share of £8 6s 8d. They contributed three shares (£25) to the *Alert*, and a half-share of £4 3s 4d for the use of a boat.

Reef Point from Perpendicular Head, Antipodes.

In May 1881, Waddel & Co's 27-ton auxiliary ketch *Anna* was sent to the Bounty Islands under command of Captain Burke. She left a sealing gang ashore and returned to Bluff on 7 June. Nine days later she sailed on another sealing voyage to the Auckland and Campbell Islands. However, stormy conditions forced her to shelter in Port Pegasus until 19 July, and she did not arrive at Port Ross until the 23rd. Twelve days later she departed for Campbell Island where a gang was landed. She then picked up the Bounty Island party and returned to Bluff on 26 August. The *Anna* sailed south again a few days later and returned with the Campbell Island gang on 9 December.[31] No details of any of her catches were published. However, 15 years later Edwin Lukins wrote of speaking to an "old time sealer" in Halfmoon Bay, Stewart Island:

> This man was one of three, he told us, who were left on the Bountys for six weeks while their vessel went on to another island. During the time they were on the island they caught so many seals that at the then value of the skins, 25s a piece, they had earned £70 each, but seal skins now are worth but 18s.[32]

This sealer could well have been one of the gang left ashore by the *Anna* in 1881, for the high price per skin quoted was right for that period. Allowing for usual practice of the sealers receiving one share each of skins caught, while three shares were retained for the vessel, for the three sealers to have each made £70 then the total haul must have been about 336 seals.

On 1 November all sealing in New Zealand waters was prohibited and this complete ban continued for 10 years. In 1891 there was once again an open season for seals, but it was short and confined to July and August. New Zealand was still in economic depression and sealers were active, although the price for skins was low. Southland newspapers recorded sealing cruises to Fiordland and Stewart Island by various cutters, and to the Snares, Auckland, Campbell and Macquarie Islands by the *Janet Ramsey* and the *Gratitude* – but none to the Bounties or Antipodes.[33] In 1893, F.R. Chapman published a paper entitled "Notes on the Depletion of the Fur-Seal in the Southern Seas" in which he reported that the "comparatively large number [of fur seal skins] obtained in 1891 caused some surprise to experts". About a thousand skins were obtained at the various islands, most of them from the Aucklands and apparently most from young animals. Regarding the Bounty Islands, Chapman remarked that "the late open season seems to have yielded some hundreds of seals". However, as no sealers are recorded to have visited the Bounties that year perhaps he was referring to the take of the *Anna*'s gang of 1881.[34]

There are no further records of fur seals being taken at either the Antipodes or Bounty Islands. In the year 1886 the American barque *Alaska* (Charles W. Fisher, master) on a four-year-long whaling voyage to the south-west Pacific Ocean used both the Bounty and Antipodes Islands as way points. Two entries from her log read:[35]

> Wednesday Jan 27. This day light winds from N.E. to E.N.E. Course SW by S at 2 PM see the land Bounty Islands. Thick fogy weather.
>
> Saturday April 24. This day; light wind from NNW to W with fog Steering by the wind and N by E At 9AM see the Island of Antipod Employed in mending the cuting [cutting] stage.

A closed season for seals existed in New Zealand from 1891 until 1913, but because of poaching – which was impossible to stop – the seals barely increased. Open seasons for fur seals were declared from 1 July to 30 September 1913, and from 1 June to 30 September in 1914 to 1916, inclusive. In 1913 a total of 490 sealskins were taken – all but 45 from Fiordland and the Snares Islands. The annual tallies for sealskins exported in the years 1914 to 1917 were 490, 710, 1876 and 1377 respectively, but most of these came from Campbell and none from the Antipodes or Bounty Islands.[36] Since then, the only legal sealing in New Zealand waters has been some 530 fur seals taken under special license at Campbell Island during 1922–1930, and 6187 from the Fiordland and Stewart Island coasts in 1946.[37]

THE TOTAL HARVEST

After carefully studying the literature, I estimate that the total number of fur-seal skins reaching port from the Antipodes was about 330,000. [*See* Table 1: Antipodes Island – Shipping and fur seal harvest 1805–1880] However, this estimate makes no allowance for wastage, both on the island and during transport, which could have been as high as 15 per cent.[38] From similar sources, John Ling[39] recently estimated the total Antipodes Island take for the same period at 383,287 fur seal skins – some 50,000 more. However, several of his listed cargoes are in error. For example, he credited the *Ceres* with shipping 20,000 Antipodes Island skins to London in January 1804, and the *Independence* with taking 59,000 skins from the Antipodes to Canton in 1805–06. But we have seen that the first sealers did not land on the Antipodes until February 1805; that the *Ceres* made her only trip to the Antipodes in January 1806; and that the *Independence* was lost in the Southern Ocean some time before March 1806, and never sailed further north than Norfolk Island.

My estimate of the total number of Bounty Island skins to reach port is 56,700 [*See* Table 2: Bounty Island – Shipping and fur seal harvest 1807–1881]. This is only slightly higher than Ling's estimate of 54,448.

TABLE 1: Antipodes Island — Shipping and fur seal harvest 1805–1880

Year	Month	Vessel	Occasion	Seal skins loaded
1805	Feb	*Independence*	First sealing gangs landed	nil
1805	July‡	*Independence*	More sealers landed	nil
1805	July‡	*Favorite*	More sealers landed	nil
1805	Oct‡	*Honduras Packet*	With gear & provisions	nil
1805	Nov	*Venus*	Sealing gang landed	"few skins"
1805	Nov‡	*Governor King*	More sealers landed	nil
1806	Jan	*Honduras Packet*	Called for skins	27,000* (to London)
1806	Feb	*Governor King*	Called for skins	100 (lost/wreck)
1806	Feb	*Ceres*	Called for skins	18,507 (to London)
1806	Feb	*Favorite*	Called for skins	60,000 (to Sydney)
1806	May	*Star*	With provisions & for skins	56,692 (to Sydney)
1806	Aug	*Favorite*	Called for skins	55,000 (to Canton)
1806	Aug‡	*Star*	More sealers landed	nil
1806	Nov	*Star*	Called for skins	14,000 (to Sydney)
1807	Feb	*Perseverance*	Relieved gang & for skins	40,000* (to Canton)
1807	Mar‡	*Commerce*	Uplifted sealers & skins	39,000 (to Sydney)
1807	Apr‡	*Star*	Called for skins	5,823 (to London)
1807	Dec	*Antipode*	Had gang ashore	4,000 (to Sydney)
1807	Dec	*Topaz*	Called at island	nil
1809	Jan/Feb	*Antipode*	Left gang ashore	4,000 (to Sydney)

Year	Month	Vessel	Occasion	Seal skins loaded
1809	Nov‡	*Antipode*	More sealers landed	1,000* (to Sydney)
1810	July?	*Unity?*	Uplifted Antipode's gangs?	1,000* (to Sydney)
1825	Oct‡	*Prince of Denmark*	Sealing gang landed	100* (to Sydney)
1826	Mar‡	*Sally*	Visited	nil*
1826	May	*Prince of Denmark*	Uplifted sealers & skins	460 (to Sydney)
1828	Nov	*Haweis*	Left 10 sealers ashore	140* (to Sydney)
1829	Jan	*Rob Roy*	Sealing Three crew deserted	nil
1829	Mar	*Rob Roy*	Returned for deserters	nil
1843	May	*Rodney*	Visited	nil*
1880	Aug	*William and Jane*	Landed. No seals seen	nil
1880	Sept	*Alert*	Left sealing gang ashore	nil
1880	Nov	*Alert*	Uplifted gang. No seals seen	nil
Total fur seal skins loaded at Antipodes Island (minimum): 330,000				

NOTES:

‡ Month approximate, depending on time taken sailing from, or to, Sydney.

* Estimate based on likely proportion of total cruise catch, or other evidence.

TABLE 2: Bounty Islands — Shipping and fur seal harvest 1807–1881

Year:	Month:	Vessel:	Occasion:	Seal skins loaded:
1807	July‡	*Brothers*	First sealing gangs landed	38,000 (to Sydney)
1807	Dec	*Commerce*	Visited enroute to Aucklands	unknown
1808	Feb	*Santa Anna*	Left gang on islands	nil
1808	Sep/Nov	*King George*	Sealing at islands	7,500 (to Sydney)
1808	Nov‡	*Santa Anna*	Uplifted sealers and skins	8,000 (to London)
1809	Jan	*Santa Anna*	At islands	unknown
1809	Jan	*Swan*	Called to post letter	nil
1809	July‡	*Star?*	Had a gang ashore	2,000 (to Sydney)
1824	?	*Mercury?*	Left gang on islands	nil
1825	?	*unknown*	Rescued above gang	unknown
1826	Mar	*Sally*	Visited	nil*
1828	Nov	*Haweis*	Left 2 sealers ashore	200* (to Sydney)
1830	Jan	*Rob Roy*	Landed sealers	28
1831	Dec	*Tula & Lively*	Landed. Only 5 seals seen	nil
1846	Dec	*Alert (US whaler)*	Visited	nil
1880	Aug/Sep	*William and Jane*	Sealing at islands	347 (to Bluff)
1880	Aug	*Alert (NZ schooner)*	Left gang on Depot Island	25 (to Bluff)
1880	Sept	*Alert*	Sealing & loading skins	191 (to Bluff)
1880	Nov	*Alert*	Uplifted sealers & skins	57 (to Bluff)
1881	May	*Anna*	Left gang on Depot Island	nil
1881	Aug	*Anna*	Uplifted sealers & skins	336 (to Bluff)
Total fur seal skins loaded at Bounty Islands (minimum) : 56,700				

NOTES:

‡ Month approximate, depending on time taken sailing from, or to, Sydney.

* Estimate based on likely proportion of total cruise catch, or other evidence (see text).

CHAPTER FIVE

Hazards to Shipping

The shortest and quickest course for sailing vessels leaving Australia for Europe lay on the Great Circle Route via Cape Horn. This course took them southwards to pick up the strong westerly winds that then drove them westward. The subantarctic islands to the south of New Zealand, particularly the Auckland Islands, straddled this general track, and rough seas, overcast skies and fog combined to make them notorious as a trap for sailing vessels. The Antipodes were north of the usual course, but variable weather and highly inaccurate charts led numerous sailing ships into close encounters with their shores. The weather and sea conditions experienced south-east of New Zealand by the barque *Emu* (Captain William Howard) in early March 1839 appear typical. During the second week out from Hobart on a voyage to England:

> Unfavourable weather, with gales and fog, was experienced . . . For eight

> days it was impossible to use the sun for an observation, and as the ship's course was ESE, and the Auckland and Antipodes Islands lay in that direction, some anxiety was felt. This was very real to the Tasmanians, as a first-class ship, the *Rifleman*, had left Hobart Town only two years previously and had never again been heard of; it was assumed that in such weather as this she had crashed into one of these islands and been lost with all hands . . .

On Friday, March 7, the Chief mate thought he saw land, the Aucklands being in the vicinity. At 5 p.m. it came up foggy with increasing winds to gale force. In the evening an anxious look-out was kept and as the wind was increasing, the vessel was put about for the night and sails shortened.[1]

A few days later, on 12 March, Antipodes Island was sighted and the ship closed to within three miles. As it was 6 p.m. the captain was not able to honour a promise he had earlier made to the ship's surgeon, William Crowther, that he could land to collect natural history specimens. Crowther described the island in his journal:

Earliest known sketch of Antipodes Island – William L. Crowther, Barque *Emu*, 1839. *(W.L. Crowther Library, State Library of Tasmania.)*

> It seemed at first sight to be very high land, which it was, about 1200 ft. above sea-level, extending 5 miles in length and about the same in breadth. It had a most singular appearance, being guarded as it were on its two extremities. On its north end a rock or small island like the Mewstone [a small islet off southern Tasmania], equally as high and perpendicular; on the south-east is seen another very high and more massive. As we approached closer the whole island seemed to be comprised of a quantity of hills which terminated in the most horrible precipices. The island seemed solid rock without soil or vegetation excepting a scrub or broom of brownish-green colour. The bluff crags or precipices were only inhabited by seafowl in the most wonderful variety.[2]

From this, and an accompanying sketch, the *Emu* clearly approached the group from the south and then bore eastwards past Albatross Point. The smaller islands mentioned and sketched are West Windward and Leeward islands. Obviously, Crowther was disorientated, as regards compass directions, by almost 90°.

THE CHANGING POSITION OF THE ANTIPODES ISLANDS

In 1800, Captain Waterhouse determined Penantipode Island's position as 49° 49′ S 179° 20′ E. Forty years later, in March 1840, Lieutenant O.H. Wilson, RN, wrote to the *Nautical Magazine* and *Naval Chronicle* enclosing a sketch of the island and pointing out a major error in its generally accepted longitude. On two voyages he found it to be at 178° 42′ E, a position confirmed in 1846 by Captain Benjamin Darley of the *Ewerettа*.

Surprisingly, the corrected longitude was slow to be included on charts and in sailing directories. In further correspondence to the *Nautical Magazine* in June 1859, Captain Stevenson of the *Maidstone* reported that the islands were still incorrectly positioned on charts and in sailing directories, and that "instead of one, as described", they numbered at least "four detached islands, with clear channels between". He gave the following comparison between his observations and those previously published: "Long. by my chronometers, mean of three 178° 40′. Horsburgh 179° 30′ E; Raper 179° 42′ E; Norie 179° 40′ E." The editor commented: "It is very remarkable that these lonely isles should have remained so long incorrectly placed on the chart, which here is sufficient authority now to correct."

However, the problem remained, as further reported in the *Nautical Magazine* for July 1865. The barque *Fugitive* had recently returned to Plymouth from Sydney and "her commander, Captain Barwood, having good chronometers, under favourable circumstances, and with a clear sky, made the centre of the Island of Antipodes to be 178° 43′ E, which is forty-five miles west of the position given in his chart".

After checking that the then current Admiralty chart agreed with Barwood's observations, the editor commented on the continued use of outdated charts: "If such seriously erroneous charts are to be perpetuated by remaining thus uncorrected, what is to become of our mercantile marine? No ship should be allowed to navigate with such disreputable documents in these days when the Government liberally places at the command of the public, on the most moderate terms, the same charts as those by which Her Majesty's ships are navigated . . . the seaman must be cautious how he trusts merchant ship's charts that should have been corrected five and twenty years ago!"

Nevertheless, even Her Majesty's ships sometimes fell into the trap. In 1865, HMCS *Victoria* — following two different almanacs and a chart published in January 1853 — spent over 10 hours searching for the Antipodes. The captain eventually found the islands where Lieutenant Wilson had said they were 25 years before, but 51 miles west of where the *Victoria* had started looking. In 1868 the brig *Amherst*, on an official mission for the New Zealand Government, was still using charts showing the Antipodes in the wrong location.

In 1875, James Imray and Son of London published a large chart of the Western Pacific showing the Antipodes Islands in near-correct position — at 49° 43′ S, 178° 42′ E. However, as late as 1888, Captain Douglas reported to Melbourne Customs that on his last voyage to London in the *Ben Cruachan* he found that the Antipodes Islands were 75 miles further westward than shown on his chart — which had been published by H.R. Norrie of London in 1873 with the claim that it was based "chiefly from documents lodged at the Hydrographic Office of the Admiralty".

All charts and nautical almanacs published after the mid-1870s contained near-correct co-ordinates for the Antipodes, but it is possible that in 1893 when the *Spirit of the Dawn* ran onto the islands there were still many old editions in use on merchant vessels. Alternatively, if that ship was carrying the 1875 edition of *The New Zealand Pilot* — published by the Admiralty, London, — a misprint in the text, which gave the wrong longitude (170° 43′ E), could have led to the belief that the Antipodes Islands were already well astern.

There are still minor discrepancies shown on the most modern maps and charts of the islands. According to the latest Lands and Survey map of Antipodes — NZMS 272/4 (1978) — Mt Galloway, the highest point, is at 49° 41′ 25″ S latitude; 178° 47′ 03″ E longitude. Chart NZ 311 published by the Hydrographic Office of the Royal New Zealand Navy (1992), shows Mount Galloway at 49° 41′ 03″ S; 178° 46′50″ E.

The opening up of the Victorian goldfields in the early 1850s caused a flood of migrants. The Australian population increased rapidly, more than doubling in a decade, to number over a million by 1860. This greatly increased ship traffic to and from Europe and unexpected encounters with the Antipodes, other subantarctic islands, and icebergs, became commonplace.[3] One such ship was the *Maidstone* bound from Melbourne to London in

1859. Her master, Captain W.P. Stevenson, was following published sailing directions and decided to steer the "most direct passage" for Cape Horn. He later reported:[4]

> As the ship approached the southern latitudes, the wind veered to the westward, and on the 7th of February passed half way between the Snares Rock and the Auckland Islands, blowing a heavy gale; bar. 28.80 [inches of mercury].
>
> From noon of the 9th February (morning and afternoon sights to correspond), in lat. 49° 26′ S., long. 177° 5′ E., I shaped a course to pass to the southward of the Antipodes Island, allowing the position assigned, and calculated the difference at noon between our latitude and longitude and that of the island. The result proved by bearing and distance 84° S., 105 miles E. Consequently we did not expect to approach the island till 11h. p.m. However, at 6h. 30m. p.m. the look-out forward reported icebergs ahead. I directly made use of a powerful telescope, and distinctly observed the sea breaking high about four miles on the starboard bow, bearing E.S.E., the weather misty, with a fresh westerly breeze. We shortened sail and altered our course to N.E., and followed along until we discovered the icebergs proved to be *insula firma* – the Antipodes! But instead of one, as described, we numbered four detached islands, with clear channels between . . . according to our calculations, the islands are placed 42 miles too far to the eastward.
>
> These islands do not appear to be noticed by navigators, although much in the way of the homeward-bound . . . and from the reason of their being immediately in the track of ships steering for the Horn, deserve further attention, and a more correct position assigned to them.

The look-out's initial identification of the islands as icebergs is not surprising. For many decades during the late 19th and early 20th centuries, icebergs were often encountered well north in the Pacific and Indian Oceans, and sometimes reached 43° S off the east of New Zealand.

ICEBERGS

During the 19th and early 20th centuries, collision with an iceberg was a real risk for any vessel plying between Australasia and Europe. Of the scores then lost without trace, many probably met this fate during storm, fog or darkness. In some years, bergs were commonly encountered along the usual sailing tracks in the Pacific, off Cape Horn, and in the South Atlantic often as far north as 37° S. The seas off the Cape of Good Hope and the South Indian Ocean also had their share of icebergs entering the shipping routes. In one extreme case, in January 1850, a berg was in sight from the Cape of Good Hope at latitude 34° S.

Historical records compiled by H.C. Russell during the 1890s suggest that icebergs appeared in the shipping lanes in unpredictable swarms. For instance, in the latter part of 1854 "alarming accounts of ice in the southern ocean began to come in. In November, both in the outward and homeward tracks, more particularly between Cape Horn and Cape of Good Hope, many icebergs were seen". In the Pacific Ocean, an iceberg was reported at longitude 170° W and latitude 40° S in 1855. Icebergs of prodigious size were sometimes encountered and navigating a safe course past them could be hazardous. One huge berg reported by 21 ships from the vicinity of Cape Horn in 1855, was described as: "A solid mass of ice, measuring sixty miles on one side, forty miles on another, and in the third side (for it was triangular), there was a great bay, into which three vessels unconsciously sailed — two got out by tremendous exertion, and the third became a total wreck."

A similar berg was encountered at 47° S in the Atlantic by the *Wasdale* and *Strathcathro* on 11 January 1893. They "sailed all unconscious of danger into a horse-shoe shaped bay in an iceberg" — the bay was 20 miles long, 10 miles across in the middle, and four miles wide at the entrance.

In 1862, Admiral Fitzroy wrote of the occurrence of icebergs on the usual shipping route between New Zealand and Cape Horn: "In the South Pacific, between 150° and 100° W longitude, and 50° to 60° latitude, every ship that risks a passage through it finds numerous and some enormous masses of ice. Immense islands rather than icebergs have been passed thereabouts, eight hundred to one thousand feet above the sea and several miles in circumference."

Starting in late 1891 and lasting until 1897, "another remarkable outburst of icebergs" occurred on the southern oceanic trading routes right around the globe. Very many bergs were encountered to the east of New Zealand, particularly in 1892.

In early October 1892, the *Coptic* and *Aorangi* reported many icebergs "within 24 hours of leaving Lyttelton" at 46° S and 174–180° W. Similarly, shortly after sailing from Lyttelton, on 19 October the *Star of England* saw a huge iceberg and soon the ship was "completely surrounded by icebergs, nothing but ice three hundred feet high could be seen from aloft". For a while the engines had to be stopped. During the afternoon the ship cleared the worst of the ice and "kept away to the north of the Chatham Islands". The next day at 43° S, 170° W, she passed another large iceberg.

On 29 October 1892, Mr Gascoigne, the Resident Magistrate of the Chatham Islands, reported that several icebergs were off the island and that some had stranded at Pitt Island: "One five hundred feet high, another nearly half a mile long; they remained in sight a few days and then broke up." Another account suggests that there were eight or more bergs all around the Chathams and through Pitt Strait. They were in view for "about a week or more", some eventually breaking up and others drifting off to the east. According to the *New Zealand Pilot* it was "an occurrence never before recorded", and there has been no recurrence since.

Icebergs were commonly seen from Campbell Island in the years 1892 through to 1906. On 30 November 1897 while at the Antipodes Islands, the Government steamer *Hinemoa* saw 17 icebergs. Four were stranded onshore, and three off to the west were estimated as 300, 250, and 200 feet high and "one mile around". The ship's Chief Officer drew a sketch showing the disposition of the bergs around the islands. Later that night, about half way to the Bounty Islands, the *Hinemoa* passed another large berg, one mile long and 350 feet high.

Further icebergs were reported between the Antipodes and Chatham Islands in October 1902, and elsewhere in New Zealand's subantarctic in the late 1920s. Alex Spence, a shepherd on Campbell Island, recalled an experience while on Mount Dumas towards the end of 1929: "When we got high enough to look out to sea, away to the south-west we were surprised to see what looked like a full-rigged ship. But after peering through the telescope we realised it was a huge iceberg hull down on the horizon. When we got to the top, we saw another only six or seven miles away to the north-east. And further round there was yet another, the largest of the three — it looked like Mt Cook gone for a swim. Broken ice had stacked up all along the rocks."

In 1931, bergs were reported near the Auckland Islands and the same year one even reached the South Otago coast at 46° S. One was reported at latitude 55°, south-east from the Antipodes in 1948. Since then, no icebergs have been seen near New Zealand, and few have been sighted anywhere in the Pacific north of about 55° S. Perhaps this may be symptomatic of the recorded warming of the Southern Ocean and shifting oceanic currents. Because of their great draught (about 80 per cent under water), icebergs are impelled by ocean currents rather than directly by wind. They seem not to survive long in rough temperate seas north of the present-day Antarctic Convergence.

HMCS *VICTORIA*: THE FIRST SEARCH FOR CASTAWAYS

Following the loss of the schooner *Grafton* at the Auckland Islands in January 1864 and the subsequent rescue of her crew 19 months later, there were concerns that other missing ships may have been wrecked there. This resulted in the Government of Victoria sending the Colonial steam-sloop HMCS *Victoria* under command of Captain W.H. Norman and with Thomas Musgrave, captain of the *Grafton*, as advisor, to search the Auckland, Campbell, Antipodes and Bounty Islands for shipwrecked persons.[5] Although the *Victoria* was equipped with extra "special stores" – of bedding, clothing, food, and alcoholic beverages – to cater for any persons rescued, it was not part of her mission to establish castaway depots on the islands. She did, however, let loose a number of goats, rabbits, pigs, "game-fowls", geese and guinea-fowls and numerous "English trees" were planted at Auckland and Campbell Islands. These had been sent down by the Acclimatisation Society of Victoria to help provide for "any persons who may hereafter be wrecked or in distress upon these islands".

The *Victoria* left Melbourne on 4 October 1865 and, after searching the Auckland and Campbell Islands without finding sign of castaways, reached the Antipodes on 3 November in "heavy and continued rain". Over the next two days strong gale-force winds veered from the NW to WSW and the ship was kept "close in under the lee of the island for shelter" where no suitable landing site was seen. On the afternoon of the 4th the wind slackened a little. The ship tried to "steam round the island, by the N.W. side, but, finding the sea very heavy, had to bear up under its lee again". Later, after setting "double-reefed trysails", they were able to "beat round by the south-western shores" and circumnavigate the island, "thus obtaining a good view of the south-western and north-western shores at less than a mile off".

In their respective accounts, Captains Norman and Musgrave published the first detailed descriptions of the Antipodes Islands.[6] Norman wrote:

> Perpendicular cliffs all round the island, rising to heights varying from 200 feet to 600 feet. On the N.W. cape is an immense cave about 120 feet high; there are also several small islets from 150 feet to 200 feet high on the N.,

Icebergs at the Antipodes Islands, 1 December 1897. Sketch by Chief Officer A.S. Moys, NZGSS *Hinemoa*, "Birds-eye view" looking NE. (*NZ Journ. Marine and Freshwater Research.*)

N.E., and E. side; none of them are more than a mile off the main island; and all of them appear safe to approach or to pass between. The highest part of the largest island is apparently about 1,100 feet high. No landing place was seen, unless on the E.N.E. corner, where some rocks jut out a few yards, but at the time we passed the sea was running too high to make the attempt. The only vegetation seen on this island was some long grass and fern or scrub of a dark colour, on the top and sides of the hills.

Musgrave's journal adds further detail:

The whole group presents to the eye the most wild and dismal specimen of nature's handiwork that I have ever beheld; to look upward when close under the cliffs, makes one shudder . . . The Antipodes Island consists of a group of rocks, the largest of which is about nine miles in circumference; in shape it is something like a wedge standing on its edge, the pointed end to the northward. It is covered with a brownish colored, perished-looking grass. Its highest part is not less than 1,200 feet above the sea. It is surrounded by ten smaller lumps of rock; all of which, excepting one off the south side are high; and, like the large one, on all sides present a bold, perpendicular, inaccessible basaltic front. The two off the north point lay the farthest off – about three-quarters of a mile – the *Victoria* went twice through this channel.

No attempt was made to land and at 4 p.m. the *Victoria* stood off towards the Bounty Islands that were reached on the evening of the 5th, and inspected closely the next day. Norman describes the islands thus:

> This group, seen from a distance, has the appearance of being covered with vegetation, but nearer inspection shows them to be of a greenish color, and quite barren. A dense fog rising suddenly at 9.15 a.m., and the boat having returned reporting no possibility of any one existing, or landing even with safety on them, induced me to steam away at once for safety.

Musgrave once again provides extra detail:

> At 3.30 on the morning of the 6th, steam was got up, and we stood in towards them. Passed between some of them, and at 7.30 a.m. a boat was lowered and sent on shore in charge of the first officer, to see if there was a possibility of landing. He found a small nook on the N.E. side, where he managed to land one of his men, who brought off some specimens of rock, which is of granite formation. Seals were numerous; and from the water's edge to their summit, the rocks were all literally swarmed with penguin . . . This group . . . consists of a number of bare rocky islets, without a blade of grass or other vegetation upon them. They are probably between 20 and 30 in number (I have counted 19); and the greater part of them are, as near as I can judge, from 150 to 300 feet high, with clear channels between some of them, but the broken water in every direction around them bespeaks hidden dangers; and the whole group should be carefully avoided by passers by. Fortunately they are not in the general track of shipping.

THE CRUISE OF THE BRIG *AMHERST*

In early January 1868, the brig *Amherst* returned to Bluff from a sealing expedition having on board ten survivors from the wreck of the three-masted American ship *General Grant* which had long been missing on a voyage from Melbourne to London. With 83 people on board, she was wrecked on the western cliffs of the Auckland Islands in 1866 with the loss of 73 lives. In a vain attempt to get help for the survivors, then camped on Enderby Island, first mate Bartholomew Brown and three others of the crew had sailed for New Zealand in January 1887 in one of the ship's boats. Unfortunately they had neither compass nor chart, and apparently had decided on a course much too far to the east to make a landfall in New Zealand.[7]

In response to great public concern regarding the fate of the boat's crew, the Southland Provincial Government chartered the *Amherst* (Captain Paddy Gilroy), and sent Henry Armstrong on her as their representative, to search all of New Zealand's southern islands and to establish depots of supplies for castaways.[8] The *Amherst* carefully searched both the Auckland and Campbell Islands without result. She left depots of supplies at both groups, and liberated goats and pigs on Campbell Island. After leaving Campbell the brig "soon ran the distance to the Antipodes Islands, making the land before daybreak on the 2nd March". Armstrong records that "when close to the Island, we fired our gun, and lowering a boat, I went ashore with an officer, effecting a landing very easily under the lee (east side), although a considerable sea was running outside." The party climbed to the top of a hill in the centre of the island (probably Mount Galloway), setting fire to the tussock as they went. From the summit they carefully scanned the landscape, but "saw nothing but the tussock waving in the wind, the albatross sitting quietly on their nests, and a few parroquets flitting about". After four hours on the hill the party spread out in different directions before returning to the boat convinced that there was nobody alive on the island.

Armstrong found, as many others have before and since, that "to walk across country required a little circumspection, progress being made by hopping from one tussock to tussock, a false step causing the unwary one to subside up to his chin amongst the grass". He also commented on the geology, noting that "the rocks on the island are purely volcanic. Close to where we landed are large beds of ashes, and a feruginous scoria. From this and other indications, the conical shape of the hills, and their rounded tops, I am of opinion that the island has been the site of an active volcano". He brought back a few rock specimens – the first from the island to be examined by a scientist.[9] Near the landing place they left a small cache of articles of use to shipwrecked persons:

> Before leaving we placed a board on a high rock, securing it with stones, on which is carved "Brig Amherst, in search of castaways, March, '68; by order of the Government of Southland". With it, two bottles, one containing some matches, a flint and steel, fish-hooks, and a parcel of dressed flax; the other, a letter, in which I mentioned what had been done on the Auckland and Campbell Islands, &c.

Armstrong drew a sketch of the east coast of the Antipodes,[10] probably as the ship left for its next planned landfall at the Bounty Islands. Due to a succession of strong gales the brig was hove to and drifting to the north-east, and finished up running in to shelter at Pitt Island in the Chathams. It was not until 19 March that they made the Bounties. In his report to the Superintendent, Province of Southland, Armstrong relates:

> A few strokes of the pen suffice to tell how we were baffled in our attempts to close with these islands for a period of eighteen days (including our stay at Pitts) but they cannot convey . . . any impression of the sense of weariness and disquietude from which we suffered during that time of constant strife with the elements. On the same night as we sighted the [Bounty] island the wind changed suddenly to S.W., and blew a hard gale, a heavy sea rising with it. The brig was "hove to" (her chronic state) and at 8 a.m. next morning, being about 8 miles to the S.W., two trustworthy look-outs were stationed on the foretopsail yard, and we ran down under a close-reefed maintopsail, to within half a mile of the rocks, for such they are, a group of naked detached rocks, extending from N.W. to S.E. about two miles. The sea rose in spray to the tops of the highest (some 100 feet) and breached clean over the lower ones. There are several outlying rocks awash, at some distance from the mainbody. Of course no attempt could be made to land, but we saw every rock distinctly with the naked eye, and had there been anything as large as a goat moving on them we must have perceived it. Neither man nor beast could exist on the Bounty's,

> and had I known their nature, I would not have deemed it necessary to visit them.[11]

On 28 January 1868, within days of the arrival in Bluff of the survivors of the wreck of the *General Grant*, the Colonial Secretary of New Zealand sent a circular letter to the Governments of Victoria, South Australia, New South Wales, Queensland and Tasmania, proposing that these colonies co-operate with New Zealand in establishing and maintaining a depot of stores for shipwrecked persons at the Auckland Islands. This initiative was unsuccessful, and over the next decade it was left to Royal Navy ships to make occasional inspections of the islands and the depots left by the *Amherst*.

HMS *ROSARIO*

The first of these naval visits was in July 1870, when Captain George Palmer, commander of HMS *Rosario*, was hastily despatched from New Zealand. The warship had a double mission: first, to take possession of the Bounty Islands for the British Empire; and second, to ascertain "if there were any castaways on them from the missing ship *Matoaka*, as had been considered probable by some of the relatives of the passengers by that vessel".[12] (The full-rigged ship *Matoaka* had sailed from Lyttelton bound for London on 13 May 1869 carrying wool, gold, 32 crew and 45 passengers, including 13 women and 18 children. She was never heard of again. It was widely conjectured that she had foundered, caught fire or hit an iceberg – and that lifeboats with survivors may have reached the Bounty Islands.)[13] Until then no country had taken formal possession of the Bounties. The need to do so, previously overlooked by both Great Britain and its Colony of New Zealand, only became obvious when a British firm applied to the Admiralty for guano mining rights.[14] In December 1869 the guano merchant's solicitors Messrs Josselyn and Son of Ipswich wrote:

> Some clients of ours, a firm of merchants carrying on a very large trade in artificial manures, are desirous of knowing whether the Bounty Islands,

situated south of New Zealand, in Long. 179° 3′ east, lat. 47° 46′ south, are a possession of her Brittanic Majesty, and, if so, whether any concession has been granted by the British Government of the right of collecting any guano to be found on such islands.

Guano was first imported into Great Britain as agricultural manure in 1841, and the trade expanded rapidly to both Europe and North America. Within 30 years most of the best deposits – from the Chincha Islands off Peru – were exhausted. During the search for further sources, the Government of the United States had passed the Guano Islands Act 1856, which sanctioned US citizens to take possession of any unclaimed, uninhabited island in the world that contained guano. This led to several small islands in the West Indies being summarily annexed by American companies.

The British Government was uncertain, and surely concerned, about the potential for foreign claims on the Bounty Islands. It informed the New Zealand Government that it considered that the islands lay within New Zealand's jurisdiction, and that "it will be for the Colonial Government to take possession of them, should it think fit, if this has not already been done". In giving his opinion to the Colonial Secretary, the Attorney-General of New Zealand wrote: "I think it very questionable whether the Act of the Imperial Parliament could, should a question ever be raised with a Foreign Power, vest the territory in the Crown of England, no possession having been taken on behalf of the Crown – certainly none followed by occupation."[15]

So on 9 July 1870, with the *Rosario* anchored in rough seas off the Bounty Islands, Captain Palmer hoisted the colours and read aloud and signed the following:

I, George Palmer, Captain of her Britannic Majesty's Navy, and at present commanding her Majesty's ship *Rosario*, do hereby make known to all whom it may concern, that by virtue of an order from Commodore Rowley Lambard, C.B., A.D.C., commanding H.M. ships in these seas, I have this day taken possession of the Bounty Islands, in the name and on behalf of H.M.G. Majesty Queen Victoria, by the Grace of God of the United

> Kingdom of Great Britain and Ireland, Queen defender of the Faith, etc., and I do hereby declare the said Bounty Islands to be annexed to her Majesty's colony of New Zealand. God save the Queen. Given under my hand the 9th day of July, 1870, off the Bounty Islands. George Palmer, captain of H.M.S. *Rosario.*

The report appended to the proclamation described the islands as "rocky islets, perfectly barren, destitute of any covering, and exposed on every side to the fury of the sea". It mentions "a blow-hole in one of the Western islets [Funnel Island] through which the water and spray was forced upwards of 300 feet high". A landing anywhere was considered impracticable, and it was doubted if a footing could be obtained, "even in the calmest summer day". No sign of castaways was found.

Palmer recorded two large schools of blackfish in the immediate vicinity, and remarked: "I was by no means surprised when no traces of the guano deposits said to exist here were observed [for] an extremely small number of seabirds were to be seen either on the rocks or flying about". Of course it was the middle of winter during Palmer's visit and therefore outside the penguin and mollymawk breeding season. However, despite the multitude of seabirds present each summer, guano has no chance to accumulate on the Bounty Islands due to constant drenching by rough seas, rain and spray.[16]

New Zealand's Governor, Sir George Bowen, wrote to the British Government: "It will be seen that the Bounty Islands are merely a group of almost inaccessible rocks, and that it is not probable that there is much guano upon them. In reply to the application made by Messrs Josselyn, the Colonial Government has thought it right to acquaint them with the real state of the case, and send them a copy of Captain Palmer's report."[17]

It is interesting that an enquiry from prospective guano collectors, and an uncertain response by the British Government, led the Colonial Government of New Zealand to formally "take possession" of the Bounty Islands. The Bounty and Antipodes Islands had been considered part of New Zealand territory since 1842. On 4 April that year the British Government issued Letters Patent which defined the boundaries of Her Majesty's Colony of New

Zealand to include the Chatham, Snares, Auckland, Campbell, Antipodes, and Bounty islands. As a result, on 1 November 1842, Acting-Governor Willoughby Shortland proclaimed the Colony to extend from 33° S to 53° S and from 162° E to 173° W. However, in the New Zealand Constitution Act, passed by the Imperial Parliament in 1852, the southern boundary was changed to 50° S – because Britain had created a separate colony at the Auckland Islands – but this did not affect the territorial status of the Bounty or Antipodes Islands. Following the failure of the short-lived Auckland Island colony, the southern boundary of 53° S was restored by the Imperial Legislature through an "Amending Act to Alter the Boundaries of New Zealand, 1863".[18]

By comparison, Macquarie Island had become part of Tasmania as early as 1825 when it was decided to create Van Dieman's Land (Tasmania) into a separate colony. The Commission issued to the first Governor of the new colony included "our island of Van Dieman's Land . . . and also Macquarie Island lying to the southward of the said island of Van Dieman's Land".[19]

HMS *COSSACK*

In the decade following HMS *Rosario*'s dash to the Bounty Islands, a series of visits to the southern islands were made by Royal Navy ships of the Australia Station, based in Melbourne. HMS *Cossack* went south in 1873, HMS *Blanche* in 1874, HMS *Nymphe* in 1876, HMS *Sapphire* in 1877, HMS *Nymphe* again in 1878, and both HMS *Sapphire* and HMS *Emerald* in 1879. However, of these ships only HMS *Cossack* called at the Antipodes, and none at the Bounties.[20]

HMS *Cossack* visited the Antipodes Islands in February 1873, when Navigating Lieutenant Hallett reported:

> Sighted Antipodes islands bearing N.E.1/2 E., passed along the north shore of the large island at a distance of from one to two miles, it has a most barren and inhospitable appearance. Off the west side of the largest island is a rock having a large arch in the centre, and off the north-west point is a high pinnacle rock with apparently deep water between it and the island; close to the north-east point is an island seemingly an extinct crater.

> The cliffs are partially covered with a dark green moss-like vegetation; there are numerous large caverns in the face of the cliffs.
>
> The only place where it would be likely to effect a landing, is a little to the southward of the north-east extreme of the island, there, the cliff having fallen away has formed a shelving point on which the sea seemed to break lightly, it is sheltered also from the prevailing winds.
>
> The position of the small island [Bollons Island], at the north-east point of Antipodes island, is 49° 40′ S, 178° 49′ 45″ E.[21]

The crew of HMS *Cossack* did not land at the Antipodes to check the small supply of stores left by the *Amherst*. This cache with its marker board and two bottles, one containing a letter, appears never to have been relocated since placed there in 1868.

JOHN WARHAM

Above: Landfall Antipodes Islands. Photo taken from the approximate position of HMS *Reliance* when the islands were discovered in the early morning of 26 March 1800.

Right: Erecting the radio mast, January 1969.

Left: 1969 Expedition Camp, showing prefabricated hut and tents, castaway depot, and the position of the meteorological station.

Below: John Warham working on study skins in the expedition hut, 1969.

Woody Horning

Above: BAAS Expedition, 1978. Camp of the Bounty Island party.
Chris Robertson (left) and Gerry van Tets outside their tent.

Below: All that remained of the Bounty Islands castaway depot in November 1978.

Woody Horning

Above: Landing stores by Wasp helicopter. BAAS Expedition Base Camp, 1978.

Left: BAAS Expedition, 1978. Expedition buildings, Antipodes Island.

Brian Bell in the clinker dinghy. Antipodes 1978.

ANDY COX

Above: Salvin's Mollymawks and Erect-crested Penguins, Bounty Islands.
Below: *Anistome antipoda* and Perpendicular Head. Antipodes Island.

Bollons Island and volcanic hills.

John Warham

Point Felix Faure,
Bollons Island.

CHAPTER SIX

New Zealand Government Steamers

Government vessels were a very important means of communication before the days of road, rail and radio in New Zealand. The ships of the New Zealand Government Steamer Service were used extensively by various Government agencies for transporting parliamentarians, officials, troops, railway construction materials and rolling stock; and for laying cables, servicing lighthouses, patrolling the seal fisheries, and providing for shipwrecked mariners. In 1866, lighthouses, seals and shipwrecks became the responsibility of the newly created New Zealand Marine Department.[1]

By 1880 it had become obvious to the Marine Department that the Seals Fisheries Protection Act 1878 was being flouted, and that out-of-season poaching of fur seals was rife. While inspecting the seal fisheries that year, the Government steamer *Stella* discovered that the castaway depot in the old *General Grant* survivor's hut on Enderby Island had been destroyed by fire. In 1881 the *Stella* found further evidence of vandalism and theft from several other Auckland Island depots. Apparently, those disregarding the sealing regulations were treating the depots with similar disdain. This led to the Department instigating a full-time seal fisheries patrol at the Snares, Auckland and Campbell islands from 1882 to 1886, using the schooner *Kekeno*; and part of the crew's duty was to inspect, repair and replenish the castaway depots at those islands. Apart from two very small A-frame structures to hold stores – built by Captain McKersie of the *Stella* on Enderby Island in 1880, and by Captain Grey of the same ship at "Epigwait", Carnley Harbour, in 1881 – the first purpose-built castaway depots in the New Zealand subantarctic were erected by Captain Greig and the crew of the *Kekeno* at the Auckland and Campbell Islands in 1884.[2]

However, by 1885 no action had been taken either to establish provision depots at the Antipodes or Bounty Islands or to regularly inspect these groups for the presence of castaways. In the second half of that year, fears were held in Australia as to the fate of the ship *North American* which had left Melbourne on 4 February and failed to arrive in London. Her last known position was about 180 miles south-east of Stewart Island where she was "spoken to" by the ship *Aristides*. On 4 September the Victorian Premier alerted the New Zealand Government and suggested that the Bounty and Antipodes Islands be searched for survivors. A further telegram of 20 September read: "Applied to the Admiral who thinks hopeless. Merchant Shipping Association suggests that perhaps NZ Government will send a search party to the islands. Auckland Islands also suggested – James Service, Premier, Melbourne".

However, Lloyds of London thought it unlikely that any survivors would have reached the Auckland Islands due to winds prevailing following the last sighting of the *North American*. Also, the *Kekeno* had only recently returned from a routine inspection trip of the depots at Auckland and Campbell Islands so the priority for searching was directed at the Antipodes and Bounty Islands. On 9 October the Marine Department sent the following message to the port of Bluff to await the arrival of Captain Grey of the *Stella*:

> As soon as you return from Puysegur Point you are to fill up at once with coal and stores and proceed to the Antipodes Islands and thence to Bounty

> Islands to search for castaways. Exercise all caution in approaching these islands and should you be able to land bring specimens of rocks, soil and vegetation. If you find any castaways you will return to the easiest reached port in New Zealand, but if you find nothing you are to go to Nugget Point and continue your voyage. Let me know if price asked for coal at Bluff is excessive – W. Seed.

In the event the *Stella* searched all the southern islands, and on 7 November 1885 the New Zealand Premier sent the following telegram addressed to Honourable J. Service, Premier, Melbourne:

> Steamer Stella called today at Nuggets Lighthouse from Auckland Campbell and Antipodes and Bounty Islands, found no castaways. Two storehouses empty on Enderby Island – on Antipodes found hut which had been used, boats mast and piece of ship's head board with letter N cut into wood but could not have been recent – will send full report on arrival here of steamer. Regret search fruitless – Robt. Stout.

Grey's report records that he landed at the Antipodes on 4 November finding the old blown-down sealers hut "on the NW side". On the west side of the island they "found a boat's mast, a long boat's storm sheets [and] ship's headboard". The *Stella* inspected the Bounty Islands and a party made a landing at "a little boat harbour".[3]

The search for survivors from the *North American* led to a decision by the New Zealand Government to establish castaway depots at the Antipodes and Bounty Islands. These depots were built and stocked by the crew of the Government Steamer *Hinemoa* in March 1886. This was immediately reported to the Victorian Government with a request from New Zealand for aid with their regular servicing:

> This Government having decided to establish Depots for castaways on those islands, our steamer *Hinemoa* was dispatched for that purpose . . . and returned on 20th inst. Having placed a depot on the north east end of the Antipodes and one on the western Bounty Islands containing the stores

> specified in the enclosed lists . . . I would add that it is intended to send one of our steamers to visit the islands once a year, about February or March and I would suggest that it might be useful if your Government could find it convenient once a year."

The Victorian Premier replied that they could not help, "having regard to the remoteness of those islands . . . and to the fact that there is no Government vessel here which could be made available for the proposed visits".

As a result, New Zealand Government Steamers were left to carry out the work alone. From 1885 until 1927, the Marine Department ships patrolled the subantarctic islands every year without fail. In most of these years there were two, and occasionally three, visits. Typically the crew comprised the captain, two deck officers, three engineers, greasers, firemen, two cooks, two stewards, a bosun, six seamen and a boy. They searched the southern islands for missing vessels and castaways; built and serviced survival depots and boat sheds; liberated cattle, goats and sheep as food for castaways; transported Government officials, scientists and other paying passengers; checked for signs of seal poaching; and freighted livestock and wool for the pastoral lessees of Auckland and Campbell islands.[4]

Only once during this period was there call for a special patrol of the Antipodes and Bounty Islands to search for a missing vessel. This was in 1891 following the loss of the 83-ton iron steamer *Kakanui*, which disappeared with all hands during a violent storm in the first week of January 1891, while returning from Macquarie Island. Following searches for survivors that took the SS *Hinemoa* to Macquarie Island, the Auckland Islands, the Snares and Stewart Island, another search was made at the Auckland and Campbell Islands. Finally, on 27 February the *Hinemoa* left Wellington and "proceeded direct to the Antipodes and Bounty Islands". Here, Captain Fairchild "made a most complete and careful search for any trace of the vessel, but without result".[5]

THE STEAMERS

The vessels involved with regularly patrolling the Antipodes, Bounty Islands and other subantarctic islands for the Marine Department were the SS *Stella*, SS *Hinemoa*, SS *Tutanekai* and NZS *Amokura*. In 1894 the New Zealand Government, seeing the need to check for castaways more frequently, approached the Australian Station of the Royal Navy asking if they could mount a patrol in June and December each year to supplement visits by Government Steamers in March and September. Although the Royal Navy avoided a definite commitment they offered help, and warships occasionally shared inspection duties with the Government Steamers until 1908.

The SS *Stella* was built in 1876 by Scott & Co., Greenock, at a cost of £10,695. Ordered by the New Zealand Marine Department for lighthouse service, she was a 158-foot schooner-rigged iron steamer of 268 tons gross. She arrived at Wellington in October 1876, and in 1885 became the first New Zealand Government vessel to visit the Antipodes and Bounty islands. In 1889, the *Stella* was taken off routine patrols to the subantarctic and replaced by the SS *Hinemoa*. In 1895 the *Stella* was sold to an Auckland timber company, and in 1918 was bought by the Otago Iron Rolling Mills. She returned to the subantarctic on contract to the Campbell Island Syndicate in 1919 and 1920.[6] In 1926, she was stripped and towed to Chalky Inlet, Fiordland, to become a jetty for a fish freezer. Her hull is still there today.

The *Hinemoa* was of similar design to the *Stella* and from the same shipyard. However, at 207 feet long and 542 tons gross she was considerably larger. She was built as a New Zealand "Government and Parliamentary yacht" at a total cost, including extras, of over £25,000. She arrived in Wellington in October 1876 and was handed to the Marine Department to maintain in 1878, but for some years was engaged in transporting politicians and working for other Government departments. She made her first trip to the Antipodes and Bounty Islands in 1886 and then patrolled them regularly until 1910. This was the last visit of the *Hinemoa* to the subantarctic. By 1915 she was considered too weak structurally to return to the southern islands, although she continued general duties with the Marine Department until 1925. Further lengthy and varied service followed under both Government and

NZS *Amokura* under sail. (*Wellington Museum of City and Sea.*)

private owners. In 1944, at the age of 68 years, she became the target of a naval gunnery exercise and ended up at the bottom of Pegasus Bay, North Canterbury.[7]

The SS *Tutanekai* came into service with the Marine Department in 1896. She was specially built by D. & J. Dunlop, Glasgow, for laying and repairing telegraph cables, servicing lighthouses, and carrying out other New Zealand Government work. At 205 feet long and displacing 810 tons she had ample cargo space and was fitted with a first-class saloon and passenger accommodation. The cost of building the vessel and bringing her to New Zealand was £29,261. The *Tutanekai* made her first trip to the Antipodes and Bounty islands in February 1899, but then made only very irregular trips south (1902, 1903, 1906, 1907) until she took over the work completely in 1921.

In 1906 the New Zealand Government bought the old auxiliary gunboat HMS *Sparrow* from the Royal Navy for £800. The ship was 165 feet long, steel framed, skinned in teak, and displaced 805 tons. Her 729 indicated horsepower motor gave her a top speed of 13 knots. She also carried three masts and was rigged as a barquentine. Renamed NZS *Amokura*, she was transferred from Defence to the Marine Department in February 1907, and became a training ship for seamen boys aged 12 to 17 years. The boys were trained for both the navy and mercantile marine, and after two years were allowed free choice of which service they joined. The *Amokura* carried a full complement of 76: Captain Hooper, two officers, two engineers, a purser, four instructors, two greasers, two firemen, a cook, a steward, and 60 boys. From 1910 to 1918, as part of her duties the *Amokura* carried out all inspection trips of the southern island depots. She was deemed unserviceable for sea-going

A shore party of seamen boys from NZS *Amokura* at the Bounty Island depot. Probably in December 1912. (*Alexander Turnbull Library, Wellington, New Zealand. 1/2-056479-F.*)

service in 1918: the last boy was discharged and the vessel officially paid off in December 1921. By then more than 500 young sailors had received training on her. *Amokura* spent the next 30 years as a shipping company coal hulk on the Wellington waterfront. In 1953 she was towed to Kenepuru Sound, Marlborough, for use as a store hulk and jetty. Some of her remains still exist there.[8]

SS *Tutanekai* took over sole responsibility for routine patrols of the New Zealand subantarctic island castaway depots from January 1921. By 1923 it had become obvious that the need for the depots was past. However, on Captain Bollons' recommendation the steamer continued to visit the

Auckland Islands annually, and the other groups once in every three years. In February 1927 it was finally decided to close the depots. The Secretary of Marine replied to a memorandum from his Nautical Adviser: "The abolition of the depots will render it unnecessary for the steamer to visit the islands and therefore the intention is that she will make no further visits."[9]

Tutanekai's last inspection of the Bounty and Antipodes depots was in April 1927 and her final visit to the Auckland Islands in February 1929. She was decommissioned, and scuttled by explosives in Cook Strait in February 1931.

THE CAPTAINS

Equally renowned as the steamers that patrolled the southern islands for nearly 50 years were the men in command. Names such as Captains Fairchild, Post, Bollons and Hooper hold respected places in New Zealand's maritime history.

Captain McKersie took the SS *Stella* on her initial subantarctic voyage to the Snares and Auckland Islands in May 1880, but was relieved of his command on 6 November that year when he was apparently out of favour with the Department. The only surviving reference to this event reads: "Capt. McKersie to be dispensed with & Capt. W.J. Grey appointed Master of Stella".[10]

Grey commanded the *Stella* for seven years, taking the ship on her first patrol to the Antipodes and Bounty Islands in November 1885. He transferred to the Customs Department in 1887. Captain John Fairchild, master of the *Hinemoa*, then took over the *Stella* for two years before transferring back to the *Hinemoa*, where he remained until 1895. Captain J. Neale was master of the *Hinemoa* from 1895 until 1898, when he left the Steamer Service to become harbourmaster at Manukau.

In 1895 Fairchild was sent to Britain to bring out the *Tutanekai*, and he remained in command of her until his accidental death in July 1898: he was killed on the ship by a falling block when lifting-gear broke during loading in Wellington. Fairchild was highly respected and had been in the

Government Steamer Service since the early 1860s. His list of previous commands included the paddle-steamers *Sturt* and *Luna*, as well as the *Stella*, *Hinemoa* and *Tutanekai*.

Fairchild's tragic death led to an immediate re-allocation of commands. Captain C.F. Post, the recently appointed master of the *Hinemoa*, was transferred to the *Tutanekai*. John Bollons, mate of the *Tutanekai*, was promoted to command the *Hinemoa*. Post remained in command of *Tutanekai* for 23 years until his retirement in December 1921. Bollons transferred back to the *Tutanekai* as master in February 1922, a job he held until subantarctic patrols ceased in 1929. By the time of his death through illness in September 1929, his seamanship and deep knowledge of the subantarctic was legendary.[11]

Captain G.S. Hooper, RNR, was in command of NZS *Amokura* for the entire period of her commission (1907–1921). He was then based in Wellington as Nautical Advisor to the Marine Department, and in 1923 also became Administrator of the Ross Dependency. In this latter capacity, in the summer of 1923–4 he travelled to Antarctica on a whaling expedition aboard the Norwegian mother ship *Sir James Clark Ross* (Captain Carl A. Larsen). In January 1924, at Discovery Inlet on the Ross Ice Barrier, Hooper transferred to one of the fleet's five chasers, the 130-ton *Star I*, for a daring 10-day voyage of 1414 miles along most of the Ross Dependency's coastline.[12]

TABLE 3: Voyages by Government Steamers to Antipodes and Bounty Islands

Year	Ship	Dates at Antipodes*	References
1885	*Stella*	4 Nov	Grey 1885
1886	*Hinemoa*	16–17 Mar	Fairchild 1886
1887	*Stella*	Mar	MD
1888	*Stella*	2 Feb; 28 Sept	Dougall 1888; MD; Graffiti
1889	*Stella*	July	Chapman 1891; MD
1890	*Hinemoa*	17 Jan; Oct	Kirk 1891; Chapman 1891; Godley 1989
1891	*Hinemoa*	c.3 Mar; 3 Nov	Wilson 1891; Cumpston 1968; HBH 1891
1892	*Hinemoa*	Jan	MD
1893	*Hinemoa*	Jan; May; 30 Nov	Warham & Johns 1975; ODT 1893
1894	*Hinemoa*	15 Feb; May; 15 Oct	Joyce 1894; graffiti; NM
1895	*Hinemoa*	16 Feb; June; 16 Oct	Hector 1896; Glasgow 1895; Kerr 1976; MD; NM
1896	*Hinemoa*	10 May	Lukins 1896
1897	*Hinemoa*	9 May; 30 Nov	graffiti; Hinemoa 1897
1898	*Hinemoa*	1 Aug	graffiti
1899	*Tutanekai*	c.23 Feb	Cumpston 1968
	Hinemoa	Sept; Nov	Kerr 1976; NM
1900	*Hinemoa*	July	Cockayne 1904
1901	*Hinemoa*	14 Jan; [only 1 trip]	Hutton 1902; ANZ Dunedin; Ogilvie-Grant 1905.
1902	*Tutanekai*	22 Jan; July	Alexander 1900–04; Cockayne 1904
1903	*Tutanekai*	13 Mar	graffiti
	Hinemoa	16 July	graffiti; Godley 1989
1904	*Hinemoa*	2 Apr; ? [2 trips]	graffiti
1905	*Hinemoa*	c.12 May	Fraser 1906
1906	*Tutanekai*	5 Mar	graffiti; NM
	Hinemoa	22 Oct	graffiti
1907	*Tutanekai*	Feb	Waite 1909; Plunket 1912
	Hinemoa	21 Nov	Chilton, 1909
1908	no visit to Antipodes or Bounty Islands		

Year	Ship	Dates at Antipodes*	References
1909	*Hinemoa*	15 Jan; Sept	Aston 1909; Godley 1989; Kerr & Judd 1978
1910	*Amokura*	13–15 Mar; 21 Nov	Falla n.d.; ANZ Wgtn
1911	*Amokura*	11 Dec	Falla n.d.; ANZ Wgtn
1912	*Amokura*	31 Mar; 22 Dec	Falla n.d.; ANZ Wgtn
1913	*Amokura*	9 Nov	Amokura 1913
1914	*Amokura*	4 Apr	Falla n.d.; ANZ Wgtn
1915	*Amokura*	18 Apr; 15 Nov	Falla n.d.; ANZ Wgtn
1916	*Amokura*	22 Apr	Falla n.d.; ANZ Wgtn
1917	*Amokura*	2–3 Jan; 25 Feb; 30 Nov	Falla n.d.; ANZ Wgtn
1918	*Amokura*	16 Apr	Falla n.d.; ANZ Wgtn
1919	no visits to Antipodes or Bounty Islands		
1920	no visits to Antipodes or Bounty Islands		
1921	*Tutanekai*	27 Jan; 22 Sept	graffiti
1922	*Tutanekai*	April	Bollons 1923; Auckland Star 1927
1923	*Tutanekai*	31 Mar - 1 Apr	Archey 1923; Munro 1923; graffiti
1924	no visits to Antipodes or Bounty Islands		
1925	no visits to Antipodes or Bounty Islands		
1926	no visits to Antipodes or Bounty Islands		
1927	*Tutanekai*	4 Apr	Oliver 1927; Godley 1989

NOTES

* Bounty Island visits were made one or two days later, in each case.

REFERENCES:

MD = Marine Department Annual Report in Appendix to the *Journals of the House of Representatives*.
Graffiti = names and dates written on walls of Antipodes castaway hut.
NM = National Museum bird collections.
ANZ = Archives NZ, Dunedin & Wellington.
HBH = *Hawkes Bay Herald*.
ODT = *Otago Daily Times*.

CHAPTER SEVEN

Succour for Castaways – Depots, Livestock and Plants

ANTIPODES ISLAND DEPOT

The depot on Antipodes Island was built in 1886. On the *Hinemoa*'s return to Wellington, Captain Fairchild reported to the Marine Department:

> We reached the Antipodes at 10 a.m. on the 16 March, and, after steaming round the island, found fairly good anchorage on the north-east side, in fifteen fathoms of water . . . We at once proceeded to land the material and erect the house, which was finished at 5 p.m. on the 17th and all the stores, etc., deposited therein . . . The house is erected on the north-east end of the island, in the best-sheltered place we could find, about 100ft. above sea-level, and about 300ft. in from the shore, and can be seen a good distance off from a vessel approaching from the north-east. Enclosed is a rough sketch of the island.[1]

The Antipodes "house" or depot was constructed entirely of kauri timber.[2] It measures 4.4 m x 2.85 m and sits on 12 x 150 mm square wooden piles. Everything about its construction is solid. The floor joists are 170 x 50 mm and the framing 130 x 50. The external cladding is 250 x 25 double-rebated weatherboard, and the interior lining 150 x 15 tongue and groove. Originally, the roof was of heavy-grade galvanised corrugated iron over 130 x 50 rafters and 100 x 50 purlins. The precision jointing of framing, rafters and bracing indicate that it was taken to the island in kit-set form. During its 41 years of service to the Marine Department it appears to have needed only minor repairs and occasional painting.

In 1893 the Liverpool barque *Spirit of the Dawn* was wrecked on Antipodes Island and 11 survivors spent 88 days under miserable conditions without finding the depot. In consequence, in 1894, the Marine Department placed 65 finger posts in prominent positions on the southern islands pointing to the depots. Like the depots and boatsheds, these were all painted white when first erected and the more accessible ones repainted as opportunity offered. Five posts were put up on the Snares, 40 at Auckland Islands, 12 at Campbell, and eight at the Antipodes.[3] Remains of all of the Antipodes posts have been located since 1969, the most intact being behind Alert Bay. The others were sited in northern Ringdove Bay (one near the shore and one higher up, at the plateau edge); on the escarpment crest at spot height (219 m) to the east of Cave Point; on the southern coastal platform (one near South Bay and another about 1 km further west); and on the summits of Mount Galloway and Conical Hill.

During 1908 the French crew of the wrecked barque *Président Félix Faure* constructed two makeshift cabins up against the depot, and using shipwreck timbers built wooden benches around the inside walls of the depot to give extra sleeping space. These benches remained as historic features of the hut until 1978, but have since been removed. One of the cabins erected in 1908 was a lean-to structure along the full length of the southern wall. Roofed with sheets of zinc lining from provision boxes supported by four oars lashed to other boat wreckage, this lean-to had walls of peat, tussock and other vegetation. It first appears in a photo taken by Rollo Beck in 1926, when it

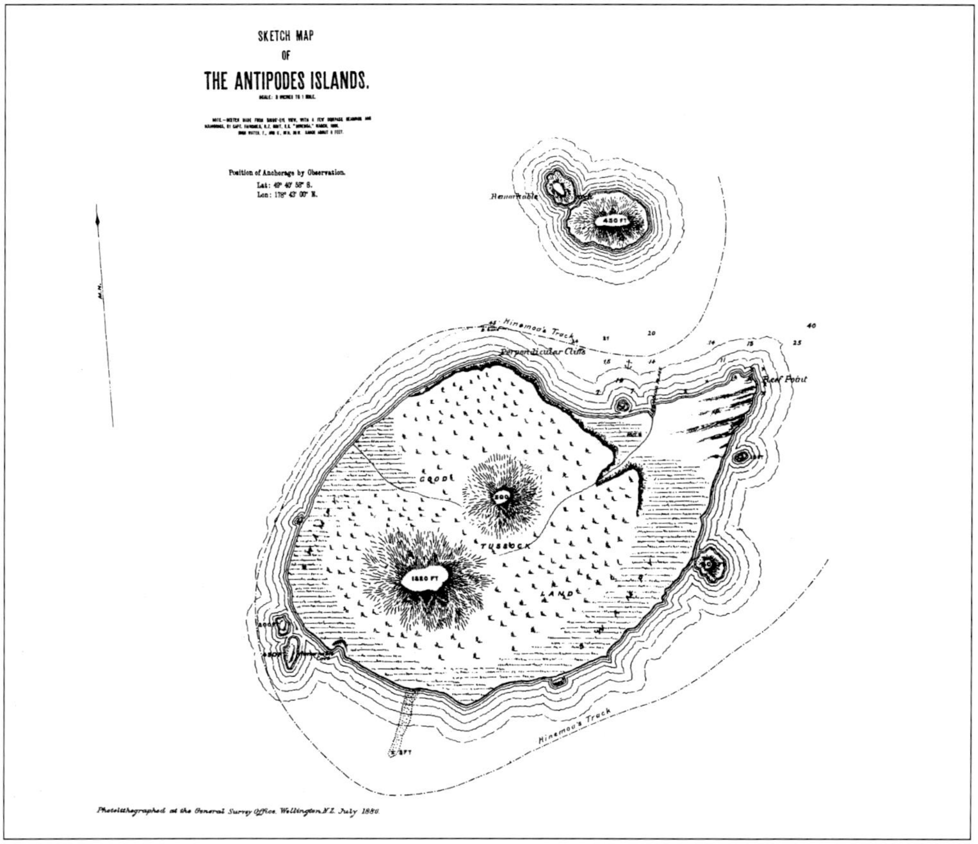

Antipodes Islands as sketched by NZGSS *Hinemoa* in 1886. (*App. Journ. of NZ House of Representatives.*)

was already in a state of disrepair. Remnants of the zinc roofing and the oars, still leaning against the hut wall, were all that remained by 1969.

In November 1950 the *Alert* Expedition found that the depot hut was "still solid and dry inside",[4] and "the stores seemed in good order, although . . . some tins had inevitably rusted. The zinc lined blanket and clothing cases were intact, and the Americans [USCGC *Northwind*, 1947] had left, with compliments, some K ration cases".[5] However, when a party from the New Zealand Oceanographic Institute visited in November 1962, they found that most of the boxes of food and clothing had been axed open and their contents scattered. Writing on the hut wall suggested that the culprits were from the fishing vessel *Chance*, from Bluff, which had called on 30 July 1958. This suspicion was fuelled in official circles by the knowledge that four years earlier a Stewart Island fishing vessel was known to have taken lifeboats and windows, and damaged stores at castaway depots and wartime buildings in Port Ross, Auckland Islands.[6]

When the University of Canterbury Antipodes Island Expedition arrived in January 1969, the door and window of the building were missing, apparently blown away, and there were five large holes in the roof. Many of the tins of food had rusted. Moisture and moths had ruined most of the contents of the axed-open boxes of clothing, blankets, tea, tobacco, matches and other supplies. The expedition members spent the best part of four days working on the depot, cleaning it out, repairing the roof with new corrugated iron and fitting a new door and window.

At the time that the building was being renovated a telegram was received from the Lands and Survey Department asking that the depot and contents "be left in original condition". It is unclear what initiated this directive, but it was doubtless conservation-orientated. To the expedition members "this request seemed absurd", as the castaway hut and its contents were fast deteriorating. Therefore, permission was obtained via radio from the Secretary of Marine to bring a large selection of the relics back to the Canterbury Museum where they reside today. That this was a wise decision has since been demonstrated by the gradual disappearance from the depot of the remaining clothing and artefacts that were left behind securely packed in a box.[7]

By 1975, visitors in the launch *Parimar* found that the depot's roofing iron, put on in 1969, had completely blown away.[8] The roof was once more replaced in corrugated aluminium by the B.A.A.S. Expedition in 1978, when further maintenance and painting of the outside of the hut was carried out. In 1985, Lands and Survey ranger John Clay and three sailors from HMNZS *Monowai* secured some loose weatherboards and corner boxes and applied two coats of paint to the exterior. A rotten floor bearer at the back of the hut, first reported by John Newton in 1978, was inspected but could not be replaced without jacks to lift and support the joists and flooring. This task, and re-piling, was finally done in 1998 by Dave Houston, who also repainted the exterior.

It is a measure of the adequacy of the depot's basic design and construction that it still stands solidly today, despite having lost its roof, door and window to the elements on various occasions since it was abandoned by the Marine Department in 1927. Inside the castaway depot, carved and pencilled names and messages bear evidence of many visits. The most practical inscription was probably written when the hut was built, and simply reads "Good water in swamp close by". The earliest ship visit recorded is that of the *Stella* in September 1888. The next oldest notes the visit of HMS *Lizard* in February 1894, followed by a note left during the visit of the *Hinemoa* in December 1897 – when the hut was almost 12 years old. Perhaps in those days it took that long before visitors felt comfortable about writing on its walls. The most detailed message reads "*Hinemoa* August 1st 1898 Dirty weather settling in Leaving for Bountys and NZ tonight Stores all in order and untouched W.F. Brown".

NZGS *Hinemoa* at Campbell Island. (*Hocken Collections, University of Otago E2709/2.*)

The many ships recorded include the *Stella, Hinemoa, Tutanekai, Amokura,* HMS *Lizard,* HMS *Ringdove,* USCGC *Northwind, Alert, Taranui, Chance, Tangaroa, Far Quest, Parimar,* HMNZS *Waikato,* HMNZS *Monowai,* HMNZS *Taranaki,* HMNZS *Tui, Totorore* and *Marine Countess.* Among the names scribed on the walls and rafters are those of officers, carpenters and seamen of warships and Government steamers, and members of early scientific expeditions.

BOUNTY ISLANDS DEPOT

In his March 1886 report Captain Fairchild records:

> The Bounty Islands were reached at 10 a.m. on the 19th, and, after finding a fairly-good anchorage in twenty-three fathoms of water on the north side, we at once proceeded to select a site and erect a house. The house is erected

> on the largest island, near the western side of the group, and is about 120ft. above sea-level, and can be seen from a vessel approaching from the north. I enclose a rough sketch of these islands, which are fourteen in number, and run from 20ft. to 290ft. in height, and are composed of coarse granite, without a speck of vegetation on them, not even a bit of moss, and no fresh water. They are covered with millions of penguins and other seabirds.[9]

Fairchild was concerned that castaways would be without firewood on the islands, and recommended that "a cheap cooking-lamp be made, which would burn penguin fat or oil". He considered:

> there would be no trouble in getting any amount of penguin oil, and by this means castaways could cook fish, etc., and, as for fresh water, I think that, as much rain falls there during a great part of the year, they might catch the rain-water, and so exist.

Obviously, he was not then aware that penguins desert the islands during winter. There is no record of what gear or provisions were left in this depot.

In March 1887, only a year after the depot was built, it was found to have been completely destroyed and "only a few fragments of it" remained. At first it was reported to have "been carried away – probably by a very heavy sea",[10] but later it was said to have been destroyed by lightning,[11] and later still to have been "blown away".[12] Initially it was considered not worthwhile replacing, "owing to the inaccessibility of these islands, or rather rocks, and the impossibility of existing on them", although by 1890 someone must have had second thoughts for a sail was provided for castaways to catch rain water.

More than four years after the original depot was destroyed another was built by the crew of the *Hinemoa* on 4 November 1891. One of the passengers on this trip was Robert Wilson, a schoolboy from Bulls. He recorded in his diary that the *Hinemoa* arrived at the Bounties at about 6 a.m., and anchored close inshore:

> As it was fairly calm, the captain started with a boatload of timber to build a depot on the largest island . . . The landing was really horrible. The boat waited close to the rock till a wave came up and then you had to jump and

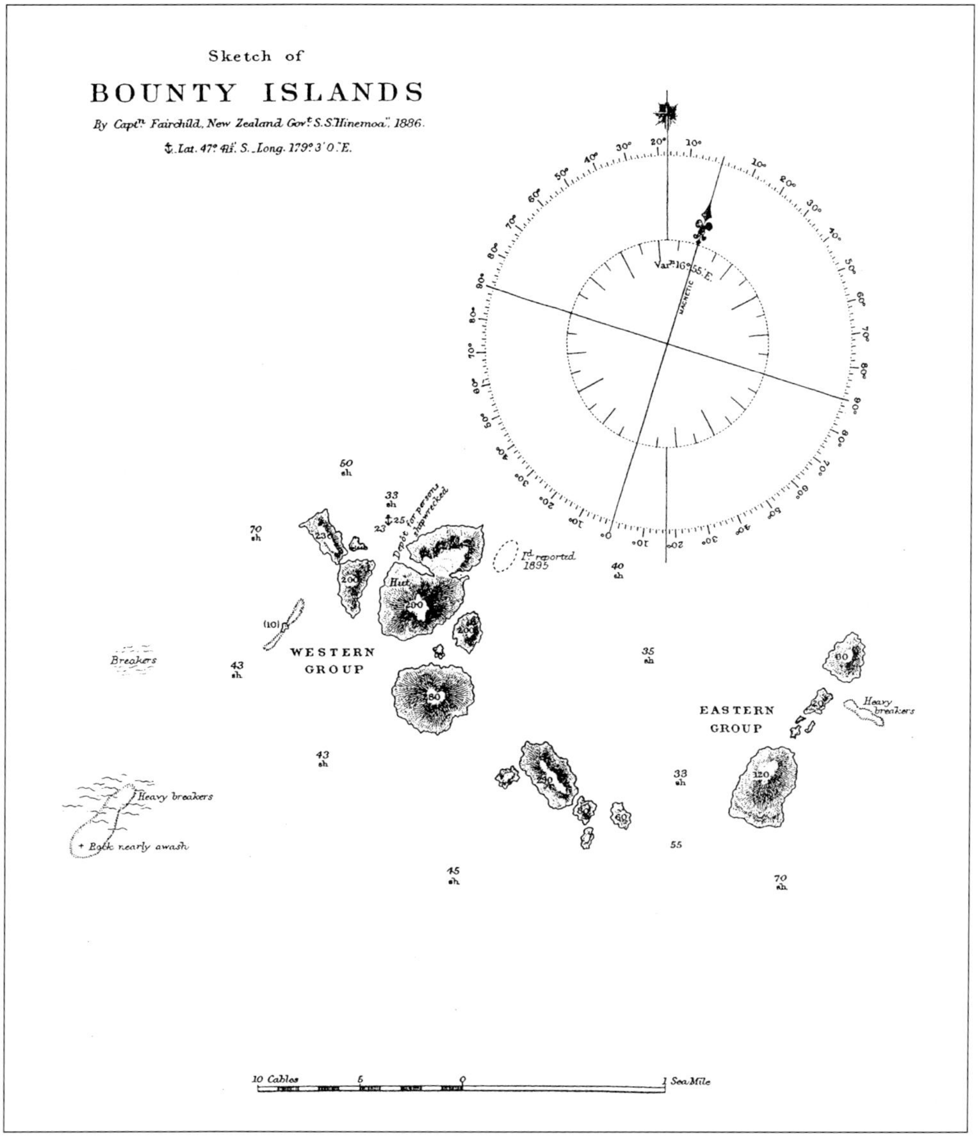

Bounty Islands as sketched by NZGSS *Hinemoa* in 1886, with additions by HMS *Royalist* in 1895. (*British Admiralty Chart 1022.*)

> trust to luck. I got ashore safely . . . The captain had the house finished by 2 [pm] so he came aboard and we headed for the Bluff.[13]

From Bluff, on 6 November 1891, Fairchild sent a telegram to the Secretary of the Marine Department, Wellington, which concluded:

> We built a house on the largest island of the Bounty Group and painted it white put the provisions and stores and fresh water in the house and left

> it in good order we have had fine weather saw no trace of wreckage or castaways at any of the islands – John Fairchild.

Although still on the same island (Depot Island), the replacement depot was at an entirely different site and no longer visible from the north, but a flagstaff was erected and the depot itself could be seen from the south-east. Whereas the first depot had been "on the top of the island" at "about 120 ft above sea-level", the second was built 300 metres away to the south-east, in a "small hollow" and only about 60 feet above the sea – suggesting that the prevailing opinion blamed lightning or wind, rather than heavy seas, for the loss of the first.

Edwin Lukins, assistant curator of the Nelson Museum, who visited the islands on the *Hinemoa* in 1896 and published a pamphlet[14] on the voyage, considered the depot's construction to be ingenious and "a great feat". He described it as follows:

> It is a low building, having somewhat the appearance of Noah's ark, for in the first place sleepers were laid down on the rocks in the hollow referred to, and on these sleepers boards were nailed to form a platform on the centre of which the little building was erected, and the sides of the platform are weighted down with pieces of rock to prevent the whole being blown away. In building the structure it was found necessary to fit the boards very carefully, for the slightest crevice sufficed to admit the fine down from the feathers of the seabirds, and before the door was fixed the building was nearly filled with feathers and down.

Lukins continued, making interesting comments on provision for a water supply and other necessaries, but made no mention of an oil stove as originally suggested by Fairchild:

> At the back of the building, which measures about 8 feet by 12, and is just high enough for a man to stand upright in, a portion of the platform is left vacant, so that a piece of canvas kept in the depot, may be laid down to catch rain water. In the building I noticed about a dozen tins of water, and a quantity of provisions, clothing and other necessaries for shipwrecked

> mariners, but I thought God help the poor sailors who might be cast away on this inhospitable rock, and I believe no man could live here when the birds are in possession, so dreadful is the stench.

The position of the first depot was marked on Fairchild's sketch map, which was published by the New Zealand Government in 1886. Surprisingly, long after this building was destroyed and replaced elsewhere, the *New Zealand Pilot* for 1891 and 1901 continued to refer to the old location:

> Depot for ship wrecked persons. On the principal island a hut, which can be seen from the Northward, is Southward of the western inlet at a height of about 120ft. above the sea. Stores for shipwrecked persons are deposited in the hut, and the islands are visited twice annually. The paucity of birds about the islands was remarkable in July.

Likewise, the depot continued to be erroneously shown in its original position on maps of the Bounty Islands published by the New Zealand Department of Lands and Survey in 1890, 1895 and 1896. The site of the second Bounty Island Depot seems never to have been marked on any map, or to have been well known – even to later commanders of New Zealand Government vessels. For after the *Amokura* returned from an inspection of all the southern islands in March 1910, Commander George Hooper reported that he had visited the Bounty Islands on 17 March and was unable to locate the depot:

> A South-westerly gale was in progress here, and there seemed no prospect of landing for an indefinite time so the Ship steamed about for a while. I tried to obtain a glimpse of the depot but could not do so; perhaps it is blown down, or perhaps it is not visible from the northward (as stated in the "Admiralty Pilot for New Zealand"). Perhaps the latter (N.Z. Pilot) is in error as I cannot recollect having seen it when at the Islands before.[15]

In March 1914 Hooper was again unable to land at the islands due to the strength and direction of the wind. The masters of Government vessels often encountered this problem at the Bounties, and would resort to blowing the ship's whistle and inspecting the rocks at close range for signs of shipwreck. As on all other occasions, "nothing alive was seen other than birds and seals". However, in his report on the voyage Hooper felt the need to comment:

> The Depot on the Bounty Islands is now very old, and may now be down entirely. I sent some of my people on shore about 18 months ago for the purpose of inspecting it. The Depot was then standing, but the contents were not examined. This Depot should now be rebuilt and restocked. I have always hoped to be able to do this, and have constantly carried the necessary material for that purpose. The task is a big one, and I now doubt if the weather will ever be smooth sufficiently long enough for me to carry it through with the boys. It will be desirable to have this matter dealt with by some other means if such an opportunity should occur.[16]

However the rebuilding and upgrading of the Bounty Islands depot was never to happen. With the passage of time the need for castaway depots on the southern islands was decreasing. The last shipwreck on any of the southern islands had been that of the *Président Félix Faure* at the Antipodes in 1908. On 14 April 1923, Captain Bollons summed up the position in a letter to the Secretary of Marine:

> The depots maintained at Antipodes Island and Bounty Rocks will probably never be used. There are no sailing ships traversing these southern seas nowadays. All the vessels lost on the Auckland and Antipode Islands were either from Melbourne bound for Europe or from Rangoon to Callao. At the present time this trade is completely done . . . I would recommend a further change. The Auckland Islands to be visited annually, the other groups once in every three years. Should it ever happen that a vessel is overdue from an Australian Port an extra visit could be made.[17]

Later that year the Marine Department published a "Notice to Mariners" advising that the provision depots on the southern islands would be visited only once in each year.

In February 1926, the Whitney South Sea Expedition of the American

Museum of Natural History visited the Antipodes and Bounty Islands in the ship *France*. They landed at the Bounties and inspected the depot. They found it "just a rotted frame" containing "several boxes with some provisions and two stone jugs half full of stale water".[18] The expedition leader, R.H. Beck, recorded in his journal: "We went ashore and around to the cabin where the stores are placed, but found the house in poor shape, the top and sides mostly gone, with the boxes open to the weather and penguins fighting for sitting places on some boxes. Nothing has been done for years evidently."[19]

On arrival of the ship in Auckland, Beck wrote to the Secretary of Marine, Wellington, enclosing photographs of the depots. Concerning the Bounty depot he wrote:

> As the latter shows no sign of recent visits by the Government vessel I wondered if you had abandoned this station. The U.S. Hydrographic Pilot Book lists it as being maintained and a member of the Marine Department in Auckland says it has not been repaired because of unfavorable weather on recent trips of the Government boat, but will be as soon as possible. We found the Antipodes station in good shape. Is it likely that Bounty Island will be visited this year and possibly repairs made?[20]

This letter, with its reminder of the depot's outdated listing in an international "Pilot Book", probably initiated another review of the policy on maintaining castaway depots on New Zealand's southern islands, for on 3 March 1927 official notice was published to mariners in the *New Zealand Gazette* that "relief and provision depots for castaways [were] to be discontinued" on the Antipodes, Bounty and Campbell Islands.[21]

In April, during a final inspection of the castaway depots in the *Tutanekai*, Captain Bollons posted written notices at the Antipodes "to the effect the vessel would not again visit the island". The Bounty Island depot was found to have completely collapsed. A passenger, Dr W.R.B. Oliver, claimed it had "been washed away", but Bollons informed the Marine Department that the Bounty Islands' "store shed has decayed and fallen to pieces. Consequently a notice was not left at the rock."[22]

Forty-one years later, on 12 January 1968, Marie Darby guided the first

The Bounty Islands castaway depot in February 1926. (*Rollo Beck, Archives New Zealand, Wellington M1, 14/3/6.*)

party of tourists to land on the Bounty Islands. Little was left of the depot hut:

> All that remains are a few wooden boxes now used as roosting places by penguins; some planks under which prions nest and where a curious insect and spider fauna exists; and an old iron kettle and two earthenware crocks bearing the trade name HUTSON, of their New Zealand manufacturers.[23]

In May 1975, Lt Commander I.A. Hunter of HMNZS *Canterbury* was winched onto the depot site by helicopter and retrieved the two earthenware crocks, fearing that they might otherwise be souvenired by crews of foreign fishing boats. The crocks, made by P. Hutson & Coy, Newton, Wellington, would originally have held mineral water as untreated water would deteriorate with long storage. One crock was presented to the Canterbury Museum and the other is in the Royal New Zealand Navy Museum, Devonport.[24]

When I last visited the depot in 1989 – 62 years after it was abandoned – the site was hard to find. A few beams, planks and smaller pieces of wood wedged between rocks, and the old rusty kettle, were all that remained.

THE INTRODUCTION OF LIVESTOCK AND PLANTS

In March 1886, at the time the Antipodes castaway depot was built, Captain Fairchild recommended that some sheep and goats "be sent there next trip of a Government vessel; also, some English grass and blue-gum and wattle seeds". The latter to provide firewood, as there was "no brush or wood of any kind on the island".

The first landing of sheep on the Antipodes is reported to have been in 1887. In February of the following year the *Hinemoa* landed three goats and seven sheep, supplied by the Invercargill Wreck Fund. Also on this trip, "assorted trees and plants, consisting of gums, firs, wattles, and scotch broom, were placed on the Aucklands, Campbells, and Antipodes".[25] Fortunately for conservation, none of these woody plants survived.

Three cattle were landed on Antipodes Island in 1889. In January 1890 it was noted that they "had begun to make tracks through the heavy tussock by the landing": two were seen, as were "some recent traces" of sheep. On this visit botanist Thomas Kirk observed that the cattle "greedily devour *Stilbocarpa* . . . eating even the rhizomes; so that some of our choicest things will soon be thinned."[26]

In October 1891 two cattle, including a bull were seen, and the skeleton found of a cow that had fallen over a cliff. Some sheep were also present.[27] In November 1893, Fairchild saw nine sheep, a cow with a calf, a big bull and a heifer – and the second mate, John Bollons, considered that there were still goats on the island. Cattle were still present when Lyttelton MP James Joyce visited in May 1894, and more may have been liberated in 1900.[28] After a visit in July 1903, botanist Leonard Cockayne confirmed that "cattle, sheep and goats have been landed on several occasions, but . . . invariably died after three or four years". Three more heifers were landed at the time of Cockayne's visit. He concluded:

> It is very easy to see how such tussock slopes and swamps as those I have described are most unfavourable for the well-being of domestic animals. Sheep, thickly clothed with wool through not being shorn, if they once fall down in such tussock meadows can never rise again, and must perish.

Part of Main Group, Bounty Islands, showing the approximate position of the first depot built in 1886 and that of its replacement (built 1891). Contours are at 10 m intervals.

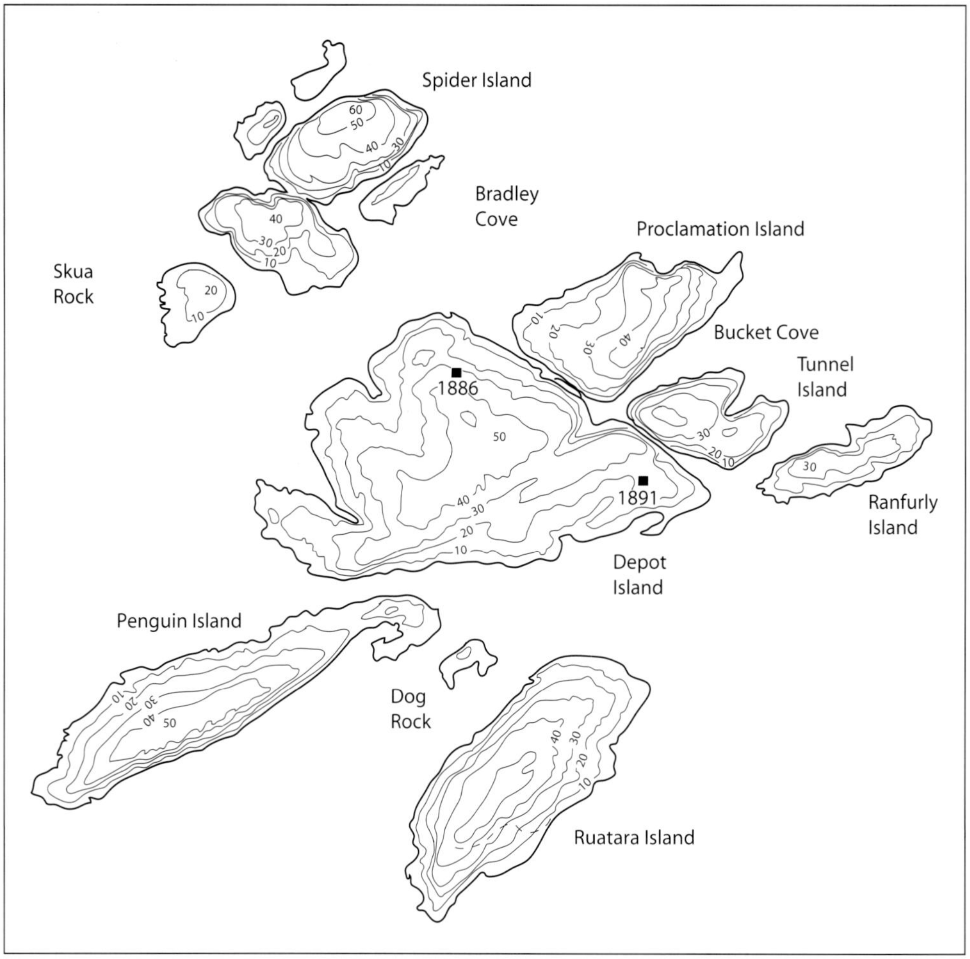

> Cattle certainly may get on better, and might make tracks through the tussocks; but whether they could thrive exposed to the furious gales in the more open lands of the interior is questionable.[29]

More sheep and goats were liberated in 1904, and this appears to have been the last introduction of stock to Antipodes Island.[30] In 1908, only one young cattle beast survived, to be then killed by the shipwrecked crew of the *Président Félix Faure*. Skeletons were the only sign these castaways found of the one-time presence of sheep and goats.

CHAPTER EIGHT

The *Spirit of the Dawn*

The *Spirit of the Dawn* was an iron barque of 716 tons gross weight and 692 tons net register. T.R. Oswald and Company built her in 1869 at Pallion in Sunderland, Durham. She measured: length 175′ 1″; beam 30′ 7″; depth 19′ 7″; moulded depth 25′ 6″; freeboard midships 3′ 6″. Messrs John Bell and Son of Dury Lane, Water Street, Liverpool had owned the ship for over 15 years. Registered No. 63151 at Lloyds, she was rated AA1 as an iron vessel built with thicker plating than the rules required. She had last been surveyed in July 1891.[1]

On 4 December 1893, Lloyds of London received an unsigned telegram from Wellington.[2] It simply read: "Spirit of Dawn wrecked Antipodes Islands". This was the first the insurers or owners had heard of the ship since she had sailed from Rangoon nearly six months earlier.

The *Spirit of the Dawn*, under Captain Robert T. Millington and with a total crew of 16 hands, left Rangoon on 17 June 1893 loaded with a full cargo of rice, bound for Talcahuano in Chile, where she was to call for further orders. She met with very squally weather through the Bay of Bengal, and after passing through the doldrums encountered variable winds veering from east to southwest.[3]

Nearing the latitude of New Zealand, overcast skies, rain and fog made navigation difficult. The ship's position was ascertained on 1 September, but during the following two days only one further sight was obtained, and this was unreliable. Throughout this period they had been beating against variable head winds in "thick weather", leaving their exact position uncertain – though Millington, a "good seaman and a splendid navigator", was sure they were well clear of any islands. We do not know what charts or sailing directories the *Spirit of the Dawn* had on board, but they could well have given incorrect co-ordinates for the Antipodes Islands.

During the early hours of 4 September there was drizzling rain, a light easterly wind and a moderate sea. The fog was so dense that those on deck could not see the length of the ship ahead. The chief officer, Mr Horner, relieved the second officer at 4 a.m. About half an hour later Able Seaman Ballard, the lookout, shouted out that he thought there were breakers ahead. The chief officer ran forward and peered out anxiously but the fog had become so thick that nothing could be seen – though the roar of the breakers was loud and unmistakable. Millington and all hands were called, and it took only a minute or two before everyone was up.

Immediately the captain ordered Third Officer Davies to take the wheel and for the helm to be put "hard-up", but the vessel was carrying very little sail and was slow to change course. Through the murk came a glimpse of surf breaking on partly submerged rocks ahead. The captain ordered that life belts should be issued and the starboard lifeboat "cleared away". However, the ship struck almost immediately and settled down so quickly that there was no time to get the boat into the davits. Millington ordered all hands to take to the mizzen rigging, which most did. The steward and the cook were not seen after the vessel struck, except that Mr Morrissey, the Second Officer, saw the steward going into the cabin as he supposed for stores. Morrissey remembered the steward saying, "We shall all go down," and himself replying,

Antipodes Island W.N.W. 8 or 10 leagues.

Profile of Antipodes Island. Sketch by Lieutenant O. H. Wilson, R.N., published in 1840. (*Nautical Magazine and Naval Chronicle.*)

"Have no fear, we shall all be right." At that hour of the morning the cook would have been up and working in the galley.[4]

At the time the ship started to sink, the Chief and Second Officers had been struggling to get the lifeboat cleared away from its station on the bridge deck. With no time to use the davits and the captain's order for the crew to take to the rigging, these officers jumped into the boat hoping that she would float off the skids as the ship went down. Fortunately, this was exactly what happened.

Once the boat floated clear, most of the men in the rigging jumped either straight into her, or into the sea to be pulled aboard. Millington, the carpenter and one seaman refused to jump. The captain, still clinging to the mizzen rigging, ordered the boat to row clear of the wreck, and almost instantaneously the ship sank, taking with her the captain and four men. The lifeboat was caught by the mizzen-stay as the vessel rolled over, and the crew shoved her clear. Then the main brace came across her, and a sailor "cut it like a fiddle-string" with a tomahawk that fortunately was part of the mandatory safety equipment in lifeboats.

The lifeboat was also fully equipped with mast, sails, oars and water. The fog was becoming thicker every minute and although the crew rowed about the position where they thought the ship had sunk they found no further survivors or wreckage. As the boat was pulling away, they fancied they heard cries from men in the water, but they were too far off to see anything, and could not tell the direction from which the calls came. They knew they were near land but could not see it. The wind and current being easterly they drifted out to sea until about 11 a.m. when the clearing fog revealed an island about seven or eight miles (12 km) to the east. Although the officers knew their approximate latitude and longitude, they were uncertain what island it was.

After a long pull of about four hours the lifeboat was close to the place where the ship had struck. The survivors described this as "a reef extending about half a mile seaward" on the island's south-west coast. This reef is shown on Fairchild's 1886 sketch map of Antipodes Island, and on all subsequent nautical charts. *Brett's New Zealand and South Pacific Pilot* for 1887–88 states "a reef runs off the S.W. end [of Antipodes Island] for about half a mile, with a rock on its outer end about 3 feet out of the water".[5] It is probable that the ship ripped her bottom out in passing over the reef, and sank in deep water on the other side. The 11 sailors rowed further along to the east searching for a suitable landing, and finally found an entrance between rocks where they were able to pull in and land – on the relatively sheltered shore of "a little harbour".[6] They were in what we now know as South Bay.

SURVIVAL ON THE ISLAND

The survivors were exhausted, wet and cold. They did not know where they were. Some were wearing little more than underclothing. After landing the oars, mast, sail, and other loose gear they attempted to haul the boat up – but there was "nothing but bluff rocks at the place where they landed", so they "made it fast to a rock by the painter".

Their first thoughts were to find food and shelter. There was plenty of water nearby but very little to eat except limpets, which some of the men recognised as edible. Despite being hungry, they were afraid to eat too many at first in case they were poisonous. But soon all had "a pretty good feed of them". The castaways explored further to look for a place to shelter. Immediately above the landing place was a narrow tussock-covered terrace about 20 metres above sea level. Behind this again were very steep tussock-covered slopes and rock ledges, towering upwards to disappear into the mist that still shrouded the island's summit. After scrambling over rock and tussock, they found "a little overhanging bluff" where they decided to camp for the night. They cut the tussock grass and cleared a space big enough to hold them all. After spreading the cut tussock straw on the ground they lay down and covered themselves with a sail. Some remained wet all night.

At daybreak the first men returning to the beach for more limpets found that the boat had disappeared. She had been beached at low tide, and during the night a rising tide and a heavy swell had caused her to break adrift. The boat was never seen again. This deprived them of the means to explore the shores of the island.

That day they walked around the coast for about a kilometre to near the reef where the ship had sunk, hoping that something of use may have been washed ashore. But no wreckage was found. The journey was exhausting, as much of it was over rough rocks and through deep tussock. They had a further meal of limpets and also killed a penguin – the only one to be seen. They shared it out and ate it raw, for they had no way of cooking or lighting a fire. Morrissey ate the heart. He later said that he "tasted it and nibbled at it like a fish at bait, and found it did not taste very bad".

After returning to camp the men discussed their predicament. They had seen that the narrow terrace terminated in steep slopes and cliffs about three kilometres to the west, and that beyond there was no route around the coast. Likewise, to the east of South Bay the land plunged near-vertically into the sea. They decided they would have to climb to the top of the island if they were to find out more of their surroundings.

The next morning Horner, Morrissey and two seamen set off with the intention of exploring the island. On the long climb up to the plateau rim at nearly 300 metres above the sea, they kept as much as possible to stream channels and old slip scars, but from time to time had to struggle through head-high tussock. These huge tussocks, of *Poa litorosa*, grew on pedestals and their interlocking leaves made it almost impossible to push between them. Sometimes the men made better progress by walking on the tops of the tussocks, but every so often would miss their step and plunge out of sight between the plants. Once they were on the undulating top of the island the going became easier, but they still had to traverse slopes of tall, thick tussock and gullies filled with near-impenetrable fern. This was extremely tiring for starving sailors not used to such exercise. By nightfall they estimated they

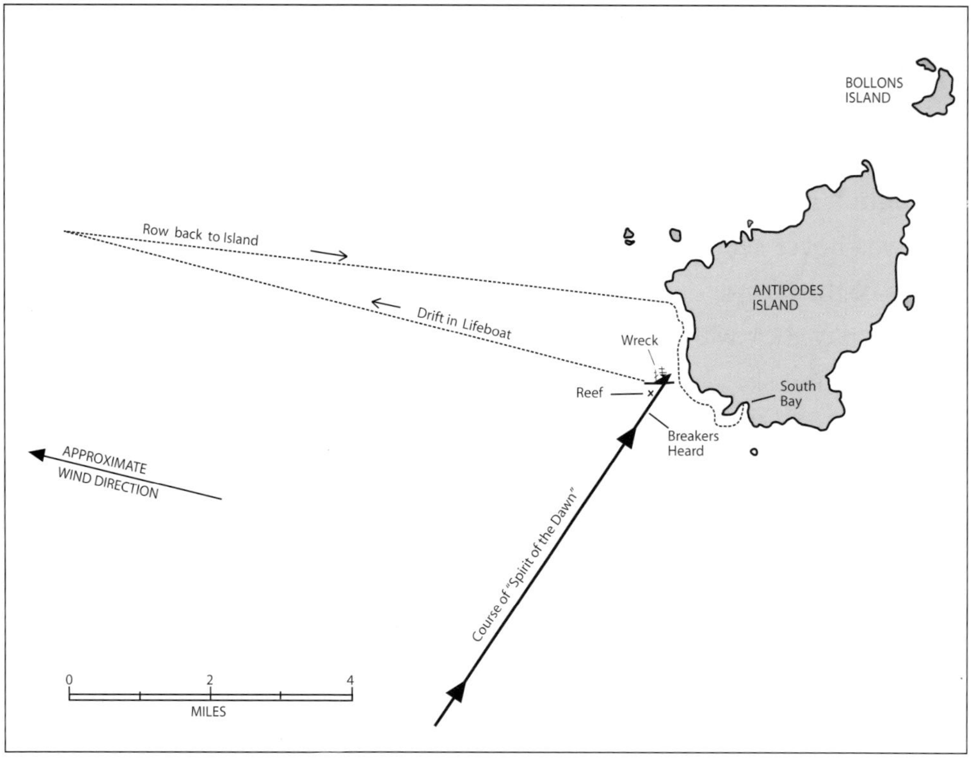

Antipodes Islands, showing the track of the *Spirit of the Dawn*, the site of the wreck and the survivors' subsequent journey in the lifeboat.

had walked about eight kilometres or halfway around the island.

That evening they killed a wandering albatross, which they skinned and partly ate raw. Morrissey recalled that they "did not eat it all – we could not quite stomach that at the time". They cut tussock straw and huddled down in pairs for the night. Overnight, the two officers got wet from the rain that fell, while the seamen apparently found a more sheltered place to sleep and remained dry.

The next morning there was a thick fog. The men breakfasted on the remains of the albatross. They were on high land but couldn't see far for the fog. It was coming on to rain, and after some discussion they decided to head back to the others. On the return journey they cut straight across country over several hills and slid down the tussock and rocks to the campsite that night – " wet, hungry, weary". They told the rest of the castaways of their ordeal and that they had found nothing significant. After that the general feeling was that there was "nothing on the island barring birds and so forth".

If the scouting party had in fact walked the distance they estimated, their overnight bivouac would have been close to the New Zealand Government Depot with provisions for castaways, sited near sea level at the north-eastern end of the island. It is probable that the difficult nature of the terrain and vegetation led them to over-estimate the distance travelled. Nevertheless, it was most unfortunate that through fog, tiredness and hunger, they decided not to continue their exploration of the island. Had they located the castaway depot they would have found ample provisions for the whole of their stay; also a stock of cooking utensils, clothes, blankets, matches, tobacco, a rifle and ammunition, as well as fishing lines. There were also a number of goats, sheep, and cattle that had been liberated as food for castaways. It is not surprising that the sailors saw no sign of them as heavy tussock kept the animals confined to a small area near the depot.

Following their unproductive survey of the upper levels of the island, the men decided to keep their camp where it was. Never again did they journey far from the narrow coastal terrace that stretches for about two kilometres between South Bay and Stack Bay on the south-west coast of Antipodes Island. They built a shelter with walls of tussocks, roofed in by the boat's sails, and nearby they erected a signal staff with the boat's mast and an oar. Several days later they discovered a Giant Petrel nesting area where the large dark-coloured chicks were easily caught. The legs were skinned and eaten raw – "we could eat nothing else of them". Besides a regular diet of limpets, they also ate the roots and leaves of several plants including "a small creeping plant resembling celery in both appearance and taste". This was native celery *Apium prostratum*.

In late winter with no means of lighting a fire, poorly clad and on this meagre diet, all the men felt the cold badly and understandably had little strength to travel far, save to harvest their next meal. One sailor, a Eurasian boy named Felix Hewbert who had shipped at Rangoon as an ordinary seaman, was not used to cold weather and suffered much more than the others. He had escaped the wreck without shoes and on the island his feet were always wet and cold. They became frost-bitten and he could barely move about. The rest of the men did all they could for him, but he eventually lost four toes off one foot and two and a half off the other. It was reported that the toes mortified to such an extent that they could be cut off with limpet shells.

About mid-September, Erect-crested penguins began to arrive in great numbers at the start of their breeding season. The castaways tried penguin for a second time. According to Morrissey, "there was any amount of fat on them and we got it scraped off their skins, and then we used to put it in leaves to keep. There was a root we found on the island . . . we used to cut it in two pieces and put the penguin fat between, and in that way we made a regular sandwich." The root was probably from the plant *Stilbocarpa polaris* – known to the early sealers as Macquarie Island cabbage.

It seems that for most of September the castaways enjoyed quite good weather with a number of sunny days. "We used to skin the penguins and then take them to the beach and keep them in salt water . . . and afterwards put them in the sun to dry; on the next day we would dislocate the birds and cut them in slices so that the sun might have more effect. That is the way we used to dry our meat, and finally we got to be as good as French cooks in regard to the penguin." Another report mentions that the penguin flesh was also "wind dried".

On the 17th day after landing, 21 September, the castaways saw a barque that passed so close they could see the man at the wheel. The very next day a full-rigged ship passed less than five kilometres from the shore. Although the men waved and yelled until they were hoarse, both ships sailed on. In their anguish they realised that if the lifeboat had not been lost they could easily have rowed out and cut the second vessel off. On two other occasions vessels were seen that had passed well eastward of the island. At that time they had only a piece of canvas for a flag, and that was down on the low terrace near their camp. Here it would not have been very obvious against the background of the tussock-covered slopes.

On 2 October, almost a month after the wreck, the castaways found penguin eggs for the first time. Previously they had noticed, as they killed penguins for meat, that eggs were developing inside them – and they looked forward eagerly to the time when the birds would lay. Eventually, a bird was killed that contained a full-size egg covered with a shell. This caused great excitement as the men realised there were eggs to be had fairly soon. The next morning when two of the sailors went to collect a penguin they found birds sitting on eggs. They shouted and "hallooed" to the others who wondered what all the fuss was about, until the pair came back with their hats full of eggs, and the news that there were many more.

The castaways wasted no time visiting penguin colonies around the coast as far away as the wreck site. Many of the birds savagely defended their nests, pecking and hitting out with their flippers. That day dozens of eggs were eaten as they were found, and others collected and brought back to camp. One sailor tied knots in the ends of his oilskin leggings and carried them home filled with eggs, feeling very proud of his haul. All the castaways felt an immense joy from at last having a satisfying and easily obtainable supply of food.

After that there was an abundance of fresh eggs for about two weeks, but then "they began to get addled" as the penguins had completed laying and incubation progressed. Still, by then the crew had gathered and stored a great quantity. Morrissey recalled that "the mate and one of the apprentices and I together hid away, I suppose, over 100 dozen in holes for a rainy day".

Towards the end of October another smaller species of penguin, Rockhopper penguins, arrived at the island and started to lay: "We thought that they would surely not keep coming, or else we would be able to live like kings. If we had only had a fire and a frying pan, we might have had omelets and scrambled eggs and so on, but as we had no fire we had to drink the eggs raw." The castaways then ate "30 to 40 a day each". They also "made a big cache of eggs – a hole 6 ft deep and 4 ft long and wide, and in it they laid a layer of eggs, and a layer of grass alternately, as a stand-by against the end of the season".

Food was no longer the men's prime concern. Bad weather seemed to be coming more prevalent. Not only did rain make it harder to dry their penguin meat, but also they realised that they must provide themselves with better shelter. Another of their troubles was how to mend what scanty clothes they possessed. In early November they shifted their camp to a place where "three caves were found along the beach, and these were made fairly comfortable by walling up the entrance with sods and by putting down a flooring of dry grass". They built two huts: probably one was for the officers and the other for the men. Morrissey described the move as:

> to a place below an overhanging bluff, and we built a wall in front of it so that we had a sort of cave to live in . . . At night we closed the opening of our cave up with tussocks, and when the hole was shut it was as dark as a dungeon, but we were alright inside our castle, and we used to lie as close together as we could in order to keep warm.[7]

The caves had rocky ledges, and before lying down at night the castaways used to "knock the tops off a number of eggs, and stand them on the ledges handiest to reach, so that they would not be thirsty during the night".[8] The boat's sail that had been used to roof their previous shelter was now spare, so they "wacked" the canvas out between them to mend their clothes. They unravelled a pair of mittens, used the wool as thread, and made needles out of albatross bones. Although they often searched for debris washed ashore from the wreck, the only things found were a red singlet, a few empty gunny bags and some small pieces of wood.

On about 14 November, after they had been on the island for about 70 days, they carved the latitude and longitude and the words "Shipwrecked crew" on a piece of wood and lashed it to a life buoy that they had brought ashore in the boat. They set the buoy adrift, "with the view of it being picked up by any vessel at sea". A few days later they removed the boat's mast from where it had first been erected and "planted it on top of a high knob". From all accounts this knob was the prominent volcanic plug about 200 metres north-west of the head of South Bay. With the red singlet, canvas and some bunting they made another flag, "so that any vessel coming within three or four miles of the island could not help seeing the flag on a clear day". From then on one or other of the crew kept watch from this point during daylight hours.

At their new camp the castaways were much better situated. When it rained they could keep dry under the rock overhang, "excepting the man on the lookout at the flagstaff, who had nothing to protect him but the tussocks".[9]

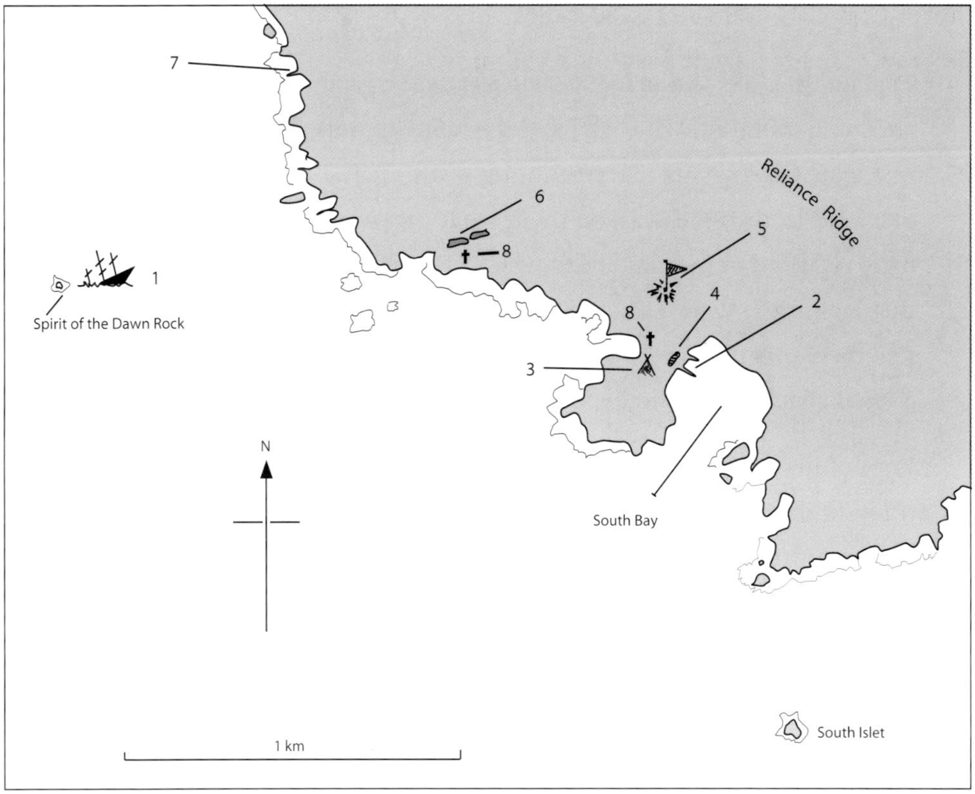

Historic sites near South Bay, Antipodes Island.

1 Wreck of *Spirit of the Dawn*
2 Castaways' landing place
3 Castaways' first camp
4 Castaways' caves
5 Castaways' flagpole
6 Remains of old sealing huts
7 Overhang with fire-site and burnt penguin bones
8 Finger posts pointing to depot

RESCUE

On the morning of 30 November, the *Hinemoa* was approaching Antipodes Island en route from Campbell Island on its six-monthly voyage to check the subantarctic island depots for shipwrecked mariners. As usual there were a number of passengers on board including Miss Seddon, the Premier's daughter. It was a fine, clear day, and from the ship's bridge a flagstaff was observed "erected on a high knob at the south-western end", and as the ship got nearer a "little flag" was hoisted up it. Captain Fairchild immediately acknowledged by hoisting the ship's ensign, and then "steamed on round to the food depot" at the north end of the island. He expected to find people there, but after blowing the ship's whistle no one made their appearance.[10] After anchoring, the captain went ashore and discovered that no one had been at the depot since the *Hinemoa*'s last visit in May. He immediately sent Second Officer John Bollons to the south end of the island to learn who was there. As Bollons recalled it 20 years later:

> Captain Fairchild said to me; "Mr Bollons, go over, and see what those men are doing over there!". It took me three hours to walk across the island: the first mate, after giving me a tight hug – they [castaways] always hug you first – welcomed me. I asked them what they were doing there, and the mate replied that they had been wrecked. I said I knew that, but why were they not at the depot? They didn't know – they had never searched. So I told them that there were on the island three head of cattle, five sheep and a lot of goats, and a food depot.[11]

Meanwhile the *Hinemoa* had lifted her anchor and steamed around the island looking for wreckage. Fairchild saw nine sheep, a cow with a calf, a big bull and a spotted heifer, but no sign of human activity. On getting around to the south coast those on board again saw the flagstaff and some men walking about on the rocks. Then, as one of the ship's passengers described it:

> a boat was lowered and sent ashore and there a pitiful sight was beheld. Eleven men, some whom had very little clothing, were found standing on the rocks – some with pieces of raw penguin flesh in their hands, which they had been eating. The first salutation from them when the boat landed was "God bless you! We have been here 88 days."[12]

Once the rescued men were on board, enough clean clothing was found for them from among the passengers and crew. Everything was provided for their comfort in the way of food and accommodation. The *Hinemoa* then steered for the Bounty Islands, and finally for Dunedin which was reached

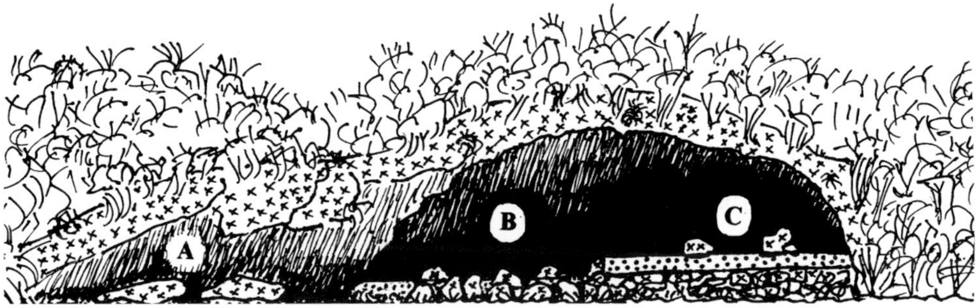

Castaways' Caves, South Bay, Antipodes Island.

A Shallow overhang with big rocks on floor – probably used for daytime shelter.
B Flattish peaty floor – probably the crew's sleeping cave.
C Raised flattish peaty floor, over stones, supported by a rock wall along one edge. Deeper than B – probably the officers' sleeping cave.

Note: The remains of a rock wall occur along the outer edge of both sleeping caves, and rocks that have fallen from the roof are scattered over their floors. (*Based on photographs and notes by K. Walker, 2004.*)

on the afternoon of 4 December. On the ship's arrival at Port Chalmers, Felix Hewbert was transferred to Dunedin hospital and the rest of the crew to lodgings paid for by the Government. According to contemporary New Zealand reports the crew, apart from Hewbert, were all in excellent condition – although a much later British account mentions that "the almost dying men were taken off [the island] and brought to New Zealand".[13] The *Otago Daily Times* and *Witness* launched an appeal for funds from their readers to assist the sailors until they departed on the next direct steamer to England. The New Zealand Marine Department expended a total of £161 12 9d on the relief of the crew. This was later refunded by the Imperial Board of Trade, since the wrecked vessel was owned in the United Kingdom.[14]

A Court of Inquiry into the wreck of the *Spirit of the Dawn* was held at Wellington on 12 December before James Martin, Resident Magistrate, and Captain Joseph T. Adams, Assessor. The ship's three surviving officers, the look-out man at the time of the wreck, and an apprentice gave evidence. The judgement of the Court was that "the *Spirit of the Dawn* was well found", but as Captain Millington was lost with the vessel, there was "no evidence to show how the vessel came into the position in which she was" when wrecked. It was however, ascertained that the final "sight" on 3 September was not reliable, and "the master, according to his reckoning, would have passed well clear of the island". The Court added that, in its opinion, the survivors did all that could be done to save the lives of those lost with the vessel.[15]

Several editorials in New Zealand newspapers were very critical of the lack of initiative of the castaways on the island. The *Southland Daily News* said about the loss of the lifeboat that "it seems scarce credible, aware, as they could not help being, that their first hope of escape lay in their boat, that they should have, so to speak, deserted it to its fate". The newspaper continued:

> We are told they were not aware of there being any depot on the Island or the men who made what they reckon half its circuit, say five miles, would have finished their task and have enabled the party to pass the time of their detention in a perfect sailor's paradise – plenty to eat, fresh meat at that, plenty of tobacco, and plenty of sport in hunting, when they chose, plenty

> of clothes to wear and warm bunks to sleep in. One almost feels inclined to say their sufferings served them right.[16]

The criticism seems severe and not based completely on the facts as related by the rescued sailors, but it only put in print the comments that were then being made everywhere. Even 20 years later, Bollons stated:

> they simply trailed the [boat's] painter over the rocks, without making it fast, and when they came to find it again the boat had drifted well out to sea. Can you imagine such folly in sailor men? . . . It seemed incredible that there should have been so little enterprise. When I asked the mate and second mate to come with me and see [the depot], I'm blessed if they would come. They must have been thoroughly ashamed of themselves. I told them straight that even a pack of women would have shown more curiosity about the island. There's one of the men working on the wharf at Onehunga still. He has never been so fat as he was on a diet of raw penguin eggs on the Antipodes.[17]

THE CASTAWAYS' CAMP

When the 11 survivors from the wreck of the *Spirit of the Dawn* landed from their lifeboat at South Bay on 4 September 1893, they "scrambled over rocks and tussocks" until they came to "a little overhanging bluff" on a "low terrace". Here they camped for the night under a tent rigged from the boat's sails and masts. A few days later they built a shelter in the same place. It had walls of tussock roofed in by the boat's sails, and nearby they erected a signal staff by using the boat's mast, an oar, and a piece of canvas.

Descriptions given by the castaways suggest that this camp would have been under the continuous line of low bluffs that runs across the isthmus of the peninsula forming the western shore of South Bay. While checking out this location in January 2001, Kath Walker and Graeme

Elliott found a low rock overhang with a dense mat of dry tussock beneath. This site, about two thirds of the way westward along the bluffs, is the most probable position of the castaways' first camp. Their signal station would initially have been on the higher ground to the south. About three weeks before they were rescued, and prompted by deteriorating weather, the castaways shifted camp "to a place beneath an overhanging bluff". Here, they "never got wet" even when it rained, and they "built two huts by placing walls of tussocks up against the cliff". The site is variously described as "an overhanging cliff", "an overhanging bluff", "a sort of cave", and "three caves . . . along the beach". It is also recorded that "the caves had rocky ledges" and that they were "made fairly comfortable by walling up the entrance with sods and putting down a flooring of dry grass".

The site that best fits all the recorded facts is a series of three continuous overhangs above the north-western shore of South Bay. A party of ornithologists led by Brian Bell checked out these caves during May 2001 and found they had fairly level floors and were roomy enough to accommodate 11 seamen. Most important, there were rocky ledges along the walls that matched the castaways' description.

At my request, Kath and Graeme further inspected the site in February 2004 and provided more photos and notes. Inside the northern-most cave, a low rock wall had been built to support a floor of stones and deep peat, apparently the remains of old tussocks. Immediately south of this is a lower area of level floor with the remnants of a rock wall across its outer edge. These were obviously two separate sleeping areas. The rest of the overhang to the south is quite shallow and its floor is scattered with large rocks. It was probably used as a daytime shelter only.

When the castaways moved their camp to the caves they also shifted their flagpole to "a high knob . . . a little way back from the shore". The man on lookout duty at the flag "had nothing to protect him but the tussocks". This site would have been on top of the tussock-covered volcanic plug immediately north from the South Bay Peninsula. Two independent searches during 2001 failed to find any remains of the boat's mast amongst the tall tussock there.

CHAPTER NINE

Ask the Navy

On 23 December 1893, as a result of the wreck of the *Spirit of the Dawn* and at Captain Fairchild's prompting, the New Zealand Government requested the Royal Navy, Australia Station, to more accurately survey the southern islands. The Marine Department was particularly concerned with the inadequate charting of the Antipodes Islands, and the need to check their latitude and longitude.

The 165-foot screw gunboat HMS *Lizard* sailed for the Antipodes early in 1894, landing a party to inspect the depot on 15 February. On return to Lyttelton, her commander confirmed that the islands were "very incorrectly drawn on the chart". He had also found that the position of the hut was "about 2 miles out in latitude and 7 miles in longitude". This was reported to the Admiralty in London asking whether a special surveying vessel should be sent. The reply received in July by the Earl of Glasgow, Governor of New Zealand, read:

> The Lords Commissioners of the Admiralty do not consider Antipodes Island to be of sufficient importance to warrant one of H.M's Surveying vessels proceeding so far out of her way for the sole purpose of examining it; but on the next visit of one of H.M's Ships to that island, endeavours will be made to have it more correctly drawn; observing that now that its position has been fixed with fair accuracy by H.M.S. "Lizard" the most important detail required for passing ships is known.

In August 1894 the Senior Naval Officer in New Zealand waters was directed by his Admiral to "visit Bounty, Antipodes and Campbell Islands as soon as convenient, and endeavour to ascertain their exact position and make a correct drawing". Surprisingly, the Auckland Islands were not mentioned. However, when asked for their opinion the New Zealand Government replied that they thought it "very desirable that the Auckland Islands should be included in the proposed survey" since Fairchild considered that the coastline and inlets were "not correctly shown on the chart".

In early February 1895 the 200-foot screw corvette HMS *Royalist*, commanded by James Goodrich, returned from a southern cruise and submitted detailed "Hydrographic notes on Bounty and Antipodes Islands". In these the navigator, Lieutenant Edward Reeves, reported that on "the present drawing of the Bounty Islands, I find they are wrongly placed relatively to one another"; that "eastward of principal island (hut) is another island . . . not shown on the plan"; and that "the western group is too far to the north relatively to Eastern Groups". He also found that the hut was not visible "until you get off the eastern group", and that breakers seen one mile to the south-west of the western island had not been charted.

Previous soundings on all sides of the group were checked and found to be correct. Measured by patent log, the spread of the group from east to west was found to be two nautical miles. Weather did not permit a landing but sights from the ship "placed the west end of the group in latitude 47° 41′ 31″ S, Longitude 179° 2′ 33″ E".

At the Antipodes, the *Royalist* found landing impossible, but Reeves' findings there generally agreed with the report of HMS *Lizard*. Rightly, he

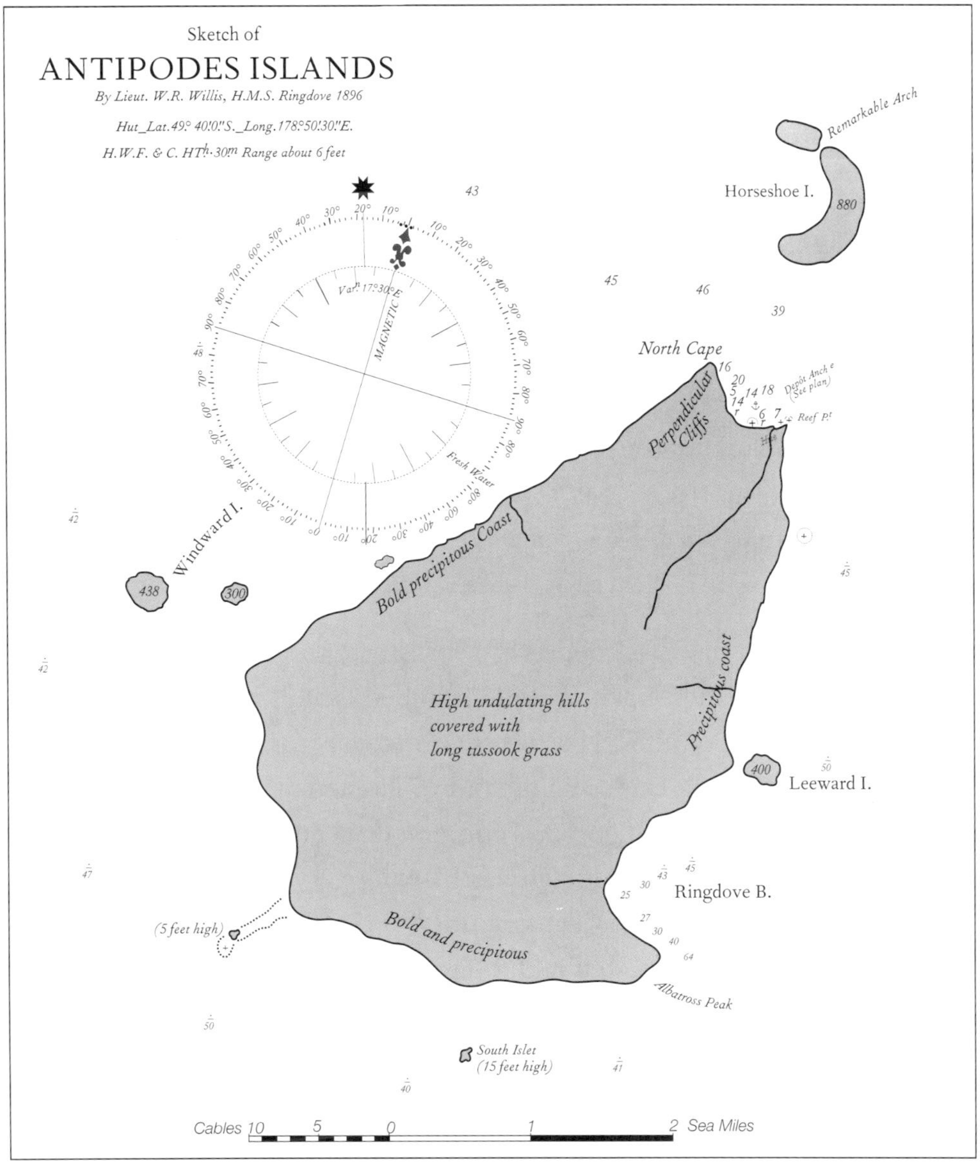

Improved chart of Antipodes Islands following HMS *Ringdove*'s 1896 survey. (*UK Hydrographic Office OCB 1002 B4.*)

considered the main island to be "at least twelve miles in circumference", and that "the 10 feet rock" off the south coast was "correctly placed as regards distance from the shore but should be further to the eastward". At the Campbell islands the weather did not permit any surveying.[1]

On one of her routine southern inspections, in October 1895, the *Hinemoa* found substantial wreckage at the Auckland Islands but no bodies or survivors. This once more raised the question as to whether the southern islands should be visited more regularly. Premier Seddon pointed out to the Governor that the *Hinemoa* could not be spared to make more than two trips a year, usually "about September and March", to check the depots and search for castaways. He suggested "that His Excellency should ask the Rear Admiral and Commander-in-Chief of the Australia Station whether he can arrange to send a man-of-war to the islands twice a year, say in June and December".[2]

In typical public-service style, Rear-Admiral Cyprian A. G. Bridge replied:

> I have the honour to inform your Excellency that, whilst I am unable to enter into any definite engagement as to the months in which, or the number of times that one of Her Majesty's Ships shall visit the islands in question, I will give instructions to the Senior Officer on the NEW ZEALAND Division of the Station which, I believe, will satisfactorily meet the case.

The Rear-Admiral was as good as his word, for within the next two months HMS *Lizard* visited the Auckland and Campbell Islands, and HMS *Ringdove* the Antipodes and Bounties. Like *Lizard, Ringdove* was a screw gunboat of 165 feet length overall. Under command of Lieutenant Bremer she arrived at Antipodes Island at 7 p.m. on 23 February 1896 and anchored overnight, keeping steam on the engines as it was blowing very hard from the south-west. A heavy swell prevented landing until 4 p.m. the next day, when with difficulty the depot was "visited and found correct, with a notice that it had been visited by the 'Hinemoa' on 16 October".

A survey of the group started at 6 a.m. on the 25th when *Ringdove* weighed anchor and steamed round the islands "taking bearings and distances and sextant angles, as the whole island appears to be wrongly charted". The ship's boats "visited all the coves for signs of shipwreck" and carried out soundings at Depot Anchorage.

Ringdove arrived off the Bounty islands at 3.30 p.m. on the 26th. Bremer reported that he steamed around and close to all islands but could not land and visit the depot owing to wind and sea. However, he "stopped close in and fired a gun on each side of the Depot-island (on which the hut and staff could be plainly seen) and had there been any persons on the islands they

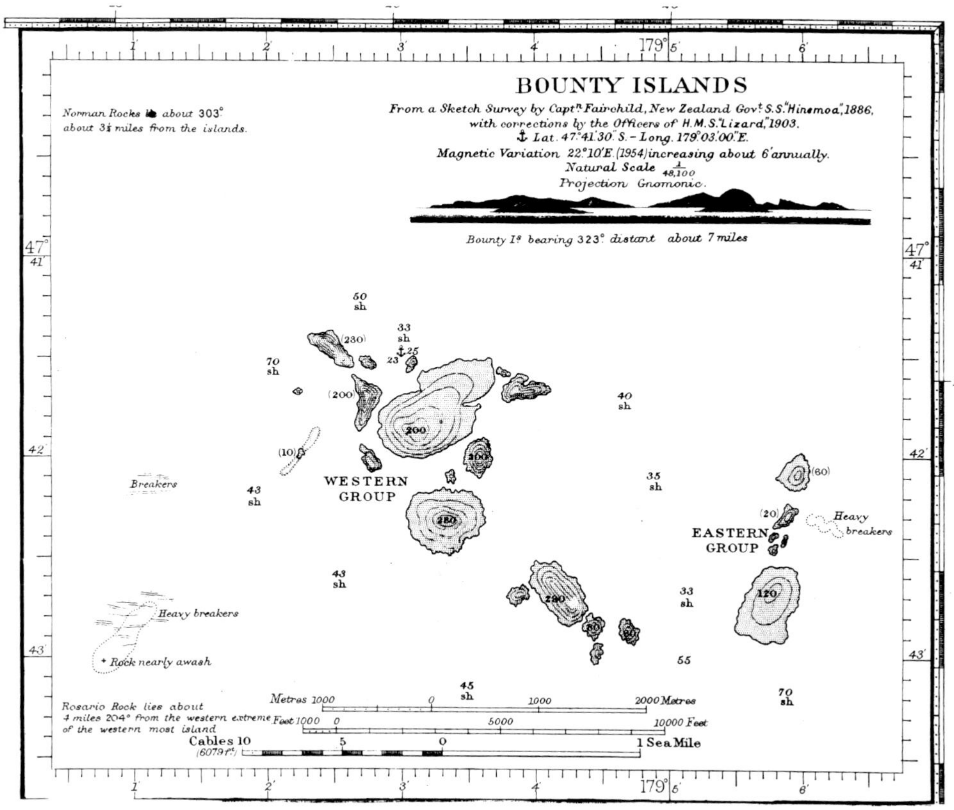

Improved chart of the Bounty Islands following HMS *Lizard*'s 1903 survey. (*British Admiralty Chart 1022.*)

must have been seen". The warship left the islands that evening as a gale threatened and the barometer was falling fast.

On 17 June 1897, the Royal Naval Standing Orders for the New Zealand Division were changed to read: "The Senior Officer in New Zealand is to cause the Bounty, Antipodes, Auckland, and Campbell Islands to be visited twice a year, and the other islands attached to his division if possible once a year." Rear-Admiral Bridge noted: "This order was given to ensure that the Ships on the New Zealand Division should get a fair amount of sea-work, most of the cruizing [*sic*] on that Division being merely coasting."[3]

Towards the end of 1897 the British Museum (Natural History) wrote to the Earl of Ranfurly, Governor of New Zealand, requesting him, if possible, to obtain for them examples of birds from New Zealand and its adjacent islands. As well as organising collections from the mainland and going himself on two voyages with Government steamers around the subantarctic islands, the Governor also contacted the Australia Station of the Royal Navy. Thus, the commanders of the various British cruisers in New Zealand waters were asked to procure bird specimens as opportunity offered.

The first results from this request occurred in October 1899 when HMS *Ringdove*, under the command of Lieutenant R.F. Ayscough, visited all of the southern islands, including Macquarie, on a 31-day cruise from Lyttelton. She encountered extremely heavy gales and at one stage while en route for Macquarie Island had to divert to the Auckland Islands, and was weather-bound there for several days. She finally arrived at the Antipodes Islands on 28 October. The depot was inspected the next day and found in good order and an Antipodes Island Parakeet was shot for the British Museum. After calling at the Bounty islands on 30 October the ship reached Lyttelton early on 2 November.[4]

The 225-foot torpedo cruiser HMS *Archer* (Commander J.P. Rolleston) carried out further routine patrols of the southern islands in 1901 and 1903. On both trips, while at the Antipodes Islands (15 July 1901 and 14 January 1903) and Bounty Islands (16 July 1901 and 15 January 1903), Rolleston and Lieutenant Kennett Dixon collected numerous bird specimens. These included Antipodes Island Snipe, Antipodes Island Parakeets, and Bounty Island Shags, including some live specimens of the last species.

In 1903 during a round of the southern islands "accomplished in thirteen days, due to the phenomenally fine weather", *Lizard* inspected the Antipodes Islands on 6 December, when, as recorded by her Commander, Lieutenant John Glossop, the castaway depot was checked and "every thing appeared to be in good order and untouched". He noted some cattle near the depot, and that there was "practically no scrub at all on these islands which would render them undesirable for settling" because of a lack of firewood.

Lizard reached the Bounty Islands the next day and found the chart to be most unreliable, "much more so than the others". In little more than three hours, the depot was inspected and found intact, and some corrections added to Fairchild's original "sketch survey". These corrections were later incorporated in the 1917 edition of the Admiralty Chart. Glossop found it strange that the New Zealand Government was advertising the islands for lease, "presumably for sheep runs", when: "The Bounties are absolutely uninhabitable being nothing more than huge rocks with myriads of sea birds of various sorts on them, so many that you could not walk without kicking them, the islands are one vast breeding ground".[5]

During a voyage in early November 1904, the 300-foot cruiser HMS *Psyche* was the next warship to visit the Antipodes and Bounty Islands. Apparently no further warships visited until 1908 when, after checking the Bounty Islands depot on 12 May, the *Psyche*'s sister ship, HMS *Pegasus*, arrived at the Antipodes depot next morning to find it overflowing with castaways.

CHAPTER TEN

The *Président Félix Faure*

The *Président Félix Faure* was a steel four-masted barque of 2803 gross tonnage and 2393 tons net register. She was built at Le Havre by Forges et Chantiers de la Médit., and launched in May 1896. The ship measured: length 311′ 6″; beam 45′ 5″; depth 24′ 9″; moulded depth 26′ 7″; freeboard midships 5′ 3.5″; and was owned by Compagnie Havraise de Navigation á Voiles. She was registered at Le Havre, and rated A1 at Lloyds.[1]

> For a considerable time before they were rescued the castaways leaned upon the slender hope of communicating their dire plight to the outside world by means of feathered messengers. On an average, two albatrosses per day were tossed high into the air and driven off, each bearing, tied round its neck, a little quill, into which a fragment of paper was deftly thrust, bearing the following information: *Président Félix Faure. 4 mâts barque Francaise naufragé sur l'Isle Antipodes, le 13 Mars, 1908, 22 hommes – Noel.*[2]

Unfortunately none of these messages got through, and it was not until a routine inspection of the islands by a British warship that the castaways were discovered and news of their rescue was telegraphed from New Zealand to the outside world. *Lloyds Weekly Shipping Index* for Thursday May 21, 1908 included the following item:

> Président Félix Faure – Christchurch, N.Z., May 15, 9 pm. – Pegasus arrived having on board the crew of the *Président Félix Faure*, totally wrecked, March 13, Antipodes, while on voyage New Caledonia for Havre. No lives lost".

The *Président Félix Faure* with a total complement of 22 hands sailed from Pouembout, New Caledonia on 16 February 1908 for Le Havre with a full cargo of 3650 tons of nickel ore. She was one of a large number of steamers and sailing ships then engaged in this trade between New Caledonia and Europe. Captain A. Noel had previously made eight voyages to France with similar cargo, and also several to Newcastle, England. The previous year he had made a fast passage home to Le Havre in 93 days. On that occasion, and on previous passages, he had passed to the north of New Zealand on the way to Cape Horn.[3]

After clearing New Caledonia in February 1908, the ship encountered bad weather nearly all the time. At first, Captain Noel attempted the favoured course around the north of New Zealand, but continuous bad weather and adverse winds forced a change of course to pass to the south of Stewart Island. After passing the latitude of southern Tasmania, very strong south-east winds and high seas were encountered, and the deeply laden vessel plunged and laboured heavily. Nevertheless, she made good progress on her homeward passage, and on the 26th day out from Pouembout was thought to be from seven to 10 miles south of the Antipodes.[4]

On the afternoon of 13 March the weather was very thick and foggy with a heavy sea running. Suddenly breakers were seen on the starboard side. The vessel was "kept up to the wind to clear the land" which intermittently loomed to starboard, and was driven towards the north of the islands. Noel "then saw breakers everywhere" and he "tried to wear ship". This manoeuvre must have been aborted, perhaps because it was bringing them too close to the shore, for the ship continued on a north-easterly course. The *Président Félix Faure* "cleared the first cape", but at about 4 p.m. the high cliffs of a second cape suddenly appeared close ahead. Again, an attempt was made to alter course but before this was possible the ship ran bow-on and stuck hard onto submerged rocks, about 100 yards out from sheer cliffs, towering above for over 300 feet.[5]

Later, Noel blamed the loss of the vessel on the thick fog at the time, and also on the lack of a detailed chart of the islands. The ship's chart of the Southern Ocean showed only one island at the Antipodes, whereas there are two major islands (main Antipodes and Bollons) separated by 1.5 kilometres of water. After interviews with the captain and crew, the *Press* reported: "The Captain, it seems, finding himself near the southerly island, which loomed up suddenly out of the fog, attempted to alter course to clear it, but ran on the south side of the northerly island."[6] Undoubtedly, the first cape cleared by the ship was the extreme northern point of the main Antipodes Island (North Cape). The second cape where the ship struck was the southwest end of Bollons Island. But for the fog, Noel would have seen the open passage between the two islands, put the helm down, and easily cleared the islands.

The masts collapsed when the vessel struck and she went down in about four minutes. Meanwhile, one of the lifeboats was provisioned and launched and all hands and their three pet dogs got safely into it. The crew rowed around for a while to get their bearings in the shifting fog, and finally decided to attempt a landing at a little cove on the north side of the main island. The breakers were running high, the boat capsized, and all were thrown into the water. The crew and the Captain's dog, Sarah, got ashore without serious mishap, but the two other dogs were drowned, the boat was smashed to pieces and all their stores and belongings, except what they stood up in, were lost. The site of landing was the eastern end of Anchorage Bay.

As the fog lifted that evening, Captain Noel looked across to the wreck site on Bollons Island. The sea was still breaking heavily against the cliffs, and the *Président Félix Faure* "was only scattered, submerged wreckage".

SAILING TERMS AND THE *PRÉSIDENT FÉLIX FAURE*

Helm hard up means to steer the ship as far as possible to windward. **Helm down** is to steer further away from the wind direction. **The vessel was kept up to the wind** indicates that the bow of the ship was kept pointing as close as could be to the wind while still maintaining headway.

A four-masted barque, such as the *Président Félix Faure*, should have been able to sail as high as six points (68°) off the wind. From the reconstruction of the ship's track along the north-western coast of the Antipodes Islands and the vessel's apparent inability to sail further away from the land on that course, it seems that the wind must have been blowing from only a few degrees west of north. Such a wind direction would also explain the high breakers encountered at the boat landing in Anchorage Bay. To beat further offshore, Captain Noel needed to turn the ship and bring the wind onto its other side.

To wear ship means to do this by first turning away from the wind and running before it. An alternative is **to about ship**, or **to tack**, which is to turn head-to-wind. To tack in a square-rigged ship was very time-consuming as all braces needed to be worked, and it would probably have been impossible in the high seas encountered. To wear ship seems to have been Noel's only option, but since this manoeuvre involved running downwind it needed considerable sea-room — and as North Cape loomed out of the fog it was aborted.

ON THE ISLAND

For the crew of a sailing ship the castaways were surprisingly elderly, a few being "distinctly venerable". The engineer was 71, most were in their 50s or 40s, and only five were under 30 (including three boys, apparently in their early teens). Noel is reported to have been "about twenty-eight or thirty

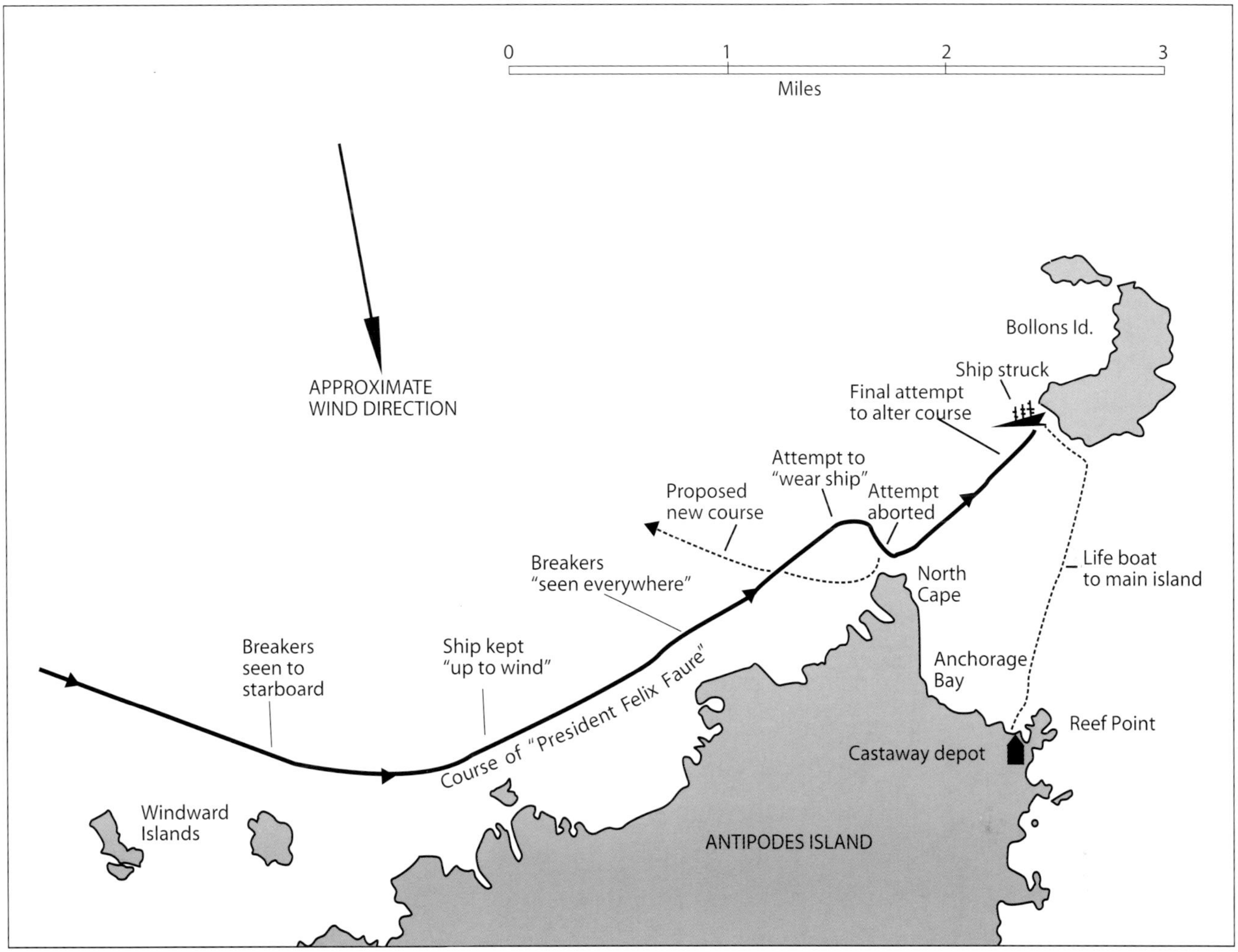

Antipodes Island, showing the track of the *Président Félix Faure*, the site of the wreck, the lifeboat journey and position of the depot.

years of age". All except the Algerian Second Mate were French, mostly from Le Havre. Only one was married.

Night was coming on. Many of the crew were poorly clad and all were soaking wet. In their search for shelter, some of the men climbed the hillside above the landing and on the other side, in a hollow, they were overjoyed to see a hut, the provision depot established in 1886. They clambered the few hundred metres up rocky slopes, low cliffs, and through dense waist-high tussock to the depot, which was tucked hard in against a tussock-covered bank that afforded it some protection from the prevailing wind. The outer walls were weatherboard, with an 11-foot stud at the back wall sloping to

8 feet in the front, where there was a door and one small window. The interior was fully lined with close-fitting planks. The hut's roof was of corrugated iron, and its timber floor was well off the damp peaty ground. In all respects, it was a solidly constructed building and completely weatherproof. Unfortunately, it had not been designed to house 22 men, as it measured only 14′ 6″ by 9′ 6″. By standing up the castaways were able to squeeze themselves in, and that was how they spent their first night on the island.

With dawn the next day all the men scouted about, the contents of the depot were examined, matches were found and a fire lit. Little trace of the ship remained, for during the night it had been "smashed into pieces" by the heavy seas. The oars and other wreckage from the lifeboat were found on the shore. There was plenty of good drinking water in a small stream that flowed past within 50 metres of the depot door from its source in a swamp higher up the hillside. As soon as possible, two additional "cabins", as the crew called them, were built against the sides of the depot. They had walls of scrub, tussock and peat; and were roofed using oars, wood from the lifeboat, the metal lining from provision boxes, and tussock thatch. These huts provided shelter for three men each, but were far from weatherproof and the drenching rain soaked through and dripped inside.[7]

A stocktake was made of the stores in the depot, and some items were shared out. However, the food started to vanish very quickly before the hungry men. Not knowing how long they would be castaways, the captain put the crew on short rations as far as the remaining provisions were concerned – 15 tins of preserved beef were rationed to one a week, and biscuits to one each a day. It was not long before the men had to seek other food supplies. The crew first tried albatrosses, which were nesting in "thousands close to the depot" and were easily killed with sticks. The flesh of the adults was "far from tasty and not very nourishing", but their newly hatched chicks were considered much more favourably. At first, the parakeets on the island were found to be very tame. Some were killed and considered excellent eating, but they soon learned to avoid people and by the fourth week were very hard to catch.

When preparing penguins for cooking, the meat was cut from the breast and thighs and the rest of the carcass discarded. The numbers of penguins were countless, and for a while the food supplies they offered were unlimited. However, on Good Friday all the penguins deserted the island on their regular annual migration away from the breeding colonies. "In the evening there were sufficient to feed a regiment, on the following morning not one was left", and that source of supply was cut off, to the men's deep disappointment.

About five weeks after the wreck, the submerged remnants of the ship broke up completely during a heavy gale, and wooden wreckage washed ashore in Anchorage Bay. The crew recovered the timber and rough wooden benches were constructed around all four walls of the depot, like bunks, to give additional sleeping spaces. These benches were still a prominent feature of the castaway depot in 1969. A report that year to the Canterbury Museum records that "the bunks are very wide and 11 men would be able to climb into them with some discomfort". After these benches were built, about 10 sailors slept in the depot at a time, six in the makeshift huts outside, "and six kept watch four hours about".[8]

A good deal of fishing was done, with hooks made out of nails from the provision boxes and pieces of wire. They were bent to the correct shape and sharpened with a file that was one of the tools found in the depot. Lines were made from threads of canvas woven into a strong cord. Without a boat the men could not get outside the band of thick kelp that grows all around the rocky shores of the Antipodes, and this interfered greatly with their lines. They started to build a raft from wreckage, but soon gave it up as impractical. Fishing, therefore, was not very productive, but sometimes they caught fish coming ashore in the breakers and "headed them off before they could get away". They also collected shellfish, mainly limpets, which were cooked in different dishes but were "tough and leathery".

The root of a low-growing plant was dug up and prepared, but was found to be "stringy and unnutritious". The men, therefore, had to keep mainly to the birds for their principal supplies of food. Cooking duties were shared. As explained later by Seaman Sicat: "We have two cooks, one week in turns, everybody. [Each week]we kill five dozen penguins and one goose [albatross]. One box canned beef every Sunday." It sounds as if their basic diet was penguin five days a week, albatross on Saturday, and corned beef on Sunday.

The monotony of their enforced exile had a depressing effect. Captain Noel found that the *New Zealand Government Gazette* notice nailed to the door of the depot "got on his nerves badly". It concerned the dates of the sealing season, and every time he entered the hut or walked past, he read the formal wording until he got it off by heart. It was all the more annoying as not a single seal was seen in all the time the men were on the island.

It appears that some of the stores left in the depot for castaways had previously been stolen – probably by seal poachers. Tools found there included an axe and a file, and there were supplies of candles and matches. There was no tea or coffee nor, apparently, any pots and pans, or eating utensils. There was a very limited amount of clothing and only five pairs of boots. One of the boys had landed without shoes, and sandals were made for him by platting tussock grass. "There were 12 small blankets, and they were cut in halves to go round." The castaways made a cooking pot out of an oil can found at the depot, and pans from the "tin lining" of biscuit boxes. Limpet shells neatly fitted with wooden handles were fashioned into spoons, and with the aid of the file, knives were made from the hoops of a barrel. Combs were made from twigs and "thorns of bushes".

LOOTING AT THE DEPOTS

From the establishment of the first castaway depots at the Auckland and Campbell Islands in 1868 there had always been problems of theft and unauthorised use of stores by sealers, sailors and lessees. The Antipodes were no exception, but unfortunately looting of the depot there following the *Hinemoa*'s 1907 visit deprived the *Président Félix Faure*'s crew of much-needed supplies.

On 27 May 1908, the *Southland Daily News* included an item headed "Robbery at Island Depots — Despicable Crime" in which a parliamentarian, J.A. Millar said: "Unfortunately, there appears to be a good deal of truth in statements made by the captain of the French ship *Président Faure*, and others, that the depots placed on the desolate southern islands for the relief of castaways are visited by unauthorised persons and that portions of the stores are stolen. It is impossible to conceive a more dastardly form of theft. Indeed, through these practices, the lives of unfortunate castaways might easily be lost, so that the crime assumes much graver proportions than mere looting. The islands being visited necessarily so infrequently, enables the practise to be carried out almost with impunity. The information to hand seems to show that people do visit these islands, but whether they are whaling or sealing it is difficult to say. It is almost certain that a good deal of seal poaching goes on down there. I have given the matter a good deal of thought, and certain proposals will be placed before the Government for a more effective supervision of the islands. My idea is that men should be kept permanently on these islands under conditions that will be suggested to parliament in due course."

Although the problem was recognised, it proved impracticable to solve or to increase the frequency of inspections by Government vessels.

All of the books and magazines found in the depot were in English, and not many of the men could read them. However, some other uses were found for them. Grass and dried leaves rolled up in pieces of paper torn from the magazines were smoked as cigarettes, for none of the sailors had any tobacco after the lifeboat was wrecked.

There was a notice at the depot saying that sheep, goats and cattle had been liberated on the island, but initially no sign of these were seen. However, on Good Friday the tracks of cattle were discovered. Twelve of the sailors hunted down a large calf, which was killed and eaten. It afforded splendid beef, and the men made a gala time of the occasion. Although there was plenty of meat, they had to eat it quickly as they knew it would not keep. Unfortunately the calf was the only one of its species left on the island. The *Hinemoa* had placed three young cattle beasts there six years previously but all had died, along with the sheep and goats – only their skeletons were found.

The calf's skin was used for mending the men's boots. Needles were made from nails, the eye being bored by twirling the point of a knife round and round; sewing thread was stripped from a piece of canvas. Previously, the men had used canvas and tussock straw to keep their boots together. Some of the sailors also made shoes from albatross skin.

There were only four days upon which rain, hail or snow did not fall. The general bleakness of the climate was hard to endure. In the words of the Captain:

> the weather. Oh that is terrible down there! Rain, fog and wind, rain, fog and wind all day and every day. We were wet all the time. That was perhaps, the worst part of it. The island seems never to have good weather. The sun seldom shines brightly there, and there seems to be hardly any warmth in its rays.

Clothing was scarce, and there were very few blankets to cover the men at night. Those on watch had to move about to keep warm. At first a fire was kept alight day and night, but it was difficult to obtain dry wood. Apart from wreckage from the ship and lifeboat, the only source of fuel was the twisted branches of stunted *Coprosma* scrub that grew in scattered patches on the island. Soon all the scrub near the depot had been harvested and the sailors had to make long walks of up to three kilometres for fuel. They seem to have had plenty of matches, for they brought some from the ship and more were found in the depot. After a time as wood became scarce, the fire was allowed to go out, being re-lit when needed.

One of the favourite methods of passing the time was to send out "messengers" to the outside world. They used the quills of the albatross, plugged with cork, as receptacles for messages giving the name of the ship and where she had been wrecked. Large numbers of albatrosses were liberated with these quills tied around their necks, carrying with them the hopes of the men that they would be captured on some vessel, where the messages could be read.

Day after day had gone by, and the men's hopes of rescue had become less keen. They kept a lookout, but it was not with the same hope as at first, and there became a time when they were almost indifferent. "As night came on," one man said, "and gloom spread over us, nothing could tell the state of awful depression that we got into, thinking that the next day would bring no more than the one already past". Scurvy appeared also and added to their depression.

THE RESCUE

HMS *Pegasus* sailed from Wellington on 6 May 1908 on a cruise of the outlying islands, her main mission being to check the New Zealand Government provision depots. Proceeding under "easy steam" she first delivered mail to Waitangi in the Chatham Islands. On 10 May, she left the Chathams for the Bounty Islands. Strong south-west winds and heavy seas were encountered but she reached the Bounty Islands in 48 hours. A cutter was sent ashore to check for shipwrecked persons. No signs of human presence were seen, and after a brief stay of three hours the cruiser started for the Antipodes. A short run of 17 hours brought her in sight of the islands, high land being visible by 8.30 a.m. on 13 May. From her reported times between the various island groups she must have been steaming at between 8 and 10 knots.

PUBLIC NOTICE.

CLOSE SEASON FOR SEALS.

Marine Department,
Wellington, N.Z., 2nd April, 1903.

NOTICE is hereby given that the CLOSE SEASON for SEALS has been extended up to the 30th day of June, 1904. Any person found killing, hunting, catching, or attempting to catch or kill Seals during this close season within the Colony of New Zealand (which includes the Auckland, Campbell, Antipodes, Bounty, Snares, Solanders, Chatham, and Kermadec Islands) will be prosecuted with the utmost rigour of the law.

W. HALL-JONES,
Minister of Marine.

Public notice "Close Season for seals" as posted on all subantarctic islands by the New Zealand Marine Department, 1904. (*Archives New Zealand, Wellington M1, 2/6/1, Pt. 1.*)

That morning two of the crew of the *Président Félix Faure* (the youngest boy, Grull, and a seaman called Remond) were high up on the island attempting to catch an albatross to send another message. They had a photo of the boy's mother with "Président Félix Faure 4-masted barque wrecked on Antipodes Island" written on the back in pencil. It was sealed in an albatross quill plugged with cork ready to tie around a bird's neck. Suddenly, they sighted smoke on the horizon. It was10 a.m., and at that time the cruiser must have been nearly 20 miles away. They raced down the hill and alerted the others. The fire was stoked up with all the fuel on hand, including the remaining wreckage from their boat. They shared out and ate the last of the stores, by then limited to a daily ration of half a biscuit. At first the *Pegasus* was heading directly towards the island. Then she seemed to change course, and for a moment they thought that she was going on past. They waved and shouted and were relieved when she turned, came close in and a boat was lowered. It gradually dawned on them that their ordeal was over.

About 11.30 a.m. *Pegasus* was rapidly closing on the island where Captain Quale was intending to land to inspect the depot. When a thin column of white smoke was seen rising from the top of the cliffs, he assumed that there were castaways on shore. Soon afterwards, a number of men could be seen frantically waving hats and coats, and even trousers. The weather was bitterly cold, with heavy squalls of hail and rain from the south. At 12.40 p.m. the cruiser was under the lee of the island and had dropped anchor in 17 fathoms of water. A 12-oar cutter was lowered, and a party of 13, including Lieutenants Baker and Bateman and the ship's surgeon, Dr Lobb, made a landing through breakers onto the rocky shore near the depot. The cutter got into difficulties, and if it had not been "for a mass of octopus seaweed [bull-kelp *Durvillaea antarctica*], which formed a fender, it would have been stove in at the cave, which was chosen for a landing". Here the boat was met by 22 bedraggled and surprisingly subdued, castaways.

Without loss of time they were taken on board the cruiser in two boatloads. Describing his feelings at the time, Captain Noel said: "I believe that I was actually indifferent. It was not until I was standing on the deck of the *Pegasus* that I fully realised that I had been rescued, and would leave behind for ever that rough little island, with its gales and rain and inclement inhospitable climate." A note of sadness to the rescue was that their surviving dog was left behind on the island. The French crew tried to get it to come as they entered the navy cutter, but as one sailor said, "he was scared and ran away. Poor old beggar. I expect he'll die all right."

The surgeon was sent with the landing party as it was thought that there might be serious cases of injury or sickness ashore, but his services were not immediately needed. Although the men had suffered severe hardship, they had very few serious medical problems. When first rescued, the castaways bore signs of the hard life they had led and were described by one British sailor as "a pretty sick looking lot. They seemed pinched up, and their clothes, such as they were, were all covered with darns and patches and mud". On board the cruiser the shipwrecked men were provided with extra clothes, hot drinks and good food, which livened them up considerably. The bosun of the *Président Félix Faure*, Julien Bodin, had been badly bitten when catching an albatross, and his hand was "out of action". Le Gall had also sustained a hand injury from a penguin peck, and Remond had his right hand bound up as a result of salvaging wreckage during rough weather. Later, one of the sailors was reported to have narrowly escaped the loss of his arm, for medical assistance reached him just in time to have prevented serious trouble.

At 4 p.m. the cruiser weighed anchor and shaped a course for Lyttelton. A few hours later, those on watch were rather eerily reminded of the fate of the French ship. At 10.30 p.m., in the gloom, the *Pegasus* passed close to a deeply laden four-masted barque heading eastward. The big sailing ship was evidently homeward bound around Cape Horn. She was running under short canvas before a heavy gale and a high sea, and was soon lost from sight.

The *Pegasus* met with very strong winds and extremely rough seas throughout the run up to Banks Peninsula: "So severe was the strain on the vessel that the head wireless apparatus aloft was wrecked, and as she rolled her boats were absolutely washing in the seas, the guns also being submerged." One of the lifeboats was carried away. The French sailors were nearly all seasick from their weakened state, long sojourn ashore and the unaccustomed motion of the cruiser. HMS *Pegasus* arrived at the port of Lyttelton at 5.15 p.m. on 15 May 1908.

Soon after her arrival, reporters from the *Lyttelton Times* and the *Press* were aboard interviewing Captain Noel and his crew, and also talking to the officers and crew of the *Pegasus*. This resulted in the publication of conflicting accounts of some aspects of the shipwreck.[9] Much of the confusion was due to the fact that most of the Frenchmen had little knowledge of English (e.g. two hours became "two days"). Also, some information was second-hand from British sailors, leading to uncertainty as to what stores were found in the depot. There was also confusion caused by the reporters' lack of knowledge of the geography of the Antipodes Islands (for instance, the south side of Bollons Island became the "the south side of the Antipodes"). Two days after the initial interviews, Noel, who spoke and wrote excellent English, wrote to the papers protesting, and correcting some of the major errors.[10]

The French Consular Agent from Christchurch, Mr G. Humphreys, met the shipwrecked sailors at Lyttelton. He arranged accommodation for them at the port and an issue of new clothing. The Shipwreck Relief Society helped with replacing their personal effects. All left Lyttelton on 21 May aboard the SS *Maitai* bound for Sydney, where an inquiry into the circumstances of the wreck was held by the French Consul General. The crew of the *Président Félix Faure* sailed for Marseilles on the Messageries Maritimes mail boat.[11]

One outcome of the wreck of the French ship was that it was brought to official attention that books and magazines in the English language were of little use to foreign castaways. Apparently prompt action was taken, for in 1969 members of the Canterbury University Antipodes Island Expedition found a package containing several copies of the *British Esperantist* magazine and pamphlets of "keys" to the Esperanto language in the Antipodes castaway depot. These papers were still in their original wrapping dated 1908, and addressed to the Minister of Marine. I have found no evidence that similar magazines were left at depots on other southern islands. For the Antipodes it was very much a case of closing the stable door after the horse had fled.

HMS *PEGASUS*

HMS *Pegasus* was a Royal Navy cruiser which served on the Australia Station from 1905 to 1913. Built by Palmers on the Tyne, she was launched in March 1897 and completed in 1899. She was one of the Pelorus class of "third-class protected cruisers" which with a length of 314 ft overall and displacement of about 2200 tons were driven by coal-fired three-cylinder triple-expansion engines and twin screws. These ships were designed mainly for patrol work and were capable of 16–20 knots. They were lively at sea, rather cramped for their crew of 230 men, and frequently plagued with mechanical problems.

Pegasus was ordered to the Australia Station in 1905. It was while she was serving with the New Zealand Division of the station that she rescued the crew of the *Président Félix Faure*. *Pegasus* returned to Sydney at the end of 1908. She was transferred to the Cape Station in March 1913, and on the outbreak of war in August 1914 was ordered to East Africa, where she joined in the shelling of the German-held port of Dar-es-Salaam, sinking an enemy gunboat and a floating dock.

Early on 20 September 1914 she was anchored off Zanzibar. Her men were servicing the boilers, repairing machinery and cleaning guns when the German cruiser *Konigsberg* closed to 9000 yards and opened fire. *Pegasus*, with steam partly blown down, was unable to get underway, and within 15 minutes the unequal fight was over. She sank in shallow water with 39 of her men killed and 59 wounded.

CHAPTER ELEVEN

An Attempt to Promote Pastoral Farming

During the latter stages of the 19th century both the Imperial Government of Great Britain and the Colonial Government of New Zealand had a strong desire to uphold British sovereignty over their outlying islands. Formal taking possession by proclamation, followed by occupation, was seen as the safest course. This led to a policy of granting leases and encouraging occupation. In 1870, the Governor of New Zealand, Sir George Bowen, wrote to the Secretary of State for the Colonies:

> The Colonial Government will always be glad to give leases on easy terms to mercantile firms or other persons willing to maintain establishments on the uninhabited dependencies of New Zealand; for, in addition to other considerations, the cause of humanity, in the event of shipwrecks thereon, would be greatly benefited by such establishments.[1]

Several official reports may have unintentionally, and erroneously, given the impression that Antipodes Island was suitable for pastoral farming – then very profitable in New Zealand. Henry Armstrong, in 1868, reported to the Southland Provincial Government that the Antipodes were "dotted with high tussock and patches of M'Quarrie cabbage and cotton plant. The soil is peaty, but drier and firmer than that of Campbell Island; of scrub there is none worthy of the name."[2] In 1886, Captain Fairchild wrote:

> The whole of the island is covered with coarse grass, and there are over two thousand acres of land comparatively level . . . there are also two streams . . . each of these discharge about five gallons of excellent water per minute . . . Sheep and goats would do well on the island, and I would recommend that some be sent there next trip of a Government vessel, also some English grass, blue gums and wattle seeds. The weather there was not so severe as might be expected.[3]

Offer of Pastoral Runs for Lease on the Antipodes and Bounty Islands, 1895. (*Department of Conservation, Southland, database T-5-2000.*)

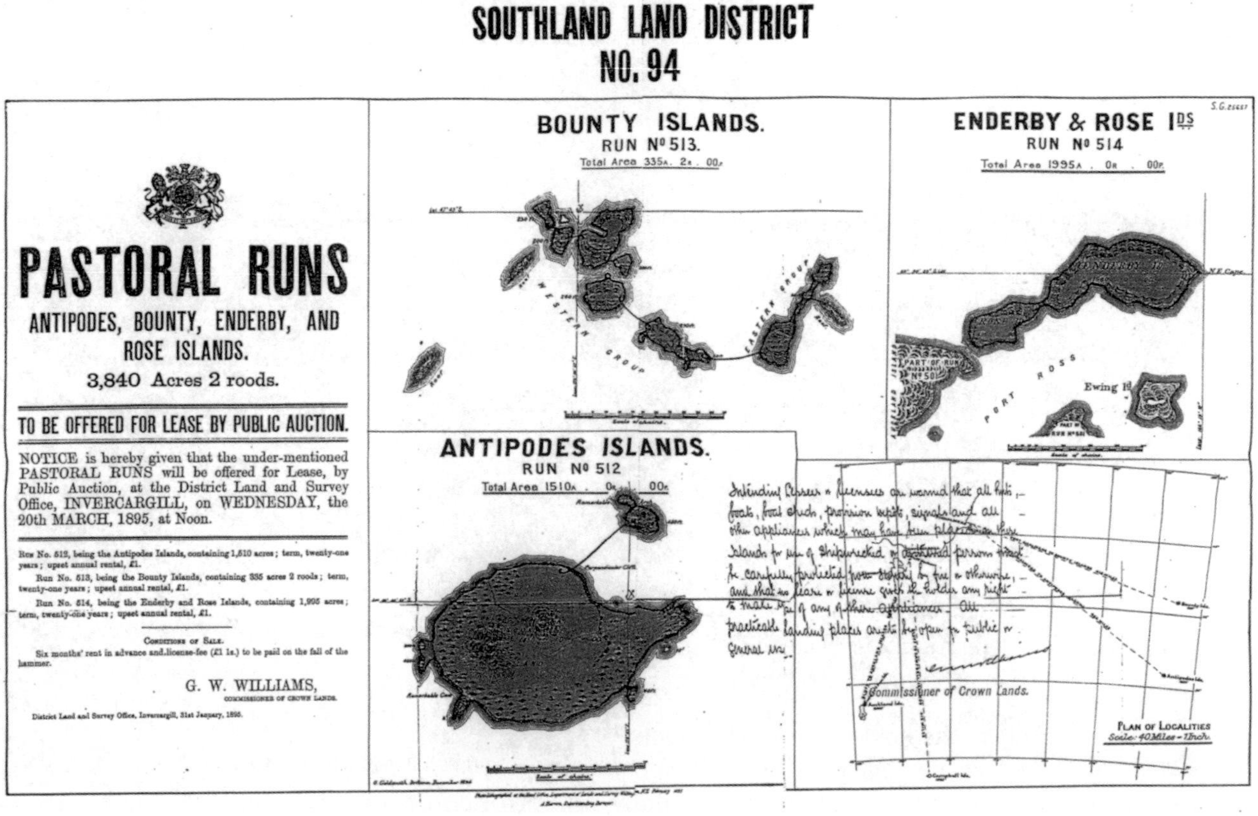

J. Macpherson, an official of the Invercargill Wreck Fund, sailed with the *Stella* on her inspection trip of the castaway depots in October 1888. With humanitarian motives he later reported to the Government on the need for "encouragement of settlement" at the islands. He considered that "ship wrecked mariners dying of starvation after they have effected a landing, presents a very strong inducement for the Government to encourage someone to take them [the islands] up and stock them". He considered that the Auckland Islands might be let as three runs, if the Government Steamer was to regularly visit twice or three times a year, "carrying stores and taking away produce". Campbell Island he "did not think so much of for stock", but concluded that "Antipodes Island is a capital island for stock but its limited area 3000 to 4000 acres is against it".[4] A New Zealand Survey map, "The Colony of New Zealand", published in 1890 had an inset of the Antipodes Islands at a scale of two miles to an inch. The main island was labelled as "good tussock land", with an anchorage, two mountains, two streams and a hut.[5]

Early in 1894 the New Zealand Government sent a team including James Joyce, the MP for Lyttelton, and James Gordon, a farmer from the Gisborne District, south on the *Hinemoa* to report on the stock-carrying capabilities of the southern islands. Joyce ranked the potential of the Auckland and Campbell Islands as high. He found that the Antipodes were of about 4000 acres and "well grassed". He added:

> There are some cattle on this island . . . Their camping places afforded proof of the beneficial influence of stock upon the texture of the peaty soil. Instead of the porous and spongy surface, a compact mould has been formed . . . The one drawback of the island is its lack of a harbour, there being only a landing place for boats in fine weather.

About the Bounty Islands, Joyce's report was clear: "A mere cluster of rocks . . . They are absolutely bare of vegetation of any kind. A more dangerous and inaccessible place can nowhere be found."[6]

James Gordon liked Campbell much better than the Auckland Islands, but in an accompanying letter asked for a lease on both. Of the Antipodes he wrote:

> This island is well grassed, fine tussock prevailing. The soil is exceedingly rich, but being so far away from New Zealand & so small a size (about 3000 acres) & without any harbour, it would be as yet of little value as a sheep or cattle grazing run.[7]

Following these reports, the Commissioner of Crown Lands, Invercargill, offered pastoral runs on the main Auckland Island, Adams Island and Campbell Island for lease by public auction. Notice of this was published on 30 August, stating that the auction would take place at the Southland District Lands and Survey Office on 21 November.[8] Probably as a result of this notice, George Jones of Auckland wrote to the Surveyor General to obtain a Crown Grant on Antipodes Island, or make some arrangement to enable him to settle there. He was referred to the Southland Land Board. On 24 October Jones wrote to the secretary requesting "that your Board may grant me land on Antipodes Island for myself and friend". He continued:

> I have given this every consideration, and have arrived at the conclusion that it will not only be satisfactory for myself and friend, but also we could take charge of the Island for your Government and would help castaways at any time if by chance a vessel were to be lost there. We would also render your board any reports at any time they might be required.

On 17 November the Commissioner of Crown Lands, Invercargill, replied that the Land Board "cannot recommend the disposal of land in freehold on this island". They did, however, "resolve to recommend to the Government to open as Pastoral Runs under Part VI, Land Act 1892, The Antipodes Island, the Bounty Islands, and Enderby Island; 21 years lease at a rental of 20/- per annum in each case". The recommendation and maps of the islands were forwarded to the Surveyor General that day.

Henry H. Martin, of Mataura, wrote to the Commissioner of the Southland Lands Board on 17 January 1895 enquiring whether Enderby Island and the Antipodes Islands would be put up for lease shortly. He also asked whether there was anything in the leases of the Auckland Islands preventing sub-letting. Martin already had a 21-year lease from 1 March 1895 on the southern part of Auckland Island for £7 10s per annum, which he had obtained at auction in November 1894. On 18 January, Martin was informed that the Land Board had recommended that the Antipodes, Bounty and Enderby Islands be "put up for lease", and that "as soon as posters arrive, one will be sent to you". On 31 January, he was told that sub-letting would not be allowed on the Auckland Islands.

The same day, the Commissioner of Crown Lands, Invercargill, published notice accompanied by detailed maps that Pastoral Runs at Antipodes and Bounty islands (and at Enderby and Rose Islands, in the northern Auckland Islands) would be offered for lease at auction on 20 March 1895: Run No. 512, "being the Antipodes Islands, containing 1,510 acres; term, twenty-one years; upset annual rental, £1"; and Run No. 513, "being the Bounty Islands, containing 335 acres 2 roods; term twenty-one years; upset annual rental, £1". Conditions of sale were: "Six months rent in advance and license-fee (£1 1s.) to be paid on the fall of the hammer." Intended lessees and licensees were warned that:

> All huts, boats, boat sheds, provision depots, signals and all other appliances which may have been placed on these islands for use of shipwrecked or distressed persons must be carefully protected from injury by fire or otherwise, and that no lease or license gives the holder any right to make use of these appliances. All practicable landing places are to be open for public and general use.

Understandably, no interest seems to have been shown in the Bounty Island run. No record exists as to how many bidders tried for the Antipodes pastoral lease. Jones and Martin may have lost interest in the Antipodes, for it seems possible that only one bid was made. "Pastoral Run No. 512. Antipodes Island. 1510 acres" was recorded as being "selected" by Mr W. Dinwoodie of Gisborne. The date on the lease was 23 April 1895, and the rent £1 per annum (the reserve price). The term was for 21 years from 1 March 1896 to 28 February 1917. Initially, Dinwoodie must have had plans to live on the island, for on 24 April – the day after signing the lease – he wrote from Deschler's Hotel, Invercargill, informing the Commissioner of Crown Lands that: "As I will be

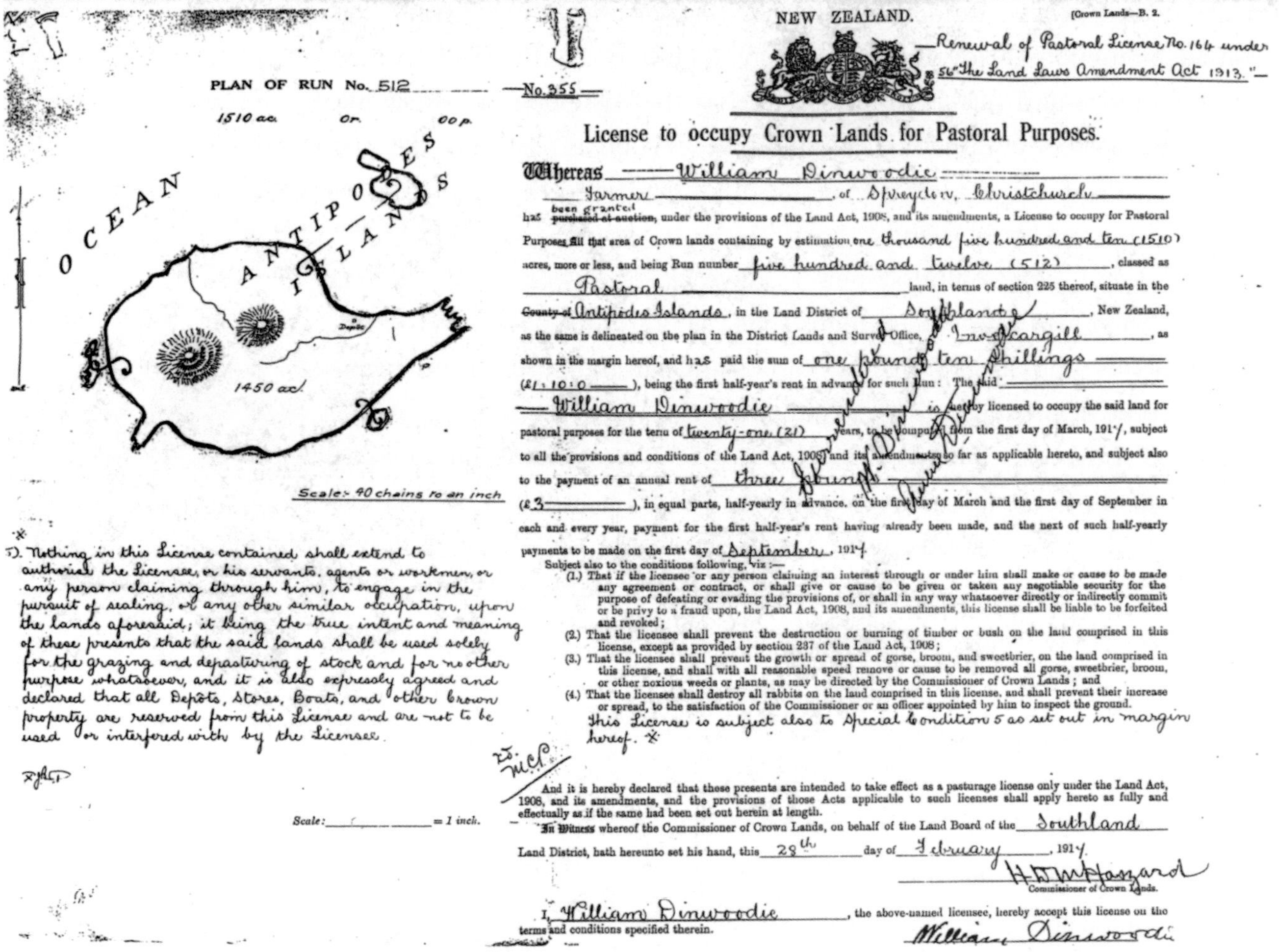

PLAN OF RUN No. 512 — No. 355 —

1510 ac. or. 00 p.

OCEAN

ANTIPODES

ISLANDS

1450 ac.

Scale:- 40 chains to an inch

5. Nothing in this License contained shall extend to authorise the Licensee, or his servants, agents or workmen, or any person claiming through him, to engage in the pursuit of sealing, or any other similar occupation, upon the lands aforesaid; it being the true intent and meaning of these presents that the said lands shall be used solely for the grazing and depasturing of stock and for no other purpose whatsoever, and it is also expressly agreed and declared that all Depôts, Stores, Boats, and other Crown property are reserved from this License and are not to be used or interfered with by the Licensee.

Scale: ________ = 1 inch.

NEW ZEALAND. [Crown Lands—B. 2.

—Renewal of Pastoral License No. 164 under 56 "The Land Laws Amendment Act 1913."—

License to occupy Crown Lands for Pastoral Purposes.

Whereas —— William Dinwoodie —— Farmer ——, of Spreydon, Christchurch —— has ~~purchased at auction~~ been granted, under the provisions of the Land Act, 1908, and its amendments, a License to occupy for Pastoral Purposes all that area of Crown lands containing by estimation one thousand five hundred and ten (1510) acres, more or less, and being Run number five hundred and twelve (512), classed as Pastoral land, in terms of section 225 thereof, situate in the ~~County of~~ Antipodes Islands, in the Land District of Southland, New Zealand, as the same is delineated on the plan in the District Lands and Survey Office, Invercargill, as shown in the margin hereof, and has paid the sum of one pound ten shillings (£1:10:0), being the first half-year's rent in advance for such Run: The said —— William Dinwoodie —— is hereby licensed to occupy the said land for pastoral purposes for the term of twenty-one (21) years, to be computed from the first day of March, 1917, subject to all the provisions and conditions of the Land Act, 1908, and its amendments so far as applicable hereto, and subject also to the payment of an annual rent of three pounds (£3), in equal parts, half-yearly in advance, on the first day of March and the first day of September in each and every year, payment for the first half-year's rent having already been made, and the next of such half-yearly payments to be made on the first day of September, 1917.

Subject also to the conditions following, viz:—

(1.) That if the licensee or any person claiming an interest through or under him shall make or cause to be made any agreement or contract, or shall give or cause to be given or taken any negotiable security for the purpose of defeating or evading the provisions of, or shall in any way whatsoever directly or indirectly commit or be privy to a fraud upon, the Land Act, 1908, and its amendments, this license shall be liable to be forfeited and revoked;

(2.) That the licensee shall prevent the destruction or burning of timber or bush on the land comprised in this license, except as provided by section 237 of the Land Act, 1908;

(3.) That the licensee shall prevent the growth or spread of gorse, broom, and sweetbrier, on the land comprised in this license, and shall with all reasonable speed remove or cause to be removed all gorse, sweetbrier, broom, or other noxious weeds or plants, as may be directed by the Commissioner of Crown Lands; and

(4.) That the licensee shall destroy all rabbits on the land comprised in this license, and shall prevent their increase or spread, to the satisfaction of the Commissioner or an officer appointed by him to inspect the ground.

This License is subject also to Special Condition 5 as set out in margin hereof. ✻

And it is hereby declared that these presents are intended to take effect as a pasturage license only under the Land Act, 1908, and its amendments, and the provisions of those Acts applicable to such licenses shall apply hereto as fully and effectually as if the same had been set out herein at length.

In Witness whereof the Commissioner of Crown Lands, on behalf of the Land Board of the Southland Land District, hath hereunto set his hand, this 28th day of February, 1917.

H. D. McHazard
Commissioner of Crown Lands.

I, William Dinwoodie, the above-named licensee, hereby accept this license on the terms and conditions specified therein.

William Dinwoodie

Renewal of licence to occupy the Antipodes Islands for pastoral purposes issued to William Dinwoodie, 28 February 1917. (*Department of Conservation, Southland, database T-5-2000.*)

unable to communicate with the Land Board from the Antipodes Island, I have instructed the New Zealand Loan and Mercantile Co. to act as my agents. Any communication from the Land Board to them will receive attention."

Dinwoodie was an associate of James Gordon, who had obtained the lease of the Campbell Island Run at auction on 21 November 1894. In 1895, Gordon formed The Campbell Island Sheep and Cattle Grazing Firm with Dinwoodie as Deputy-Manager.[9] It seems that they collaborated in the purchase of the Antipodes Island lease, maybe with the idea of running stock there in conjunction with operations on Campbell Island. Significantly, Gordon was at Invercargill during the Antipodes auction and Dinwoodie's letter of 24 April was, apart from the signature, in Gordon's handwriting.[10]

In January 1901, due to communication, staffing and financial difficulties, Gordon transferred his Campbell Island lease to Captain W.H. Tucker, also of Gisborne, but returned to Campbell Island as manager.[11]

On 31 August 1901, Dinwoodie wrote to the Minister of Marine asking about the timing of the next voyage of the *Hinemoa* to the southern islands. He explained that as "the lessee of the Antipodes Island" he was keen to get down there to "see what facilities there are for the landing of stock". After being told that the next trip would probably be in early December, Dinwoodie protested:

> When leasing the Antipodes Island, I was given to understand that the Steamer would make trips at intervals of not more than six months, and that it was intended when the island was taken up the steamers would go down there every three or four months. The steamer's last visit was in January last. That is eleven months . . . I submit the Government is not keeping faith with myself or the other lessees of the island.[12]

In the event the *Hinemoa* was replaced by the *Tutanekai* which sailed from Wellington on 26 December carrying a vice-regal party around all the southern islands, including Macquarie. Also on board was Captain Tucker, visiting his Campbell Island run, and shepherds, families and farm animals for the southern part of the Auckland Islands.[13] William Dinwoodie was not a passenger, but three months later, in March 1902, he visited Campbell Island in the 143-ton steamer *Rimu* while helping with a shipment of stock for Tucker.[14] Apparently, Dinwoodie never visited the Antipodes Islands. He made no further attempt to develop his run or take stock to the island. His subsequent actions strongly suggest that he was then holding on to the lease as a speculative financial investment. In 1899 and 1912, enquiries were made to the Commissioner of Crown Lands, Invercargill, from interested persons as to whether the pastoral lease of the Antipodes was open for application. They were informed that the lease was already taken up until 1917.

On 17 November 1915, the Commissioner wrote to Dinwoodie enquiring what stock, if any, he had on the island; and informing him that the lease was due to expire on 28 February 1917, and that the run was being reclassified. It seems that there was no reply, for a further memo asking the same question about stock numbers was sent on 16 December 1915, begging a reply by return mail. This second letter was returned unclaimed from the Dead Letter Office on 19 January 1916. Apparently by then Dinwoodie had moved his operations to Christchurch. On 5 June, Dinwoodie made contact with the Commissioner and arranged to renew his lease for another 21 years (until 28 February 1938) at a higher rental of £3 per annum. Renewal took place on 11 July 1917, with the issue of Licence No. P.R.L. 355 for Pastoral Run 512, Antipodes Islands. Southland Land Board documents recording this transaction show that the 1897 Crown valuation of the Antipodes Islands was £120.

THE ANTIPODES LEASE SURRENDERED

On 16 January 1923 Dinwoodie, responding to a circular to all Pastoral Run Holders from the Minister of Lands, approached the Commissioner of Crown Lands, Invercargill, regarding freeholding the islands or extending the lease. The Commissioner responded:

> I do not think there is any possibility of freehold being granted in your case as the policy is against the absolute disposal of Islands. Your application for an extension of lease will be considered at the February meeting of the Land Board. In the meantime will you please advise me if the Islands have ever been occupied and if any stock has been on the place during your term as licensee.

In reply Dinwoodie wrote: "I have done nothing in the way of stocking the Antipodes Islands so far. I have a would-be lessee prepared to take over the lease and stock the islands." An extension of the lease was refused by the Land Board on 15 February 1923.

The end of attempted pastoral farming at the Antipodes is summed up in a letter from the Commissioner of Crown Lands, Invercargill, to the Under-secretary of Lands: "Run 512 – Antipodes Island, 1510 acres, 21 years from 1/3/1917. £3.0.0 per annum – Rent paid to 31/8/25 – W. D. Dinwoodie,

Licensee. The above Licensee has applied to surrender and the Land Board has recommended acceptance of surrender as from 31/8/1925, pursuant to Section 92 of 'The Land Act, 1924'. Mr. Dinwoodie has never had any stock on the Islands and as we have little or no information concerning them, it is not proposed to re-offer the Run."

This whole episode sheds a very interesting light on the way the Department of Lands and Survey and the Southland Land Board approached the task of allocating and managing pastoral runs in the late 19th and early 20th centuries. As regards the southern islands they obviously worked in a state of almost complete ignorance, and lack of interest in all matters except financial return. For instance, regardless of numerous official reports describing the Bounty Islands as barren, spray-swept rocks without a scrap of herbage, they advertised a pastoral run there for 21-year lease at £1 per year. Similarly, the lease of the Antipodes Islands had been in existence for 27 years, and renewed once, before the Board realised that the islands had never been occupied or stocked. Only at that stage did it occur to them that they "had little or no information" on the islands. On the other hand, the Department and Board were highly efficient in monetary matters. On 7 October 1903 the Receiver of Land Revenue reported that Dinwoodie had not paid the six-monthly rent of 10s due on 1 September. A Land Board document dated the next day recorded that a "fine of 10% on rent due [was] to be inflicted". The rent and fine were paid later that month. Likewise, on 2 October 1912, the Commissioner of Crown Lands informed Dinwoodie:

> Run 512 . . . As you have not paid your rent on above mentioned run within 30 days grace allowed by Section 251 of the 'Land Act,1908', you have incurred a fine of 10%. The amount now payable is rent 10/-, fine 1/-, total 11/-. Please forward this amount by return mail, adding 6d. exchange if cheque be sent. Unless this amount be paid within 30 days a notice of liability to forfeiture will be inserted in the Gazette, in accordance with the aforesaid section of the Act.

The 11 shillings were paid by 7 October.[15]

CHAPTER TWELVE

Travellers, Naturalists and Scientists, 1886–1927

After 1885, the Government steamers on their southern voyages regularly carried paying passengers. In fact, travel by these vessels was almost the only way that early scientists, Government officials and the public had of visiting the Antipodes, Bounty, and other southern islands. In 1889 the charge for travelling to the outlying islands by Government steamer was 12s 6d a day, from the last commercial port of departure. Other New Zealand coastal travel was at the same rates as "ordinarily charged by first class passenger boats". Members of Parliament, Government officers, and their wives and children could travel for 7s 6d a day (children under 14 on half-rates). Passengers in the forward cabin, without individual accommodation, were charged only 3s a day. If too many people wanted to travel, the Public Service had priority – and all orders for passages had to be approved by the Minister of Marine before tickets were issued.

These were obviously times of little inflation, for in 1897 the daily rate for non-official passengers to the outlying islands was reduced to 10s – with all other charges remaining the same. Eventually, in 1922, the fares on SS *Tutanekai* were increased to "£1 per day for the general public and for public servants generally, and 12/6 per day for officers of the Marine Department".[1]

Until 1910, it was usual for between five and 22 passengers to be carried on a southern cruise. At various times these included Governors of the Colony with their families and staff, Government officials, museum representatives, scientists, animal and plant collectors, farm workers travelling to and from the pastoral runs on the Auckland and Campbell Islands, and other travellers (equivalent to today's tourists). Many of the latter were female, and a considerable number appear to have been young people – often the children of politicians, prominent and wealthy citizens and the ship's officers.

Once the training ship *Amokura* took over patrolling the depots, there was little room for passengers, though occasionally over the next 10 years she carried sealing inspectors, and a few shepherds and one scientist to Campbell Island. It was not until the *Tutanekai* resumed the full service in 1921 that scientists and tourists could once more visit the Antipodes and Bounty Islands.

Landings at the various islands became excursions in which most passengers joined, being ferried ashore in the ship's boats. They were guided by the Captain or officers to inspect castaway depots, spectacular subantarctic plants, seal colonies and birdlife. On most of the early cruises, it was usual for the ship to collect numbers of live penguins, albatrosses and parakeets for zoos and private collections. Mortality of these, both at sea and once in captivity ashore, must have been high. On one occasion it was recorded that three coal baskets full of penguins collected at the Snares Islands, at the start of a cruise, and thereafter kept in a pen on deck, were released at the Antipodes – presumably because they were in poor shape. "Fresh penguins" were then collected to take back to New Zealand. Similar collections of live penguins and albatrosses took place year after year – the demand seemed insatiable. Large numbers of plant specimens, alive and pressed, and birds eggs were also brought back.

The steamer captains – particularly long-serving ones like Fairchild and Bollons – eventually became renowned for their knowledge of the geography, history, plants and wildlife of the islands. They attained their natural history expertise not only from discussion and shared discoveries with passengers expert in various topics, but also from their own repeated observations in different seasons and years. Many of the ships' officers (both deck and engineer) also became experts at identifying plants, seabirds and marine life. The help these officers gave to passengers – with collecting and preparing specimens of plants, live birds, bird skins and eggs – was often acknowledged in reports, letters and diaries, and no doubt they were forever answering questions.

The first scientist to visit the Antipodes and Bounty Islands was Andreas Reischek, an Austrian ornithologist and taxidermist. He was a passenger on the *Stella* when she called at the Antipodes and Bounty Islands on 2 and 3 February 1888. Later that year he reported to a meeting of the New Zealand Institute in Auckland, giving a brief description of the islands, their topography, geology, vegetation and wildlife.[2] He remarked on a complete absence of seals at the Antipodes, and on the many thousands of penguins – adding that "wandering albatrosses, sooty albatrosses, molly-mawks, and Cape pigeons were hovering about, and the magellanic shag busied itself in the water". Ashore he collected specimens of two species of parakeet and a pipit, and saw snipe, skuas and White-headed Petrels. The larger green Antipodes Island Parakeet had been described and named as early as 1831, from a live male specimen taken to England by sealers and held in London Zoological Gardens. The source of this specimen was uncertain but thought to be New Zealand. It was not until Fairchild visited Antipodes Island in March 1886 that the species' true home was discovered.[3] The second species of parakeet Reischek identified was smaller and had red on the head. It differed from the mainland Red-crowned Parakeet and was new to science. He named it *Platycercus hochstetteri* after Arthur von Hochstetter, "the son of a sincere friend". The ground lark (or pipit) also differed from the New Zealand form, and Reischek called it *Anthus steindachneri* after a director of the Imperial Museum in Vienna.

Reischek found the Bounty Islands "covered with millions of birds". He noted that "the stench from the guano was dreadful, and the noise deafening".[4] This may have distracted him for he went on to record the presence of "three species of penguins" and "two species of molly-mawks", when all biologists since have found only one species of each.

A fellow passenger, journalist William Dougall, was equally impressed, particularly with the difficulties of landing on the Bounty Islands and traversing the slippery rocks. He managed to carry his large camera and tripod to the top of Depot Island to record on film for the first time the island's crowded wildlife. In a somewhat ironic vein he wrote:

> You feel particularly good humoured when you slip, and putting out your hand to save yourself your arm is buried to the elbow in a pool of semi-solid guano . . . You can smell the Bounties before you see them . . . When we got [back] to the Stella the steward blocked our way, and demanded that we should discard our unsavoury garments before entering the saloon. We divested ourselves of all the clothing we could conveniently spare, and then we were kindly allowed to pass. It was then dinner time, but, alas, we had left our appetites ashore.[5]

F.R. (later Judge and Sir Frederick) Chapman and the botanist Thomas Kirk visited Antipodes Island in the *Hinemoa* on 17 January 1890. Both later wrote of their experiences.[6] Once ashore, Chapman found it tough going:

> We started to walk through the island, and found the work very difficult. The high tussock and fern . . . Covered very treacherous ground. Mountains rise on two sides of a sort of plain or basin. We crossed this, and made for Mount Galloway, 1,300ft. by the aneroid. As we approached it we found its sides scarred by slips and deeply cut by water-worn ravines. Here grew quantities of *Coprosma* scrub, the only shrub on the island.

They eventually reached the top of the mountain and found "a good deal of flat ground up there, which was literally alive with albatrosses". Kirk commented on the volcanic nature of the island: "Most of the rocks observed were basaltic". He was "not quite certain", however, whether the entire island was volcanic for at a distance from the landing place he had noticed what appeared to be a mass of finely bedded reddish sandstone. He had no chance to check this out. About the vegetation he reported:

> Large portions of the interior are more or less swampy, and the bulk of the vegetation consists of coarse sedges and grasses, amongst which many small herbs are concealed. There is an almost total absence of ligneous vegetation, the only woody plants observed being three species of *Coprosma*, two of which are of prostrate habit or nearly so; and the largest . . . rarely exceeds the stature of a low bush. Altogether when seen on a dull day the island presents a most desolate and unattractive appearance.

Kirk made the first collection of plants from Antipodes Island, and identified a total of 55 species. Three of them were introduced – a small grass, *Poa annua*, a soft thistle, *Sonchus asper*, and chickweed, *Stelleria media*. Surprisingly, these three remained the only introduced plants recorded up until 1990. Four others weed species have been found since, and the total number of known terrestrial plants now exceeds 150.

Kirk and Chapman were not alone on their excursions, for as Chapman later wrote of the Antipodes: "We have all gazed with interest on this island on the map in our school days, and we had now taken to it six school boys – the only ones who have ever visited it. The whole adventure must have been to them like the realisation of Robinson Crusoe."[7]

Chapman landed at the Bounty Islands the following day. Like many visitors, before and since, his impressions were of inhospitable rocks with innumerable penguins (his rough estimate was one million on shore) and other birds, together with their deafening noise and awful stench:

> We watched the penguins swarming over the rocks for awhile. The great nellies swam about us; the molly-mawks sat beside their big young ones among the penguins on the rocks; the whale-birds, too, made their homes in the deeper crevices. It is good to think that some creatures can stand the smell of penguins. Heavens! What a place to be marooned in!

These scientific pioneers were followed in November 1891 by a journalist, Robert Carrick, and a 16-year-old schoolboy diarist, Robert Wilson. At the

Antipodes on 3 November, Wilson records that the ship's crew gathered three or four buckets of fresh penguin eggs – presumably either to eat or as specimens for the passengers. He also says: "When we pulled back to the ship the head steward was then going snaring, so I went with him. A party had gone on shore before this snaring." In the end "about 8 green and 12 red-headed parakeets were caught". Wilson noted the different stage of laying of the two penguin species and found two skuas' nests (taking the eggs for his collection) and a pair of Light-mantled Sooty Albatrosses: "To my joy I saw one had an egg. I killed the albatross and secured the egg. The other albatross flew away. Sooty albatross eggs are extremely rare." So much for the curse of the Ancient Mariner!

At the Bounty Islands the next day, Wilson found "The mollymawks eggs were too far gone to blow. The penguin eggs were quite fresh." In those days an interest in collecting birds and eggs was common, and nearly all the passengers were interested in natural history souvenirs. Wilson records helping Fairchild "pack a lot of boxes of Auckland Island plants for the passengers and the captain's friends", and the crew made extra money by collecting skins and eggs for passengers. To the present-day historian or naturalist, Wilson's diary contains far more of substance and insightful interest than Carrick's rather flowery 70-page report published by the New Zealand Government Printer.[8]

The next visitors, aboard the *Hinemoa* in February 1895, were the Earl of Glasgow (Governor of New Zealand), geologist Sir James Hector, nurseryman and plant collector Henry Matthews, zoologist Professor T.J. Parker of the University of Otago and his assistant, taxidermist Edwin Jennings. Reference to their dairies, published articles and reports, lectures, subsequent discussions, and later research on their collections, shows the rapid advancement then taking place in the scientific knowledge of the islands.[9]

In May 1896, Edwin Lukins, a 35-year-old Assistant Curator from the Nelson Philosophical Society, visited all of New Zealand's southern islands aboard the *Hinemoa*, and subsequently published a pamphlet on the voyage. He had only a few hours ashore at the Antipodes on 9 May and left with regret, considering it the most interesting of all the islands visited. At the

Bounties two days later he had more time and recorded vivid descriptions of the islands, their birds and seals – and much detail on the castaway depot. He brought back a large natural history collection from the southern islands for his society's museum, and two Antipodes Island Parakeets for aviaries in Queens Gardens, Nelson.[10]

In 1901 and 1902 the then Governor of New Zealand, Lord Ranfurly, made two trips to the subantarctic islands to collect birds at the request of the British Museum. On both of these journeys he was accompanied by two aides-de-camp – the Hon. H. Butler and Captain Dudley Alexander. Also in the official party during the 1901 voyage were Captain F.W. Hutton, curator of the Christchurch Museum, and Dr Collins of Wellington. The expedition called at the Antipodes on about 19 January and the Bounty Islands the next day. Alexander described Antipodes Island as "an island that everybody has heard about but few seen – it is popularly supposed to lie under London". He went on:

> A charming bird here is the small green paroquet. He is fairly tame, and can be caught with a long stick or fishing rod with a noose at the end . . . The high perpendicular cliffs near the Anchorage are very fine. There are no sealions or seals now, nor are there any shags or gulls. Each island is therefore in its way different . . . We went around Bollons Island in our pinnace, a trip which will probably not be done again for a long time, and has never been done before, the sea this time being quite calm. It was a marvellous sight to see these enormous cliffs hanging right over the little boat, the water a deep blue, with no bottom, & the yellow kelp or seaweed surging about. It was about the finest thing we had seen. Some of the party were on shore snaring paroquets, & bought back alive about 150 of these pretty little birds. For the Br[itish] Museum we potted 2 Redheaded paroquets, 2 green paroquets, 2 larks, 1 petrel.[11]

The almost unbelievably large number of live parakeets caught by the crew in only a few hours reflects the lucrative market then flourishing in specimens of rarer New Zealand birds. For example, it is recorded of one of Lord Ranfurly's trips that:

> A gentleman went round the crew of the Government steamer, prior to its sailing from the Bluff, and offered £3 10s. to any of the men who would procure a skin [of an Auckland Island Merganser] for him. As this offer was made with a view to reselling, probably at a large profit, the rareness of this duck may be easily understood.[12]

On 14 January 1901, Captain Bollons first climbed the island that now bears his name and brought back a live albatross with "wings 13 ft long, (tip to tip)". This may have been a Wandering Albatross that had crash-landed on Bollons Island, for none are known to have ever nested there – and in those days mollymawks of any species were unknown at the Antipodes.[13] The bird specimens shot for the British Museum were preserved in formalin in large jars. Hutton also studied insects and other invertebrates, and collected for the Christchurch Museum.[14]

At the Bounty Islands the official party did not venture on shore, but shot two shags and a tern for the British Museum from the ship. According to a later Dunedin newspaper report, "Bounty Islands was so unpromising that the Governor and his party did not land", but apparently their lack of enthusiasm had another cause, for Alexander wrote: "The stench is appalling, & no one would land, except a few sailors to see if the depot was alright . . . There is not a single spot without a penguin on it. Those who land have to throw away the clothes they wore."

It seems surprising that the entomologist in Hutton did not lure him ashore, for he had previously described a new and very distinct genus of weta found by Fairchild in February 1894 "under rocks" on the Bounty Islands. Perhaps it was through a desire to conform to the rest of the Governor's party, that he missed his golden opportunity to discover more of the Bounty Islands' unique invertebrates.[15]

Lord Ranfurly's second cruise was in the *Tutanekai* (Captain C. F. Post) almost exactly one year later. On this occasion the Governor was accompanied by Lady Ranfurly and their two children, together with three female and three male servants. The others in the official party were Miss B. Douglas, Mr Charles Worsley (an artist), and the two aides-de-camp – Butler and

Alexander. Captain W.H. Tucker, the lessee of Campbell Island, was also on board to check on sheep run there. After visiting other southern islands, including Macquarie, the *Tutanekai* anchored at Antipodes Island on 22 January 1902. The day was fine but the seas rough and Alexander recorded that "the landing was none too good on the rocks & before it was accomplished a big wave broke over the boat wetting some of the party". Alexander, Worsley and others climbed on up to the higher country of the North Plains to see the nesting Wandering Albatrosses.[16] Worsley painted four watercolours showing coastal views, albatrosses and penguins, which are now held by the Alexander Turnbull Library.[17] The ship reached the Bounty Islands in very rough weather two days later, but it was impossible to land as the sea was running in from both the north and south and sending sheets of spray "over the lower islands and half way up the higher ones".

In July 1903 the eminent botanist and plant ecologist Dr Leonard Cockayne visited the islands on the *Hinemoa*. This visit was the first made by any scientist in mid-winter, and the first by a botanist interested in "plant-formations" and plant ecology, rather than in listing flora and describing individual species. Also on the trip was Mr Edwin Jennings, a collector and taxidermist from the Otago Museum. Jennings was somewhat of a subantarctic veteran, having previously been to the Auckland and Campbell Islands in HMS *Nymphe* in 1878, on a five-week voyage to Macquarie Island in the ketch *Gratitude* in 1894, and around the other southern islands aboard the *Hinemoa* in 1895.

At Antipodes on 16 July, Cockayne saw the entire coastline from the ship, but as was usual for passengers he had limited time ashore – and the winter's day was short. After landing he could examine only the vegetation on the rocks and slopes behind Anchorage Bay, the valley of Hut Stream, the North Plains as far as "the base of Mount Galloway", and both sides of the ridge behind Alert Bay. He wrote:

> It will be seen from this that the whole western side of the island and the greater part of the southern side is still botanically unexplored, and this comprises somewhat about one-half of the island, small as it is. All the same, I think there will hardly be any other plant-formations of any

> importance than those described below, unless it be a swamp-formation . . . and perhaps the actual summit of Mount Galloway may have a different combination of plants.

The plant-formations and sub-formations he described were: maritime rocks; maritime tussock slopes; flat tussock meadow; inland tussock slopes; scrub; bog; inland rocks; stream and swamp. Concerning future exploration he added: "During a long summer's day, if the weather kept fine, it would be easy for an active man to travel over the greater part of the island, especially if he had an assistant to carry some of the impedimenta."

One of Cockayne's interests was the effect of animals on vegetation. Here on Antipodes he noted that on areas of almost "bare ground manured by the giant petrel" there existed a distinct plant association "of which the endemic *Senecio antipoda* is the dominant plant". This led to an idea that he was to follow up later:

> It is a very curious fact that, both here and in Chatham Island, in situations frequented by certain sea-birds there should be an endemic [plant] species peculiar to such stations . . . *Cotula featherstonii* of Chatham Island is . . . growing in ground near the holes of mutton birds . . . I do not see why rich heavily manured soil should not be just as much a factor in determining the life-form of a plant as illumination, moisture in the air, wind, or any other ecological factor."

While he was at the Auckland and Campbell Islands, Cockayne had the opportunity to study the degrading effects of cattle, sheep and rabbits on subantarctic vegetation and was not impressed with the changes he recorded. Of the Antipodes he wrote: "Were the place to be turned into a sheep-run, where the sheep were annually shorn and the tussock burnt off, then, indeed, the face of nature might be changed, and one of the most wonderful natural museums in the world be destroyed, which would, indeed, be a scientific calamity in no wise to be compensated by the trivial and problematical gain that would be acquired by sheep-farming."

At the Bounty Islands the next day, Cockayne and Jennings took the opportunity, neglected by Hutton 15 months previously, of landing. Here they discovered that the island had a rich invertebrate fauna. To quote Cockayne: "Mr. Jennings, of the Otago Museum, and myself had the great pleasure of discovering a peculiar fauna rich in individuals; indeed, in some places the guano beneath the stones was fairly alive with amphipods, beetles, spiders, and small flies, while larger flies were in great numbers on the bare warm rocks." The spiders collected were of a new genus with their nearest relatives then to be found in "the south of South America". This was early evidence linking the Bounty Islands to the ancient continent of Gondwana. They searched for land plants but found none save for "an alga clothing the rocks and giving them a greenish hue in places". Cockayne collected specimens but these were "unfortunately lost". He rightly concluded that: "Probably these islands are a remnant of a much larger land-area, and the alga not the forerunner of a more extensive future vegetation, but the last survivor of one long passed away."[18]

In February 1907 the Governor of New Zealand, Lord Plunket, sailed on the *Tutanekai* around the southern islands. He described his companions as "a somewhat novel staff, the usual Private Secretary and A.D.C.'s being on this occasion strengthened by two University scientists, one taxidermist, and two Press photographers". The scientists were Edgar Waite of the Canterbury Museum and Professor W.B. Benham. The party had a whole day ashore at the Antipodes – Benham and Waite reached the summit of Mount Galloway and made extensive collections and notes. The Governor and others " tried some sea-fishing, but found that, though the sea was full of fish, the fish were full of worms, which was a great disappointment to everyone except the scientists". At the Bounty Islands rough seas made a landing impossible.

During the course of the Philosophical Society of Canterbury's expedition to the Auckland and Campbell Islands in November 1907, Bollons proceeded on with the *Tutanekai* to check the depots at the Antipodes and Bounty Islands. On about 21 November he collected 12 live Antipodes Island Green Parakeets on behalf of the New Zealand Government. These were later liberated on Kapiti Island, a bird sanctuary off the west coast of the North Island, where several survived until at least 1923.

In January 1909 Mr B.C. Aston, Chief Chemist of the Department of Agriculture, travelled on the *Hinemoa* around the southern islands. The Antipodes were visited on 15 January and the Bounty Islands three days later. At the Antipodes, Aston collected a number of plant specimens for New Zealand museums. He also collected, and later analysed, samples of soil, rock and guano. He noted that where the birds roosted on the Bounty Islands "the rock is covered with a smooth polished crust, as if a coating of calcic carbonate has been deposited on it". On subsequent analysis this was found to contain "over 25 per cent of mineral phosphate", while the guano sample had values of P 22.8 : N 8.9 : K 0.8 – the makings of "a very powerful fertiliser". Likewise, the volcanic soils on the Antipodes proved to be "very rich in plant food".[19]

Gilbert Archey, Assistant Curator of the Canterbury Museum, travelled on the *Tutanekai* in 1923. At Antipodes on 1 April he noted that the Wandering Albatross chicks were just starting to hatch, a month later than the reported first hatching that year of Royal Albatross chicks on Campbell Island. Archey and Bollons observed an albino Erect-crested Penguin and the captain "secured a fine specimen of the King Penguin". The ship reached the Bounty Islands on 2 April, but enormous seas made a landing impossible.[20]

The final inspection of the Antipodes and Bounty Islands for castaways by a New Zealand Government steamer was in March–April 1927. This cruise had several scientists and naturalists on board including W.H. Guthrie-Smith, a well-known writer, ornithologist, and bird photographer; Dr W.R.B. Oliver, botanist and collector for the Dominion Museum; Dr G. Einar Du Reitz, a Swedish botanist whose speciality was lichens; and George Turner. On 4 April the party of 13 passengers landed at Alert Bay, Antipodes Island, and had four or five hours ashore – and four hours on the Bounty Islands the following day. Many of Oliver's ornithological observations were included in his later book on New Zealand birds,[21] and Turner later submitted an article to the *Independent News*.[22] Guthrie-Smith gave a popular account of the voyage in his book *Sorrows and Joys of a New Zealand Naturalist*. He was obviously fascinated by Antipodes Island, and was frustrated that the time ashore far too short:

> Alas! that there should not have been days, weeks, months to be spent when there were only hours . . . Oh! if only on the Antipodes Islands I could have recovered days sad in the loneliness of cities, wasted in futilities, squandered in the daily ineptitudes of life.[23]

Both botanists made collections, Oliver's including both land plants and seaweeds – while the bryophytes collected by Du Reitz increased the known species from six to 24. Apparently while ashore on the Bounty Islands Du Reitz was "unremitting in his search for lichens", but was unable to find any. One can only imagine his mixed emotions when, while searching the rocks through binoculars as the ship departed, he discovered "that some lichens actually do exist there".[24]

THE MYTHICAL LAKE ON ANTIPODES ISLAND

Both Andreas Reischek and photographer William Dougall relate how in 1888 Captain Fairchild told them of a freshwater lake on the top of Mount Galloway, which they did not have time to visit. Dougall gives the following description: "The principal hill, Mount Galloway, is 1200 feet above the level of the sea. From seaward this hill looks conical or dome shaped, but on reaching the summit a beautiful clear lake, covering an area of thirteen or fourteen acres, is found, a lake which a little later in the season than the time of our visit is much frequented by albatross, being virtually surrounded by thousands of these birds."

No such lake exists. Fairchild had first climbed to the top of Mount Galloway only two years before and in his report of that trip described the interior of the island — its sources of freshwater, grasslands, albatrosses, and lack of woody vegetation — without mentioning a lake. Chapman was the next to climb Mount Galloway, in January 1890, recording that due to dense fog he "failed to see a clear lake said to exist there". As late as 1903 Cockayne still believed there was a lake "of 13 or 14 acres" — noting that the "lake on the summit of Mount Galloway requires a careful examination for water plants".

Why did this myth about a lake last so long? It seems that, after Fairchild's and Chief Engineer Galloway's initial assent of the mountain in 1886, and Fairchild telling Reischek and Dougall of the lake's existence in 1888, the only other party to reach the top of Mount Galloway was Chapman's, and he ascribed not seeing the lake to fog.

The question remains — why did Fairchild say he had seen a lake in the first place? Perhaps, as some have since suggested, Fairchild and Galloway also climbed into drifting fog and saw a large patch of the silvery-leafed *Pleurophyllum antipoda* on the high Central Plateau. Or perhaps it was a joke taken seriously, and once in print difficult for the captain to retract.

CHAPTER THIRTEEN

Expeditions and Visits, 1926–1969

WHITNEY SOUTH SEA EXPEDITION, 1926

In February 1926, the Antipodes and Bounty Islands were visited by the Whitney South Sea Expedition in the motor schooner *France* (E.A. Stenbeck, master). This expedition, led by Rollo H. Beck, was on the southernmost leg of a cruise through the western Pacific collecting bird specimens for the American Museum of Natural History. Also on board were Mrs Ida Beck and an assistant collector, Jose G. Correia, and his wife. On 16 February as the ship approached the Antipodes Islands seabirds were all around and Beck was typing his journal on deck:

> The barometer is high, 30.02 . . . fog hangs over the islands, but it is clear outside . . . Four cape pigeons have followed us now a half mile from the

> north point of the island. Black, forbidding cliffs face the eastern side close to the water, but higher up grass is seen . . . I shot fifty-one birds before breakfast at eight o'clock.[1]

Beck remarked that this was the most he had ever shot before breakfast, and that four or five were species he had not previously collected. The captain looked to anchor in Anchorage Bay but it was too exposed, so he tried Ringdove Bay but could not "get bottom" there. Eventually the schooner "went to sea and laid off all night".

The next morning they anchored close in and Beck and two men landed, apparently at Alert Bay. They climbed inland "up onto a level plateau with rolling country about" where Wandering Albatrosses and shearwaters were found nesting. This area is now known as the North Plains. Beck collected bird specimens (albatross, petrels, two pipits and one parakeet) and took photographs. Later, back at Alert Bay, he went along the shore in a small boat and shot several giant petrels, about ten skuas and various petrels. On the morning of the 18th the wind turned to the north and with rocks only 200 yards astern they had to leave in a hurry. Beck noted:

> The propeller fouled in the kelp and the engine could not help, but we got out safely, and went around south of the island, seeing dozens of albatrosses sitting on the water, several of them sooty. There are perhaps fifty pairs of sooty [albatross] on the island, while maybe a thousand or more wandering . . . Off shore a little way, blackbellied petrels were feeding and the high flying albatrosses and skuas indicated the coming gale the rapidly falling glass warned us was ahead.

The next day, the gale blowing strong and Stewart Island "over 400 miles to windward", Beck decided to run back to the Antipodes and from there to the Bounty and Chatham Islands, although this meant "cutting out the other islands where other species of albatrosses nest. The ship and crew are not fitted for cold weather and the foresail is old:. They were then sailing with only a double-reefed foresail and staysail. Gales had been blowing for over half of the previous 20 days and they had "been hove to most of that time".

On 21 February Rollo and Ida Beck, Correia and a boat's crew landed near Reef Point. They visited the castaway hut and the Stella Bay penguin colony, collected two albino penguins and several pipits, took photographs, and observed Elephant Seals and bird life. Correia later remarked on the difficulties of travel ashore:

> From the sea the land looks very smooth, but when we landed, the aspect changed entirely. I have been to South Georgia three times and I landed at three different places and crossed parts covered with grass, but nothing like this. Here it takes an hour to go a couple of hundred yards.[2]

The following day it rained and Beck worked on board preparing skins, but others were ashore all day. On the 23rd, Beck and Hicks (one of the crew who took an interest in birds and taxidermy) climbed Mt Galloway and found albatrosses "right on top nesting, while the shearwaters were commoner on slopes and in the valley. Four snipes were seen and two of them secured". Like all visitors before and since, the party found the going through dense tall tussock very difficult and tiring. The 24th seems to have been given over to preparing specimen skins from the birds collected. Correia was not able to help, for as Beck commented with feeling: "Correia is out of commission, with his hands tied up from arsenic poisoning, not being able to get it through his head that arsenic cannot be handled like flour or cornmeal. He rubbed it on penguin skins with his hands when the spoon did not satisfy him."

The Whitney South Sea Expedition's Schooner *France*. (*AMNH, New York.*)

The following day the *France* left the Antipodes at daybreak with a fresh breeze for the Bounty Islands. Beck and Hicks continued working below decks finishing the skins. Taxidermy, using scalpels and knives, on a schooner at sea was a tricky and painful business. Rollo Beck recorded that Hicks "has a few cuts and I only have seven on the right hand with a few on the left. Correia counting carefully yesterday obtained a census of eighteen on his two hands".

The *France* approached the Bounty Islands early on 26 February. Over the next two days the two ornithologists and Ida Beck landed several times on Depot and Proclamation Islands, collecting bird specimens, taking photographs and inspecting the castaway depot. They were impressed with the immense number and tameness of the birds. Mollymawks had chicks "beginning to feather". Penguins were moulting and a very few of their young were still in down. Prions "were everywhere under rocks", calling. Shags were roosting on the cliffs and 10 were shot. They saw a few Dominican gulls, two brown skuas and one starling: "Fur seals were playing in the kelp and a couple of dozen or more young were seen. We saw probably fifty or so seals which were so tame that they came up to the boat and to the oars in the water".

On 28 February, Correia went ashore for the last time "for a few albatrosses", and at 1 p.m. the expedition left for the Chatham Islands.

RRS *DISCOVERY II*, 1938

The Royal Research Ship *Discovery II* visited the Antipodes Group on 10 January 1938 during a circumpolar voyage from Cape Town, "east about". After leaving the Balleny Islands, the ship visited Campbell Island on 27–28 January, called at Dunedin and then cruised to the south-east, carrying out oceanographic research. She was off the Antipodes Islands on 9 February. The next day, during a close-in circumnavigation, stations were worked and soundings taken – but no one landed.

Discovery II was under the command of Commander Leonard C. Hill, with Dr Henry F.P. Herdman the scientific leader on board. They later reported some error in the island's charted position.[3]

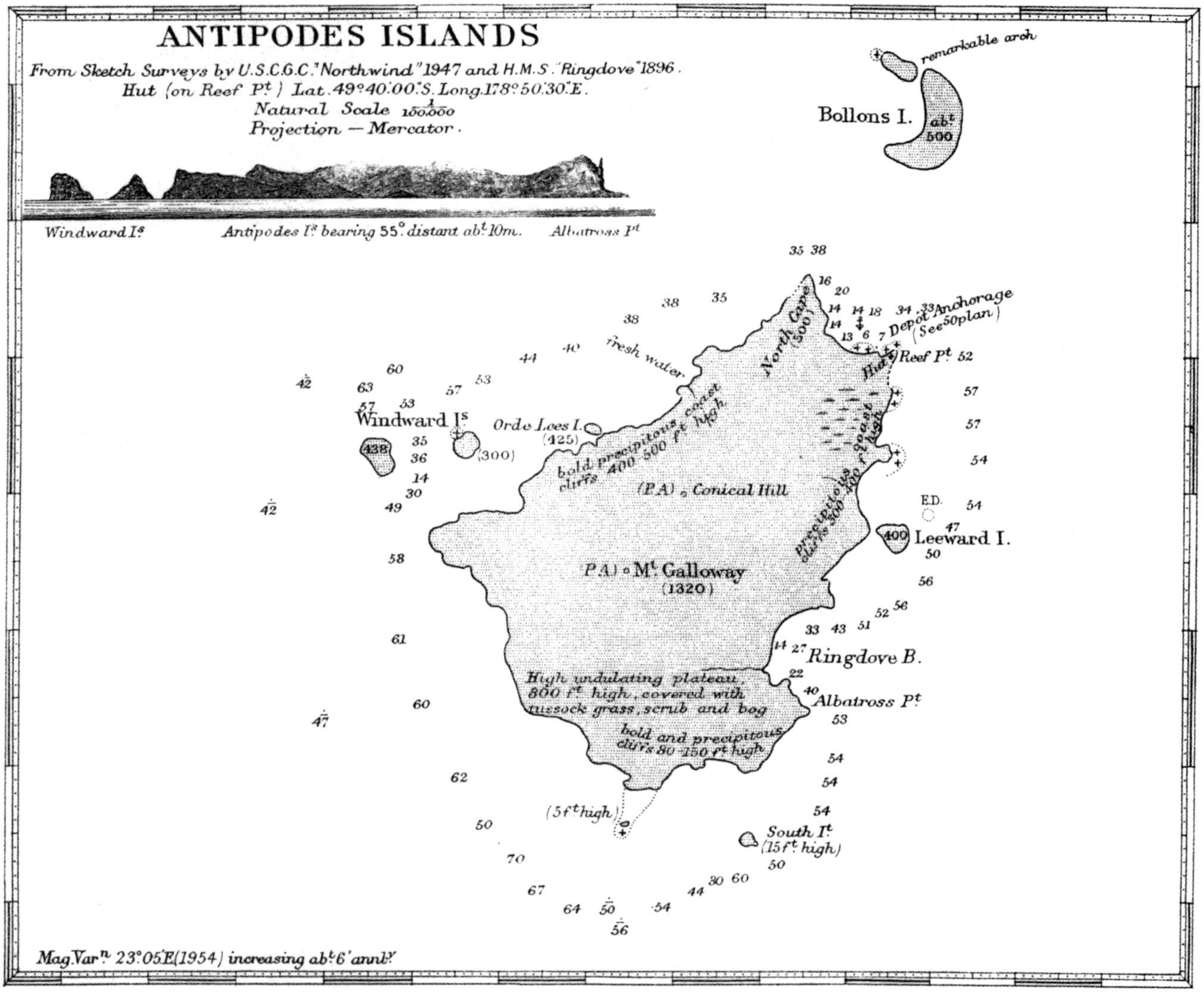

Revised chart of Antipodes Island following the March 1947 survey by USCGC *Northwind*. (*British Admiralty Chart 1022*.)

THE WAR YEARS, 1939–1945

During World War II the New Zealand Government set up bases and deployed coastwatchers at the Auckland and Campbell Islands to report sightings of enemy shipping. The operation, code named "CAPE Expedition", did not include the Antipodes or Bounty Islands, since these had no harbours or other strategic importance. However, towards the end of the war, as weather reporting became the top priority, consideration was given to setting up a meteorological station at the Antipodes.

In January 1944, inspections of Ringdove Bay, other Antipodes anchorages and a potential station site were planned to have been carried out by Captain W.R. Webling of the 28-metre auxiliary ketch *New Golden Hind* while returning from relieving the Campbell and Auckland Island stations. However, the mission was aborted just short of the Antipodes when dangerously rough seas forced the ketch to divert to Dunedin.[4]

In early July 1945, a Royal New Zealand Air Force plane based in New Plymouth was on a navigational training flight to the Bounty and Campbell islands. At one stage, it descended through cloud to make the first reported sighting of the Bounty Group since 1927. The aircrew "spent about a quarter of an hour circling the main collection of rocks at [the] Bounties, photographing from a low altitude". The navigator, Flight Lieutenant A. McCredie, later reported to the Marine Department that "the rocks, especially on their northern slopes, were densely covered with seals – apparently of all sizes". Low-level flying conditions were "extremely bad" and the aircrew found it impossible to estimate the number of seals seen, though they considered them to be "extremely numerous".[5] These observations on the apparent recovery of the Bounty Island fur seal population were very timely and much appreciated by the Acting Secretary of Marine. Particularly since his Minister, under pressure from fishermen, had just gazetted an open season for fur seals in parts of Fiordland, Stewart Island and eastern Otago.[6]

USCG CUTTER *NORTHWIND*, 1947

In early March 1947 the icebreaker USCGC *Northwind* commanded by Captain Charles W. Thomas called at the Antipodes Island Group while returning from Antarctica – where she had played a leading role in the US Navy expedition Operation Highjump. While accompanying other ships of the Task Force northwards from the Antarctic Circle, Thomas found sea conditions so stormy that he "could not hope to keep station so zig-zagged up through the sixties and fifties with the wind alternately on bow and quarter". A zag took them to the Antipodes.[7]

The ship's log[8] records that at 7.47 a.m. on 4 March they picked up land

Above: Northern Ringdove Bay and Leeward Island, Antipodes.

Below: View across Stack Bay towards Cave Point and Windward Island, Antipodes.

John Warham

Above: View across the south end of Stack Bay to Spirit of the Dawn Rock (right distance).

Below: South coast of Antipodes Island from the sea.

Above: Sectoides Stream, Antipodes.

Below: Dougall Stream and Mount Galloway.

Above: Erect-crested Penguins and coast north of Orde Lees Island.

Below: Natural bridge at Orde Lees penguin colony.

JOHN WARHAM

Above: Rob Stanley at finger post erected in 1894 behind Alert Bay, Antipodes Island.

Below: Castaways' Caves, South Bay. The high knob on which they flew their flags is in the right distance.

GRAEME ELLIOTT

KATH WALKER

Above: Two sealers (Alexander Foster and Willam Rook) were buried on this ledge, above Stella Bay, in 1825.

Left: Stone bottle from sealers camp, south coast Antipodes Island.

Above: Remains of glass bottle from sealers camp, Reef Point Antipodes Island.

Below: Tourist "zodiac cruise" at Bounty Islands, January 1993.

Ringdove Stream waterfall after rain. Pat Taylor on MV *Pacific Ruby*, 1993.

"believed to be Antipodes Islands on air search radar bearing 053° T [degrees right from true north], distance 33 miles". Needing smooth water to clean the exhaust lines of two generators, Thomas changed course for them. The Antipodes were sighted, through fog and at a distance of three miles, at 9.50 a.m. After entering Ringdove Bay, the ship investigated the coast northwards and anchored in Depot Anchorage at 10.48 a.m. Here, Boat 1 was launched:

> A landing party under Lieutenant Langenbeck and Lieutenant Abe Siemens, the Assistant Engineer, went ashore. This little known and still less frequented group is precipitous with reaches above the cliffs covered with tussock grass and reeds which was so difficult to traverse that it kept the shore recco patrol close to the island's sole 10 yards of beach.[9]

Their landing was at Hut Cove, where they visited the "shipwreck station", left a few cases of emergency rations, "established Kilroy's presence for posterity", and also obtained the second record of Elephant Seals for the island.[10] Deciding to use the time to best advantage, Thomas planned a topographic and hydrological survey using the ship, helicopter and boats. One boat took soundings of Anchorage Bay while another investigated the North Cape area. The ship's helicopter carried out two reconnaissance flights but fog prevented systematic aerial photography. By 3.30 p.m. all sailors were back on board – the last boat returning with nine live penguins. After weighing anchor, the *Northwind* circumnavigated the main island at a distance of "1000 yards off the headlands". Regular soundings were recorded, and radar used to good effect to photograph and chart the intricate outline of the coast. At 5.10 p.m. they passed between the

Sailors from USCGC *Northwind* landing in Hut Cove, Antipodes Island, April 1947. Photo by Mashburn, US Coast Guard. (*Elliot Dawson collection.*)

Windward Islands, and 30 minutes later entered Ringdove Bay for the second time. After anchoring, the motor surf-boat was lowered and made two trips to the shore, finally "bringing back a total of forty-eight (48) penguins". A scientist from the Woods Hole Oceanographic Institute asked to go ashore to obtain samples of some "rare white rocks" seen from the ship. He was disappointed, after attacking them with a geological hammer, to find they were quite ordinary – only covered with penguin guano. By 8 p.m. *Northwind* was once more underway and leaving the islands.[11]

This survey of the group was only the third attempted, following a crude sketch drawn by Captain Fairchild of the *Hinemoa* in 1886 and a more detailed survey by *Ringdove* in 1896. The *Northwind*'s "sketch survey" of the Antipodes Group was published on a US Navy Hydrographic Office chart later the same year, and on the 1948 edition of British Admiralty Chart 1022.

On the morning of 7 March, the *Northwind* reached Wellington in company with Admiral Byrd's flagship, USS *Mount Olympus* and the USS *Burton Island*. Here, *Northwind*'s captain and officers met an Antarctic "survivor" from Shackleton's *Endurance* expedition, Thomas Orde Lees, who had settled in Wellington. He made such an impression on them that they gave his name to a small Antipodes islet and took him on a helicopter flight over the city.[12] Four of the Antipodes penguins were presented to the Wellington Zoological Gardens. One Rockhopper Penguin and the zoo's curator, C.J. Cutler, were flown by *Northwind*'s helicopter to Newtown Park where they were greeted by "J.E. Perkins the biologist to the Byrd Expedition, a group of zoo officials, and cheering crowds of school children . . . The penguin seemed undisturbed by the first flight of its life". Another Rockhopper and two Erect-crested Penguins were taken to the zoo by road. The remaining 50 or so penguins were destined for the Washington Natural Zoo. They were transferred to the *Mount Olympus* and left for Norfolk, Virginia, on 14 March.

THE *ALERT* EXPEDITION, 1950

In 1950, the first New Zealanders to spend more than a few hours ashore on Antipodes Island in over 70 years were members of a private scientific expedition organised by Alex Black of Dunedin and led by Dr Robert Falla of the Dominion Museum. The *Alert*, a 72-foot converted harbour defence motor-launch, left Dunedin on the evening of 2 November and 38 hours later made landfall on the Antipodes Islands from seven miles off in clear weather. These conditions were later described as "sailor's luck", for there was low cloud or fog on all of the next eight days that the *Alert* remained at the islands. The *Alert* was equipped with depth sounder, compass and radio direction-finding equipment, and when the sky was clear the navigator obtained positional fixes using a sextant.

Bob Miller (*right*) and Rod Litt surveying on the Bounty Islands, November 1950. (*Alex Black*.)

The nine men on board were: Alex Black, owner and skipper; Alister Thomson, navigator; Alf Birchall, crewman; Jim Ollerenshaw, photographer and field officer, Wildlife Branch, Department of Internal Affairs; Graham Turbott, ornithologist, Auckland Museum; Robert Falla, Director, and Dick Dell, conchologist, from the Dominion Museum; and Bob Miller and Rod Litt, surveyors from the Lands and Survey Department. Most had previously sailed with Black on the *Alert* – Falla to the Snares Islands in 1947 and on seal surveys around Stewart Island and Fiordland in 1948; and Miller, Litt, Dell and Ollerenshaw during the New Zealand–American Fiordland Expedition in 1949.[13]

Before leaving Wellington, Falla visited the RRS *Discovery II*, which was then in port, and talked with Henry Herdman, the scientific leader on board. Herdman had been on *Discovery II* when she visited the Antipodes in 1938, but now the British whaling research ship was due to leave on 2 November directly for the Antarctic ice edge, and eventually return to Dunedin.[14] When Falla mentioned that he was also sailing on 2 November for the Antipodes Islands, he was left in no doubt that those islands were "no place to go in a

Robert Falla filming a Wandering Albatross, Antipodes Island, November 1950. (*Alex Black.*)

Harbour Defence Launch" and that he would be lucky to find them.[15] So, on *Alert*'s arrival in Ringdove Bay, Falla – with tongue in cheek – sent off the following message, via Awarua Radio: "HERDMAN. R.S. DISCOVERY II. Found Antipodes. Wishing you similar success ice edge and Dunedin. FALLA."[16]

The expedition made its first landing during the early afternoon of 4 November on rocks in northern Ringdove Bay, below a very large penguin colony. From here the best route to the top of the island was through the penguins, which from the ship had presented the appearance of an "unusual black and white scree". The distribution and habits of the two species of penguins were to receive much attention, both then and throughout the rest of the trip. After several hours ashore, and a climb by some of the expedition to reconnoitre the top of the island, all returned to the ship for the night.

On 5 November the surveyors, having decided to camp ashore, packed their "heavy loads" of equipment and camping gear up the steep slopes through the squawking, pecking penguins, which Litt described as "the most unusual tramping hazard I have yet encountered". They set up camp, one small pup tent among the windswept tussock and fern, near the plateau edge about 200 metres above the sea – and from here set about their mapping project. Over the following days the surveyors were hampered by the weather. Not only were there cold south-west winds with snow and sleet on two days, but also fog and mist was common – which confined sightings and the taking of bearings to the "fair periods in between". Falla and Turbott had both served terms as coastwatchers on the Auckland Islands and were impressed with the novelty of the Antipodes climate. Falla considered that the Antipodes, even on their highest peaks, were much drier than the other subantarctic islands – in spite of constant fog and mist – and, significantly, the castaway depot at the Antipodes was the only one he knew where the stores "showed no mould". The temperature "was mostly in the low forties [5–7°C], and was seldom below freezing, even on the tops".

With the lack of good campsites ashore, the rest of the party found it easier to return to the ship each night, although the ornithologists did spend some time ashore observing the "nocturnal activities of the petrels". On foggy nights, when the searchlight was being used to maintain safety margins from the shore, huge numbers of petrels were attracted to the ship. As Ollerenshaw reported:

> Seabirds showered on to decks, into cabins, in fact everywhere possible. Some birds were not found until the "Alert" reached Dunedin. They were hitting all parts of the vessel like showers of hailstones. Many birds were stunned, and a few of them killed outright. To go on deck brought hard hits to body and head; one bird hit me a smack on the head following which I retired to a safer place.

Turbott noted that these birds included abundant Grey-backed Storm Petrels, Black-bellied Storm Petrels, Common Diving Petrels and White-headed Petrels; a number of Fairy Prions; and a few Sooty Shearwaters, White-chinned Petrels and Cape Pigeons. Even one Giant Petrel came aboard. The Dominion Museum had a permit to obtain bird specimens, and most of the petrels brought back were collected dead or stunned from the ship's deck.

Each day the scientists landed, climbed inland, and spread out – documenting the birds and collecting specimens of flies, spiders and other invertebrates, plants, peat and rocks. Much time was spent on the higher parts of the island – studying and photographing the Wandering Albatrosses, with their well-feathered young, on the uplands; and the beautiful Light-mantled Sooty Albatrosses, with freshly-laid eggs, that nested around high-level bluffs. Black was able to get ashore on two occasions, recording penguins, albatrosses, the surveyor's camp, and upland and coastal views on movie film.

The four species of land bird also received much attention, Turbott taking particular note of the characteristics, behaviour and food habits of the two parakeets. A total of 17 parakeets were collected, 15 being brought back alive to aviaries in Tauranga and Dunedin. A few Subantarctic Snipe were seen or heard: Ollerenshaw accidentally trod on one, so it was "collected" as a museum specimen. As well as observing birds, Dell and Turbott "ranged widely for the smaller animal life". In particular, Dell collected marine life both around the shore and with a dredge at sea.

In the late afternoon of 6 November a south-east swell rose in Ringdove Bay, and the *Alert* shifted to a more sheltered anchorage on the north side of Leeward Island. Next morning, she sailed north to Reef Point, and the vicinity of the castaway hut, but no landing could be made here because of rough seas. Once back at anchor near Leeward Island, getting ashore was difficult, and a well-timed jump from the dinghy onto a rock among the swirling bull-kelp was required. The party then clambered over slippery boulders to a gravel beach at the north end of the bay (since named Alert Bay), where a small breeding group of Southern Elephant Seals were found. From here there was good access to the top of the island via short, narrow ledges. The scientists then reached the Northern Plains and walked overland to the castaway depot.

The depot was found to be sound and dry inside, and the stores in good order – although after 20 years a few tins were inevitably rusted and some books had been chewed by mice. The zinc-lined cases containing blankets and clothing were intact, as were the ration boxes left by the USCGC *Northwind* in 1947. The *Alert* stayed two nights anchored in Alert Bay. On 8 November, with the weather improved, she circumnavigated the group – passing around Bollons and Archway Islands and between the Windward Islands. During the circuit, Dell was surprised to see a pair of Bounty Island Shags on a high ledge on Bollons Island. These were the only ones seen at the islands, and they have not been reported there since.That night the ship returned to anchor in Ringdove Bay where she remained until the expedition left the Antipodes.

One of the objects of the voyage was to see whether New Zealand Fur Seals had re-established a population on the Antipodes, since their numbers had recently improved at other New Zealand islands. Disappointingly, only one aged and decrepit bull "on his last flippers" was seen at the south end of Ringdove Bay. However, several small herds of Southern Elephant Seals, with new-born pups, and a solitary Leopard Seal were found.

On 10 November the surveyors struck camp and at 6 p.m. the ship was once more underway dredging for bottom samples along the eastern coast. As she passed close to Bollons Island it was seen that the two shags were still on their well-used ledge; and that Cape Pigeons, Black-browed Mollymawks and possibly Grey-headed Mollymawks were breeding on the cliffs. At 7.30 a course was set for the Bounty Islands.

The vicinity of the Bounty Islands was reached on dead reckoning, after an all-night run. All hands were on deck early on the 11th, trying to locate the islands through dense banks of fog. Black instigated a box-search after deciding that they must have passed the islands. Unfortunately the first leg of this was to port, taking them further away, and it was four hours before Falla sighted one of the East Group, bearing SW one mile distant, through a gap between fog banks. Ollerenshaw recorded the great relief of all on board:

> Up to this time feelings had been rather tense and mingled with disappointment. Shortly after . . . we were cruising past the rocky eastern islets upon which seals, and many penguins and other birds were observed. Anchorage was sought in the channel near the largest of the group and after a meal all went ashore. With cameras and instruments to carry, this proved to be a risky business . . . the granite surface of these islets were

> entirely devoid of vegetation and soil, and worn smooth. Nailed boots proved useless . . . Rubber soles were more effective but treacherous on wet surfaces. Mr Black's use of sugar bags tied over boots seemed to me the most suitable device for ascending this surface.[17]

The visitors found Depot Island "covered with birds, the penguins alone numbering millions". Many photographs were taken, and a pair each of Fulmar Prions, Salvin's Mollymawks, and Bounty Island Shags collected for the Dominion Museum. The New Zealand Fur Seal population of the group was estimated to be about 5000. In the few hours available, the surveyors attempted observations to help improve the inaccurate chart of the islands, but they met considerable difficulties. Litt was frustrated by his footwear and agreed that "nailed tramping boots are about as useless as a pair of skates", legs of tripods became entangled with penguins, and the steel survey tape was rendered useless when mollymawks cut it with their beaks.[18]

The *Alert* left the Bounty Islands shortly before 6 p.m. and after encountering moderate seas, and a group of migrating humpbacked whales, arrived in Dunedin at 5.40 a.m. on 13 November.

NEW ZEALAND FISHERMEN, 1950s

Occasionally, from the mid-1950s on, fishing vessels searching for new rock lobster grounds visited all of New Zealand's subantarctic islands.[19] One fishing boat from this period whose crew left its name carved on the wall of the Antipodes depot was the *Chance* from Bluff, which appears to have called on 30 July 1958.

Fortunately, no crayfish or other in-shore commercial species were found to encourage a "rush" on the Antipodes – something that may have led to far greater damage to the islands than the mere vandalism these visitors wreaked on the boxes of old castaway stores and provisions.

The Antipodes castaway depot in February 1926. (*Rollo Beck, AMNH.*)

OCEANOGRAPHIC CRUISES, 1961, 1962, 1965, 1969

Early in 1961, the Scripps Institution expedition Monsoon on the converted ocean-going tug RV *Argo* (Barnes Collinson, master) followed Captain Bligh's original track from south of New Zealand to Tahiti. On 28 February, five scientists – S. Calvert, H. Craig, H. Menard, W. Nesteroff and C. Russell – were landed on one of the larger Bounty Islands to collect rocks and other specimens. The granite samples were later analysed for composition, and dated at 189 ± 5 million years.[20]

In both November 1962 on MV *Taranui* (Captain Ron Matheson) and January 1965 on HMNZS *Endeavour* (Commander P.R.H. Silk), research teams from the New Zealand Oceanographic Institute (NZOI) of the Department of Scientific and Industrial Research (DSIR) spent three weeks studying the biology, geology and morphology of the Antipodes and Bounty Islands region. During both cruises samples were collected from the sea and the surrounding sea floor, and teams led by Elliot Dawson landed at the Bounty and Antipodes Islands. At both groups they banded nesting albatrosses, obtained geological specimens and collected inter-tidal animals. The 1962 party stayed at the Antipodes castaway depot overnight. They found that most of the old metal-lined boxes of food and clothing which were intact in 1950 had been axed open and their contents scattered. On 29 January 1965, during their second cruise, the Institute's scientists found both the hut and new supplies they had left there were "in good order", and it appeared that no one had visited since 1962.[21]

As part of the November 1962 programme, T. Hanley of the DSIR's Geophysics Division established a magnetic station on the northernmost point of Tunnel Island, Bounty Islands, and another above Stella Bay at the Antipodes. The NZOI party collected rock samples on Depot Island at the Bounties,[22] and also erected a large T-shaped wooden marker on totara posts on a low knob near the Antipodes depot. It was orientated by compass so it could be used for aerial photography – which eventually was flown in 1973, with the subsequent mapping published in 1978. (This marker board lasted well. I set up meteorological stations on it in 1969 and 1978, and it was still solidly in place when I last checked in 1989.)

In 1969, as a result of these cruises, David Cullen published a pioneering paper on the geology of the Antipodes Islands.[23] It was based largely on characteristics of the surrounding sea floor and the islands' structure and morphology as seen from the ship. Chemical analysis and radiometric age determinations were done on island rock samples collected by his colleagues for, as one of them later related, Cullen "opted not to get his feet wet".

In late 1962, the Russian whaling and oceanographic research ship *Slava* was also working in the vicinity of the Antipodes and Bounty Islands, and a landing was made at the former Group. When the *Slava* later called at Wellington, G.A. Solyanik, then the Soviet Director of Exploration in the Antarctic, visited both NZOI and the Dominion Museum and gave a verbal account of the landing. Dawson recalls that this included the claim of having seen a Gentoo Penguin at the Antipodes.[24] At the time, Falla, dismissed this as unlikely, but at least two vagrant Gentoos have been recorded there since.

The third visit was in *Taranui* (Captain Matheson): during the Bounty Hydrology Cruise of 1969, Norman Ridgeway and a shore party landed at Hut Cove on 3 February to visit the Canterbury University Antipodes Island Expedition base camp.[25]

THE *ELTANIN*, 1967

The USNS *Eltanin* (Captain Lawrence G. Wirth) left Wellington on 30 December 1966 and called at the Antipodes Islands on 2 January 1967. This 3900-ton ice-strengthened ship was a floating research station administered by the US National Science Foundation's Antarctic Research Program (USARP). On board for "Cruise 27" were 35 scientists and technicians attached to nine science programmes which included upper-atmosphere physics, meteorology, geomagnetics, and physical, chemical and biological oceanography. Between Wellington and the Ross Sea, scientific work centred on continuous seismic and magnetic profiling along the ship's track. However, bottom- and mid-water trawls were operated successfully near the Antipodes, "giving buckets full of sea life". Seabird numbers were monitored and specimens collected for the Dominion Museum and the Smithsonian Institution.

A party that landed on the Antipodes near Reef Point included New Zealand ornithologist Peter C. Harper from the Dominion Museum. He reported seeing a few hundred New Zealand Fur Seals ashore, mostly yearlings and sub-adults – a major increase from the one old male seen by the *Alert* in 1950. University of Miami scientists studying the distribution of marine fungi collected soil and inter-tidal water samples. Dr George A. Llano, USARP representative on board, made a collection of flowering plants and ferns that are now in the US National Arboretum in Washington DC.[26]

THE *MAGGA DAN*, 1968

On 12 January 1968 the Danish vessel MS *Magga Dan*, commanded by Captain F.E. Bang, called at the Bounty Islands. She was under charter to the Holm Shipping Company of New Zealand and carried 24 naturalists participating in the first tourist expedition, organised by Lindblad Travel of New York, to McMurdo Sound, Antarctica.[27] Lars Lindblad was Expedition Leader, and his staff included Captain Edwin McDonald (US Navy, retired), a consultant on Antarctic matters, and New Zealander Marie Darby as lecturer and scientific advisor. Later, Darby was to write:

> Dawn broke on a great, grey heaving ocean empty of the sight of land. Then there was a solitary bird – a grey-backed mollymawk; then another – a cape pigeon; and yet a third – a sooty shearwater. By 7.30 am, birds were everywhere: storm petrels . . . prions . . . mollymawks . . . wandering albatrosses . . . sooty shearwaters and penguins. At 8.15 am a dark grey shape loomed against the grey sky and sea – it was the Bountys. The dark grey shape divided and multiplied into many barren rocks, baring their jagged teeth through the surface of the ocean, miles from anywhere.[28]

By 10.30 a.m., *Magga Dan* was anchored close inshore. One of the passengers, Gladys Moore, records that the motorboat was then launched and Lindblad, Darby and McDonald went on a scouting trip along with the third mate and some seamen. After two attempts the passengers succeeded in getting ashore in a sheltered cove on Depot Island with the aid of a rope they had fastened to the top of a cliff.[29] Darby further describes their difficulties in landing:

> At several places, the [boat's] bow nudged into the kelp-fringed shore, only to be sucked away and down several feet in the trough of a wave. Everybody aboard was soaked in the sea-spray. The islands are sheer and smooth-surfaced, and are eroded in places to form great caverns and pinnacles. Water, pushed through narrow channels, ballooned out on the other side before rushing gurgling, sucking back again . . . One jumped ashore and scrambled up a slippery, greasy, penguin path, arriving on the top-most slopes to experience at last, in flesh and feathers, this avian Ascot. We were like Gulliver in a Lilliputian world of mollymawks and penguins.[30]

They also found that "the lower ledges were filled with New Zealand fur seals in great numbers".[31] By midday all passengers were ashore. They had about five hours on Depot Island, watching and photographing the birds and seals, and visiting the castaway depot. *Magga Dan* was underway again at about 5.30 p.m. She passed the Antipodes at 5 a.m. the next morning but the islands were not sighted through "fog, drizzle and rain".[32]

CHAPTER FOURTEEN

University of Canterbury Expedition, 1969

By 1968 the Antipodes Islands remained biologically the least known of all New Zealand's subantarctic islands. To help fill the void, the Zoology Department of Canterbury University – which had been active in field research on many New Zealand southern islands, but particularly the Snares – commenced planning an expedition that would "represent the major scientific investigation undertaken there [at the Antipodes] up to the present time".[1] The expedition aimed to study both plant and animal communities, including the littoral marine zone. Dr John Warham, Senior Lecturer in Zoology, was appointed leader and the selected expeditioners included Zoology Department staff and invited scientists (I was fortunate to be one) from other organisations active in subantarctic research. The party of eight men, all with previous subantarctic experience, comprised Warham, Peter Johns and Ian Mannering from the Zoology Department; Rob Stanley from the Marine Department; Brian Bell from the Wildlife Service, Department of

Internal Affairs; and Eric Godley, Willie Kuschel and myself from the Botany, Entomology and Ecology Divisions, respectively, of the DSIR.

For laboratory and mess facilities the Zoology Department workshop constructed a 20 x 12 ft prefabricated hut in 4 x 4 ft plywood-covered modules bolted together, floored with particle board and roofed with corrugated iron. The hut was equipped with benches, shelves and a central table. For sleeping, two 14 x 14 ft tents each weighing 180 lb were borrowed from the NZ Army. When received the tents were "very part used" and in poor condition. Knowing they would have to survive innumerable subantarctic gales, Mrs Pat Warham spent many hours patching and reinforcing them by hand. The university workshop also constructed 18 extra 4 x 4 ft plywood modules as floors for the tents.

HMNZS *Endeavour* (Commander D.G. Bamfield) left Lyttelton on 4 January 1969 with the expedition on board, sleeping in the hold with all their equipment and supplies. The Navy tanker and supply ship planned to first visit the Antipodes and then call at Campbell Island before proceeding to Antarctica. After leaving port there were following winds and swell from the northeast. Consequently, when the Antipodes Islands were reached – in heavy mist at about 4 a.m. hrs on 6 January – rough seas were pounding the north and east coasts, where the only feasible landing places existed. Waves were also washing over the low tank deck amidships, making it extremely difficult to load and lower boats. After circling the island until about 9 a.m. hours it was decided to continue on to Campbell Island as weather reports suggested similar conditions for the next 15 hours – the new plan being to leave us there for about three weeks until *Endeavour* returned north, when another attempt could be made to land at the Antipodes.[2]

We reached Campbell Island on the evening of 7 January and by 10 a.m. next day we were all ashore at the wharf below the Beeman Cove Meteorological Station with hut components, tents, food and other gear. In fine, sunny weather the station tractor and sled moved everything to a flat but very exposed location on Beeman Point. The hut was temporarily erected on wooden bearers (rather than piles) and the two sleeping tents pitched over their wooden floors. After a quick evening meal at the weather station, work

Personnel of University of Canterbury Antipodes Island Expedition, 1969, outside newly-erected prefabricated hut at Campbell Island. From left: Taylor, Bell (*front*), Kuschell, Warham, Godley, Mannering, Stanley, Johns. (*John Warham.*)

carried on until the hut was externally complete at 11.30 p.m.

Day two brought rain and 30-knot winds, but by its end the hut was fitted out – and guyed down against the gales – and most of the gear unpacked. During the day we had frequent visitors from the meteorological station, who we suspected were waiting to see our entire camp being blown away. By that night we were self-contained and independent, except for visiting the station for an occasional shower and once to see a film. Although frustrating at the time, this "practice run" at setting-up camp eventually paid off when we later relocated to Antipodes Island.

Following pre-arranged contingency plans the Campbell Island field programme was underway on 10 January. During the next 16 days all members of the party were actively engaged in various projects such as collecting plants, invertebrates, litter and marine samples; surveying vegetation; and studying penguins and other birds. Brian and I spent most of the time carrying out a census of feral sheep and Southern Royal Albatross – a job completed only the day before our departure.[3]

On its return from the Ross Sea, the *Endeavour* reached Campbell Island on 26 January. We were re-embarked with all our equipment and collections by late morning, the hut sections and timber being stowed forward on the tank deck ready for offloading. After leaving Campbell the sea remained fairly calm, with no white caps, so we were surprised when the ship suddenly changed course to the south. At the time some of our party surmised that this was to avoid a fast-moving front behind us. They couldn't have been more wrong; later we were told it was to allow the officers to hold a celebration dinner without being inconvenienced by the ship rolling.

ANTIPODES AT LAST

The *Endeavour* reached the Antipodes at about 2 a.m. hours on 28 January, and at first light the island was clearly visible free of mist. The sea was fairly calm. The first exploratory landing was made at about 5 a.m. hours when John, Peter, the bosun and a Petty Officer radio technician left in an inflatable *Gemini* headed for a bay (later named Stella Bay) to the south of Reef Point.

None of us had been to the island before and on the aerial photos the beach here had appeared readily negotiable and close to the castaway hut. On arrival the *Gemini* party soon realised that landing here was a mistake. They found very heavy kelp and large slippery boulders; the tide being rather low made landing difficult. To get ashore they had to jump into the sea and scramble out over big smooth boulders and slimy kelp. Peter and John then managed to get their packs and bedding rolls out, as the inflatable had meanwhile lifted with the surge and came further in finally ending broadside-on and embedded in the kelp, requiring a tow from another boat to eventually get out of the weed. These two and the bosun meanwhile pressed through a reception committee of penguins and seals, climbed a short cliff and forced a passage through shoulder-high tussock to the depot about 200 metres away.

The deep gut below the depot hut (which we later named Hut Cove) seemed a much better landing, with less kelp and at that time very little slop. A ship's motorboat with Willie and I and some boxes of gear had looked for an alternative landing on the rock shelf in Anchorage Bay. Those at the depot saw that this site was hopelessly distant for landing the expedition's massive amount of equipment, and contacted *Endeavour* via hand-held radios. The ship eventually got a signal through to No.1 boat to abort work at the rock platform, reload stores, and go to the aid of the Petty Officer on *Gemini* stuck in the Stella Bay kelp. However, I stayed ashore at Anchorage Bay and climbed overland through penguins and heavy tussock to meet up with the other three at the depot.

Meanwhile, No.2 boat with more stores managed to get to the beach in Hut Cove. One of its crew jumped ashore and assisted the bosun and me with the offloading. This boat then backed out, taking a line which the sailors attached to a buoy and anchor just outside the mouth of the cove. When No.1 boat arrived, with *Gemini* in tow, it moored to the buoy and off-loaded its stores into the inflatable. Then Willie, aboard *Gemini*, hauled her by the line on to the stony beach where those ashore were waiting to unload. Willie then hauled himself back out to get a second load. Thereafter a system began to get established with more sailors coming ashore to help unload and help get the gear to the top of the cliff – a height of about 18 metres.

John located his heavy 100-foot rope. This was rigged up to the cliff top and we started, with some difficulty because of snags, to haul the stuff up. Later a second, lighter, rope was manned from the far side of the cove to pull on the load and keep it out from striking the cliff. The work proceeded like this for about an hour when an engineer officer and more men arrived. The crew ashore worked hard under the drive and abuse of the engineer, who was the only officer to land. They installed a second ropeway with tackle brought from the ship, which really speeded things up.

About 10 a.m. Ian came ashore and reported that all of our cargo was off *Endeavour*. As well as the hut components, tents, tools and scientific and personal gear, this included a radio transmitter, several 12-volt batteries, radio aerials and masts, a generator, two-burner kerosene stoves, Primus stoves, cooking utensils, Tilley lamps, 80 gallons of kerosene, 20 gallons of petrol, and four gallons of methylated spirits. Among our general stores were eight sugar bags of potatoes, two bags of onions, 100 lb of flour, 50 lb of bacon, 40 lb of cheese, 48 lb of butter, 70 lb of sugar, six dozen small fruit cakes and 30 dozen eggs. There were cases of canned vegetables and fruit, bags of porridge oats, numerous packets of rice, dried fruit, Maggi soups, egg powder, milk powder, tea, coffee, drinking chocolate, Horlicks malted milk, barley sugars and 54 dozen small cakes of chocolate. For meat dishes we had a large supply of Alliance single-serving freeze-dried packs with mouth-watering names such as "Beef, Curry & Rice" and "Beef Steak Stew". There was also 50 lb of trail biscuits manufactured by Cadbury Fry Hudson. These were produced to NZ Antarctic Division specifications and supplied in 1/2 lb packets packed in large wide-mouth tins, "2 tins per wooden crate".

By the time the ship's crew left the island, about two hours later, the heaviest loads and about two-thirds of all gear were at the top of the cliff. *Endeavour* left the islands at about 1 p.m. Her farewell – a siren blast that reverberated around the cliffs – seemed to have a derisory tone, for the sailors had clearly thought we were mildly crazy in choosing to stay in such a gloomy and inhospitable place.

We decided to erect camp on the level area east of, and close to, the castaway depot, where shelter from the worst of the prevailing north-west wind was provided by the depot and the low bank behind it. Space was cleared for the two tents by levelling the tall tussocks with axe and mattock. The last of the floor modules were hauled up the cliff and assembled, and after our practice on Campbell Island the tents were soon pitched. We then started to clear the site for the prefabricated hut. Meanwhile, a couple of us got busy setting up a makeshift cookhouse in the draughty castaway depot. By the time a substantial meal was over everyone was ready for bed and all turned in at about 8 p.m.

The next day dawned fine and sunny, but there was a considerable surge in the cove, making us appreciate the calm seas encountered during yesterday's landing. Rob devised a water reservoir to hold runoff from the valley drainage for, although heavily peat-stained, the stream water was quite drinkable. By dark we had cleared the site for the hut, dug in the piles and erected the floor, walls and roof supports. Between jobs on the hut, Ian erected the latrine, John cleared a track through the dense tussock towards Stella Bay, and Eric started pioneering a similar path to give access to Anchorage Bay.

On 30 January, everyone was immediately on to the major job of hauling the last of the gear up from Hut Cove. The benches were put in the hut, followed by the roof. The site was tidied up, surplus gear and supplies stowed, and Peter and Ian erected the radio aerial. When our hut was finished the radio "went on the air", but we failed to make contact with New Zealand or Campbell Island. That afternoon I started to set up the Meteorological Station near camp at the site of the T-shaped marker boards erected by the Oceanographic Institute in 1962. The met station consisted of a Stevenson screen with wet-bulb, dry-bulb and max./min. thermometers, and a 4 inch rain gauge. There was also a hand anemometer (measuring wind speed), and a precision aneroid (to record barometric pressure). Also, a continuously recording barograph was housed in the castaway hut. From 1 February routine weather observations were carried out each day.

On 31 January, Ian erected the spouting and tank to collect rainwater from the roof, allowing an alternative supply for drinking to the brown, peat-stained liquid from the stream. It was so murky that, one evening, Brian overlooked adding tea to the brew and served up "hot peat-water and milk". We all took a few surprised sips before someone worked out what was wrong.

The camp was now firmly established, and research and exploration could begin in earnest. Not that science had so far been ignored. Many new observations had already been made and, in fact, Eric had discovered a new species of bull-kelp in Hut Cove, almost immediately on landing. There was much to engage all our scientists in the immediate vicinity of Reef Point, with its novel vegetation, penguin and seal colonies, and accessible shores, so it was a few days before we travelled much beyond the Northern Plain. Although the island was less than seven kilometres long, it took a hard three hours from our camp to reach the south coast, as much of the going was extremely tedious due to the massive size of the close-growing *Poa litorosa* tussocks. But we had learned all about these on the first day ashore, about which John later wrote:

> From the rim of the island at Stella Bay where we landed to the castaway

> depot is only about 200 metres but took some 15 exhausting and humiliating minutes to cover. The tussock crowns are about one metre across and arise from pedestals about two metres high. You can either try to force a way between these "niggerheads" or attempt to stride from crown to quivering crown. In practice we used both methods but generally spent much of the time on hands and knees.[4]

It was abundantly clear why the cattle, goats and sheep first liberated at the depot as food for castaways in the 1880s had been unable to travel far and rapidly died out; and the sheer impracticality of earlier schemes to farm the island was obvious. As Rob said: "Imagine living there with a family. You would soon lose the kids in these tussocks."[5]

At higher elevations the tussock was lower and less dense, but the shortest distance between two points was seldom a straight line. We found it easiest to avoid, if possible, areas of dense tussock, swamps and deep fern-filled gullies, and tack along the many small ridges where the vegetation was thinner and albatross trails often eased the way. On steeper hillsides, the best route was usually via old landslides or beside watercourses. Not all of our explorations could be conducted on day trips from the camp, and on many occasions expedition members camped out using either a small tent, or overhangs and small caves as shelter.

PEOPLE AND PROGRAMMES

Eric's mission was to study the flora and vegetation of the island. He made a herbarium collection of all land plants seen. Twenty-two species new to the island were found – two flowering plants, four ferns, one lycopod, and also eight new species of mosses and seven of liverworts. Eric also spent much time studying certain plants in great detail, particularly the endemic *Gentiana*, *Senecio* and *Coprosma* species. He also sampled and described the different vegetation associations (tussock lands, swamps, herb fields and so on) and their distribution over the island. Ian studied the marine life, making extensive collections of seaweeds, fish and marine invertebrates. Most of his

Canterbury University Antipodes Island Expedition setting up camp beside the castaway depot, 28 January 1969. (*John Warham.*)

work concentrated around Anchorage Bay, Hut Cove, Reef Point and Stella Bay, but he also visited the South Coast and the shores of Ringdove Bay.

Willie and Peter were the expedition's entomologists. Nothing from earthworms to fleas could escape their attention. Both were relentless in surveying and collecting terrestrial, freshwater and shore-dwelling invertebrates, and bird parasites. Willie specialised in litter dwellers and moths, while Peter's specialities were beetles and flies. Peter also undertook a compass survey of the island, and was also our radio technician/operator, keeping in touch with ham-radio operator Phil Howell in Christchurch, and at other times with *Endeavour* and Campbell Island station.

Four of the team – John, Brian, Rob and myself – worked on birds, helping each other with measuring, banding, and recording data. Our combined sightings added a number of species to the island's known fauna, including several self-introduced passerines. Some specimens were made into study skins, and the skeletons of others, found dead, were collected for the Dominion Museum.

John studied the two species of penguins – which were moulting during our stay – and concentrated on weight changes, behaviour and vocalisations. He obtained high-quality sound recordings and motion pictures of both penguins and petrels for later analysis and comparison. Rob assisted with the penguin research and studied the density and relative numbers of old and new Wandering Albatross nests on the island. He also collected data on the size and status of the island's pipits.

Brian's main task was to make a census of as many species as possible, and map their distribution. In this he concentrated on the Wandering Albatross and the colonial nesting species, especially the two penguins and the Giant Petrel, but he also investigated the distribution of the other smaller petrels. During this work he banded over 793 albatrosses, and over 900 seabirds in total.[6]

Marking birds with metal leg bands (each engraved with an individual number and return address) helps with many ornithological studies. When a bird is banded as a chick its age will be known if it is recaptured later, so if enough are recaptured over many years one can learn such things as average age of first breeding and longevity. Movements of birds can also be studied – for instance, two of the albatrosses we banded at the Antipodes were later recaptured from a fishing boat off Malabar Head, New South Wales, and a third was found dead in the Tuamoto Archipelago.[7]

My major project was a study of the island's two endemic parakeets – small parrots with long pointed tails. Most people associate parrots with tropical regions and find it strange that some live in the New Zealand subantarctic. Red-crowned parakeets – of different sub-species to those at the Antipodes – also occur on the Chatham and Auckland Islands, and were previously at Macquarie Island until killed out by wild cats around 1890. However, these are not the most southern parrots in the world. This distinction belongs to the Austral Conure of Chile and Argentina, which ranges as far south as the islands near Cape Horn.[8] As it was somewhat unusual to have two closely related parrots on such a small isolated island, I was interested in how the Antipodes Island Parakeet (green) and Reischek's Parakeet (red-crowned) differed in numbers, distribution, movements, nesting and feeding habits, and what ecological factors prevented them from inter-breeding. Using a hand net, I caught 78 birds of both species and marked them with plastic leg bands in different colour combinations so that each could be individually identified. I also undertook a census of the fur and Elephant Seals around the entire coastline, investigated the house mouse population, looked after the weather station and co-ordinated the keeping of standard meteorological records.[9]

At 6 a.m. on 3 February the camp woke to a loud blast on a ship's siren. The MV *Taranui* had called while on a hydrographic cruise for the NZ Oceanographic Institute. Three hours later a party of five came ashore led by Norman Ridgeway, who had camped with me on Enderby Island in November 1954. After a cup of coffee the visitors explored Reef Point while several of us wrote letters home to be posted in Wellington in a week's time. Our visitors left at midday, but their ship remained at anchor for another six hours, occupying a temperature and salinity station between Reef Point and Bollons Island.

INITIAL EXPLORATION

Brian and I shared the common interest of inspecting the entire coastline and reaching all parts of the island. After a few day-excursions to places such as the Northern Plain, Leeward Island, Conical hill, North Cape and south along the north-western cliffs, we decided to camp out to investigate more southern parts. On 3 February, Eric and Peter had returned from an overnight trek to the central parts of the island and reported "many errors in the existing map – mainly that there were two ridges south of Mt. Galloway".[10] They had also left the expedition's only portable tent on the Central Plateau as a semi-permanent field base. However, we were initially interested in more coastal places, and on 7 February left for Ringdove Bay and Albatross Point intent on sleeping out and hopefully finding dry ledges or caves if the weather turned rough.

That day, as usual, we made notes on parakeets, albatrosses, giant petrels, and other birds. We also banded albatrosses and mapped the distribution of penguin colonies and seals from above the cliffs. Eventually we worked our way along the plateau edge behind Ringdove Bay and right out along the ridge leading to Albatross Point. Here progress was very slow, and views down into many of the small bays hindered by the rugged terrain and thick tussock. Later that evening we returned to our packs at Ringdove Stream, and as the night was fine, camped out among low scrub behind the cliff top. Just on dark a little mouse turned up to try to share our evening meal. As we were later to discover, these introduced mammals occurred all over the island, and we often saw their burrows in the sides of old albatross nests. Here and everywhere else where we camped out at night, Brian and I spent time after dark spotlighting with our torches to record the nesting and activity of the smaller, night-flying petrels.

The next morning we were up by 6 a.m. and – after a breakfast of cold rice and dried apricots, cooked the night before, a mug of tea and a few trail biscuits – were soon investigating the birdlife of the valley. Pipits and parakeets of both species were common and unconcerned by our presence. A green parakeet visited and promptly investigated our milk tin, prying and picking at its edges and label. Later, not far away, the rapid and unusual feeding behaviour of a red-crowned female soon led me to its nest in a clump of hard fern. The nest was at the end of a tunnel elbow-length through the thickly tangled fronds, well above the ground, and lined with soft fern fragments. It contained one chick covered in grey down through which feathers were starting to appear.

Around mid-morning we packed up and set off up the southern branch of Ringdove stream towards the highest point of a high ridge to the south, counting pockets of nesting albatrosses on the way. From the top of what is now called Reliance Ridge we could see much of the south coast. There was the rugged eastern part, with steep slopes and high cliffs descending direct to the ocean, and to the west a wide coastal terrace covered with scattered penguin colonies. There was also a little bay sheltered by a peninsula, not shown on our map, on which we could see at least 10 fur seals. The steep slopes below us were almost 1000 feet high, covered with tall dense tussock and interspersed with steep bluffs. It was clear that the best route down was well to the west. Eventually we descended via old slip scars and watercourses to a large penguin colony west of South Bay. Three hours later – after passing through thousands of penguins, banding a group of giant petrels, and traversing less than two kilometres of the coast to the west – cliffs and thick tussock hindered further progress and we headed up once more. Going uphill with a heavy pack through the impenetrable, tall tussock was horrendous. It took all of two hours to reach the ridgeline, even though we tried to keep to what appeared to be the most open ground. From here our route back to base was via the unknown tussock plains and boggy swamps to the west of Mount Galloway. At 9 p.m. that night, almost five hours after leaving the southern coast, we trudged into camp at Hut Cove very tired and hungry, more than satisfied with our journey, and full of information on the geography of the island. This trip had confirmed all our previous suspicions as to the sheer inaccuracy of the 1948 British Admiralty map.

AIRDROP ON THE ANTIPODES

By 8 February we had had no clear radio contacts. Usually when we transmitted there was no answer from either Christchurch or Campbell Island, but occasionally we could hear snatches of messages for us from Campbell. A further problem arose when, after a few days of efficient service, our generator for charging the radio batteries refused to start. All these problems were transmitted to Campbell but without any clear response. We were therefore surprised two days later to hear Campbell Island loud and clear for the first time, saying that an airdrop of a generator had been arranged. On 13 February, Campbell Island was again on-air with the news that a RNZAF Bristol Freighter would carry out the airdrop in a few days time.

Saturday 15 February began calm and overcast with a light north-west wind and occasional drizzle. There was an air of expectation in the camp – this was the day of the first airdrop on the Antipodes, and everyone had an allotted task. The Bristol Freighter was due at 12.20, but at about 9 a.m. Brian came rushing in to say that there was an aircraft approaching, and everyone sprinted to their stations. Peter called by radio and had an immediate reply

– three separate bundles would be dropped. The first parachute came down very close to our marked target and contained a new radio from Phil Howell and a Honda 300 AC/DC generator from the Marine Department. The second chute carrying a package of apples, oranges, bananas and plums was caught by a light breeze and came to rest on the top of one of our radio masts. The third drop contained bread, meat, more fruit, and a copy of that morning's *Press*.

The aircraft made three more circuits (evidently taking photographs), fired a flare and then returned to Christchurch – the whole journey taking about 8 hours and 40 minutes. We were all very impressed by the operation's efficiency, and appreciative to the RNZAF and the Army for the extra goodies. Peter spent most of the day rigging up a new aerial system and that evening had a successful "sched" with Phil Howell in Christchurch. This marked the end of our radio problems. From then on we had reliable contact with Christchurch and when appropriate with the *Endeavour*, although the link with Campbell Island remained unpredictable.

A NEW SPECIES

On foggy nights petrels were attracted to the lights of our camp, and many crashed into the hut, or hit the aerial masts and wires. If we reacted quickly to a thud on the roof or twang of a wire, then often the bird could be caught by hand before it had a chance to take off. These individuals were brought inside and identified, measured, checked for breeding and then released. Only occasionally, either as a result of a prior museum request or the discovery of a new species for the island, were specimens collected. John also had a powerful 100-watt spotlight, which when connected to a wet-cell battery or direct to the generator could be used to lure the birds to crash-land nearby. Further from camp we used our headlamps and torches for the same purpose. The species most commonly attracted to lights were White-headed Petrels, Common Diving Petrels, Grey-backed Storm Petrels and Black-bellied Storm Petrels, but we also saw Sooty Shearwaters, White-chinned Petrels (shoemakers) and others.

I enjoyed these occasions, as one never knew what species, or rarity, would next appear. Probably my most exciting find occurred on the night of 12 February. Brian and I had spent most of that day around camp catching, measuring and banding parakeets, so after dinner – for something different to do – we decided to go spotlighting along the track to the North Plains. While in the lead in thick tussock country about 300 metres above camp, I picked up an odd-looking, mid-sized petrel in the air. I kept the spot directly on it until, disorientated, it eventually crash-landed almost at my feet. It was a *Pterodroma* petrel of a species I had never seen before.

When the bird was examined closely in better light at the hut we were all, at first, uncertain of its identity. John later decided it was a Soft-plumaged Petrel (*Pterodroma mollis*) – a species that had never before been reported in New Zealand, and whose nearest known breeding place was the Crozet Islands, about 8300 kilometres away in the Indian Ocean. The birds were not uncommon in the stream gully above the hut, and three more were caught the same night. The next day John and I prepared study skins of all four birds, two of which were later sent to the British Museum of Natural History for comparison with specimens there.

FURTHER EXPLORATION AND RESEARCH

Immediately following the airdrop, Eric, Brian and I left camp for the south-west part of the island. After negotiating the swampy ground behind what is now called Mirounga Bay (after the Southern Elephant Seals that come ashore there) we crossed several deep fern-filled gullies and climbed various coastal hills while headed in the general direction of Cave Point. The day was calm and parakeets of both species were flying over the plains at heights of up to 200 ft, and for distances of 500 metres or more before landing. So much for the early theories that the Antipodes green parakeet "seldom takes wing" and was losing its power of flight.

There were two Giant Petrel colonies on the high cliff tops, the second on the northern headland (129 metres) of the prominent unnamed Bay ESE of the Windward Islands; and on the boulder beaches and rocky shores below were 21 fur seals. After partly descending towards the bay we found the going too tough, so cut back up to the plateau rim and followed this around to the south where we made camp in the deeply incised stream bed, finding shelter beneath its overhanging banks.

The next morning, before breakfast, I watched a green parakeet feeding a chick just upstream from the camp. The parent called once as it flew across the gully and landed on a solitary bush of the only really woody plant that grows on the island, *Coprosma rugosa antipoda.* After nibbling briefly on a few fresh shoots it flew directly to the top of a tussock covered bank, where a well-grown chick emerged and started to beg with a repetitive high-pitched call – something like "Aw dit dit – aw dit dit dit dit". The chick was fed in a way I had witnessed on several previous occasions. During regurgitation and transfer of food the parent tilts its head sideways while the chick's bill remains upright. This chick was fed several times in quick succession and repeated its distinctive call before each feed – the final note coming just as the bills were interlocked. After six feeds the chick quickly turned and disappeared between the bases of the thick tussocks, presumably back to its burrow. The parent then carefully wiped its bill on a clump of moss before flying off.

Later that morning we headed for higher ground to the west and found the remains of an old castaway signpost dating from 1894 on top of a 219-metre high peak. Cave Point was only one kilometre away. This was a great site from which to assess the distribution of albatrosses, but because of the thick vegetation few were nesting on this corner of the island. Indeed, the tussock here was so thick that it took another two and a half hours to reach the coast directly above the huge sea cave that gives the point its name. Hereabouts we found three Giant Petrel colonies, and had some excitement catching and banding these large aggressive birds. Returning uphill we were surprised to meet Rob, who was exploring and photographing far from base, and then turned north-east across a wide plain towards the western flanks of Mount Galloway. We had hoped to find caves or dry ledges to camp under, but had no luck and eventually decided to spend the night in a creek bed behind the Orde Lees Penguin colony. The day had been fine with scattered cloud but mist came in after dark, much to our delight for it made it ideal for spotlighting and identifying petrels. However the welcome mist was soon followed by drizzle, and then by steady rain. The over-hanging banks of the gully provided a little shelter, and here we huddled in our sleeping bags and their so-called "waterproof" covers.

By dawn our bags were drenched. Brian and I were up early, getting organised and making a brew, but Eric was content to lie in – only the end of his pipe and its smoke, emerging from his tightly closed sleeping bag, indicated that all was well. The rain drove us back to the hut, and for the rest of the day our wet bags drooped from the rafters while the mist and drizzle continued outside. Late that night after a successful radio sched with Christchurch, Peter wrote in the log:

> Brian is outside spotlighting and says that the air is full of mist and birds. The sleeping bags are still wet and hanging from the roof so it looks as if it will be a late night for the birdmen . . . Birds are now crashing on the roof accompanied by the cries of Brian that the sky is full of birds – it seems that the weather is *perfect!!!* for them . . . The wind is definitely getting stronger and I think we are for another bad night.

Thursday 20 February was "a real summer day, calm, dry, and warm" with a smooth sea. Everyone was out collecting, recording, banding, and photographing as far afield as Ringdove Bay, Waterhouse, Galloway and North Head. Several of us had a shower under the waterfall down in Hut Cove, and Rob even had a swim. Ian found the very calm sea ideal for his work, and at low tide collected three species of fish from a pool in Anchorage Bay. However, later in the evening a big swell came in and filled the cove with thick froth. The following day was a complete contrast with fog and drizzle confining work to the vicinity of the huts. By now the airdrop bread was finished and scone-making once again became part of the daily routine.

On Saturday, John, Rob, Ian and Peter left on a fly-camping trip towards the south of the island. After reaching the tent camp on the Central Plateau, Peter left for the Cave Point area to do some surveying, while the other three headed for northern Ringdove Bay. The descent into the bay was along the bank of the northernmost stream – at first through heavy fern and finally through a colony of Erect-crested and Rockhopper Penguins. In two tiny coves to the north of the stream were about 70 fur seals, and they saw others along the coast. Ian made notes and collections on the shore, and the party then returned by the same route. Mist and rain set in during the climb and once over the top they at first went too far to the north, but eventually reached the rock shelter near which the tent was pitched. Wet through and cold they cooked a meal and crawled into their sleeping bags – all four sardined into the two-man tent.

The next day dawned calm and sunny. The southern party went to Reliance Ridge where Peter left them to continue his survey work. The others descended on a reasonably good route to the south coast about 1 kilometre west of South Bay. At their lunch stop near the coast Ian found an ancient fireplace made by early sealers from flat stones, and later Peter found another similar fireplace nearby and also an old stone bottle, which was collected for the Canterbury Museum. Ian researched the marine life of the area, while the others explored the coastal platform further to the west. All returned to the tent on the Central Plateau that night, and were back at base the following morning.

On 25 February, Peter finished off his survey on a high-speed trip with our accurate aneroid barometer to measure the height of the island's high spots – taking in Mounts Galloway, Waterhouse, Reliance and others. The same day, Eric, Brian and I set off for our last three-day trip. South of Orde Lees we encountered dense mist and light rain. Above Stack Bay we, at last, had success in locating dry rock shelters – below rocky bluffs right where the stream plunged over the edge of the plain. The largest, under overhanging rocks, was big enough for cooking and eating, but would sleep only two. However, I soon found another snug hole, just big enough for one, in the side of a lava flow about 50 metres further down the gully. Beyond a raised threshold, it had a dry, level floor of fine rock debris and appeared to have been formed by a bubble in the original lava flow. If only we had been able to find similar shelter on the other rainy nights we had camped out!

The following day was spent on the south coast, where we found a pair of Mallard Ducks in a rock pool. That night we were back up on top of the island

and camped just where Ringdove Stream drops over the cliff into the bay. At the camp site Eric found a new fern for the island, *Blechnum fluviatile.* As was usual at our overnight camps, Brian and I went spotlighting after dark. Petrels of all the most common species were attracted to our lights, but here, also, we were obviously on a White-Headed Petrel colony with the birds landing all around looking for their burrows. I was shortly to gain an insight into how and why there were so many skeletons and partly-eaten corpses of White-Headed Petrels scattered all over the island. The sound of screaming led to a White-Headed Petrel being attacked on the ground by a pair of Subantarctic Skuas. Other similar kills were seen or heard that night. Once ashore in the dark the petrels appeared to have little defence, and like rabbits cornered by a stoat, tended to just sit there, scream and be pulled to pieces. When lit up in the torchlight the skuas on the ground were unperturbed, walking about and waiting to pounce on incoming birds.

The next morning Eric returned to base, botanising on the way, but Brian and I descended the banks of Ringdove Stream almost down to the shore. Once below the mist we had good views of the coast as far north as Leeward Island and counted over 200 fur seals in the southern half of the bay. We encountered green parakeets all the way down the tussock-covered slopes but no red-crowned birds, that species preferring more open ground. In the afternoon we returned to base in light rain, banding albatrosses on the way.

That night was foggy, so the spotlight was rigged direct to the generator and its beam soon lit up the sky. Before long, as John recorded:

> We were bombarded by diving petrels but equally numerous were white-headed petrels, with smaller numbers of shoemakers, mutton birds, black-bellied and grey-backed storm petrels, grey petrels and, the bird Rob and I had lit up 2 nights ago but failed to get, a little shearwater. We eventually got one of these down and later another while Willie Kuschel picked up 3 more and found a better location for luring petrels – the tip of the bank above Stella Bay where we watched till midnight.[11]

PREPARING TO LEAVE

On 28 February we started preparations for leaving the island. Willie picked up his pitfall traps from the North Plains, Brian started to catch three pairs of both species of parrot for taking back alive to New Zealand, and Rob worked on the final repairs to the castaway hut. In the afternoon some of us rigged up an A-frame at the top of the cliff and sent down several loads of boxes and other gear. That night we heard from Campbell that *Endeavour* would arrive at Antipodes at noon on Monday 3 March expecting to "load immediately and sail at sunset". For some time stocks of a few food items had been running low. To eke these out, Peter – who had been appointed quartermaster – allocated a daily ration to cover all hands. A notice was nailed up in the galley:

> Restricted Items:
>
> Sugar. 400gms/day
>
> Trail Biscuits. 2 pkts/day for hut, extras for overnight field parties.
>
> Cake. 2 blocks/day
>
> Butter. 1 lb/day
>
> Cheese. ½ lb/day – a little extra may be taken by overnight field parties.

But otherwise our food and fuel supplies were holding well. Packing of surplus supplies, gear and collections continued the next day. That afternoon Peter and I went up to the North Plain and positioned two markers to assist aerial mapping of the island. These were three-foot square sheets of corrugated iron, painted white, each raised above ground on four stakes, and accurately placed 500 yards apart.

The whole of 2 March was spent in continued packing, dismantling the laboratory hut and getting it down to the shore via the A-frame and pulley. Radio contact continued with the *Endeavour* during the day, and we heard that that she was now arriving earlier than expected – 8 a.m. hours tomorrow. We set up the kitchen in the castaway hut and took down the higher of our two radio aerials. Brian's captive parakeets, which had settled in well to their cages, were moved to a small cave above Hut Cove.

Monday started badly with high winds around midnight, which sent several of us out to fix failed tent guy ropes. The seas were soon pounding into the Cove, and at about 3.30 when John looked over the cliff it was to see that waves were reaching some of our gear. All hands were immediately called to action. Although the seas were huge, the tide high and white foam everywhere, none of our gear had actually been lost. We shifted a few items higher, re-fixed a tarpaulin, and returned to bed to spend a restless night.

At 6 a.m. Peter called *Endeavour* – after repairing a broken radio mast – to hear that the ship was only four miles off and proposed launching a boat and testing conditions. We sent Commander Bamfield greetings on returning to Antipodes Island on the 169th anniversary of its discovery by Captain Waterhouse in HMS *Reliance*, but told him we could see no chance of getting off with our gear in these conditions. Heavy seas continued to pound into Hut Cove all day, as the ship remained off the eastern coast of the island. Whenever she patrolled north into our view, it was clear that she was manoeuvring with difficulty in the prevailing winds and sea. After waiting until 5 p.m., *Endeavour* sailed for Lyttelton to offload its passengers, advising us that she would return by 8 March.

STRANDED

The next day dawned with a moderate north-west wind and an almost clear sky. The sea had reduced considerably and we felt that, with patience, boats could have been worked in the Cove that day without undue risk. In the morning all hands, except the cook, were busy hauling essential food and gear back up the cliff. Peter had a couple of schedules with Phil Howell and heard that the *Christchurch Star* had featured a headline "Scientists Stranded on Island". In the accompanying story the reporter assured readers that the party had sufficient food and "no fears were held for their safety". By mid-afternoon heavy rain set in and the temperature dropped. The castaway depot, now used for cooking and eating, was surprisingly comfortable and cosy with eight people crowded in – and some were reluctant to leave for the great outdoors or the chilly tents.

Brian had brought commercial parrot seed to feed the 12 captive parakeets during their journey back to the Mount Bruce Native Bird Reserve, but that

HMNZS *Endeavour* and ship's boat off Hut Cove, Antipodes Island, 1969. (*John Warham.*)

was insufficient now that our stay was prolonged. The answer was to sustain the captives on one of their natural foods, *Carex appressa* seed. This was easily done by collecting seed heads from the nearby swamp, which became a daily chore during the rest of our stay.

Over the next few days everyone found unfinished research to complete. As well as continuing work on parakeets and seals, I unpacked some of the meteorological gear and continued weather observations. There were many times when boats could have worked Hut Cove, but the *Endeavour* remained in port waiting for a favourable forecast from the Weather Office. On the evening of 7 March we heard, with disquiet, that she was still in Lyttelton, and were told the same on Saturday – with the extra news that they did not expect to leave before Monday. By this time supplies of some foods were completely exhausted, and we gratefully took 6 lb of sugar and a packet of powdered cream from the emergency rations left in the depot seven years earlier by the Oceanographic Institute.

However, overall we had plenty to eat and drink, and were far from starvation. Our two smokers suffered the worst deprivation as they had finished all their tobacco by 2 March in anticipation of a plentiful supply of cigarettes on board *Endeavour* the next day. In fact, the smokers' dilemma had its beginnings right at the start of the expedition. Willie wanted to quit smoking and thought that his prolonged stay at the Antipodes would be a great opportunity. His plan was to take only enough cigarettes to get him to the island and then, once away from the pressures of the office, he would be able to stop. Of course it did not work that way, and he soon needed a smoke. Eric, the only other smoker, generously shared his cigarettes so eventually – even with rationing – these ran out. Eric was not greatly concerned as he still had his pipe, a good supply of tobacco, and it was only three weeks before the *Endeavour* was due. However, Willie still craved tobacco and by using the tissue paper from around bars of chocolate (and adhesive paste) was able to roll cigarettes from pipe tobacco. By efficient rationing, Eric made sure that this supply would last and eked it out right up to the eve of our projected departure. Unfortunately, when the ship failed to pick us up we were left with two smokers without smokes. They then resorted to a few Camel cigarettes left in the castaway depot 22 years before by the *Northwind*. The Camel's label claimed "Choice Quality", but they were now very mouldy and apparently far from satisfactory; nor did the 60-year-old "Strong Plug Tobacco" among the castaway provisions make a satisfying roll-your-own.

On 9 March we were able to speak on the radio with Lieutenant Wilson from *Endeavour*, who explained that the ship was waiting for a favourable weather report for our area, that the USS *Burton Island* might be diverted on its way back from Antarctica to pick us up by helicopter, and that an airdrop of food could be organised if needed. John reiterated that sea conditions changed rapidly and that Wellington could not give an accurate assessment of the situation at the Antipodes. It was necessary to have the ship at the island to take advantage of the periods when conditions were okay, several of which had occurred since *Endeavour* left.

Monday 10 March was one of the most pleasant days of our stay, and Hut Cove remained calm throughout. However, strong winds started to blow from the north-west that evening. After dinner we received advice on the radio that *Endeavour* had left port and would be arriving at dawn on Wednesday. This was great news, except for the fact that the wind outside the depot was then increasing rapidly, and we anticipated an approaching storm. By 11 that night there were gusts of up to 60 knots, together with driving rain. During one particularly violent squall, both sleeping tents began to collapse. In my tent (which was shared with Eric, Ian and Willie) the windward end pole broke in half striking Eric in the back, fortunately without serious injury. This collapse allowed rain in on to the floor where Ian and I were sleeping. At the same time the fly at the other end of the tent flailed loose, and one section and several guy attachment points were ripped. Almost simultaneously the other tent's ridgepole snapped and its fly was destroyed. This tent was lowered and the occupants and their essential gear evacuated to the castaway depot.

As we contemplated the devastation, the wind changed rapidly 90° to the south-west. The neighbouring hills now gave more shelter from the full force of the wind, and we were able to re-erect our tent using a pole from the other. However, our fly could not be made fully secure and one corner of the tent remained exposed, so I moved into the castaway hut as well, where five of us occupied the sleeping benches erected by the shipwrecked crew of the *Président Félix Faure.* As the night wore on the wind dropped to a stiff breeze. In the morning the lowered tent was dismantled and packed. The other could still be used so was straightened up, but it was obvious it would not survive another storm.

The day was sunny with only occasional showers, so gear could be dried out and most remaining equipment was packed and lowered down to the cove. Eric retrieved some of his specimens that had been blown away by the wind, and collected fresh plants to take back alive. Throughout the day the wind slowly decreased. Breaking waves could be seen well offshore. In the strait between Reef Point and Bollons Island the sea was rough and confused due to opposing swells from the east and west. As a result the cove was subject to heavy swell even though the wind was offshore. Towards night the seas began to subside and we hoped for a calm morning to come. On the night's sched *Endeavour* said they expected to arrive at 8 a.m.

Wednesday dawned fine, with moderate westerly winds. The sea conditions looked good, which we reported to *Endeavour* by radio. She arrived on time and came in close, obviously intending to anchor in the shelter of North Cape. However, the ship then told us that the wind and sea made this impossible and she cruised around to the east of the island. The Navy's apparent uncertainty was worrying, as Anchorage Bay and Hut Cove looked as workable as we had seen them in the last 44 days – except for one or two rare occasions. If they could not get us off under these conditions, they never would!

Eventually one of the ship's motorboats came around Reef Point and anchored a buoy at the mouth of the cove. Then, with some difficulty, it reversed into the beach – a mistake, as it had to stand well off for fear of damaging the rudder and propeller. However, I managed to throw them a long rope which we had attached to a rock ashore. This was taken back out, pulled tight and tied to the buoy. There were some anxious moments while the boat turned and became entangled in the kelp in the narrow entrance, but eventually it was able to work its way back bow first into the cove while fastened fore and aft to the taut rope. An engineer officer with a field radio landed. There was a fair amount of slop on the beach and the Captain said he wanted the most important things loaded first, as he was not happy with the sea conditions. He was treating our evacuation as an emergency operation. Meanwhile some of us had been moving the last of our camping gear down to the beach, except for the radio and its batteries. The first boat away carried the captive parrots and boxes with specimens and scientific equipment. Presently a second boat arrived and loaded other priority gear. The boats then continued to load, unload and return, about four times each. Ian went aboard *Endeavour* on the third load to organise the stowage of our various items.

Conditions on the beach were difficult because of the slippery boulders and the breaking seas, which kept the heavy ship's boats too far out for ease of loading. The Captain had agreed to put at least 12 men ashore to help, but apart from the engineer and a radio operator, who both worked hard, there were only two other seamen ashore for part of the time. A lot of heavy lifting was needed, and as John later wrote:

> The brunt of the burden fell on Brian, Rowley and Rob, with Eric a little further back. All of them . . . at times were over their heads in the sea. . . . At first the boat crews weren't adept at pulling out into deeper water when the larger seas came in and one [boat] took several hard knocks on the rocks. A number of boxes got dipped in the sea. Most of them are too large for . . . these conditions where it may be necessary to hang onto a box for several minutes while up to the waist in water until a chance is presented of getting it up and onto the boat's gunwale . . . . . well above head height.[12]

At one stage it looked as though we were going be able to load the hut as well, but the officer ashore was clearly concerned for the safety of the boats. Despite our enthusiasm to finish the job, we were eventually told that the Navy was not prepared to risk the five or six more boatloads needed. We helped Peter get the radio and batteries down the cliff with the block and tackle. Fortunately the radio was loaded safely but the heavy batteries all got soaked and two were dropped when waves caught the loading party, and were last seen in six feet of water.

At Eric's suggestion we then stacked the hut modules, timber and other remaining gear into a cave-like recess at the back of the beach where they would be above all but exceptional seas. The second-to-last boat took some of our party and all our packs, and the rest of us left in the last boat after casting off the fixed rope. Once the two boats were hoisted aboard *Endeavour* she immediately set a course for Lyttelton.

We had been forced to abandon our hut, what remained of the army tents, sacks of marker pegs, bundles of wire netting, the two radio masts, drums of kerosene and petrol, and several empty drums, as well as the A-frame at the top of the cliff. The Navy also left behind their anchor buoy and quite a lot of rope on the beach. During the two hours we had been loading, the sea conditions had changed very little. Although there was clearly some risk of damage to the boats coming in to the boulder beach – particularly to the one that had no forward stem and was therefore difficult to hold bow-on – we felt that the rest of our gear could surely have been uplifted. To us, the trouble seemed to be that *Endeavour* was too unwieldy for inshore use in these latitudes where 30-knot winds are normal, and the heavy ship's boats were too cumbersome for use on a kelp-infested boulder beach. For some reason the inflatable *Gemini*, which had been invaluable when we first went ashore, was not used during off-loading. This was the last major expedition to the island using heavy ship's boats as the main means of inshore support.

CHAPTER FIFTEEN

Expeditions and Visits, 1970–1978

HMNZS *ENDEAVOUR*, 1970

Endeavour called at the Antipodes Islands on around 16 February 1970 to collect the prefabricated laboratory and other gear abandoned at the back of Hut Cove by the Canterbury University party in 1969. She also had a mission on behalf of the New Zealand Wildlife Service to collect more live parakeets. Two geophysicists on board, Peter Fitchett and Keith Dick from Victoria University, were given the task and managed to capture two green and two red-crowned birds which eventually went to the Mount Bruce Native Bird Reserve.

The ship then called at Campbell Island to embark a team of which I was a member. We had been building a fence across the island and shooting the wild sheep off the northern half.[1] The Navy had instructions to transport the prefabricated building from the Antipodes to the University Field Station on the Snares Islands. When it was being prepared for unloading we noticed that at least two of the packages could contain mice, and found droppings in both. One was a large box of wood wool and the other an old army tent – both originally destined for back loading to the mainland. If we had not been aboard they would have been unloaded at the Snares. This showed just how easy it is for undesirable animals to be landed on unmodified islands.

RV *ACHERON* AND *AQUATIC EXPLORER*, 1972

In November 1972 the 76-foot research vessel *Acheron* was chartered by Lester Peterson, a bird photographer of Chicago, in a bid to complete his photographic coverage of all the penguin species in the world. At that date the one species still eluding Peterson was the Erect-crested Penguin, which breeds only at the Antipodes and Bounty Islands. The *Acheron*'s owner Alex Black invited several other people to also take part in the trip.[2] She sailed from Dunedin on the evening of 17 November and moored at the southern end of Ringdove Bay two days later. On board were Alex Black (skipper), Ken Middleton (navigator), Lester Peterson, Gordon Nichols (National Parks supervisor), Lester Ricketts (surveyor), Alan Baker and Frank Climo (Dominion Museum biologists), and Sir Thaddeus McCarthy (a retired Supreme Court judge who was along as Alex's guest).[3]

The next morning Lester Ricketts and Gordon were put ashore to complete survey work started by Bob Miller in 1950, which was needed for ground control for an improved map of the islands. That day, they established four survey stations and took altimeter readings, but cloud defeated any solar observations; Peterson took his first Erect-crested Penguin photographs; and the biologists collected specimens of plants and animals round Ringdove Bay.

Next day, rain and very poor visibility meant no landings, photography or surveying, but the biologists were able to conduct marine trawls to 40 fathoms – in the vicinity of Leeward Island – and collect specimens of seabirds for the Dominion Museum. Conditions improved on the 22nd and most of the party landed, the surveyors being ashore all day. Base lines were measured and bearings taken from four survey stations, including the summit of Mount Galloway, but a murky sky, strong winds and biting cold made the work difficult. All day there were heavy south-west gales, and the seas were building. One squall flipped the alloy dinghy while it was moored to *Acheron*'s stern. An oar was lost and the outboard motor doused. Later the ship had to move to safer anchorage near Leeward Island.[4]

On the morning of 23 November shifting winds forced the ship back to Ringdove Bay, but continuing squalls and heavy surf made landing impossible. Much of the afternoon and that night were spent coping with a dragging anchor.

Late on the morning of the 24th, while anchored in Ringdove Bay with visibility down to 200 metres, Alex switched on the radar to check that the anchor was holding. The next minute the crew heard: "Will you look at this?" Alex was pointing to the screen and there, quite unexpected, about five miles away was an approaching ship. Eventually, and literally out of the mist, came an extraordinary-looking vessel. Shortly, the radio crackled and an American voice asked politely: "White vessel identify yourselves, if you please."[5] The strange vessel turned out to be the *Aquatic Explorer*, a state-of–the-art oil exploration ship fitted out for acoustic research, and operated by Western Geophysical of Houston, Texas. Under command of Captain Denis Wolstenholme, she was conducting seismic surveys for Hunt International Petroleum Company in their various concession areas.[6]

It is claimed that, at first, the Americans thought they were seeing a ghost ship, for they had been at sea for months without sighting another vessel, and the *Acheron* was of traditional design. The *Aquatic Explorer* anchored nearby, helping the New Zealand surveyors by obtaining an accurate fix of latitude and longitude from four satellite passes – then a very novel navigation method for New Zealand. This fix was, in turn, related to one of the survey sites ashore by means of the ship's radar.[7]

Rough seas and snow showers to sea level continued throughout the day, but four people – including Peterson – were able to land near the castaway hut. Once again cloud made solar observations very difficult and the thick vegetation put an end to any further surveying, but Alan did a seal count at Reef Point and Frank was put ashore on Leeward Island to collect inter-tidal specimens. That evening the *Aquatic Explorer*'s captain and first officer visited *Acheron* but were forced to stay longer than intended, for gale-force squalls made their return by dinghy too dangerous. It was not until next morning when Alex manoeuvred *Acheron* up to the survey ship's stern that the two officers were able to jump back aboard.

On the 25th the *Acheron* sailed for Dunedin, reaching it on the morning of 27 November. It had been an eventful and successful trip and, despite being seasick for most of the time at sea, Lester Peterson was thrilled to get his penguin photographs.

KETIGA, 1973

On 15 November 1972, Gerry Clark left Kerikeri in his home-built 6.5-metre plywood bilge keeler *Ketiga* on a circumnavigation of New Zealand, which was to include the subantarctic and Chatham Islands. This sponsored solo voyage was to raise money for the Kerikeri Stone Store Preservation Society.

After rounding Cape Reinga he sailed south through the Tasman Sea, well offshore, and did not see land again until reaching the Auckland Islands on 11 December. After 10 days there and a similar stay at Campbell Island, Gerry left for the Chathams on 2 January. He sailed past the Antipodes Islands in a fog without sighting land, but knowing it was there because of the many seabirds about.

He reached the Bounty Islands on 9 January when, under calm conditions, *Ketiga* motored through to be greeted by four inquisitive killer whales. High among Gerry's impressions of these remote islands were the "clouds" of birds, the smell of guano and the silhouette of a seal in the golden sunset: "The islands were so unspoiled that Gerry found it difficult to imagine anybody had been there before him."[8]

After a stopover of a week at the Chatham Islands, *Ketiga* reached Kerikeri on 6 February. This was a daring and remarkable voyage – without today's aids of satellite navigation, radio transmitters and emergency locator beacons

– considering the small size of the yacht, and that its only auxiliary power was a 4.5 hp Seagull outboard motor.

MAPPING THE BOUNTY AND ANTIPODES ISLANDS

Until 1974 the most recent map of the Bounty Islands was a small inset (1:100,000) on Admiralty Chart 1022. This was based on two sketch surveys carried out in 1886 and 1903. The official map of the Antipodes Group was also on the same chart, on the same scale, and entirely the result of sketch surveys – the last by the *Northwind* in 1947. On 10 December 1972, at the request of the Department of Lands and Survey, the Royal New Zealand Air Force carried out aerial photography to aid more precise mapping of the Bounty Island group. The first new map was Aerial Plan No.1036/5 produced by the Department's Photogrammetric Branch in April 1974, on an approximate scale of 1:14,400. For the first time all the Bounty Islands were shown, and in correct position relative to one another. However, the naming of the individual islands had to wait another four years.

Finally, in 1973, weather conditions permitted the RNZAF, on Sortie 63, to achieve adequate vertical photography of the Antipodes Islands for mapping purposes. Aerial Plan No.1036/4 was produced in 1974 on an approximate scale of 1:27,600. The current official map was published in 1978 as NZMS 272/4 at a scale of 1:25,000.

Further photography was done on subsequent RNZAF sorties to the Bounty Islands during patrols of New Zealand's Exclusive Economic Zone, and was used to estimate the fur seal population of the group.[9] Both fixed vertical large-format cameras and hand-held cameras for oblique photography were employed during flights on 29 November 1978, 29 December 1980, 5 December 1983, 13 December 1993, 7 January 1994, and 9 November 1995. As well as air force photographers, staff from other agencies assisted the project. Lands and Survey photographer Gavin Woodward flew in 1978, I was on board in 1983 and 1994, and Karl Blass of the Department of Conservation took oblique photographs in 1993.

On 24 May 1974, HMNZS *Canterbury* (Lieutenant Commander Ian A.

Hunter) visited the Bounty Islands, with one task being to check the recently drafted Lands and Survey plan. A series of low-level oblique photographs were taken of all the islands from a Wasp helicopter, and were later used to help estimate the numbers of fur seals there.[10] The helicopter was also used to winch the captain on to the castaway depot site where he retrieved two old earthenware water crocks dating from 1891.

CONTENTS OF THE DEPOTS

At first, in 1886, there were sufficient supplies left at each of the two depots for only six castaways. There were medical supplies, blankets and clothes, but no boots — and the only food was biscuit, fat, tinned meat and salt. Shipwrecked persons were supposed to find and prepare other foods with the fishing gear, knives, matches and cooking gear provided. Gradually, boots, tea, sugar, pipes and tobacco and other useful items were added — and the number of castaways catered for at each depot increased to 12. Still sometimes, as happened when the *Président Félix Faure* was wrecked at the Antipodes with 22 survivors, there were insufficient clothes and blankets to go around.

In later years, the standard Marine Department list of depot contents was 12 each of the following personal effects: woollen blankets; underpants; woollen singlets; flannel shirts; pairs woollen socks; three-piece woollen suits; pairs leather boots "watertight bluchers"; cherry pipes. The clothing found in 1969 at the Antipodes depot was of good quality New Zealand and English manufacture. Included were waistcoats (in shades of black, brown and orange) some bearing the price tag of 4s 9d, warm grey or navy flannel shirts, and heavy single-breasted tweed jackets and matching trousers. Some of the suits (displaying price tags of up to 49s 6d) were quite colourful in small checks of red, black and green. Surprisingly, the woollen blankets were also brightly coloured in checks of black, brown, red, yellow and blue.

Food, medical supplies and other consumables consisted of: 12 cwt cabin bread (biscuit); 100 lb beef dripping; 4 cases of preserved meat (beef and mutton) in 4 lb tins; 25 lb tea; 56 lb sugar; 2 dozen tin boxes of matches 250s; 6 lb of strong plug tobacco; 1 pint castor oil; 1 pint carbolic acid and oil; 100 laxative pills; 1 jar zinc ointment; lint and wadding; silk for sewing wounds; 1 packet of surgical needles; 1 pair scissors; and 14 lb yellow soap.

Other gear provided included: six fishing lines "3 hapuka and 3 cod"; 3 dozen assorted fish hooks; 2 sheath knives; 10 lb assorted wire nails; 2 skeins of twine; 1 ball of lamp wick; one packet of sewing needles; 6 sail needles; 1 seaming palm; 12 reels of strong white cotton; 4 packets white tape; 2 Bibles; 1 board game (draughts); and several books and magazines (including *Esperanto Magazine* after 1908).

All the above were packed in sealed, zinc-lined, wooden boxes. In addition each depot contained a shovel, a tomahawk or hatchet, a hand saw, a hammer, a file and/or sharpening stone, a kettle, a frying pan, and a camp oven. At one stage the Antipodes' depot contained a rifle and ammunition for shooting the farm stock that were liberated there. A supply of "mineral water" in earthenware crocks was also provided at the Bounties.

FAR QUEST AND *PARIMAR*, 1974–75

Early in 1974, Bernie Anderson, a fisherman based at Kaiangaroa, Chatham Islands, loaded his boat, *Far Quest*, with crayfish-pots and headed to the Antipodes and Bounty Islands in search of rock lobsters.[11] Apart from a faded inscription in the Antipodes depot reading "Far Quest, B J Anderson, D Karsten, McCutcheon" nothing is recorded of this voyage, but obviously it failed as a commercial venture.

In March 1975, the 62-foot Dunedin launch *Parimar* took two "charity hitch hikers" to Antipodes Island. Nicholas Boyd and Thomm Sandberg, both 23, were attempting "the first true Round-the-World hitch hike from London to the Antipodes and back". When the *Otago Daily Times* reported that if successful they would win thousands of pounds in bets for a British charity for crippled children, local businessman Cliff Skeggs (later to become Mayor of Dunedin) offered his boat *Parimar* for their final passage to the island. A crew was then found – Bill Cobb (master), Ian Kerr (mate), Andy Hopkins (engineer) and Harvey Perkins (deck hand). Also on board were a Television New Zealand camera crew of John Keir, Bob Brown and Ken Saville, and Skeggs' father-in law Bill Ledgerwood.

The launch left Port Chalmers on the evening of 18 March but was forced to return later that night due to a minor engine problem. She finally got underway again at 10.30 next morning and encountered "gale-force winds and 20 ft seas" until Antipodes Island was reached 44 hours later. She anchored in Ringdove Bay for four hours while the hitchhikers, who had obtained an entry permit, went ashore. The launch then circumnavigated the islands before setting sail for Port Chalmers, arriving on 22 March.[12]

In late September *Parimar* returned to the Antipodes while searching for the three-man crew of the missing ketch *Veronica*. Previous RNZAF Orion searches of a wide area of ocean, including that between New Zealand and the Chatham Islands, had proved unsuccessful. *Parimar*'s was the first ship-based search for shipwrecked sailors at the Antipodes and Bounties since *Tutanekai*'s last visit in 1927. The use of the *Parimar* was again donated by Cliff Skeggs to the "Southern Friends of Veronica" search committee, and her 14-man volunteer crew was described as "about the most experienced you could get". Apart from Captain Ken Middleton of the Otago Polytechnic Nautical School, they included "fishermen, yachtsmen, a mechanic, an engineer, a doctor and a representative of Radio Otago".

Parimar arrived off the Antipodes at dawn on 29 September and anchored at Depot Anchorage. The first call was at the depot, as it was hoped that the missing men could have found a haven there. The old hut, however, would have offered little comfort to any survivors as its roof had recently blown off. Nine searchers spent a full day ashore, climbing to the top of the island, but found no sign of the missing ketch or its crew. After an extensive search of the coast of the Antipodes, *Parimar* sailed for the Bounties. Atrocious weather

Tunnel Island, Bounty Islands Group, February 1926. (*Rollo Beck, AMNH.*)

ruled out a landing there, but all the islets were thoroughly scanned with binoculars. The launch returned to Dunedin on 2 October.[13]

RV *TANGAROA*, 1976–78

RV *Tangaroa* (Captain Neil Gillstrom) visited the region on two short scientific cruises in 1976. During the first, on 2 November, a slight northerly swell made for an easy landing on the south side of Depot Island in the Bounty group, but Sandy Bartle and John McDougall had only one hour ashore due to a thick fog that delayed landing for almost six hours. "Huge numbers" of

Erect-crested Penguins, Salvin's Mollymawks, and Fulmar Prions were found to be incubating eggs. "Several hundred" Bounty Island Shags were seen: about half were immature, indicating that this endemic shag was far more abundant than previously thought, and was breeding well. This was the most important finding of the visit. Six Fulmar Prions were collected for taxonomic studies during a cruise around the islands. Bartle collected a few spiders and insects for the National Museum, but no geological specimens were taken owing to the solid granitic rock.[14]

The second cruise was for seismic and magnetic research. At Tunnel Island on 18 November, the geophysicists (A.L. Burrows and M.M. Gill) found it impossible to reoccupy the magnetic station established in 1962 as it had been commandeered by a very aggressive bull seal, with harem and pups. A new station was established "at a lower level and . . . marked by a survey peg wedged into a crack in the rock". They landed at the Antipodes and repeated magnetic observations at the 1962 station above Stella Bay. The party also reported that the roof had gone from the depot, and that its contents were rusted, wet and rotten.[15]

On a subsequent cruise by *Tangaroa* in September 1978, Cameron Hay of the NZ Oceanographic Institute made the first seaweed collections by scuba from Antipodes and Bounty Islands. Dives were made in Stella and Crater Bays on 24 September, and at the Bounty Islands two days later.[16]

CHAPTER SIXTEEN

BAAS Wildlife Service Expedition, 1978

In 1978 an expedition led by Brian Bell and organised by the Wildlife Service visited the New Zealand subantarctic islands aboard HMNZS *Waikato* under command of Captain Ian Bradley. Named the BAAS (Bounty, Antipodes, Auckland and Snares) expedition, this voyage positioned scientific parties on both the Bounty and Antipodes Islands. I was a member of the Antipodes Island Party. *Waikato* also carried ship-based scientists and administrators on short visits to several sites in the Auckland Islands. A planned stopover at the Snares had to be abandoned because of atrocious weather. Altogether, a total of 26 scientists and other civilian personnel were involved.[1]

After leaving Devonport with some expedition members, building materials, stores, small boats and gear on 1 November, *Waikato* sailed for Lyttelton where the main party came on board. The ship left Lyttelton on 6 November and a day later arrived at the Bounty Islands. Here the first task was to find a site to land the shore party – Chris Robertson (leader), Gerry van Tets, and Woody Horning – with their gear and enough stores and fresh water for a month's stay.

AT THE BOUNTY ISLANDS

A strong westerly sea made Depot Island inaccessible, but a suitable landing was found on the rocky north-eastern point of Proclamation Island. Here, using rubber boats, sailors and expedition members landed tents, food, fresh water and equipment amounting to almost two tonnes in weight, most of which was then packed up a very slippery granite slope to near the top of the island. All available ground on the lower slopes was occupied by fur seals, and the higher ledges and crevices were filled with nesting penguins and mollymawks. Fortunately a suitable campsite was found about 30 metres above the sea where a larger than usual sloping rock ledge, sheltered on two sides, was relatively devoid of nesting birds. Here, Chris's two specially designed canvas tents were erected on their wooden floors and anchored to the rock with pitons.

I assisted with the landing and carting, and spent two hours ashore on Proclamation. While this work was underway Captain Ian Bradley, three navy divers, a boatman, Cameron Hay and Woody set out to check diving conditions. They headed for the shelter of the tunnel at Tunnel Island, for Woody's idea was to get rigged up there, and then dive elsewhere. But as he recorded in his Dive Log:

> The captain was an eager fellow and he leaped into the sea as soon as we were ready. So we made a short "reccy" dive. He followed me and I pointed out interesting sights such as nudibranchs, spider crabs, pauas, and sponges. The view was fantastic. Algae drop out at 10 metres or so and the near vertical rock walls are covered in crustose red algae. Animals are scattered here and there and are by no means dense. The walls have the appearance of being swept clean. There must be a tremendous surge through this tunnel area at times.

After 15 minutes they returned to the Zodiac. Later Cameron, Woody, Ian and a navy diver explored the "south gutway" of Spider Island during a 30-minute dive. Cameron collected mostly seaweeds and Woody mainly sponges, echinoderms, and other invertebrates, including a spider crab. A school of 15 small subantarctic cod (nototheniids) swimming close to a patch of weed were the only fish seen.[2]

One of my official projects was to carry out a survey of seals at the Bounty and Antipodes Islands, so later in the day all islets in the group were reconnoitred from the ship's Wasp helicopter with John Newton, of the Lands and Survey Department, and myself on board. In about 30 minutes' flying time I was able to map where fur seals were ashore, make some brief notes and, with John's help, obtain aerial photographs from which counts of seals on all islands could be made. During much of the time the Wasp was flying at between 80 and 115 metres altitude. Despite the great density of wildlife at the islands, there was no problem with birds in the air and no evidence that seals, nesting penguins or mollymawks, were disturbed by the helicopter.

When the photos were later enlarged, counts showed around 2660 seals hauled out on the rocks. However, early November was not an ideal time to get an estimate of the total number of seals associated with the islands. At any rookery the numbers ashore vary seasonally, even hourly with changing weather and tides. The optimum time for a fur seal census is after the cows give birth in December and January. At that stage the number of new-born pups can be accurately assessed, since they are easily recognised and confined to the shore. The total population is then estimated by allowing for species-specific factors such as average age at first breeding, age-related mortality and longevity. Over the next two years further analysis, assisted greatly by photographs taken at the Bounty Islands by RNZAF Orions in November 1978 and December 1980, revealed that well over 3000 pups were being born their annually, and that the total fur seal population of the islands was over 16,000.[3]

Later, before HMNZS *Waikato* left for the Antipodes, Captain Bradley dressed in historical naval garb re-read the proclamation of possession as originally delivered in 1870 by Captain Palmer aboard HMS *Rosario* – only this time the ceremony was ashore on Proclamation Island.

The three-man Bounty Island party camped on Proclamation Island for 13 days until the *Waikato* next called on 20 November. They were the first to spend more than one day at the islands since the Whitney South Sea expedition in 1926, and the first to camp on the islands since sealers from the *Anna* stayed three months there in 1881. Chris's main study was on the breeding Salvin's Mollymawks, Gerry concentrated on the ecology and behaviour of the resident Bounty Island Shag, and Woody made extensive underwater collections and studies. He also collected terrestrial lichens, algae and invertebrates on Proclamation, Tunnel and Depot islands.[4] After Woody attached fixed ropes across the channels, Chris visited Depot and Tunnel Islands by swimming, and Gerry used a telescope to observe nesting shags and other bird life on adjacent islands. Chris and Gerry's survey of bird numbers on the different islands was later expanded with the help of our aerial photos. They obtained population data on nine species, six of which were breeding – but the only land bird seen was a lone starling. Woody discovered about 20 species of terrestrial invertebrates additional to the 12 already known from the islands. At this stage none of the islands had individual names, but the party had copies of draft maps only recently compiled by the Lands and Survey Department from aerial photography. Woody recalls:

> The three of us named all the islets. One evening we sat on an abandoned mollymawk nest with a map on our laps. After examining possible names, we decided on one and had a toast to the newly named islet with overproof rum that the New Zealand navy gave us. Lion Island was so named because from where we sat, the islet looked like a lion sitting down. Spider Islet was not named because there were spiders on it, but because I collected a spider crab there. Needless to say by the time we named all the islets, we were feeling pretty good indeed![5]

During the marine biology programme, Woody found that:[6]

> Diving conditions were strenuous because of the tremendous surge and cold water. Landing on small rock platforms in a heavy swell, and

> collecting small organisms while being swept by the surge were particularly difficult . . . Nevertheless in nine dives, more than 80 samples, containing algae, colonial invertebrates, molluscs, starfish, crustaceans, and other invertebrates, were collected from rock walls, crevices, and ledges down to a depth of 43 m.

He was the only diver, and usually Gerry was his surface attendant. Woody recalled years later:

> He passed equipment down to me on ropes and hauled specimens up cliff faces. If I got into trouble, he was to fish me out of the water. It was not until we were nearly back to Auckland at the end of the expedition that I found that he could not swim!!! . . . What I did at the Bounties, diving alone, was not a good safety idea. I was very experienced and was extremely cautious but still got caught out one time . . . we would not want to encourage people to do what I did.[7]

The occasion he referred to occurred in the gut between Proclamation and Depot Islands while he was trying to prise off an entire kelp plant at its holdfast, 13 metres below the surface. A huge wave set came in above, creating a heavy surge, and he was swept out of the gut, and "ended up at 3 metres depth and about 50 metres away".

AT THE ANTIPODES

HMNZS *Waikato* arrived at the Antipodes early on 8 November and disembarkation was quickly underway. A large permanent hut was to be built near the castaway depot by the Lands and Survey Department so there was much to offload, including the stores and equipment for 13 people – some 18 tonnes in all. The ship's helicopter was used to fly all this (and most of the Antipodes Island party) directly to the site.

This only left the expedition's two boats – an inflatable Zodiac and a 12½-foot wooden clinker dinghy – to be motored the kilometre or so to the island. After the Zodiac was made ready Brian drove it in to land at the rock platform in Anchorage Bay where we planned to store the boats. I was to take the dinghy. The outboard motor was clamped in place and checked ready to go. The only load was a spare motor and fuel tank, and these were laid on the floorboards amidships. The boat was then rigged to the ship's derrick, I climbed in and she was lowered into the sea. While casting off the sling I noticed water inside the dinghy, but took a few moments to realise just how quickly it was rising. After checking the drainage bung and deciding the problem lay elsewhere, it was far too late to be hoisted back up – there was nothing for it but to quickly start the motor and head for shore.

My main concern was for the spare motor, which was slowly being submerged in salt water. Bailing furiously I headed for Hut Cove, as there appeared to be no one on shore in Anchorage Bay. The dinghy's speed dropped markedly as she settled lower in the sea, and when finally beached at Hut Cove there was over 20 cm of saltwater on board. Before being shipped at Auckland, the dinghy had apparently been in storage and had dried out, causing the seams between her planks to open. After a few days soaking in seawater at the Antipodes this problem disappeared, and thankfully minor stripping and prompt attention meant the spare motor was none the worse for its soaking.

Materials for the new hut amounted to about 222 packages and weighed some 11,000 lbs. (the Navy had not converted to metrics). Some 26 loads slung in a net below the helicopter were required to get the materials to the island. All day we were busy unloading the helicopter, sorting stores and hut modules, selecting a site for the new hut, cleaning out the castaway depot, setting up the meteorological station and pitching tents. The old depot was covered with a large tarpaulin and became the cookhouse, radio room and radio-operators' accommodation. The rest of us slept in six two-man tents.

The initial shore party left at the Antipodes comprised: Brian Bell, Phil Moors, Andy Cox, Johnny Kendrick and Mike Soper (Wildlife Service); John Newton and Chris Stewart (Department of Lands and Survey); Rohan Wahrlich (Army); Cameron Hay and myself (DSIR); and Neil Harraway, Bob Brown and Errol Samuelson (Natural History Unit, TVNZ). Brian led the expedition and was involved in many projects, but his main interests were completing a census of the Wandering Albatross population and a general bird survey with special emphasis on the outer islands. In this work he was assisted by Andy, and also later by Chris Robertson. The Wandering Albatross population was found to be larger that previously estimated, and 1200 birds were banded. Some of the mollymawks breeding on Bollons Island were identified as Subantarctic Black-browed, and several of the outer islands were found to support populations of the endemic parakeets, snipe and pipits.

Phil's main study was on the distribution, numbers, breeding and foods of the mice, the only introduced mammals on the main island. He determined their movements and home ranges by live-trapping and individually marking animals. He was also interested in Subantarctic Skuas, studying their foods, breeding and the growth of chicks.[8]

Cameron carried out a survey of inter-tidal and sub-tidal flora and fauna, and made a comprehensive study of the bull-kelp in Stella Bay. After 20 November he was joined by Woody, and together using scuba they dived at 11 sites around both Bollons and the main Antipodes Island, collecting 87 samples of marine algae and invertebrates from depths down to 20 metres.[9] I continued the studies of the parakeets,[10] fur seals and Elephant Seals that I had begun during the University of Canterbury expedition in 1969.

Rohan was an army radioman sergeant seconded to the Expedition as communications officer, medic and cook. Johnny gathered sound recordings, adding 14 new species to the National Sound Collection of birdcalls, and recorded the flora and fauna on both movie film and still photography. Similarly, Mike Soper – a medical practitioner, bird photographer and veteran of many previous Wildlife Service expeditions to the subantarctic – added to the photographic record of the island's birdlife. The television team collected material for documentary films showing aspects of the natural history of the subantarctic, including habitat, animals and plants, the operation of the expedition, and *Waikato*'s fisheries patrol.

On 20 November the *Waikato* returned from Wellington and the Bounty Islands bringing Mike Imber (Wildlife Service), Chris Robertson and Woody; and to take off Mike Soper, Johnny, Neil, Bob and Errol. The ship also carried Bob Falla, Gerry van Tets, John Jenkins, Neil Cheshire, Gerry Rowan, Buzz

Burrows and Mike Gill, all of whom came ashore for part of the day. Bob was a guest of the Navy, John and Neil were on board to record the distribution of birds at sea for the seabird mapping scheme, Gerry Rowan was chairman of the Outlying Islands Reserves Committee, and Buzz and Mike Gill re-occupied the magnetic station for the NZ Geophysical Survey.

The ship's helicopter took me on a flight along the southern coast of the island counting seals between Cave and Albatross points, for at that stage I doubted if we would ever get a chance to survey this coastline adequately from the boats. *Waikato* also collected votes for the General Election from those expedition members who had not already cast a special vote at home. She then sailed for Campbell Island, the Auckland Islands, the Snares and then back to Lyttelton. Election night was 25 November – and we all sat around in the hut, had a few drinks, ate peanuts and raisins, and listened to the radio as the results came in. The National Party with Prime Minister Rob Muldoon was re-elected for another term.

The job of our new scientist, Mike Imber, was to investigate the status, distribution and breeding biology of the small petrels. As most of these are nocturnal, much of his work was done at night using lights. His daytime observations concentrated on skua-killed remains and on burrow and nest surveys. In some burrows, he observed the birds' routine by digging a shaft to the side of the nesting chamber and fitting a lid. The BAAS expedition made several new discoveries regarding petrels because of its timing (November) and the availability of small boats for coastal surveys and visits to the offshore islets. Breeding was confirmed for the first time for Snares Cape Pigeon, Subantarctic Fairy Prion, Soft-plumaged Petrel and Grey-backed Storm Petrel. However, the big petrel discovery concerned the Subantarctic Little Shearwater. Contrary to expectations it was found to be a spring breeder, and on Bollons Island there was a huge population of hundreds of thousands of breeding pairs – certainly the largest colony of this species in the south-west Pacific.[11]

A NEW HUT FOR THE ISLAND

The main task of John Newton and Chris Stewart was the erection of a permanent eight-bunk hut on Antipodes Island. The drive for permanent accommodation arose from a mix of conservation and political concerns. In January 1978 the Minister of Lands requested his Department to provide a preliminary report on "the implications of establishing a presence on the outlying island reserves". The Department saw the objective of establishing people on the islands as primarily one of "on-the-spot supervision and protection, to reduce the risk of unauthorised entry . . . and in appropriate cases to carry out research or programmes of work for the eradication of introduced plants and animals". However, there was the additional political concern: "To reinforce claims of sovereignty and reaffirm that the islands (or some of them) are capable of sustaining human life, a big factor in terms of international agreement for the acceptability of any land as a base for claims to a territorial sea and exclusive economic zone."[12]

In the event the review failed to initiate any further "permanent presence", other than that already existing at the meteorological stations on Campbell and Raoul Islands. However, it did lead to the building of the Antipodes hut as well as a substantial new biology wing at the Campbell Island station. The Antipodes hut had been designed, pre-cut, and partly made up in sections under John's direction at the Department's training centre, Turangi. The hut was L-shaped with a lean-to roof, and a floor area of approximately 42 square metres. There were two bunkrooms each sleeping four, a large central room with sink unit and kerosene stove, a storeroom, and an enclosed entry porch for wet clothes and boots. The windows were glazed in ¼-inch plate glass. Two 900-litre water tanks collected rainwater.[13]

A site close to the castaway depot was chosen for its good wind protection and solid rock below the peat surface. Although the piles were seated on rock, the soft peat caused problems in obtaining a static base for the hut's foundations. This was overcome by digging in "dead men" and bracing the corner piles with wires and steel waratahs. Once the foundation was fixed and the particleboard flooring laid, few problems were encountered. The hut's outer walls had been pre-built in sections already covered with insulating foil paper and vertical timber boarding. The largest measured 2.8 m x 1.6 m and weighed about 150 lb. With the help of other expedition members in shifting and lifting, these and the interior partitions were all up by the end of the third day, and a start had been made on laying the plywood ceiling on top of the rafters. The ceiling was insulated with fibreglass bats sandwiched between two layers of foil. The aluminium roof went on late on the fifth day, an event celebrated with bottles of wine. John and Chris slept in the new hut that night. All walls except the entry porch were then lined with plywood and the bunks installed. Further members of the expedition moved in for the sixth night as the interior was being finished. Next day the kitchen was finished and food supplies were shifted inside. The hut was in full use on the eighth day with only painting and odd finishing jobs to be done.

The castaway depot was now used as the "radio shack" and Rohan's living quarters, while one bench near its door became the "biology lab". On 19 November John and Chris built a stand behind the new hut's storeroom for the two plastic water tanks and connected up the water supply from the roof. While the hut was being built field work was quickly underway. On 9 November some of us spent a few hours cutting tracks through the tussock to Anchorage Bay, Reef Point, and towards the North Plain; and the first regular daily meteorological readings were taken at 9 a.m. hours.

Later John and Chris worked on repairing and documenting the castaway hut and helped out with other projects. On one occasion they were dropped off by the boats at South Bay and, with Brian, further investigated the old fireplaces found on the south coast in 1969. Here they discovered further old ruins, which John measured up and sketched.

THE BOATS

The small boats were the greatest asset of this expedition, enabling the marine scientists to dive on all coasts, close-in surveys of seals and seabird nesting sites, and visits to the offshore islands, none of which had been landed on since the days of Captain Bollons. Occasionally, they were also used to drop offshore parties in Ringdove Bay and South Bay. Both boats were stored in

Anchorage Bay, high on the rock platform, and we checked them last thing at night before turning in. They were used on 16 of the 29 days the expedition was at the islands. The coastline of the group was circumnavigated four times (twice by clinker and twice by Zodiac), and the entire eastern and western coasts were surveyed on several other occasions. All the offshore islets and stacks were investigated close to or landed on. The most important landings were three on Bollons, two on Archway and one on East Windward Island.

On the second day at the Antipodes (9 November), Brian and I commenced the seal survey in the *Zodiac* from North Head down the eastern coast to beyond Albatross Point. We found a total of 79 fur seals and 131 Elephant Seals, about 73 of the latter being young pups. On the way back, Cape Pigeons were observed landing on the cliffs around Leeward Island and at Albatross Point.

Three days later, with Cameron and Andy, Brian and I took the *clinker* down the western coast on a 5½ hour survey trip, around Cave Point to the start of Stack Bay and return. My diary records:

> We counted and mapped the distribution of fur seals and Elephant Seals. Poked into all coves and caves, etc. Saw a starling half way down the coast, also lots of [light-mantled] sooty albatross, cape pigeons and [fairy] prions. Black-backed gulls plentiful. Circumnavigated Windward Islands. Penguin colony [erect-crested] on the SW side of inner island. Landed in first cove south of North Cape while Cameron dived for ½ hour.

In all, 31 penguin colonies, 10 fur seals and 27 Elephant Seals (10 pups) were found between North Cape and the Windward Islands. Comparing the ease of finding these seals from the boats with the difficulty of checking on them from land during the 1969 expedition highlighted just how indispensable small boats must have been to the early sealers left at the Antipodes.

On a later trip with Brian, Mike and Phil, we circumnavigated the entire coastline of the islands in the clinker on a seal and seabird survey. There were no fur seals around Bollons Island, but we saw 13 on the west coast to Cave Point, six on the southern coast to Albatross Point and 257 on the east coast back to Perpendicular Head. Most were yearlings and there was no sign of harems forming – clearly fur seals had not yet re-colonised the Antipodes for breeding. It was obvious that numbers had built up in the three weeks since we arrived, and that the favoured hauling ground was the sheltered eastern coast. In the classification of fur seal sites, Antipodes Island best fitted that of an "immature colony", one where young animals congregated in summer to escape the aggression and mayhem at the breeding rookeries. Probably most of the young animals turning up at the Antipodes at that time were from the Bounties.[14]

Mike mapped colonies where small petrels were breeding or prospecting, finding the largest concentration of Cape Pigeons (about 80 occupied sites) on the north side of Archway Island. On the west of the main island, Fairy Prions were found breeding in rock falls and sea caves. Calm weather enabled us to circle both Windward Islands and cruise close in along the shore of Stack Bay, well inside the offshore rocks. In these conditions the clinker was ideal for survey work: it was stable enough to stand up in for a better view and I preferred it to the smaller Zodiac.[15]

On the morning of 22 November both boats started for South Bay, Brian, Mike, Chris Robertson and me in the clinker, and Andy, Cameron and Woody in the Zodiac. The plan was for the two divers to dive at South Bay and for Andy and me to be left there to spend three days at the south of the island. However, the wind soon increased and once around Albatross Point we encountered a big south-westerly swell as well as a nasty chop. We decided to turn back just short of our destination while abreast of South Islet over which waves were breaking. The divers then worked the south end of Ringdove Bay with Chris in the Zodiac, while Andy and I were put ashore with our packs near the outlet of Ringdove Stream. The surging sea made for a difficult landing, with the clinker being almost swamped when it got caught up on a rock ledge by a descending swell, but Brian's astute seamanship saved the situation.

I had climbed most of the way down the cliffs here and back up again with Brian in 1969, and the vaguely remembered route to the top looked fine from the sea. However, on this occasion, with our heavy packs, it took about one hour's hard climbing. The trick is to enter the deeply incised ravine at the top of the initial debris fan, and then as soon as possible climb out on its true left. At first we went too far up the ever-narrowing ravine and had to turn back at a waterfall. We eventually found a spot just inside the mouth of the ravine where, with shedding and then passing up of packs, we could scramble up the near vertical northern bank. Once out of the stream, it was a simple but hard climb around bluffs and up steep vegetated slopes to the plateau rim at about 180 metres above the sea.

We camped for two nights in the head of Ringdove Stream, visiting the south coast, Reliance Ridge, and the slopes above Stack Bay, before returning to the hut via the Orde Lees valley. Our main object was to record bird distribution, and I was particularly interested in parakeet behaviour. We found both Green- and Red-crowned Parakeets in the valley of Ringdove Stream and throughout the steep fern- and tussock-covered slopes leading down to the south coast – but saw red-crowns only about the penguin colonies. Most of the penguins were guarding chicks (some newly hatched), and were very aggressive and noisy. We found five Mallard Ducks on small pools on the coast and two in a stream east of Orde Lees. In the valley of Ringdove Stream we saw three snipe, and found one of their nests – containing a very small chick and an egg that was just pipping.

Broadly speaking, the daily routine of the parrots living in the patchy vegetation of tall fern, tussock and megaherbs along the valley bottom of the Ringdove Stream started with very active feeding from first light tapering off in intensity till mid-morning. They then gathered at pools to bath, later sitting in the fern along the stream bank to preen and bask in the sun – often dozing with eyes closed and head tucked in near a wing. At one pool, I counted seven red-crowned and three greens within 10 yards of each other. Both species preened using bill and feet but also rubbed their crowns on the edges of *Stilbocarpa* leaves. Later in the afternoon activity increased, with many birds moving higher up the slopes to feed on the short tussock plain. Feeding continued till dark when birds retreated for the night to roost sites in dense vegetation.

THE OFFSHORE ISLANDS

The small islets and stacks lying off Antipodes Island are unmodified gems. A few have been landed on occasionally – some never. We first visited the northern pair of Bollons and Archway Island on 21 November when we mapped all penguin colonies from the sea; we saw no seals. It was far too rough to land on the western side of the group, but Chris Robertson and Rohan got ashore on Bollons Island's eastern reef. From there they telescoped the Black-browed Mollymawks on the cliff ledges above, deciding that some had dark-brown eyes and were possibly of the subantarctic sub-species rather than the commoner New Zealand form. On 29 November, Chris, Phil, Mike, Andy and I landed on Bollons Island for about four hours, while Brian stood off in the clinker.

Our landing was onto a steep rock slope near the middle of the western bight. Mike immediately set off to investigate petrel burrows, Phil to look for any sign of mice, and Chris and Andy headed over the ridge towards the mollymawks. I then climbed up 200 metres to the summit via one of four small penguin colonies. These Rockhoppers were nesting in clearings in dense tussock, and intent on incubating two-egg clutches. Another three colonies were located near the island's northern end and contained mainly Erect-crested birds, many with small chicks. At higher levels Subantarctic Little Shearwater burrows, containing large chicks, were everywhere – as were their skua-killed corpses. I saw three Black-backed Gulls and several skuas. Two skua nests each contained two chicks, and another had a very well-grown youngster. Light-mantled Sooty Albatrosses were flying about and appeared to have nests on the eastern cliffs. Mike discovered Grey Petrels nesting near the summit, and a dead Black-bellied Storm Petrel. Fairy Prions were seen landing on the south-western cliffs, and near here Chris and Andy managed to climb down to a group of 12 mollymawk nests and confirm their identification.

Reischek's Parakeets were plentiful over the entire island, whereas Antipodes Island Parakeets were mainly in taller tussock on the upper slopes. I estimated that Bollons Island probably supported about 180 Reischek's and 60 Green Parakeets. Subantarctic Snipe appeared common: two were seen and others heard. Pipits were everywhere. So also, were Starlings – in ones, twos, and up to eight in a flock. Other introduced birds seen were four Dunnocks (Hedge Sparrows) and one Redpoll.

Bollons Island is very exposed to the prevailing westerlies. There is no scrub or tall fern, and on its accessible western side there is practically only *Leptinella*, windswept *Poa foliosa* tussocks and native nettles low down, and dense *P. litorosa* tussocks interspersed with sedges, *Senecio*, and stunted megaherbs on the upper slopes. As usual I looked for places where sealers or shipwrecked mariners may have found shelter in the past, or where future expeditions could camp. I saw no trace of early residents but did find a potential, if somewhat draughty, campsite under a rock overhang some hundreds of metres north of the landing place and about 20 metres above the sea. It was just south of a stream notch in a line of rocky bluffs, and had enough room to pitch two pup tents on its fairly level floor.

On the afternoon of 2 December, Chris Robertson took Andy and Rohan over to Bollons Island in the Zodiac and then dropped me off on Archway Island. In three hours ashore I had a good look at all parts of this fascinating little island which in many ways is a smaller edition of Bollons, but with an east-west orientation. The easy slopes are to the south, where the best landing is directly below a penguin colony. About 150 pairs of Erect-crested birds and their chicks were in residence, but there were only a dozen or so Rockhoppers nesting, on eggs, and mostly under an overhang at the western edge of the colony. Towards the eastern end of the island, I found three Light-mantled Sooty Albatrosses incubating eggs. The burrows of Subantarctic Little Shearwaters were everywhere amongst the tussock. Four skua nests were found, all with eggs or chicks. Antarctic Terns and Fairy Prions were flying about and landing on the cliffs, and up to 100 pairs of Cape Pigeons were nesting on ledges at the eastern end of the island. At the time of my visit, Archway Island appeared to have about six resident Reischek's Parakeets and three Antipodes Island Parakeets, but one of these flew the narrow 50-metre gap to Bollons Island, so probably there are no true "residents". Pipits were in pairs and very common – I counted more than 20 birds. I did not hear or see snipe, but they had been recorded here earlier by others on our expedition.

The only introduced species were Starlings, and there were signs that many of these were roosting on ledges under an extensive rock overhang high up on the western end. This same overhang, being well-protected from all wind directions except the south-east, is the only place anyone could find shelter on the island. There was no sign of previous human occupation, but I estimated it would easily sleep up to six persons. The island has no streams, but I found freshwater seeps at the western end.

We investigated the Windward Islands many times from the sea, either while cruising past or while "anchoring" the boats by holding onto the fringing kelp. The two islands are steep, rugged and windswept. From the boats we saw parakeets on both, and Cape Pigeons nesting on the cliffs of East Windward Island. The latter island's northern slopes support sparse vegetation of *Poa foliosa, P. litorosa, Carex appressa, Senecio* and *Stilbocarpa,* with a little *Polystichum* fern in sheltered pockets. Near the bottom of the slope, above the spray zone, was a small colony of about 20 pairs of Erect-crested Penguins. On the more sheltered eastern side the steeply sloping top above 80-metre sea cliffs are clothed in windswept *P. litorosa* tussocks.

In good weather it is possible to land on the northern end of East Windward Island and climb to the summit. Rohan with the Zodiac put Andy and Phil ashore here on 3 December. They saw three pair of green parakeets and one red-crowned bird, recorded snipe and pipits, and along the summit ridge found dense breeding burrows of Little Shearwaters. Most likely these petrels also dominate the tussock cap of West Windward Island which is in two parts, separated by a narrow chasm. We could not land on either the main portion or the adjacent stack – and their vertical rock walls suggest that future investigators will require helicopter support.

The only other outlier on the western coast of Antipodes Island is Orde Lees Islet, a steep-sided 107-metre pinnacle lying about 60 metres offshore. There is a very large colony of penguins on the adjacent mainland, but the only birds seen on the islet were Cape Pigeons, breeding or prospecting on the upper cliffs. There is a sparse scattering of vegetation on the pinnacle's steep slopes and ledges, and its near inaccessible summit is crowned with a tiny cap of tussock where perhaps a few petrels may have burrows.

The second-largest offshore island in the Antipodes Group is Leeward Island. It is also the most sheltered – as its name implies – lying close in to the main island's eastern coastline. Encircled by vertical cliffs from 40 to 130 metres high, the island is roughly circular with an irregularly raised rim surrounding three sides of a level summit. Many visitors to the Antipodes have gazed up at its jagged cliffs from the sea, or down on its 11-hectare amphitheatre-like top from the main island. A few have even landed, fleetingly, on rock ledges near sea level – but no one has ever trod its uplands.

The plant life appears diverse with "inland" slopes clad in tussock and fern, and a large level marshy area of tall sedges draining through a gully system to the lower western cliffs, where the vegetation of the steep outward-facing slopes shows a maritime influence. Cape pigeons nest on the cliffs and parakeets have been seen flying overhead, but otherwise the island's natural history remains a mystery. A helicopter landing is the answer, but perhaps managers and scientists should not rush to discover the secrets of Leeward Island. Retaining its pristine, primeval condition should be the first priority.

PENGUINS, SEALS, PLANTS AND PARROTS

While out in the boats or around the coasts checking for fur and Elephant Seals, I also mapped the positions and relative sizes of the penguin colonies. There were 95 distinct breeding colonies, most containing both Erect-crested and Rockhoppers. The largest were three to the west of South Bay, and another near Orde Lees Islet. The latter has a spectacular setting. The main nesting area is on a rock terrace about 20 metres above the sea, backed by tussock slopes and towering bluffs. On the seaward side, the thousands of penguins breeding here can land only on one small, steep rocky point that juts out from the cliffed coastline. There is constant penguin traffic up and down to this point and also across a natural rock arch, about five metres wide, which bridges a deep watery chasm bisecting the two halves of the colony. As the surface of the bridge is covered with nesting birds, for those travelling over it was very much a case of "keep moving, and look straight ahead". Surprisingly, while I watched, very little strife occurred. It seemed that those nesting on the bridge were habituated, and more tolerant than most, to constantly passing traffic. Other penguins recorded during the expedition were two vagrants seen in Anchorage Bay, well north of their usual haunts – a Chinstrap Penguin from Antarctica and a Gentoo Penguin from Macquarie Island.

Another survey, carried out both from the boats and shore, was mapping the distribution of *Coprosma rugosa antipoda* scrub, the only tree-like plant growing on the island. This was confined to the main island where it grew on well-drained, sloping ground, its greatest concentration being on the northern slopes of Mount Galloway. It was completely absent to the south of Reliance Ridge, on plains and plateaux, and generally above about 260 metres.

We saw a strange fur seal on 3 December as the Zodiac was passing a rocky point south of Stella Bay. It had a prominent white chest, and on our closer approach a tuft of dark hair on its forehead became erect to form a noticeable crest. To avoid further disturbance we landed on an offshore rock and from there, with telescope and binoculars, obtained good views. It turned out to be a Subantarctic Fur Seal, a species seldom seen in New Zealand waters as its usual haunts are islands in the South Atlantic and the Indian Oceans. This young male had obviously just arrived and although it remained in the same area until our expedition left, it kept aloof from the New Zealand Fur Seals nearby.[16]

One of our last jobs before packing up to come home was to capture some live Antipodes Island Parakeets for "breeding stock improvement" at Mount Bruce. The species was then held in captivity at four localities – Mount Bruce, Wellington Zoo, Te Anau Wildlife Park and New Plymouth Parks and Reserves aviaries, but all their birds were descended from one male (Y.2385), caught at the Antipodes in 1969, and one female (Y.697), captured in 1970. We had no trouble catching females, but the males were scary and much harder to catch – and it was males that the aviculturists desired. On 5 December, in desperation, I went with Andy and Chris Stewart to Crater Hill, Alert Bay, and to Dougall Stream below the waterfall in an all-out attempt to capture male birds. We saw three males and chased the last one through the tussock and fern for about two hours without success. He had three females in attendance

Penguin colony behind Anchorage Bay, April 1947. Photo by Eichorn, US Coast Guard. (*Elliot Dawson collection.*)

The same penguin colony in December 1989.

and spent much of his time beneath the heavy tussock, where perhaps he was brooding or feeding chicks. During our search we unintentionally caught two females, but released them. In the evening, to our delight, a male perched on the cages of two captive females outside the hut, and I was able to catch him in the net. He was lousy with fleas and had a well-used brood patch, contrary to the condition of 14 females previously captured. This reinforced my theory that once the eggs have hatched the males do most of the brooding and feeding of the chicks. Later that night we heard that the *Waikato* would be arriving at 4 a.m. So this male and two females were the only parakeets we took back to New Zealand. Unfortunately these three birds were not much help to the breeding programme, for none had yet bred when I checked with Mount Bruce two years later.

On 6 December the expedition's personnel and gear were picked up by the *Waikato*'s helicopter and efficiently lifted aboard. The ship then returned direct to Auckland, arriving on 8 December.

THE DECLINE OF THE PENGUINS

During the last 50 years certain crested-penguin populations in the New Zealand subantarctic have undergone dramatic change. At the Antipodes Islands a massive reduction has occurred in the numbers of Rockhopper Penguins, and this trend continues. By comparison, Erect-crested Penguins remain numerous even though their population is reduced.

Several references from the Antipodes in 1950 and earlier indicate that Rockhopper Penguins then far outnumbered Erect-crested, and that both species were much more widespread than they are today. These changes are best illustrated at what was once the largest penguin colony in Ringdove Bay — which 50 years ago stretched almost continuously from the shore to the plateau edge at 200 metres above the sea. Graham Turbott has described the colony as it was in

November 1950: "On the northward portion of the bay we could see the big straggling patches of the penguin colonies . . . the rocky slopes were worn bare by massed birds . . . The more desirable nesting sites had been taken by the big-crested penguins before the arrival of the rockhoppers . . . [which] had established outlying colonies almost as high as the 600–700ft crest . . . It was pleasant after the climb through the congested and deafeningly-noisy penguin colony to come out on the cool plateau."

In the words of one of his companions, Rod Litt, this "mighty penguin colony" had the appearance from the ship of a "black and white scree" slope. Another colleague, Robert Falla, commented that the nests of the Erect-crested Penguins were surrounded and outnumbered by those of Rockhoppers, and that "some nests are on beach boulders near the tide mark, and the penguin suburbs go up the hills inland as high as 800 feet". Photos and movie film taken at the time by Alex Black confirm these descriptions.

By 1969 the upper levels of this once-huge colony had completely disappeared. The previous high-altitude nesting sites were covered in thick tussock and fern. A few smaller colonies of both species still existed nearer the shore, but in these — contrary to the situation in 1950 — Erect-crested birds outnumbered Rockhoppers. By November 1989 there were only six very small patches of nesting penguins in northern Ringdove Bay, with a total of around 250 nests. All were near the shore, and the largest group contained about 70 adult birds guarding 15 Erect-crested and 10 Rockhopper chicks. In November 1995, a further survey found only 129 nests in the same area — 109 Erect-crested and 20 Rockhopper.

Similar decreases have happened elsewhere. A photograph taken on 3 April 1947 by the USCGC *Northwind* clearly shows a continuous mass of many thousands of penguins covering a bare slope up to the base of the basalt cliffs behind the boat landing in Anchorage Bay, about a third of the population being on the top half of the slope above about 15 metres. A later photograph, taken in March 1969, shows much the same extent of bare ground, but with markedly reduced numbers of penguins. By December 1989, there were less than 1000 birds present, and only a few small colonies on the upper slope, all of Erect-crested Penguins. Much of this higher area, which was bare and guano-covered in 1947 and 1969, had regenerated into tussock. By 2000, only one colony remained on the higher slopes where tussocks continued to increase.

The first attempt at a full mapping of penguin colonies on the Antipodes Islands was in 1978, when I found and mapped 95 distinct colonies, 86 of which contained Rockhopper Penguins. Very rough population estimates made that year were 50,000 breeding pairs of Rockhoppers and 115,000 pairs of Erect-crested Penguins.

By 1989, 10 of the original 95 colonies had completely disappeared. Further declines have followed. In 1995 a DOC survey of all coasts found only 52,000 Erect-crested and 4000 Rockhopper nests, while a University of Otago study in 1999 reported "a very concerning trend in Erect-crested Penguins, with a second successive population crash since 1995".

However, although there has clearly been a massive decline over 50 years in the numbers of Rockhopper Penguins breeding at the Antipodes Islands, the extent of change in the Erect-crested population has not been as large, and its documentation is not as clear-cut. In the latter case, the perceived decrease may have been exaggerated by comparing earlier rough estimates with later, more accurate counts.

In 1986 Phil Moors documented a very large decrease, since 1942, in the numbers of Rockhopper Penguins nesting at Campbell Island. We also know that the relatively few crested penguins breeding at the Auckland Islands have likewise declined. There is no reliable information on changing numbers in the still flourishing population of Erect-crested Penguins at the Bounty Islands, but this is not surprising as the first accurate census of an entire island population there was not until 1997. Without careful study involving colony mapping, and accurate nest counts at comparable dates, it is hard to detect changes at high density — say between 3000 and 1000 nests scattered over rough ground.

Significantly, the numbers of Southern Elephant Seal pups born at Campbell Island have slumped by over 95 per cent since 1945. The declining numbers of Crested Penguins and Elephant Seals must be linked to long-term changes in their food supply. It is probable that the now well-documented warming of the Southern Ocean over the last 60 years, and consequent changes in its circulation patterns, has altered the availability of food close to the breeding islands.

It has been suggested that this led the penguins to switch to lower-quality food — fish rather than krill — causing poorer chick survival. However, recent research by David Thompson and Paul Sagar analysing stable isotopes of nitrogen and carbon in Rockhopper Penguin feathers (many collected from old, known-age, museum specimens) shows that the composition of the Antipodes penguins' diet has not changed in the past 120 years. Rather, for the last 50 years, the birds have been unable to find enough food in a progressively less productive marine ecosystem. This has severely reduced breeding success, and led to a gradual decline in the resident population of crested penguins at Antipodes Island.

In November 1950, nesting penguins had plenty of suitable food close to the island — for at night, while the *Alert* was at anchor in Ringdove Bay, H.J. Ollerenshaw noted: "The searchlight when lowered on to the sea revealed the presence of millions of tiny fish and shrimp like organisms. Birds, especially fairy prions and diving petrels, were feeding on them in the beam of light."

As far as I know, no similar observation has been made since. The riddle of penguins disappearing from Campbell and the Antipodes Islands may finally be answered when future oceanographic research shows that this once-plentiful marine life no longer exists within their foraging range.

CHAPTER SEVENTEEN

Expeditions and Visits, 1979–1990

Further Oceanographic Institute cruises to the Bounty–Antipodes area in the RV *Tangaroa* occurred in March and October 1979, August 1980 and March 1981. Messages in the Antipodes Island depot indicate that landings were made on at least three occasions during this period – on 13 February 1980 from an unknown ship, on 13 January 1981 from HMS *Taranaki*, and on 14 March 1981 from *Tangaroa*.

On 1 February 1982 the *Lindblad Explorer* (Captain Chris Coy), en route from Dunedin to Fiji with Lands and Survey Department ranger John Mazey on board as New Zealand Government representative, called at both the Antipodes and Bounty Islands. At 6 a.m. they were off the Antipodes where passengers Zodiac-cruised for two hours to see the scenery and wildlife. Later, at 5.30 p.m., the ship arrived at the Bounties and spent over an hour cruising close to the islands.[1]

In 1983, HMNZS *Otago* (Commander R.J. Eckford) called at the Antipodes and Bounties during the course of a southern patrol (28 March–13 April) of New Zealand's Exclusive Economic Zone. On this voyage, geophysicists Don McKnight and Mike Gill of DSIR took readings at the magnetic stations on both groups. The Antipodes Islands were inspected on 9 April, when three parties of sailors carried out a census of fur and Elephant Seals at the request of Ecology Division, DSIR. The warship also transported scientists to and from Campbell and the Auckland Islands.[2]

On 5 December 1983, I flew from Dunedin with Richard Sadleir on a RNZAF Orion surveillance flight to the Antipodes and Bounty Islands. Our main objective was to check for any increase in the fur seal population of the Bounty Islands. The plane was fitted with a fixed 5" x 5" aerial camera, which enabled vertical black-and-white photographs to be taken from 800 feet. When these photos were later enlarged it was found that seal numbers at the Bounties had increased significantly in the preceding five years, and animals were now hauling out over much more of the group's surface. Of the 7271 seals counted, over 90 per cent were on Penguin, Depot and Proclamation Islands.

HMNZS *MONOWAI*, 1985

The New Zealand Navy's hydrographic survey ship *Monowai* was deployed in the subantarctic in February–March 1985 under Commander Ken Robertson. Priorities for the mission were hydrographic surveying, ground control for topographic mapping, location filming for the National Film Unit's production *Beyond the Roaring Forties* and a variety of research projects by 14 scientists on board.[3] On the second stage of her mission *Monowai* left Dunedin on the morning of 27 February and arrived at Anchorage Bay, Antipodes Island, on 1 March. The ship stayed there for four days with its Wasp helicopter and small craft kept busy surveying, photographing, and transporting film crew and scientists from ship to shore, and around the islands.

Several scientists and a Lands and Survey Department ranger camped on shore in the 1978 research hut for three nights, while others camped out on the tops. On one occasion the four members of the film crew was flown from the ship to the Central Plateau for a short afternoon visit, but were forced to remain there overnight when cloud and mist rapidly blanketed the island. Fortunately a Wildlife Service team of Chris Robertson, Brian Bell and Murray Williams had a small field camp at the Central Plateau, where the film crew obtained food and makeshift shelter. According to Murray:

> Brian and I got there about midday to find CJRR [Chris] well set up. I recall this stack of army food packs just inside his tent and asking if he expected a party from somewhere . . . prophetic words. When the film crew arrived and then got clagged in, those food packs came into their own. Two, or maybe 3 of the crew had to endure the fern and tussock shelters we made for them that night . . . one lucky fellow got to share Chris's tent and use his spare sleeping bag. There were some cold sore bodies in the morning.[4]

Late on 3 March a message from the ship warned those ashore of approaching bad weather and asked all to be ready to be evacuated at 4 p.m. the next day. On the 4th an incident occurred demonstrating the risk of rodents hitchhiking between islands – even by helicopter. A mouse entered my pack while it was lying in the tussocks waiting to be ferried to the ship, only to be caught and killed when the pack was opened on board. That evening the *Monowai* sailed for the Bounty Islands. There, because of rough seas, landings could be made only with the Wasp helicopter. Surveying, filming and shipboard tasks were able to proceed, but most scientists did not get ashore until 7 March.

With most of the surveying finished, and improving weather, the *Monowai* returned to the Antipodes overnight, allowing another full day ashore there to finish off science projects previously cut short. The Bounty Islands were briefly visited again on 9 March to retrieve a satellite receiving instrument placed there, and the improved weather allowed the use of both the helicopter and Zodiacs to get most scientists ashore. The ship returned to Wellington, via Port Underwood, on the morning of 13 March.

The National Film Unit personnel – director Conon Fraser (expedition leader); cameraman Bayly Watson; sound recordist Steve Upston; and film production manager John Cooper – came back with excellent footage, including aerials and underwater sequences, for a major television documentary.[5]

Surveyors Ron Keen (deputy expedition leader) and John Hesseling, in close co-operation with the Navy hydrographic staff, established sufficient survey control to enable future accurate topographical maps to be prepared from aerial photography: geoceiver sites were established on Mount Galloway and at the trig on Depot Island; sun azimuth observations were also completed at the latter site to confirm the precise orientation of the Bounty Group; tidal benchmarks for mean sea level were established at both groups; and 13 photocontrol points were surveyed (12 ground-marked) and photographed from the air at the Antipodes. At the Bounties, the surveyors landed by helicopter on Spider, Penguin, Ruatara, Lion, Funnel, Castle, Molly Cap and North Rock. These eight new trig stations were connected radially to the existing station on Depot Island.[6]

National Museum Director John Yaldwyn was advisor to the Film Unit, and made collections of seaweeds, invertebrates, and ferns; the Wildlife Service team carried out research on Wandering Albatross and other birds. While Chris concentrated on albatross biology, Murray and Brian assessed the suitability of the Antipodes for a possible liberation of the endangered Campbell Island Teal, which were then confined to Dent Island, a small rat-free islet off Campbell Island. During a three-day circuit they skirted the eastern cliff tops, descended to the southern coastal platform, traversed the Central Plateau and returned to Reef Point via the western side of the island. Murray recalls:

> When you think about it, it [relocating Campbell Island Teal to the Antipodes] was an idea that was never going to get off the ground or past the Outlying Islands Committee. We had just taken the first teal off Dent Is. And there was this natural enthusiasm to find them a new home, given that rat eradication from Campbell was clearly impossible (how little we knew!) . . . Back then we were really in a bit of a dilemma . . . There was clear evidence of Dent Island being a tenuous last outpost for teal . . . The reluctant decision was to take some into captivity – but what to do with them if they adapted well and bred . . . so the thinking extended to finding an island refuge somewhere.

Murray and Brian decided that Antipodes Island was really too dry for the species and did not provide suitable shoreline foraging sites. However, they wondered about Bollons Island, "it being without mice, and whether the amphipod population was sufficient" to support a few teal pairs. As we will see later, this could not be checked out until 1994. (Campbell Island Teal were later bred successfully in captivity in New Zealand, and surplus birds released temporarily onto Codfish Island – west of Stewart Island. Then in 2001, following ongoing development of aerial poisoning techniques, the Department of Conservation eradicated Norway rats from Campbell Island. Now, finally, about 50 descendants of teal first captured on Dent Island in 1990 have been liberated back onto Campbell Island.[7])

The 1985 Wildlife party also captured five Antipodes Island Green Parakeets to supplement the captive breeding stock at Mount Bruce. At the Bounty Islands, aerial photographic censuses were made of mollymawk and penguin colonies, and 1000 Salvin's Mollymawk chicks were banded.[8] Lands and Survey ranger John Clay carried out maintenance on the Antipodes Island hut and castaway depot.[9] A highlight of botanist Colin Meurk's research into the plants, soils and vegetation of the Antipodes was the finding of three new species for the island. He made the first systematic collections of lower plants – lichens, bryophytes and algae. Martin Foggo worked with Colin studying vegetation, peat soils, and plant pathogens. On the Bounty Islands they found four crustose lichens and at least two species of terrestrial algae.[10]

Geologist Chris Adams discovered that the Antipodes were dominated by ash eruptions rather than lava flows as previously thought. At the Bounty Islands he discovered and sampled what appeared to be volcanic dykes within the granite rock. Murray Gregory, from Auckland University, studied pelagic litter and shoreline pollution, and assessed the islands' sensitivity to possible oil spills.[11] At sea, around and between the islands, geophysicist Kim Rose obtained magnetometer and gravity meter readings. Gravity readings were also taken on the Antipodes and Bounty Islands with a portable meter.

Cameron Hay studied, photographed and collected submarine and intertidal flora and fauna: a wide range of specimens was collected at both island groups including molluscs, crustaceans, and several new species of fish, as well as a undescribed species of subtidal bull-kelp. Kim Westerskov, marine biologist and photographer, carried out coastal and submarine photography for the National Film Unit and also made collections of undersea life for various institutions. A 20-foot white pointer shark with a red stain in the water near its mouth – no doubt indicating a recent fur seal attack – was seen in a channel between the islands.[12]

Working with Richard Sadleir, I studied the distribution and numbers of parakeets at the Antipodes Islands. We also made observations on the breeding of Antarctic Terns and New Zealand Fur Seals at both island groups. Seven fur seal pups were found at Antipodes Island – confirming that breeding was once more taking place – 150 years after the island's fur seal population was wiped out by sealers, and over 30 years after fur seals started to return again as visitors. In contrast, at the Bounty Islands there were about 1000 pups on Penguin Island alone.[13]

On 1 April 1987 the Lands and Survey Department, which had administered New Zealand's outlying islands for well over a century, was disestablished and superseded by a new Department of Conservation (DOC), which also took over the functions of the also disestablished New Zealand Wildlife Service. Within the next year the Outlying Islands Reserves Committee – which had advised the Director-General, Lands and Survey Department, for nearly 20 years on research and management of outlying islands reserves – was to meet once, under DOC, before also being "dissolved".

THE OUTLYING ISLANDS RESERVES COMMITTEE

This inter-departmental committee was first established in 1967 as the Sub-Antarctic Reserves Committee to advise the Director-General, Lands and Survey Department, on management issues concerning the Bounty, Antipodes, Snares, Auckland and Campbell Islands. In 1971, when the Kermadec Islands were included in the committee's brief, its name changed to the Outlying Islands Reserves Committee (OIRC).

Subsequently the committee also became advisory to the National Parks and Reserves Authority when several of these island groups achieved National Reserve status.

The chairman was the Deputy Director of National Parks and Reserves. He was the only Lands and Survey representative on the committee. Other committee members were appointed (by the Minister of Lands) because of their experience and scientific knowledge of the islands, or their involvement with island administration. At least two of the original appointees had been members of the wartime CAPE expedition. Government agencies with long-term representation included Ministry of Transport (meteorological stations), Ministry of Defence (surveillance and transport), DSIR (research — geology, botany, zoology, marine, etc), Wildlife Service (protected fauna), National Museum (national repository and research), Forest Service (animal control), and the Marine Department/Ministry of Agriculture and Fisheries (marine mammals, fisheries).

During its 20-year term, the OIRC developed policies on such important issues as entry permits, rodent and plant quarantine, tourism, mining, new buildings, historical resources, research, taking of specimens, and the eradication of introduced animals and plants. It also had a small scientific subcommittee to advise on the value of proposed research projects and their priority. The OIRC helped organise several major expeditions to the subantarctic, played a major role in several related conferences, and was involved in the production of management plans for all of the subantarctic island reserves. One of the OIRC's great benefits was the close liaison that developed between the Navy, Lands and Survey Department and other agencies represented on the committee. This resulted in tentative naval operational plans and management needs being discussed well in advance, with the Navy then often taking the initiative in offering ship and helicopter support for many projects and major expeditions.

Lands and Survey considered the OIRC one of its most successful and effective advisory committees. It worked well because the collective experience of the members was directed to the resolution of issues, followed by a firm recommendation. With the formation of the Department of Conservation in 1987, and a subsequent Government review of the need for various "conservation quangos", the OIRC was disestablished early in 1988.

MS *SOUTHERN CROSS*, 1989

In 1989 the Television New Zealand Natural History Unit was producing a two-part series called *Islands*. One story line[14] involved the co-existence of penguins (associated in many minds with the Antarctic) and parakeets (similarly associated with the tropics) on the one small island – so film was needed from the Antipodes. In November that year TVNZ arranged to charter the *Southern Cross*, a 62-foot ketch-rigged motor sailer owned by Alex Black for a trip to the islands. Originally Alex was to skipper the boat but had to withdraw, so at the last minute it was arranged for Gerry Clark to take command. Gerry had wide experience with small craft in the Southern Ocean having sailed solo around New Zealand's subantarctic islands in his little 21-foot yacht *Ketiga* in 1972–73. And later, in the 1980s, he circumnavigated Antarctica during a voyage of three years and eight months in his 36-foot sloop *Totorore*.

Others in the crew of *Southern Cross* were Julian Matsen (mate/engineer) and Greg (deckhand/cook). The television team comprised producer Rod Morris, cameraman Mike Lemon, and their assistant, Craig McKersey. The eminent American botanist Sherwin Carlquist was scientific advisor to the programme, and I was along as guide and DOC representative. *Southern Cross* left Dunedin on 30 November. The trip out was uneventful, except for minor problems with injectors on one of the twin 172 hp diesel engines. But aided by sail we reached the Antipodes at dusk on 2 December, strong westerlies making Ringdove Bay the preferred anchorage for the night.

After dark the wind increased to gale force and violent katabatic gusts screamed down from the high cliffs buffeting the vessel. In the early hours I was awakened by Julian, who was on watch, coming into the after cabin (which I was sharing with the skipper) to say that the anchor had dragged and that we were close inshore. Gerry replied, "I'll come up. Start the engines.", and then calmly got up and started dressing.

I decided it was best to keep out of his way and ask no unnecessary questions, so I stayed in my upper bunk looking out of the porthole. In the glow from the deck lights it appeared as if the moving wave-drenched cliffs were only about 20 metres away. To me it seemed ages before a motor started up – fortunately it fired second time – and even longer before the skipper had finally finished pulling on his sea boots. As Gerry climbed to the bridge I heard a short exchange of voices and the *Southern Cross* was immediately underway. By then I was up and quickly on deck but we were already rapidly leaving the cliffs behind, for on reaching the bridge Gerry had engaged the engines and steered for the open bay pulling the anchor along with us. Later the wind eased and the anchors were reset further out, and the night ended without further incident. As on later occasions when navigating past submerged rocks, I formed an enduring impression of Gerry's astute seamanship and exceptional calmness under pressure.

Later that morning, we landed at a penguin colony near Ringdove Stream. It was immediately obvious that the penguins were having a very poor breeding season. Of 30 pairs of Rockhoppers with nests, 20 had chicks less than one week old but the other nests were empty. There were about 200 pairs of Erect-crested Penguins nearby, but more than half the nests were empty and the oldest chicks were much younger than usual for that time of year. In the afternoon the film crew, Sherwin and I were landed at Anchorage Bay and set up camp in the 1978 expedition hut. We remained based here until we left the island on 8 December. The TV crew filmed around Hut Point, Anchorage Bay and the North Plains over the next three days.

On 5 December I was taken in the *Southern Cross* to investigate the penguin and seal populations between Albatross Point and Stella Bay on the east coast. The weather was fine and Julian was able to take the rubber dinghy close in around the shore, probing into all the bays, coves and caves. I made numerous landings and counted penguin chicks, Elephant Seals and fur seals. There were 16 penguin colonies between Albatross Point and Leeward Island, but only 227 chicks in total – 42 Rockhopper and 185 Erect-crested. One colony at the south end of Ringdove Bay had 60 Erect-crested Penguins standing near empty nests and only one live chick; two nearby colony sites were completely deserted. Obviously the birds' normal food supply at sea had failed.

On 6 December, all of the shore party walked overland to the point adjacent to Orde Lees Island where there was a massive penguin colony of both species. Here breeding success appeared better, at about 50 per cent. The camera team obtained much footage of parakeets, pipits, penguins,

Orde Lees Island and penguin colony on main Antipodes (foreground).

skuas, Wandering Albatross, Light-mantled Sooty Albatross and Antipodes Island Snipe – but at the end of the day still had not got the desired, but elusive, shot of parakeets and penguins in the same frame.

The next day Gerry and Julian took me on another ship-and-Zodiac excursion around the rest of the Antipodes coastline, including all offshore islets. In total, we found 85 penguin colonies – 78 on the main island, five on Bollons Island, one on Archway Island and a tiny one of 20 birds on East Windward Island. Five of the mainland colonies, we estimated, contained more than 1000 successful breeding pairs each. Apart from Orde Lees, the other four big ones were to the west of South Bay. Many colonies contained only Erect-crested Penguins, but some included up to 20 per cent Rockhoppers. Only one pure Rockhopper colony was located – 30 pairs inside a snug cave well above the shore between Orde Lees Islet and Cave Point. Landings on Archway and Bollons Islands showed similar poor chick survival, with only 370 Erect-crested and 140 Rockhopper chicks in the six colonies there. Ten small colonies that I had mapped on the Antipodes 11 years earlier had completely disappeared.

Overall, in early December 1989 there were probably about 20,000 pairs of penguins still brooding chicks, with over 90 per cent being Erect-crested. This survey and the one in 1978 showed the tremendous decline that had taken place in the penguin population from earlier times. For instance, 1950 reports and film show that there were then large colonies of Rockhoppers up to 200 metres above the shore on the slopes behind northern Ringdove Bay, whereas nowadays there are six, or fewer, very small colonies of mainly Erect-crested penguins in this locality. The decline has been much more severe for Rockhoppers, particularly on the eastern and northern coasts of the island.

By 8 December the TV camera team had at last achieved some footage of parakeets in a penguin colony. They also saw and caught a Reischek's Parakeet wearing a leg band. It turned out to be a male that I had banded in November 1978. Other highlights of the trip were the discovery of a lone Subantarctic Fur Seal amongst the New Zealand Fur Seals at Reef Point, and the abundant flowering of the colourful endemic plants such as *Senecio*, *Anisotome* and Gentians. On 8 December we packed our gear, and in the late afternoon regretfully left for the Bounty Islands.

At the Bounties the next day the seas were light and the weather fine. We landed for a few hours at Depot Island. The fur seal breeding season was at its height and the rookeries were full of aggressive bulls and harems of cows. We found that the first pups of the season were just being born – the few we saw still had the placenta attached. The rocks were covered with nesting Salvin's Mollymawks, Fulmar Prions and Erect-crested Penguins, the latter seeming to have had a better season than their compatriots at the Antipodes. Noise was incessant. The air over the islands was full of mollymawks and prions, and the surface of the sea, beyond the fringe of surging giant kelp, abounded in penguins – some groups porpoising, some swimming and diving, and others bathing.

A few of us made a quick pilgrimage to what remained of the old castaway depot, while the camera crew filmed. After a rough trip home *Southern Cross* reached Dunedin at daybreak on 12 December.

HMNZS *TUI*, 1990

In 1989, three scientists from the Department of Zoology, University of Canterbury, began planning for a four to five-month-long expedition (September 1989–February 1990) to Antipodes Island. Their main aim was to "describe the breeding system of the Erect-crested Penguin, focussing on behaviour during egg-laying and incubation, and to determine breeding densities and breeding success of the four endemic land birds, fur seals and Elephant Seals".[15] Despite careful planning the expedition failed to eventuate, due to transport and other difficulties. However, over a year later, two of its proposers, Colin Miskelly and Peter Carey, were invited to join a very much shorter expedition organised by the Department of Conservation.

HMNZS *Tui* (Commander Owen Hanley) left the port of Gisborne on 9 October with its main mission being to refuel the meteorological station at Campbell Island. On board were a party of 10 – including DOC staff, zoologists, geologists, and a professional photographer. Late on 11 October the ship arrived at the Bounty Islands where a planned landing was thwarted by fading light and rough seas. However, the zoologists were able to survey Lion Island from inflatable dinghies, and observe Bounty Island Shags, prions, terns, gulls and other seabirds.

Tui reached the Antipodes Islands on the morning of 12 October, and then circumnavigated the group to enable the geologists to obtain an overview of land formations and cliff exposures. At 10.30 a party of 12 were landed at Hut Cove before the ship departed for Campbell Island. The shore party comprised: Ian Thorne (leader), Tim Higham (journalist) and Brian Patrick (entomologist) from DOC; Jane Forsyth and Ian Turnbull (geologists) from the DSIR; Tony Reay (geologist) from the University of Otago; Peter Carey, Colin Miskelly and Simon Pollard (zoologists) from the University of Canterbury; Andris Apse (photographer); and Kevin James and Phillip Donnelly (field assistants) from the Navy. This party spent four nights on the island.[16]

The three geologists, assisted by Ian Thorne, spent two nights camping out to survey as much of the island as possible. The afternoon of the first day ashore was spent on the geology of the Reef Point-Crater Bay area. On the second day, Tony and Ian Thorne travelled to Stack Bay via the north-west side of Mount Galloway and the cliffs near Orde Lees islet, while the DSIR party inspected the east coast as far south as Albatross Point. The following day both teams reached South Bay from different directions. On 15 October, Tony's party returned north via the two highest peaks and the Central Plateau, while Jane and Ian carried on along the south-west coast towards Stack Bay before climbing up and returning over Mt Galloway. The final morning was spent in the Anchorage Bay area.[17]

Colin and Peter concentrated their work on the penguin colonies close to the hut, with occasional trips further afield for work on snipe and seals. Their main study was on egg-laying and egg-loss in Erect-crested Penguins, a subject of great interest to penguin biologists. There had been no previous studies on the topic, since this was the first scientific party to visit the species' breeding grounds during the laying period.

Brian collected invertebrates, particularly moths, often using a butterfly net over the vegetation and lights to attract night-flying insects. He added six Lepidoptera (moth) species to the island's known fauna, and collected 20 of the 22 different moths now known from the island.[18] Simon's mission was to survey the spiders. As only about four species had previously been collected, all from vegetated areas, he concentrated on rocky coastline habitats. In all he discovered about a dozen additional species, one – a small jumping spider – being by far the most common.[19]

The two sailors provided support about camp and in the field where needed; and the photographer and journalist roamed the island, camping out overnight "in search of headlands that looked dramatic at dawn and dusk".[20]

On 16 October HMNZS *Tui* returned from Campbell Island and embarked the shore party that afternoon. After an unsuccessful attempt to land the geologists by inflatable at the western end of Anchorage Bay the ship left for Dunedin, via the northeast side of Bollons Island.

CHAPTER EIGHTEEN

Changing Times

The year 1990 marked the start of a new phase in the history of the Antipodes and Bounty Islands. Human contact was to dramatically increase, becoming more frequent with one or more visits each year, though often with much smaller land parties than in the past. Several factors were involved. The main three were the advent of annual subantarctic tourist cruises (no landing permitted), the enthusiastic involvement of Gerry Clark and sailing research vessel *Totorore* in seabird research, and the initiation of a long-term study into the effect of fishing on the Wandering Albatross population.

In mid-December 1990, some 80 ornithologists from the International Ornithological Conference held in Christchurch visited the islands south of New Zealand in Society Expeditions' ship *World Discoverer* (Captain Olaf Hartmann). After a stop at the Chatham Islands they reached the Bounty Islands on 11 December. DOC had issued a permit allowing any passengers who wanted to land to do so, but only 24 would be permitted ashore at one time. In the event only a few people got ashore for a short time on Depot Island before landings were cancelled due to difficulties with swells against the rocks and aggressive fur seals. However, all passengers had extensive tours by Zodiac close in around Depot, Tunnel, Ranfurly and Proclamation Islands. Good views were obtained of all the resident seabirds and Starlings were seen flying over the rocks and "some sharp eyes even noted a Redpoll".[1]

SRV *TOTORORE*

Sailing Research Vessel (SRV) *Totorore* was designed and built, between 1975 and 1982, by Gerry Clark in a fruit-packing shed at Kerikeri. Gerry needed, and constructed, a "good strong boat" to support his dream of studying the seabirds of the Southern Ocean whilst circumnavigating Antarctica at high latitude, in some of the roughest waters in the world. This he did with various crews of two or three ornithologists, and sometimes alone during an epic voyage of 38,413 nautical miles, made over three years and eight months during 1983–1986.

Given the Maori name for the Antarctic Prion, the *Totorore* was broadly based on a plan by Alan Wright. She measured: length overall, 11.1 m (including bowsprit); length at waterline, 8.5 m; beam, 2.9 m; draft, 1.3 m; and had a light displacement of 5.5 tonnes. Built mainly of kauri covered with synthetic cloth and epoxy resin, the yacht was of particularly strong construction, and had twin ballast keels.

She was cutter rigged with furling spars on twin fore stays, and on an inner forestay for a staysail. Each headsail was reefed to suit (from genoa down to storm jib), and had a poling-out spar and one sheet. Downwind the twin headsails were easily set. The mainsail was roller-reefed and furled on the boom. When built, *Totorore* was powered by a Volvo Penta (25 hp) 2-cylinder diesel motor. A new engine, a Volvo 20/30 (30 hp) was fitted in 1998.

The *World Discoverer* arrived off the Antipodes before breakfast the next day and anchored in Ringdove Bay. Zodiacs spent most of the day touring the eastern and southern coasts of the island giving passengers close-up views of parakeets, penguins, many other bird species, seals, kelp-lined shores and magnificent sea caves. The ship then visited Campbell, Auckland and Macquarie Island before reaching Hobart on 21 December.[2]

From 17 to 19 February 1992, Gerry Clark and Grainger Brown anchored in Ringdove Bay towards the end of a three-month trip that took Gerry's yacht *Totorore* to the Three Kings Islands, Fiordland, Bluff and the Auckland, Campbell, Antipodes and Chatham Islands. They did not land at the Antipodes. In fact, Grainger recalls:

> We spent two nights anchored on the south east side of the big island and never went ashore. Gerry was a stickler about only going where he was allowed to. I remember the two of us spending all day cleaning the bilges. We didn't visit the Bountys. Another few days found us at Pitt, where I walked across the island, and then Chatham, before coming home to Kerikeri in mid March. *Totorore* was immaculate everywhere we went except Fiordland where we just had to let the sandflys take over.[3]

During the 1992–93 summer the company Southern Heritage Expeditions, owned by Rodney and Shirley Russ of Christchurch, chartered the 43-metre ship MY *Pacific Ruby* to carry travellers to the subantarctic islands. That season, *Pacific Ruby* – under command of Captain Gerry Clark and usually with Rodney as expedition leader – called at the Antipodes on 24–25 December, 2 January and 14 February; with the Bounty Islands being visited on 26 December, 1 January, and 15 February. During the December visit Rodney and Brian Bell landed (under permit) on the Antipodes to obtain research samples from Giant Petrels. However, under long-standing regulations the 20 passengers were not permitted ashore but were confined to cruising the shoreline in inflatable boats. This voyage was also the last on which tourists were permitted to land at the Bounty Islands. *Pacific Ruby* was at the Antipodes and Bounties again on 14 and 15 February 1993, and 11 and 12 February 1994.[4]

A further aerial census of Bounty Island fur seals was carried out in 1993–94. Karl Blass, from DOC Southland, made the first attempt to obtain suitable photographs during a RNZAF Orion surveillance flight on 13 January 1993, but was defeated by misty weather. On 7 January 1994, I made another attempt on an Orion out of Christchurch when we obtained vertical monochrome photographs covering the whole Bounty Islands Group from altitudes of 1200 to 3000 feet. In addition, oblique colour photos were taken of parts of many breeding rookeries and haulouts from only 300 feet. Another series of photographs not used in the census were shot by the RNZAF on 9 November 1995. When all the photos were enlarged and seals counted, it was estimated that there were around 4380 new-born pups on the islands, and that the overall population numbered about 21,500 fur seals – up by 33 per cent since 1980. The January 1994 flight also took in the Antipodes Group where photos were taken of the mollymawk nesting areas on the cliffs of Bollons Island.

In 1994, Southern Heritage Expeditions returned to the subantarctic islands in the newly chartered *Akademik Shokalskiy*. This 72-metre ice-strengthened Russian vessel was built in Finland in the 1980s for oceanographic research, and was later converted to carry 38 paying passengers as well as expedition staff. Manned by a Russian crew of about 30, she arrived at the Antipodes on 10 December. Strong westerlies confined boating to the eastern coastline. Supplies that were to be delivered to the hut for a forth-coming *Totorore*-supported research expedition had to be left in northern Ringdove Bay. Here, among sub-adult New Zealand Fur Seals, I recorded a male and a female Subantarctic Fur Seal, the first time a potential pair of that species had been seen at the Antipodes. *Akademik Shokalskiy* called at the Bounty Islands the next day, but the weather had not improved and prevented Zodiac cruising. She visited again the following summer, being at the Antipodes and Bounties on 6 December and 7 December 1995, respectively.[5]

ECOTOURISM

The first tourists to visit the Antipodes and Bounty Islands were paying passengers on the New Zealand Government steamers *Stella*, *Hinemoa* and *Tutanekai* during the period 1885–1909 when these ships provisioned castaway depots and searched for shipwrecked seamen at least once, and sometimes three times, a year. In 1910 the NZS *Amokura* took over servicing the depots, and a lack of cabin space curtailed tourist opportunities to the Antipodes and Bounties, until *Tutanekai* returned to carry out the last five patrols to those islands between 1921 and 1927.

The first contact by a designated tourist vessel with New Zealand's subantarctic islands was on 12 January 1968 when Lindblad Travel of New York, in association with the Holm Shipping Company of New Zealand, landed 24 passengers from the *Magga Dan* at the Bounty Islands during a voyage to Antarctica.

The first modern tourist vessel to call at both the Antipodes and Bounties was the *Lindblad Explorer* in February 1982, during a voyage from Dunedin to Fiji. In December 1990, about 80 passengers from the *World Discoverer* "Zodiac-cruised" the coastline of both groups, and a few passengers and guides landed on the eastern shoreline of Depot Island. Since 1992 there have been regular tourist visits to both island groups by Heritage Expeditions of Christchurch — at first with *Pacific Ruby* carrying 20 passengers, later with *Akademik Shokalskiy* carrying 38 to 46, and now with *Spirit of Enderby*.

DOC, as manager of the subantarctic island National Nature Reserves, has the responsibility of preserving the islands' natural ecosystems and heritage values in perpetuity, and visits have been closely regulated since 1967. Although ecotourist landings are permitted under tight guidelines at Auckland, Enderby, and Campbell Islands, they are now prohibited elsewhere.

On both the Antipodes and Bounties all visitors, other than officials, are limited to Zodiac cruising. This offers superb scenery and wildlife viewing. The semi-rigid inflatable boats (Naiads) can approach within inches of the shore. They provide great close-up views of spectacular cliffs with sea caves and arches, deep blue seas, swirling golden kelp, coastal vegetation, a variety of seals, penguins, petrels, shags and other seabirds — as well the two parakeet species on Antipodes Island.

TOTORORE, 1994–95

In February and March 1994, an expedition organised, led and partly funded by Gerry Clark visited the Antipodes Islands.[6] Its main aim was to carry out a census of the Wandering Albatross population and do other albatross research. Its members had also been asked by DOC to assess Bollons Island as a site for temporarily holding a second population of Campbell Island Teal until rats could be removed from Campbell Island. This was Gerry's seventh voyage to the Antipodes. Accompanying him were Gus McAllister, Jacinda Amey and Colin Lougheed, who was providing most of the expedition's funds: his aim was to record its activities using audio, video and still photography.

Totorore sailed from Bluff on the morning of 6 February. She made Alert Bay shortly before midnight on the 12th and unloaded at Anchorage Bay the following morning. During the voyage they had experienced engine problems, so Gerry and Colin sailed her back to Dunedin for repairs, leaving Gus and Jacinda at the hut to carry on with the census and to establish an albatross study area. They also searched for nesting petrels and selected penguin colonies for future monitoring.

Totorore returned on 25 February and stayed for another month. Because there is no consistently safe anchorage at the islands, Gerry had to remain on board most of the time, observing seabirds and surveying their breeding sites. However, he did get ashore on the main island for five days to help Gus and Jacinda and to search for Soft-plumaged Petrels. The result of the albatross census, after over five weeks careful searching in parallel strips, was a tally of 4522 Wandering Albatross sitting on nests with eggs – more that four times a previous estimate of "as many as 1000 pairs" made in 1969. Unfortunately the difference was probably not real, but rather a reflection of the hugely increased effort.

Another important discovery of the expedition was that White-capped Mollymawks nested on Bollons Island, for until then Black-browed were the only Mollymawks known to breed at the Antipodes. On 27 February, Gerry took *Totorore* close in under Bollons Island's south-eastern cliffs. Using binoculars, he identified several White-capped Mollymawks flying about and identified five birds of this species "at nests with chicks", and also Black-browed taking off from ledges where mollymawk chicks, of unknown species, could be seen among the tussock.

On the morning of 12 March, Gerry, Gus and Jacinda landed on Bollons Island to check out its suitability for holding a teal population. Colin then took the yacht offshore as there was nowhere to anchor. The heavy tussock made travel difficult, but the shore party was able to investigate most of the western slopes and over the main ridge towards a nesting colony of White-capped Mollymawks. There had been little rain for over three weeks and the island was very dry, but they found one small trickle of water near the northern end. On top of the ridge were eight non-breeding Wandering Albatross awaiting wind to take off, and one "out-of-use" albatross nest which appeared to be that of a pre-breeder: it will be interesting if, in time, Wandering Albatross start to breed on the island. It was decided that the island was far from ideal as a temporary home for Campbell Island Teal, mainly because it was difficult to access and lacked suitable shoreline or freshwater habitat.

The expedition left the Antipodes on 24 March, and as the yacht passed East Windward Island several White-capped Mollymawks were flying about. One took off from a ledge on the islet – Gerry thought they could be "nesting or prospecting there". *Totorore* arrived at Lyttelton on the morning of 29 March.

Later that year Gerry returned to take the *Totorore* on a second expedition to the Antipodes. This time with Mike Imber, Mark Milner and Christine

Hanel, he left Lyttelton on 13 December and reached the islands on the 17th. They located and recovered supplies left for them in Ringdove Bay by the *Akademik Shokalskiy*. Over the next eight days counts were made of albatross chicks in the study area, and Mike led a search for the Chatham Island Taiko, a rare endangered petrel which it was thought might possibly occur at the Antipodes. This latter work included spotlighting at night and collecting bird skeletons. No taiko were seen, but two taiko-sized skulls were found. *Totorore* stayed around the Antipodes coast throughout the expedition. Poor weather prevented a landing on Bollons Island, but the mollymawk colonies were surveyed and counted from the yacht. The party left the Antipodes on the evening of 25 December and arrived in Bluff on the 30th.

For most of January 1995, *Totorore* was at the Auckland and Campbell Islands. Here its crew investigated the breeding of Wandering Albatrosses on the South West Cape area of Auckland Island, counted Yellow-eyed Penguins, and transported DOC researchers around, as and when required.[7]

On the morning of 5 February, *Totorore* left Bluff once more for the Antipodes with Gerry Clark, Christine Hanel, Gus McAllister and Jacinda Amey aboard, and arrived at the island at noon on 9 February. The main mission was to carry out a complete census of breeding Wandering Albatrosses, and also to undertake the measuring and banding of birds in the previously established study area. The result of the census was an unexpectedly high total of 5757 breeding pairs. A landing on Bollons Island was once again impossible. The population of Soft-plumaged Petrels was closely observed and it was concluded that these birds had increased significantly since their discovery in 1969. From the yacht, the team also counted Light-mantled Sooty Albatross nests and landing places on the eastern side of the group, from Archway Island to South Bay. The expedition left the Antipodes on 27 March and arrived at Lyttelton on 2 April.[8]

While *Totorore* was at the Antipodes another yacht also visited. The 17-metre steel ketch *Koloa* from Wellington, crewed by owner/skipper Ron Palmer, Gavin Stichbury, Vince Belgrave and Alan Knowles, arrived on 26 February. Their voyage was on behalf of the New Zealand Institute of Geological and Nuclear Sciences and was part of an international project to measure deformation across the Pacific/Australian plate boundary. After leaving Bluff on 3 February they had called at Port Adventure, Port Pegasus and the Snares, and spent 7–11 February at Auckland Islands where they set up a GPS station for three days near Pillar Rock at the northern end of the main island. Campbell Island was reached on the 13th, and a GPS receiver operated for three days on Beeman Hill, Perserverance Harbour. Here they were delayed until the 23rd due to bad weather. At the Antipodes, surveyor Vince Belgrave had intended to establish a new GPS survey station near the huts. However, weather conditions precluded a landing there and, after meeting up with Gerry Clark aboard *Totorore* in Alert Bay, a site was chosen on the highest part of the point between Alert and Crater Bays where there is good dinghy access from a deep cove on the northern side. Here a bronze plaque was grouted into the rock and GPS observations made. Later Alan walked overland to the huts to spend the night and much of the next day with the albatross researchers. The ketch sailed direct for Wellington on the evening of 27 February and reached port on 3 March.[9]

While on various trips to the Antipodes, Gerry Clark noted the devastating effects of severe storms on the kelp beds around the island. During the December 1994 visit he was struck by the complete absence of the offshore kelp *Macrocystis pyrifera*, compared with its abundance the previous summer. It was not until March 1995 that "new growth became visible several metres below the sea surface". Similarly, he recorded: "During a particularly severe storm in mid March '95, *Totorore* was forced out to sea for a day and a night, where long stretches of *Durvillaea antipodensis* [the fringing bull-kelp] were observed which had been torn off exposed cliffs on all sides of the island."

SEARCH FOR THE TAIKO, 1995

Ever since a few unidentified petrel skulls were found at Antipodes Island in 1978, the presence there of a breeding colony of the rare Chatham Island Taiko (Magenta Petrel) had remained a possibility – especially since Mike Imber found similar skulls in December 1994. This led to DOC organising an expedition to the Antipodes in 1995, during the most likely season for locating a possible colony. The chartered 45-foot yacht *Breaksea Girl*, owned and skippered by Lance Shaw and crewed by Paul Brimecombe and Mickey Squires left Bluff on 27 October and arrived at the Antipodes early on the 30th. The scientific party comprised: Pete McClelland (leader), Mike Imber (Taiko expert), Graeme Taylor, Alan Tennyson (seabird scientists) and Andy Grant (marine mammals), all from DOC; Terry Greene (terrestrial birds) and Reg Cotter (seabirds/ meteorology); and John Marris and Angus McIntosh (entomologists) from Lincoln and Victoria Universities respectively.

On arrival in relatively calm seas, Alan, John and Angus were landed on Bollons Island to do a brief entomological and ornithological survey to compare this mouse-free outlier with the main island. The rest of the personnel and stores were then offloaded in Hut Cove. All gear was hauled up to the huts and stored, and the three people collected from Bollons Island shortly after midday. As there were only eight bunks in the hut, the two entomologists set up their accommodation in the castaway depot. The *Breaksea Girl* then returned to Bluff in deteriorating weather.

In their search for Chatham Island Taiko over the next four weeks, Mike and others spotlighted on all suitable nights at about a dozen sites scattered over the island. Petrels were captured and banded at most of these stations, but the team concentrated on identifying flying birds. The species sighted in order of decreasing abundance were Subantarctic Diving Petrels, White-chinned Petrels, Grey-backed Storm Petrels, Fairy Prions and Black-bellied Storm Petrels. Soft-plumaged Petrels were locally common in the area from the hut to Alert Bay. In the gully above the hut this species had increased ten to 15 times since 1978. No Chatham Island Taiko were seen and it was "concluded that there are no taiko breeding on the Antipodes Islands". Further collecting of bird skeletons from all over the island produced two more taiko-sized skulls, but it is now thought that these are possibly from rare hybrids between Soft-plumaged and White-headed Petrels.

The timing of the visit allowed Pete to lead a continuation of the Wandering Albatross project. The 156 nests marked in the albatross study area during the previous February were checked and all 118 chicks present were measured and banded – giving a survival-to-fledging rate of 74 per cent.

SRV *Totorore* in Bucket Cove, Bounty Islands 1997.

Jacinda Amey

JACINDA AMEY

Gerry Clark aboard *Totorore*, Bounty Islands 1997.

Jacinda Amey

Above: Sandy King using the desalinator, Bounty Islands 1997.

Below: Heritage Expeditions' ship *Akademik Shokalskiy* at Antipodes Island.

Aaron Russ

Above: New Zealand Fur Seal, Antipodes Island.

Below: Two-week old Southern Elephant Seal pups, Antipodes Island.

New Zealand Fur Seal pups, Penguin Island, Bounty Islands.
9 March 1985.

Above: Juvenile New Zealand Fur Seals and bull-kelp, *Durvillaea antarctica,* Antipodes Island.

Left: Antipodean Wandering Albatross on North Plains.

Above: Antipodes Island Green Parakeet.

Below: Antipodes Island Red-crowned Parakeets.

Jacinda Amey

Above: Leeward Island, with *Totorore* at anchor in Alert Bay, 1994.

Right: Rockhopper Penguin, Antipodes Island.

A total of 2001 fledging chicks were banded.

Alan and Graeme co-ordinated a survey of all penguin colonies. The dimensions of large colonies were measured and counts of average nest densities were then used to calculate the numbers of pairs. Many other colonies had to be estimated from vantage points or from the sea. Totals of 52,000 Erect-crested and 4000 Rockhopper nests were obtained. Two vagrant penguins were seen, a Gentoo and a Snares Crested. Terry carried out further comparative studies of the feeding and breeding of the two parakeets. He made novel observations on the carnivorous habits of Antipodes Island Parakeets, which were found to be killing incubating Grey-backed Storm Petrels in their nest holes. Although the scavenging habits of Antipodes Island Parakeets on bird corpses had often been noted before, this was the first time they had been recorded actually hunting and killing vertebrate prey. Notes were also made on all coastal and terrestrial bird species.

John carried out an extensive survey of the terrestrial invertebrates, concentrating particularly on the beetles, while Angus studied the impact of mice on the main island by comparing its invertebrate fauna with that of Bollons Island, where mice are absent. He also looked at the numbers of mice and invertebrates in areas of different vegetation and altitude, and sampled mouse diet at these different sites. Both entomologists found that the invertebrate fauna of Bollons Island was more diverse, and for some species more abundant, than on Antipodes Island. They concluded that mice were having a major impact on the numbers and composition of Antipodes Island invertebrates, and may already have caused the local extinction of some species. Other work of the expedition included counts of fur and Elephant Seals, and daily meteorological observations.

When *Breaksea Girl* returned to pick up the expedition on 26 November, a northerly swell made both Hut Cove and Anchorage Bay unworkable. Luckily, Stella Bay was still marginal and with three people in wetsuits and the dinghy "hove to just outside the surf" most of the gear was lowered down the cliff on ropes and ferried out to the yacht. However, some large bulky items, such as a generator, had to be left behind in the hut. Finally, after a long and difficult walk, all personnel and their packs were loaded into the dinghy off a very steep and slippery rock on the eastern side of Reef Point. After circumnavigating the group to check penguin colonies, the ship left for Bluff, which was reached on the afternoon of 29 November.[10]

ALBATROSS RESEARCH, 1996–97

On 18 January 1996 an albatross-research team of Graeme Elliott, Kath Walker, Les Moran and Richard Cuthbert left Bluff for the Antipodes in the chartered vessel *Marine Countess.* After a calm voyage the ship arrived at Hut Cove on the afternoon of 20 January. Over the next few years the *Marine Countess* and her crew of Tony Pollock (skipper), Roger Birch (engineer), Nash Norton (cook) and either Mickey Squires or Tom Sawyer (deep-sea navigators) became very experienced at landing expeditions and their gear at the island. Kath recalls that they soon were "very slick about getting their stabicraft craned off the Countess, all the gear up from the hold into the stabicraft, and all our stuff for a 2 month expedition ashore or off the island in about 2.5 hours".[11]

The purpose of the expedition was to establish a long-term study into the effect that commercial long-line fishing in the Southern Ocean was having on the Wandering Albatross population of Antipodes Island. This project, which actually had its beginnings in the work of the *Totorore* expedition of February 1994, was eventually to span more than a decade. Whereas previous expeditions had concentrated on describing the distribution, numbers, and ecology of the plants and animals of the island, the new long-term study involved detailed research on a single species – the Antipodean Albatross. Each summer from 1994, small teams spent two months on the island based in the 1978 research hut near Reef Point. By 1994, the hut had been used for less that 90 days in the 15 years since it was built, but in the following seven years it was occupied for over 360. These regular trips also provided opportunities to gather information and samples for other scientists' studies of Antipodes Island birds, seals and plants.

The albatross teams worked mostly in a 30-hectare study area on the North Plains. Here, each year, all nesting albatrosses were banded with individually numbered metal and colour bands, to be recaptured in subsequent years to assess their survival.

The 1996 party also studied the timing of egg-laying, and started research that monitored the foraging locations of breeding and non-breeding adult albatross by attaching satellite transmitters to seven males and eight females during their first incubation shifts. All this generated a great deal of data, and to cope with it the researchers brought computers and printers, powered with solar panels and an array of car batteries. This party was picked up by Lance Shaw, Tom Sawyer and John Fogarty in *Breaksea Girl* on 9 March and arrived back in Bluff on 12 March 1996.[12]

THE ANTIPODEAN ALBATROSS

Antipodean Wandering Albatrosses are long-lived, usually pair for life, do not breed until about 10 years of age, produce one chick (which is fed for nine months) every two or three years, and spend most of their lives searching for prey — mostly squid — over vast areas of the South Pacific and Southern Oceans. Each year over 5000 pairs nest on Antipodes Island, virtually the species' only breeding ground except for Campbell Island with about 10 pairs.

Being attracted to offal, Antipodean Albatrosses have frequently been caught during the last 40 years on long-lines, baited with squid, being set for bluefin tuna by both foreign and New Zealand fishing boats. It is thought that this increased mortality may threaten the species, particularly as reduced survival due to fisheries by-catch is held responsible for a significant decline in breeding Snowy Wandering Albatrosses in the South Atlantic and Indian Oceans.

Only a few years ago, the population size of Antipodean Albatrosses (and the closely related Gibson's Albatross of the Auckland Islands) was unclear, and almost nothing was known of their ocean wanderings. In 1994, work started on census, banding and breeding studies. Since

1996, Kath Walker and Graeme Elliott have investigated albatross foraging flights during incubation and early chick-rearing using satellite telemetry. Radios, transmitting intermittent signals, are attached as a backpack on breeding birds of both sexes during incubation shifts. The transmitters are attached by a harness or adhesive tape, and are recovered when the parent bird returns to the nest, if they do not fall off earlier as feathers moult. Foraging flights are monitored using the Argos satellite network.

Both sexes of the Antipodean Albatross typically make trips of about 10 days during the 80-day incubation period, and then shorter flights of between one and three days during the three weeks they are guarding their chick. The birds' movements at sea varied little over five seasons. Males tended to forage just south of the Chatham Islands, though some made much longer flights far to the east and south of the Antipodes. In contrast, females foraged north of the Chatham Islands and off the east coast of New Zealand. Within these zones, most individuals appeared to have favourite areas.

It is now clear that both the Antipodean and Gibson's Wandering Albatross are at risk not just from long-line fishing in New Zealand's Exclusive Economic Zone, but also from similar activity within Australia's EEZ and from unregulated fisheries in the Tasman Sea and Pacific Ocean and on the west coast of South America.

On 6 December 1996, Southern Heritage Expeditions' *Akademik Shokalskiy* arrived from Campbell Island and landed supplies at the hut for the Albatross team. This was the last time that I was ashore on the Antipodes. Also on board were Ian Turnbull and Jane Forsyth of the Institute of Geological and Nuclear Sciences, who made a hasty Naiad trip to take readings at the GPS site at the south end of Crater Bay. The next day the ship was at the Bounties.

On 3 January the *Akademik Shokalskiy* was at Antipodes Island again, this time from the Auckland Islands, before departing for Commonwealth Bay,

Antarctica. On board were Kath Walker, Graeme Elliott, Peter Dilks and Belinda Studholme, who had hitched a ride this far to continue the Albatross studies. Their first jobs at the island included banding a sample of 500 chicks in or near the study area, assessing last year's breeding success and determining mean dates of chick fledging and egg-laying. Further satellite telemetry was done on seven albatrosses. Through concerns that poor weather would not allow a landing near the hut during the few hours the cruise ship was at the Antipodes, the albatross team took with them an aluminium Stabicraft dinghy and motor. This was to help ferry stores should they have been landed a long way from the hut, as happened in December 1994. The dinghy was brand-new, on loan, and hauled high up in the penguin colony in Anchorage Bay for safekeeping. Unfortunately, in mid-January, Cyclone Drina hit the Antipodes, throwing the boat – with engine, oars and a climbing rope – into the sea, smashing her against the rocks. Kath writes that the northerly gales sent waves crashing into Reef Point with such force that: "The hut constantly shook on its piles like a moving train for most of the day, and the salt spray sent horizontal 'rain' lashing the hut, though the sky above was still blue."

Fortunately, the cyclone had no lasting effect at the Antipodes, though it caused widespread and serious damage on the east coast of the North Island. On 3 February the *Marine Countess* picked up Graeme and Peter and dropped off Pete McClelland, Mike Avis and Shannel Courtney to help with the albatross programme. She returned again to take this party to Bluff on 27 February. As the researchers were carting their gear piece by piece down to the Anchorage Bay wave platform, they found the climbing rope in its sack in shallow water. It was retrieved and used again for the next seven years as a flying fox to get gear up and down the Antipodes cliffs.

BOUNTY ISLANDS, 1997–98

In 1997 and 1998 Gerry Clark organised an expedition to the Bounty Islands, mainly to study the breeding ecology of the Fulmar Prion. This was a major undertaking.[13] In Gerry's words:

> There were four major legs to the expedition, as well as the voyages of the yacht *Totorore* to Lyttelton from Kerikeri, her home port, and after the expedition, from Lyttelton back to Kerikeri . . . During the period of the expedition the weather pattern was much influenced by "El nino", which gave us generally windy conditions with heavy swells around the islands . . . As there is very little shelter anywhere at the Bounty Islands, and the water is deep, anchoring conditions for *Totorore* were not good. In bad weather, which was frequent, much difficulty was experienced in trying to maintain station at the islands. The anchor was usually stuck among the rocks on the uneven bottom and a great deal of time was expended in retrieving it. Altogether at Bounty Islands we lost three good 20kg Bruce anchors and two 80m lengths of 8mm chain.

The first leg was used to transport gear and stores to the islands, choose a campsite and set up camp in readiness for the researchers. Gerry, Roger Bacon and Donald McDonald left Lyttelton on 1 October and anchored in Bradley Cove, Bounty Islands, four days later. The plan had been to establish the camp on Depot Island, but no suitable site was found, all being too rocky, too exposed and full of nesting birds. The next night they anchored in Bucket Cove, between Proclamation and Tunnel Islands. On the morning of 7 October, in 30-knot south-west winds, they made a thorough, but unsuccessful, search for a campsite around all the Bounty Islands. Eventually, they returned to Bucket Cove, which was the only place where the sea was not breaking heavily. Between squalls a landing place was found on the south-east side of Proclamation Island with a climbable way up the cliff. Don and Roger landed and soon found a suitable camping site on a small rock slab sloping at only about 15°, and protected by a low rock wall on two sides. Next day *Totorore* manoeuvred into Bucket Cove in squally weather to land equipment and stores. The gear was ferried by rubber dinghy, hauled ashore on ropes and then carried in heavy pack loads up the cliff. To be in close touch with his crew ashore, Gerry anchored just outside the cove where there was less swell, but during the afternoon the anchor let go in a very strong squall and the yacht drifted rapidly offshore. He later wrote:

> Using the engine I cleared Blackfish shoal (sticking out from between Lion and Ranfurly Islands) but the sea was already too violent to motor against it so I let her go. My crew called on the V.H.F. so I told them that I would probably be back the following day. That night for them was pretty miserable. They had erected one tent – not easy to secure on a flat rock – and had food and the desalinator (without the instructions how to use it) but had neither sleeping bags nor extra clothing. The temperature that night fell to 3°. The desalinator gave them fresh water, but without instructions they misused it and ruined the membrane so that it never worked very efficiently again.

Away from the islands there were up to six-metre swells, but the wind slowly eased and *Totorore* was back at Proclamation Island to pick up the castaways after an absence of over 24 hours. Throughout the following day changing winds forced her to continually seek shelter from the seas and no landing was possible. However conditions improved on 11 October, when almost all the gear was landed and carried to the camp. Early the following morning, changing winds forced Gerry to anchor closer to Blackfish Shoal, where "occasionally a sea came over the bowsprit, and sometimes another would half fill the cockpit. The close reef had fearsome seas on it, but farther away it was too deep" to anchor. On 13 October the crew were able to make the last adjustments to the camp before Gerry landed for a final inspection. The camp was then packed up and wrapped in a large tarpaulin to protect the gear from the weather, birds and seals. To help with re-erection of the tents, all securing places had been marked with paint. On the 14th, *Totorore* sailed for Timaru, arriving there early on 18 October.

After repairs to the engine, windlass and anchor, *Totorore* sailed again for the Bounty Islands on 23 October with Gerry, crewman Jeff Richards and researchers Jacinda Amey and Sandy King on board. They arrived three days later and immediately landed the two researchers on Proclamation to set up their camp. The yacht moored outside the cove, and the following morning Jeff helped land and carry up the last of the gear and stores. Jacinda's and Sandy's main task was to study the first half of the Fulmar Prion breeding season, which included collecting data on egg-laying dates, incubation and breeding success. They carried out an accurate census of the numbers of breeding Salvin's Mollymawks and Erect-crested Penguins on Proclamation Island. During this, Sandy had a fall on slippery rocks and seriously injured her arm. Jacinda was experienced in first aid and with help from Bluff Radio diagnosed it as badly bruised, fortunately not broken. Even so, Sandy had it in a sling for several days.

While this research was proceeding ashore, the crew on *Totorore* carried out a survey of nesting areas for Bounty Island Shags around all the islands. These shags nest mainly on ledges on steep cliffs high above the water, so counting individual nests was impossible even when Jeff tried by landing at a few sites. They also mapped the landing places of penguins and made many observations on other seabirds and seals. A surprise sighting was a hen Chaffinch seen on Tunnel Island on 29 October. Like all other vagrant European land birds recorded at the Bounties, it was probably blown there from the New Zealand mainland.

On 18 November *Totorore* was sheltering between the north end of Ruatara and Depot Island when in the early hours of the morning the east-north-east wind increased to gale force. The sea rapidly became very rough and it was soon too late to try and raise the anchor. According to Gerry's report:

> The space between our islands and the rocks off the eastern end of Penguin Island was a frightening maelstrom by 0600hrs, so we kept the engine running in case we needed it in a hurry. The huge seas were breaking 20m up on Ruatara and we were very conscious . . . that if any of our anchoring gear failed, nothing could save us. We thought of the girls camping on Proclamation and hoped that the two tents were holding up in the 45 to 50 knot wind. During the afternoon the wind direction changed gradually round to W about 35 knots, and then SW and *Totorore* swung away clear of Ruatara, although still in white water. At 1815 hours the 18mm nylon rope on the end of the anchor chain parted and we rapidly drifted away clear . . . Jeff and I were so pleased that it had not carried away when *Totorore* was in the dangerous area that we hardly minded the loss of anchor and chain.

The camp on Proclamation Island came through the gale virtually unscathed and on 19 November *Totorore* was able to return and embark the researchers and their personal gear. The camp was once more packed up and lashed down on site before the yacht sailed for the Antipodes. *Totorore* reached Alert Bay on the 20th and next morning Jacinda and Sandy were landed at Hut Cove and moved into the hut. Over the next four days, while the yacht anchored in Alert Bay – using two lightweight anchors in tandem and the last remaining short length of chain – the shore party counted and banded about 120 albatross chicks in the study area. They were picked up on the afternoon of 24th and the yacht reached Lyttelton on 29 November. Here, Gerry replaced *Totorore*'s lost and damaged mooring gear, purchasing a new Bruce anchor, 80 metres of chain, and 45 metres of heavy nylon rope. Further engine repairs were also needed.

On 5 December, Andrea Booth, Frances Schmechel and Marinus La Rooy came on board and *Totorore* sailed once again for the Bounty Islands, reaching them on the morning of the 9th. Andrea and Frances set up and occupied the camp and that night *Totorore* anchored in the usual place off Bucket Cove. When they tried to weigh anchor the next morning, the new chain broke at half length, so another anchor was lost. After delivering further stores and fresh water to the camp, the yacht sailed for Lyttelton to obtain a new anchor and chain. They sailed again for the Bounty Islands on the 16th, arriving back three days later. The weather for this third leg of the expedition was generally better than for the previous one. However, those on *Totorore* still had their moments. On Christmas Eve the yacht put to sea when the wind freshened, and returned the next evening to anchor near Ruatara. The next morning they found that the anchor was once again stuck in the rocky bottom. Then followed a sequence of misfortune. To quote Gerry:

> We shortened it to just chain, then a series of 30 knot squalls struck *Totorore* while she was pitching heavily in the swell. The bronze pawl holding the gypsy on the windlass flicked out, and the chain ran away. It was stopped by its terminal retaining rope, but *Totorore* had paid off and was taking the wind on her beam. The rope slipped off the bow roller and jammed down beside it.

> Like that, we tried to reduce the strain on it by manoeuvring with the engine, but without success and the rope parted – so we lost our third anchor.

Gerry then decided to head for the shallower water of the Antipodes where he could anchor with his spare short chain and remaining light anchors. He had expected to keep in touch with the researchers on the Bounty Islands by radio but soon could not hear the camp although they could hear the yacht's stronger signal. *Totorore* anchored in Alert Bay for three days and then returned to the Bounties.

While all this was occurring at sea, Andrea and Frances, ashore, were collecting information on Fulmar Prions – including hatching dates, the rate of chick-growth and a census of all nests on about half of the island. They also completed a study, set up early in the expedition, to measure the impact of the research on the birds. By comparing intensively studied sites with undisturbed control areas, it was found that the investigations had affected the breeding success of Fulmar Prions but not of Salvin's Mollymawks or Erect-crested Penguins. During this leg of the expedition a few Black-backed Gulls, a few starlings, a Spur-winged Plover and a lone Rockhopper Penguin were also seen on Proclamation Island.

Living on the steep rocky island among thousands of seabirds had its difficulties as well as novel moments. Frances wrote:

> The camp was set up on a flattish shelf of rock, one of the only ones on the island. We brought most of our fresh water with us, but also used a hand-pumped desalinator. All the washing was done in salt water. We cooked on a two burner camp stove (burritos, pasta and couscous featured prominently in our diet). The sleeping pads (Thermarests) were very comfy, which was fortunate since the bit of ground under mine was actually rocks stacked up to make it flat. Towards the end of the trip the mollymawks were taking up residence right in camp, roosting on buckets where we stored our gear and on rocks I had moved to anchor one corner of my tent. Occasionally the mollies landed on the tents or tried to take off from them, a bit disconcerting when you're inside.[14]

Attempts from the yacht to grapple for the lost chain and anchor were unsuccessful, and eventually led to the loss of another, smaller anchor and chain. After this they did not anchor again at the Bounties. Andrea and Frances were finally embarked on 6 January. The trip back home took five days after *Totorore* was caught in a gale, ended up at Kaikoura and then had to motor south to Lyttelton.

On 18 January 1998, *Totorore* sailed on the final leg of the expedition to collect the remaining camping gear from Proclamation Island. On board with Gerry were Edward Snowdon and Carl Harmer. They arrived at the islands in calm weather on 23 January and soon had everything aboard the same day. After a quick look around all the islands they left for Lyttelton, which was reached five days later.

ANTIPODES, 1998–99

Albatross researchers Kath Walker and Graeme Elliott were again at the Antipodes from 15 January to 1 March 1998 to assess population changes and survival of banded birds, and to fit further satellite transmitters. They were transported to the island from Lyttelton by the Wellington yacht *Phantom of the Straits*. This vessel, formerly an entrant in a Whitbread Round-the-World Race as *Lion New Zealand*, was a racehorse not particularly well equipped for subantarctic work. Kath recalls that the yacht:

> arrived at the Antipodes without sufficient fuel for the inflatable dingy to get the expedition's stores ashore. A rope was set up in Stella Bay from ship to shore, and the dinghy pulled in and out by hand. This turned out to be a good way of getting through the treacherous beds of giant kelp over huge slippery boulders which had long deterred landings at Stella Bay. Chairs for the hut, to replace the wooden forms, plus a pile of wood for board walk construction around the huts was bought ashore in this fashion.

Nevertheless, the more reliable *Marine Countess* was used to get the albatross team safely back to Bluff at the end of the summer.[15]

On 15 September 1998, three penguin researchers from Otago University, Lloyd Davis, Martin Renner and David Houston, left Dunedin for the Antipodes Islands aboard the *Breaksea Girl*, crewed by Lance Shaw, Mickey Squires, Russell Squires and Barry Eaton. They arrived at the island in the early hours of the 17th, the prevailing swell dictating a difficult landing in Stella Bay. The purpose of the trip was to carry out research into the breeding behaviour of Erect-crested Penguins. This species lays two eggs, but invariably only the much larger second egg survives to hatching. This research provided new insights into how the first eggs are lost from the nest, and why they are laid at all. In addition, the party conducted a census of selected penguin colonies, banded all the chicks produced in the Wandering Albatross study area, and replaced the piles on the castaway hut. *Breaksea Girl* picked them up on 2 November and returned to Bluff three days later.[16]

Albatross work resumed at the Antipodes on 20 January 1999 when the *Marine Countess* arrived with Sheryl Hamilton and Alan Wiltshire. As had become the pattern, their job was to assess adult survival and population changes, and to deploy a further 10 satellite transmitters. The *Marine Countess* returned to pick them up on 26 February.[17] In June the *Totorore* returned to recover the transmitters and carry out further seabird research.

CHAPTER NINETEEN

The Wreck of the *Totorore*

THE VOYAGE

Gerry Clark was to make one more voyage south in the *Totorore* – sailing from Lyttelton late on 30 May 1999 with crewman Roger Sale to carry out seabird research and transport two albatross researchers, Martin Renner and Anja Schulze, to the Antipodes Islands. Since the Bounty Island expedition, a new Volvo 20/30 engine of 30 hp had been fitted.[1] At first the little yacht encountered strong north-west winds, rough seas and three- to four-metre swells, and both passengers were seasick. As on all of Gerry's voyages, seabirds encountered were routinely recorded and this activity started at daybreak. At least 12 different species were noted that day. In the afternoon the winds eased and the following day was overcast, with light airs and decreasing swell. The researcher's log recorded that all crew were well, and that upwards of 18 different types of seabirds were seen. As the northerly wind died away in the late afternoon the motor was started. However, a south-westerly change followed and they were under sail again before midnight, and soon encountering rough seas and four-metre swells. By the morning of 3 June *Totorore* was less than 100 miles from the Antipodes. There were still many seabirds around: 17 species were recorded. All the albatrosses now flying about the ship were the Antipodes Island species, whereas earlier in the voyage up to three different types had been seen.[2]

Totorore arrived at the Antipodes on the morning of 4 June, passing Bollons Island at 6.30 a.m. and dropping anchor in Anchorage Bay. The weather was calm, the air cold, and unloading of the researchers and equipment commenced at 9 a.m. Using the inflatable dinghy, Roger, Martin and Anja got all the equipment and supplies safely ashore at Hut Cove by midday. Roger helped the others carry their gear up to the research hut, which was found to be in good shape although the outside toilet had blown over. They set up the radio aerial and tested the radio, solar panel, satellite phone, gas cooker and other essential gear. By mid-afternoon Roger was back on board, and *Totorore* sailed for the safer anchorage of Alert Bay.

Over the next seven days, while based at Alert Bay, Gerry maintained regular evening radio schedules with the research hut, and also with the marine radio station at Russell, Bay of Islands, and with operator Meri Leask at Bluff Marine Radio. The main job of the two onshore researchers was to recover radio transmitters from previously marked Antipodean Albatrosses. This entailed checking known albatross nests on the North Plains, and catching tagged birds when they returned to feed their chicks. These birds had been radio-tagged several months earlier and were being tracked during their two- to three-week long foraging flights by satellite receiver. The location of returning birds, and their anticipated date of arrival, was radioed to Martin and Anja daily by Graeme Elliott and Kath Walker in Nelson either by satellite phone or via the single sideband radio.[3]

The weather on 11 June was recorded at the hut as: "Min 5°C, max 7°C, wind west 20 kn., overcast, sunny at times, rain showers in morning, dry in afternoon." Martin and Anja received their last radio message from *Totorore* at 7.45 p.m. She was in Alert Bay and reception was good. Gerry mentioned he would be taking the yacht around to South Bay as soon as conditions permitted.

The next day the westerly was down to 10 knots and easing. The morning had sunny periods; there was drizzle in the afternoon, then a "beautiful starry night". That evening the hut spoke with Graeme and Kath in Nelson, but reception was poor and the hut's batteries obviously lacked charge. No contact was made with *Totorore*, but because Gerry and Roger had earlier mentioned difficulties with charging the yacht's batteries, those at the hut felt no concern, particularly as they had their own radio problems.

The weather on 13 June was: "Dry, sunny for a good part of the day . . . Wind west 5–10, almost calm! Min 2°C, max 4°C." Again that evening there was no contact with *Totorore*, but as before this gave little concern – although the hut log did mention "batteries a bit of a worry". On the evening of the 14th the *Totorore* again failed to answer radio calls. By this time Meri Leask was becoming concerned and, after ascertaining that no other station had heard from the yacht in the previous two days, she informed the Invercargill police. It was decided that those on the island should check to see if the yacht was in Alert, Ringdove or South bays as soon as possible.

THE SEARCH BEGINS

Martin and Anja left the hut in the dark next morning at 6.15 and reached Alert Bay in little over an hour. There was no sign of *Totorore*. Anja returned to work at the albatross study area while Martin continued the search to the south in increasing north-west winds and deteriorating weather. His log entry reads:

> Up on the tops visibility was rarely better than 100 m. Drizzle set in by 1030 turning to increasingly strong driving rain during the afternoon. Reached Ringdove Stream Flats by 1100, but got a bit disorientated about my exact position. Lots of fern ahead. Got to, what turned out to be, Reliance Ridge by 1145 and down to South Bay enough to see the coastline through the

> fog/cloud by 1215 . . . I could see the entire shoreline of the bay and a bit to either side: not much offshore though due to dense cloud/fog/rain. Sea is very calm in the bay . . . Had a very careful look . . . but no signs of *Totorore*, crew, or whatsoever.

On the way back to the hut Martin also checked out Ringdove Bay as far as the steep cliffs, gale-force winds and fog would allow. He summed up the day's search: "Conditions were about as bad as can be, but I'm pretty confident *Totorore* is not around – all other bays are exposed to SW or W which were the prevailing winds in the last days. Whereabouts of *Totorore* is a mystery to us, especially considering that the weather has been pretty good until today."[4]

On the radio schedule that night the lack of contact with *Totorore* was discussed, as was the pick-up day (17 June) when the yacht was expected to embark the hut party. Meri Leask informed the Search and Rescue Coordination Centre of her concerns, and the police then contacted Marjorie Clark at Kerikeri – but she was used to such dramas and not anxious. It was considered possible that Gerry had moved away from the dangerous shores of the island when experiencing battery trouble, or was even sailing back to New Zealand for repairs as he had been forced to do during the Bounty Island expeditions. It was decided to wait and delay further action, if needed, until the 18th.

Over the next two days the island party wound down their albatross and Grey Petrel research, and frequently scanned the sea for sign of the yacht. Radio communication between the island and New Zealand became more frequent. On 18 June the Rescue Coordination Centre organised for a RNZAF Orion P3 to fly from Wellington and search the Antipodes area over the next two days. On the 19th the Orion was overhead at 9 a.m., searching the entire coastline several times before flying off to search the sea area to the east and around the Bounty Islands. The plane returned to the Antipodes again at 4 p.m. before landing at Dunedin. Next day the Orion's day-long search was of the area between Bluff and the Antipodes, the seas around and to the east of the island, and finally the area between the island and Lyttelton. The total

South Bay from Reliance Ridge, Antipodes.

area searched included the Antipodes coastline, the Bounty Islands, 18,000-square-kilometres of sea east of the island, and the sea routes between the island and Wellington, Lyttelton, Dunedin and Bluff. Nothing was found.[5] On the evening of the second aerial search those on the island were asked to try to get back to South Bay, descend all the way down and check out the shoreline. They were also told that a vessel had now been organised to join the search and bring them back to Dunedin – the motor ketch *Ranui* was on its way.

The following morning was crisp and clear, with a thin covering of hail and a cold southerly wind on the tops. Martin left the hut at 6.30 a.m. and by 11 had reached sea level at the western end of South Bay. The bay was exposed to the wind and had "2 m waves running through it" and a four-metre swell offshore. He first searched the small caves on the peninsula for sign of Gerry and Roger, but without success. At 11.30 he found several small bits of wreckage along the tide line, in two coves in the north-western corner of the bay. Amongst the wreckage were some pieces, such as parts of the hull and grey-painted lockers, immediately recognisable as being from *Totorore*. One of the coves was inaccessible without climbing aids, but in the other Martin recovered a 40-centimetre structural part of the upper hull to take back to the hut, and moved other wreckage to higher ground. He later wrote in the log:

> Obviously discovering that was quite a shock. So far we had been looking for a ship and/or signs of life . . . Size [of the bits of wreckage] and the fact that pieces from the interior are involved indicate that *Totorore* has been completely destroyed . . . All the pieces found can float, [they] might have drifted into South Bay just today by strong southerly winds. I tried to spend less time with the wreckage and rather search for any signs of Gerry and Roger.

After further fruitless searching along the north side of the bay and on the peninsula, Martin left for the hut at 1.05 p.m., returning through hail showers and heavy snow falls that cut visibility down to 20 metres. The log records: "When the cloud lifted the whole island was covered in a white blanket. Strange kind of emotional mixture, the beauty of the evening scenery with the sombre news from South Bay."

RANUI

The motor ketch *Ranui* was chartered to join the search, and also to retrieve Martin and Anja. This vessel has long been associated with New Zealand's outlying islands, being designed expressly for southern waters and built of local timber at Port Pegasus on Stewart Island, where she was launched for the "island trade" in 1936.[6] *Ranui* later saw continuous service with the coast-watching expeditions (1941–45) to the Auckland and Campbell Islands.[7] In 1999 she had undergone a major refit and was now owned by Richard Allen of Dunedin. She sailed for the Antipodes on the evening of 20 June, but was forced to return to Port Chalmers next morning as her newly installed radio was not working properly. She left again that evening with a crew of Richard Allen, Fossy Fisher (deep-sea skipper), Charles Brassell, and Roy Godman. Also on board were searchers Gus McAllister and Jacinda Amey, who had been with Gerry on *Totorore* during his two-month expeditions to the Antipodes in 1994 and 1995. Shortly after clearing Otago Harbour, *Ranui* heard on the radio the news that wreckage from *Totorore* had been found.[8]

The ketch arrived at the Antipodes at 7.30 on the morning of 24 June. Roy took Gus and Jacinda ashore at the hut with some camping gear and food. They talked with Martin and Anja about Gerry's intentions, what areas had been searched, and what had been found – and confirmed that the piece of wreckage retrieved by Martin "was unquestionably from *Totorore*". Roy then loaded Martin and Anja, and their gear, onto *Ranui*, for Richard was keen that the entire party and all equipment should be aboard each night, if possible. Leaving the hut at 10.30, the searchers navigated through thick fog and drizzle down the eastern side of the island to Reliance Ridge, searching for human sign and calling all the way. From the ridge's eastern saddle they picked up a lichen-covered slip and followed it down to well below the layer of cloud and fog which was blanketing the tops. From a small bluff above the head of South Bay they searched the bay and its shores through binoculars. There was no sign of life except some debris, just discernible in the gloom, on the north-western boulder beach. With a three-hour trek back, and few daylight hours left, there was no time to descend further and they returned to the hut. As the predicted weather was unfavourable for sailing back to Dunedin it was decided they should stay in the hut to enable an early start to further searching.

On 25 June Gus and Jacinda worked to a predetermined programme:

> Traverse a high route across the island, one known to Gerry and that encompasses good vantage points for route choice and hut finding.
>
> To ascertain if possible where Totorore was wrecked so we can focus search effort on most likely outcomes.

> Thoroughly search South Bay area, concentrating on likely exits from the water, exits from South bay and any places affording shelter.
>
> Cover ground, looking, calling and listening.
>
> Retrieve all possible wreckage.[9]

Following this plan they crossed the North Plains, climbed a slip on the north face of Mt Galloway, traversed the Central Plateau to the western end of Mt Waterhouse and followed high ground to the west of Reliance Ridge. From here they descended a prominent lichen-covered slip, ending up some hundreds of metres to the west of South Bay. Here, Jacinda found footprints Martin left when he was leaving the bay on 21 June.

A moderate south-westerly swell was rolling into the bay, crashing high onto its steep cliffs. Gus and Jacinda carefully scanned its surface and searched most of its coastline, getting to the shore and looking into the water where possible. Like Martin four days earlier, they found wreckage of *Totorore* only on two small beaches. From the northern-most cove they retrieved the three pieces from the high ledge where Martin had placed them, but no new debris was ashore there. On the inaccessible beach just to the south, they counted 16 large and 10 smaller pieces of wreckage. This was far more than recorded by Martin (mainly from memory back at the hut) on 21 June. However, most of the extra pieces seen were small bits of grey plywood and tan-coloured foam that could well have broken off wreckage already on the tide line four days earlier. Some of the wreckage was partly covered by thick clumps of bull-kelp that had also been washed up on the beach by the recent, rough south-west weather.

A wave platform just south of this boulder beach afforded the most feasible landing site in South Bay. While frequently calling and using a metal rattle, the searchers checked nearby caves, overhangs, and tall tussock, and traversed around the lower slopes to a rock overhang at the bay's eastern corner, checking out a large cave en route. Here they saw *Ranui* in heavy seas about 300 metres off the entrance of South Bay and made contact on VHF radio, to learn that the weather forecast was poor for the next five days. It was now mid-afternoon and time was fast running out if they were to reach the hut before dark, so they climbed directly uphill and took the shortest route back.

The next morning Gus and Jacinda returned directly to South Bay and assessed the feasibility of abseiling down the 25-metre cliff to the inaccessible wreckage. No obvious new pieces had been washed in overnight, despite a huge south-west swell. The next areas to check for signs of the *Totorore*'s crew were the now-abandoned penguin colonies to the west of the bay, and more western slips providing access up onto Reliance Ridge. From that ridgeline and many other vantage points, including Mounts Waterhouse and Galloway, they scanned the surrounding country. Bright sunshine between the squalls made for excellent visibility. Once they saw reflected light, and checked it out, but it proved to be just hail on plant leaves. Throughout the day they had regularly sounded the rattle, called, looked and listened without success.

During the first night at the island *Ranui* anchored in Anchorage Bay, but shifted to Ringdove Bay the next day when the weather deteriorated. She stayed at anchor here except for the one occasion, seen by the searchers ashore, when she ventured around Albatross Point into the heavy seas off South Bay. On 27 June the plan was to try and gain access to the wreckage in South Bay, using equipment that was still on *Ranui*. Richard, Roy, Martin and Anja went ashore that morning at the outlet of Ringdove Stream, with Martin's 50-metre climbing rope and abseiling gear, to meet Gus and Jacinda at the top of the cliffs. At first the climbers tried to find a way above the waterfall, but found this impracticable. They then attempted to scramble up the very steep slopes just to the south of the stream, but after half-an-hour's effort turned back as it was too unstable and dangerous.[10] The climbing party returned to the *Ranui* in squally conditions, and the other two to the hut. It had been "a frustrating day, with much effort for little return".[11]

The next day found weather conditions even worse. Very strong south-westerly winds kept *Ranui* tucked hard in the southern corner of Ringdove Bay, with no chance of getting the abseiling gear ashore. By now all felt that "the chance of Gerry and Roger still being alive was minuscule".

On the morning of 29 June the wind had swung back to the west, Hut Cove was workable, and the forecast was favourable for a return to Dunedin. The hut was left with the SSB radio still set up with a fully charged,

120 amp/hour, 12-volt battery. It also contained warm clothing, a cooker, fuel, food and other equipment. At midday the *Ranui* sailed for New Zealand. Blue Petrels were seen on each of the three days of the return voyage. On 1 July, Martin wrote in the researchers' log: "A rather quiet day – little wind, few birds only. Nice to see all the Blue Petrels. Gerry was very fond of them, and proud having discovered a colony at Cape Horn. It was a bit like him following us."

The *Ranui* reached Port Chalmers shortly before dawn on 2 July.

SNOW CLOUD

In September, Roger Sale's brother Chris took his 11.2-metre yacht *Snow Cloud* from Northland to the Antipodes in a further search for traces of *Totorore* and her crew. Chris was a good friend and sailing companion of Gerry's, having been aboard *Totorore* for six months in 1985 during her Antarctic voyage from Punta Arenas to Cape Town. Knowing that everyone who made it ashore from previous shipwrecks at the Antipodes had survived, he was concerned that the *Ranui* party had been unable to search closely much of the western and southern coastline of the island.

From his analysis of weather conditions at the time of *Totorore*'s disappearance, Chris thought it unlikely that South Bay would have been tenable on 12 June, the most likely day of the wreck. He reasoned that Gerry would have been unable to judge conditions in South Bay until rounding Albatross Point and then, finding the bay too rough, may have continued to make observations along the coast. If so, the yacht could have been lost beyond the area searched by the *Ranui*, especially since all of the debris found in South Bay "was of the floating type", and items normally associated with the immediate vicinity of a wreck (e.g. rope, sails, and clothing) were missing.

Snow Cloud left Lyttelton on 8 September and reached Anchorage Bay on the evening of the 12th. On board were owner/master Chris Sale, John Wood, Marianne Wood and Lloyd Knauf. The following day they landed and visited the research hut, but no one had been there since *Ranui* had left. The hut's radio was still in working order. The yacht then proceeded down the western coastline, close inshore with Lloyd as lookout up the mast, checking out all possible landing points and frequently sounding a very loud foghorn. On the southern coast a swell of two to three metres, or more at times, was running into the shore. They passed across Stack Bay but could not investigate it closely, as it was "full of awesome reefs that appeared out of the large swells like great teeth and then disappeared beneath the swells again, we passed inside the rock to the south of Stack Bay but decided not to do so again because of the uneven nature of the bottom".[12]

Snow Cloud continued around to Albatross Point before returning to stand off South Bay. She passed outside of South Islet both times, as there were large breakers on the hidden reef that runs from east of South Bay to the islet. Chris and Marianne motored into South Bay in the inflatable dinghy. Although there was considerable backwash at the entrance, once inside the surface of the bay was calm, apart from surges. It was "like a mini harbour". Chris wrote in his report:

> We marvelled at this beautiful place and I understand what would draw Gerry to such a place, as one could watch penguins at close range and probably many other birds as the breeding season got underway . . . Also I have nothing but admiration to those that made the journey over the island to search, the country is very steep to get in and out of .

The eastern side of the bay was steep with guts running in behind islets and rocks, from which surf foamed out into the bay; the north side was sheer and appeared to offer no landing places. The pair then closely searched the three coves on the western shore and sighted many small pieces of wreckage from *Totorore*. They managed to land in the middle cove, on the boulder beach that had been inaccessible to previous searchers. It was "littered with *Totorore* pieces mainly below the water bits of hull, a bit of a life ring, cupboards, floorboards". The one thing that stuck out was that "wreckage from the top half of *Totorore* is just not there".[13]

Marianne then used a facemask to peer over the side and search underwater as they slowly motored around the bay. The water was crystal-clear, and near the shore the surge of the sea conveniently moved the kelp to reveal every part of the bottom. The rock in the middle was close to the surface and very obvious. Chris reported that:

> Absolutely no wreckage was seen on the bottom, which led to the conclusion that *Totorore* almost certainly would not have been in South Bay when wrecked as there would be large parts that would not move such as the keels, engine, etc.

They then moved around to Ringdove Bay, but weather conditions did not allow a landing. That night they hove-to offshore in north-north-east winds of about 15 knots and rain. On the morning of the 14th they anchored in the shelter of Leeward Island but by midday the wind had freshened from the north-east and the sea became rough, forcing them to sail for the western coast and anchor close in, to the south of Cave Point.

The following day they attempted to revisit South Bay, but sea and weather conditions prevented the use of the inflatable. *Snow Cloud* then returned to the western coast of the Antipodes, to anchor off Orde Lees Island. During all of these manoeuvres they searched for signs of people and wreckage, but the only traces of *Totorore* were those found in South Bay. Other flotsam seen were two orange floats, one onshore in Ringdove Bay and another in the eastern corner of Stack Bay, but these were very unlikely to have been associated with the missing yacht. Late on 15 September, a weather forecast predicted deteriorating conditions, so *Snow Cloud* sailed for New Zealand that night. She arrived in Akaroa in the early morning of 19 September.[14]

TIAMA

The 15-metre yacht *Tiama*, owned and skippered by Henk Haazen, was at the Antipodes Islands over the Christmas/New Year period. This was a Greenpeace project that involved being the first to see the sun on 1 January 2000, and sending emails using solar energy from that first sunlight of the new millennium. *Tiama* arrived at the Antipodes about five days before the turn of the century and stayed about the islands – the passengers sightseeing and photographing – until the New Year. The weather was good, mainly overcast with some rain, but little wind.

Tiama's crew spent most of one day in South Bay searching for wreckage, and saw some debris including a life buoy and small bits of ply on the tide line in the north-west corner. A search was also made for wreckage on the bottom of the bay by towing a swimmer equipped with snorkel and facemask around on a manta-board. The water was clear but in places seaweed obstructed the search. They had anticipated locating large heavy objects, such as *Totorore*'s anchors, mast, engine and keels – but nothing was found.

At dawn on 1 January they saw the sun 10 minutes earlier than other parties watching from the Chatham Islands, and took a photograph of their yacht lit with the first rays of sunshine. This photo – "Rise of the New Dawn" – and some video footage was then beamed out over the Internet via a satellite phone. With these images went a message of hope for the new millennium to be forwarded to thousands of people around the world.[15]

AKADEMIK SHOKALSKIY

On 9 January 2000, Heritage Expeditions' ship *Akademik Shokalskiy* – en route to Campbell Island and the Ross Sea – anchored in Ringdove Bay after a good overnight run from the Bounties. Later that morning the passengers were taken on natural history cruises of the eastern coastline in the ship's three semi-inflatable Naiads.

Expedition leader Rodney Russ then decided to take two of the Naiads around to South Bay to look for traces of *Totorore*. Rodney had first met Gerry Clark at the Auckland Islands when *Ketiga* called there in December 1972. Later the two became good friends and sailed together aboard *Ketiga* in the Bay of Islands, and in 1992–94 Rodney employed Gerry to command *Pacific Ruby* on her four tourist voyages to the subantarctic. Rodney had hoped to help with the *Totorore* search during two earlier visits (16 December and 3 January), but sea conditions had been unsuitable. On this occasion, judging by the favourable overnight run and conditions in Ringdove Bay, the weather and seas certainly looked better. Rodney and his son, Nathan, took wet suits and dive gear with the intention of conducting an underwater search. Rodney writes:

> As soon as we poked our nose around the corner from Ringdove Bay I realised that it was not a day for South Bay – but was determined to have a look. Overhead conditions were good, there wasn't a lot of wind but there was a very large S-SW swell rolling through with a bit of a chop on top. But, it was the size of the swell that was impressive – 5 to 6 metres. We got to South Bay without incident but once there it was obvious we weren't going to dive or even get in the water. The swell was rolling in! There was no wreckage to be seen on the shore anywhere.

The water was very clear, and the two boat crews spent some time leaning over the sides of the Naiads, peering underwater, around an area where Rodney considered he would have anchored had he had a yacht there. Although they could see the bottom in places, there was no sign of anchors or wreckage. It was not the sort of day to hang around in South Bay, so they started back for the ship. Rodney continues:

> We came out of South Bay and headed directly towards Albatross Point – we were running with the swells. I was in front and remember coming up on top of this particularly large swell and thinking it was larger than the others. As it started to fall away I remember looking over the side and all I could see through the water was rocks and kelp – we had crossed a reef between South Islet and the south coast. A few seconds later and we would have been smashed onto the reef. I turned and waved frantically to the Naiad behind, to make sure they avoided it. I think I was the only one that saw, or at least fully appreciated, just how close we had been to another shipwreck.

Once back aboard *Akademik Shokalskiy*, Rodney checked the chart. It shows an area of water of less than 10 metres inside of South Islet, but no reef or foul ground anywhere nearby. He writes that because of the very large swell encountered, it is hard to know just how shallow the sea above the underwater reef actually is. His Naiads had passed over the rocks, into the swell, on their way to South Bay and not seen them. He was left wondering if, after leaving South Bay, *Totorore* had tried to run with a big swell "inside of South Islet and not been as lucky as we had been".[16]

A FINAL SEARCH

During their time at the Antipodes those on *Snow Cloud* were prevented by rough seas from closely searching the coast to the east of South Bay – and Chris Sale left the islands feeling certain that other debris would have washed up there. Obviously this was an area where answers to many questions might be found. So in January 2000 Sheryl Hamilton and Alan Wiltshire were asked to check out this stretch of coastline while they were at the Antipodes for the albatross research project. They arrived at the Antipodes on 3 January aboard the *Akademik Shokalskiy*.[17]

Early on 24 January Sheryl and Alan left the hut and headed for Reliance Ridge. From the high point at 326 metres they dropped down to the coast above the first cove to the east of South Bay. However, there was no way down to the water, for the little gut was completely surrounded by steep cliffs. They then climbed up about 100 metres, through thick tussock to get around to the next cove to the south. This one was accessible from above, and was backed by a large rock platform with a blowhole and penguin colony – but access from the water onto the high rocks, through thick kelp, would have been difficult. There was a small dry cave, about five metres deep, above and behind the platform, but there was no sign of anyone having been there. However, behind rocks in the eastern corner of the cove they did find a piece of blue, high-density, closed-cell foam matting, about 40 mm thick and measuring about 60 x 40 cm.

They continued east along a steep tussock slope, up to 400 metres wide, above 10-metre sea cliffs. At the top of the slope were towering cliffs with rock overhangs, which they investigated as they progressed with much climbing up and down. At one place they could descend and closely search a short section of rocky shore, but found "no sign of anything". Further east the thick tussock gave way to shorter tussock, cushion plants and bare scree.

It was very steep, with small bluffs, forcing them to climb high before they could safely get back to the coast. After travelling about 300 metres through penguin colonies, investigating a shallow cave and scanning a cluster of offshore stacks, they reached a cove similar in size and shape to Hut Cove "but without the vegetated access at the back". It was inaccessible from above, but had easy access from the sea onto a small boulder beach. Thorough searching with binoculars revealed no sign of wreckage. From here on, into the next bay to the east, they were confronted with huge cliffs straight up from the water. This meant retracing their steps some way before they could climb back up to Reliance Ridge, and into thick fog.

Sheryl and Alan reported that "you could probably get ashore in a few places" where seals and penguins were landing on the stretch of coast adjacent to the rock stacks near the end of their traverse. But the kelp was thick and they saw no sign of anyone having been there. Apart from the closed-cell matting, which may or may not have been from *Totorore*, they "saw no general rubbish washed ashore" anywhere during their search – which had carefully covered about 1.5 kilometres of very rugged coastline.[18]

After completion of their albatross studies, the two researchers were taken off the island by the *Marine Countess* on 14 February.

A MYSTERY UNSOLVED

The Maritime Safety Authority (MSA) completed its report into the wreck on 2 December 1999. After considering all available evidence, the investigators, Frank Little (MSA) and Gary Park (Police), found that "the cause of the loss of *Totorore* is unknown, therefore the factors surrounding the accident must remain unspecified". They concluded that *Totorore* was "overdue" through an unknown catastrophic event that most likely occurred "whilst navigating in or close to South Bay or at anchor in the Bay".[19]

Exactly what happened to the *Totorore* will probably never be known. There was early speculation that she may have got caught at anchor in South Bay by a sudden change in sea conditions. Perhaps the anchor failed and she drifted onto the rocks. The bay is quite small, and on previous visits the yacht had anchored right in the middle to get enough swinging room. Once, after hauling up the anchor, Gerry is said to have reversed out as there was no room to turn against the wind and seas. If *Totorore* was wrecked because her anchor dragged or failed, the anchor and chain should still be on the bottom of South Bay along with her engine and keels, but no sign of these have so far been found.

The crew had reported having "battery trouble" earlier on the fatal voyage, so perhaps when forced to leave by changing weather, they were unable to start the motor. The accident inspectors pointed out that starting a diesel engine in cold conditions can be demanding on batteries, and with weak batteries it could be impossible. They also noted that the engine had no hand-starting device, but this is usual with most modern marine engines. *Totorore* was fitted with only a hand-operated windlass, and the anchor and chain would have had to be hoisted, or jettisoned if stuck, before she attempted to leave South Bay. Gerry would have tried to sail out only under favourable wind conditions, but a lack of motor power may have influenced his choice of course once outside.

Gerry had been to the Antipodes many times and was well aware of the underwater reef inside of South Islet. He was also a master at reading the sea's surface for indications of submerged rocks. When I sailed with him around the Antipodes in 1989 he took *Southern Cross* right into Stack Bay between underwater reefs that he pointed out well in advance. On that occasion we were counting seals, the sea was calm, and we hugged the shoreline whenever possible. However, even though we passed inside Spirit of the Dawn Rock, Gerry opted to avoid a course inside of South Islet. I am certain he would only have taken this passage if there were no other option.

Following his fruitless September search in *Snow Cloud*, Chris Sale concluded it was "fairly certain they were not in South Bay when they were wrecked, but probably not far from it". He suggested that the yacht may have been leaving and "foundered outside the entrance to South Bay probably on the submerged reef that runs out to South Islet". He added: "if this was the case they may have put out a Pan Pan call before attempting to set off, but because of the very steep and enclosed nature of South Bay and possibly low batteries and the time of day, they were not heard."

Chris also speculated that the loss of the *Totorore* might have been due to a liquid petroleum gas (LPG) explosion. He came to this conclusion after finding no large pieces, and no part of the cabin tops/superstructure among the wreckage. The accident inspectors were unconvinced, considering that seas could have broken up larger pieces of wreckage in the two months between the accident and *Snow Cloud*'s search. Nevertheless, an explosion remains a possibility, for large pieces of wreckage or parts from above the deck were never found, even during Martin's first search on 21 June. LPG was used on *Totorore* for cooking, a new stove had recently been fitted, and the gas bottles were stored in an aft cockpit locker. Gerry and Roger were very aware of the dangers of LPG on boats and were always careful. Chris had hoped that the wreckage found, especially a squab, could have been tested for evidence of an explosion but this was not possible. He wrote in his report:

> What bothers me most is the missing part of *Totorore*, basically everything from the decks up, as this was very strongly tied to the rest of the hull and would not just pop off, also there was not much upper hull, the only thing I can think of that would make sense of all this would be a large LPG explosion blowing the top off the boat, the rest of the boat sinking probably in less than 20 metres of water as if it was much deeper it would be unlikely to break up.[20]

In this scenario, once again, the accident would have occurred immediately outside South Bay – most probably on 12 June – with the shattered top half of the yacht being carried offshore by the prevailing westerly wind. Over the next few days pounding seas, particularly at low tide, would have broken up the submerged hull, and the incoming tide would have carried floating debris into the bay.

It seems most likely that *Totorore* was overwhelmed by an unknown disaster just outside South Bay, possibly on the reef inside South Islet. Her engine, keels or anchors have not been found in the bay, whereas floating wreckage was cast ashore there – but not found elsewhere, despite searches of the adjacent coastline to both the east and west.

CHAPTER TWENTY

Natural History

MARINE LIFE

At the Antipodes and Bounty Islands, the common inter-tidal and submarine fauna of cliffs, rocks, and the sea floor include sponges, coral-like bryozoans, sea squirts, sea anemones, starfish, small sea urchins, small mussels, yellow-footed paua, limpets, sea snails, whelks, chitons, hermit crabs, spider crabs and large barnacles.[1] However, many other species that the layperson might expect to find are missing or very rare, including the usual, much-sought-after edible crustaceans, shellfish and fish of southern New Zealand, although some of these, such as crayfish (rock lobster) live further south at the Snares and Auckland Islands. There are no black-footed paua, scallops, blue cod, tarakihi, butterfish, leatherjacket, wrasses or spotties, all of which are plentiful at the Chatham Islands. The only common resident fish of any size are nototheniid cod – but these are unappetising, with their body cavity and flesh usually infested with large parasitic worms. Octopuses have been found at both the Bounties and Antipodes.

Of course, seasonally, pelagic species such as small crustaceans (krill), squid, and fish – of all sizes – abound in these waters. At the Bounty Islands, small fish and krill are the main items in the diet of Antarctic Terns and Fulmar Prions; and Bounty Island Shags feed mainly on fish and squid. Southern blue whiting aggregate to spawn near the Bounties and, along with squid, are regularly harvested nearby by commercial fishers. The occasional white shark is also attracted to both island groups by the ever-present and increasingly plentiful New Zealand Fur Seals.[2]

Thirty-three species of seaweed have been recorded from the Bounty Islands, of which 18 per cent are not found elsewhere in the New Zealand subantarctic. By comparison there are 116 different species at the Antipodes of which 13 per cent are absent on the other islands. However, many of New Zealand's commonest brown, green and red seaweeds have not so far been found at the Antipodes or Bounties. Of particular interest is an endemic Antipodes Island species of bull-kelp first collected in 1969. It is attached to the rocky bottom in shallower places, has broad non-buoyant solid blades and a stout, erect, bright-yellow stipe (stalk). At low tide, the top of the stipe and base of the blade can arch above the water. In these respects it differs from the common *Durvillaea antarctica* found at all subantarctic islands, which is attached by its holdfasts to the inter-tidal zone and has flexible stalks and floating blades divided into narrow six- to seven-metre-long thongs. Also confined to the Antipodes and Bounties is a robust form of the brown seaweed *Marginariella*, as yet unnamed.[3]

LAND VEGETATION

Antipodes Islands

There are 70 native species of vascular (higher) plants on the Antipodes. These comprise three club mosses, 17 ferns, seven grasses, six sedges, two rushes, four orchids, 27 other herbs, two low-growing woody plants and one species of shrub. Sixty-eight per cent are found widely elsewhere in New Zealand and 26 per cent are on other New Zealand subantarctic islands. The others occur only at the Antipodes: they are the endemic species *Gentiana antipoda* and the endemic subspecies *Senecio radiolatus antipodus*, *Coprosma rugosa antipoda* and *Stellaria decipiens angustata*. In addition, about 17 species of lichen, 36 liverworts and 21 mosses have been recorded.

Antipodes Island is strikingly free of weeds. Six introduced species have been found growing on the island. *Poa annua*, chickweed and sow thistle have been there for well over a century without becoming abundant or dominant, and the three that have arrived since 1990, and were confined to single plants in the area of the huts, have since been eradicated.

The vegetation is predominantly tussock grass, sedge and fern with only scattered areas of shrubland. The three most physiognomically important species are the tussock *Poa litorosa*, the tall fern *Polystichum vestitum* and the shrub, *Coprosma rugosa*.[4]

The maritime vegetation of the coastal rocks and cliffs is dominated by salt-tolerant grasses, sedges and herbs, all low growing, creeping or cushion like. Behind this zone the coastal grassland of the steep seaward slopes is characterised by tall, dense tussocks of *Poa litorosa* – growing on pedestals and sometimes over two metres in height – and by the presence of coastal species such as *Poa foliosa* tussock and the ferns *Blechnum durum* and *Asplenium obtusatum*. These coastal grasslands are often so dense that traversing them becomes a slow and tiring ordeal. The few swamps found near the coast are dominated by the sedges *Carex appressa* and *C. trifida*.

In contrast, on the inland plains the *Poa litorosa* tussocks are stunted and widely spaced, with abandoned albatross nest sites scattered throughout providing a disturbed and enriched substrate for algae, liverworts, mosses, ferns, bidibids, gentians and *Senecio*. Here, lower-lying, less boggy areas are often dominated by the sedge *Carex ternaria* and the megaherbs *Anisotome antipoda* and *Pleurophyllum criniferum*. *Polystichum vestitum* fern occurs, especially along watercourses, and tall sedge *Carex sectoides* is prevalent in the wettest swamps on the island.

The vegetation dominating the slopes of the inland hills and mountains

Aerial view of Funnel Island, Bounty Group.

is tall, thick *Poa litorosa* tussockland, with small scattered areas of *Histiopteris incisa* fernland and *Coprosma rugosa* shrubland. Natural slips, caused by the weight of vegetation and periodic heavy rain, occur from time to time on the steeper slopes. These slowly re-vegetate, at first with lichens and mosses and later by other plants. Such slips provide by far the best routes either up or down the steeper slopes. Tussock becomes less dominant on the summits of Mounts Galloway and Waterhouse, where the commonest species are *Pleurophyllum criniferum* and *Anisotome antipoda.*

Coprosma rugosa antipoda is the only upright woody species on the Antipodes Islands. It is confined to the main island where it grows in scattered patches from 60 to 320 metres above the sea. The largest plant seen in 1969 had a trunk with a basal diameter of 140 mm, was well over two metres high and was over 80 years of age as shown by a count of annual growth rings. I mapped the distribution of this shrub in 1978, and found it occurred in over 140 scattered patches, always on well-drained sites, and mostly on the northern half of the island. The greatest concentrations were on the northern and eastern slopes of Mount Galloway. The species was uncommon on south-facing slopes and did not occur to the south or west of Reliance Ridge.

The Antipodes Islands were formed by volcanic action in the last two million years and have never been connected to any other land, so the arrival of the plants living there now must have been assisted by wind, birds, ocean currents or man. The principal sources of the island's vascular flora have been the New Zealand mainland to the west and the Chatham Islands to the north, or the Auckland and Campbell Islands to the south-west.[5]

Eric Godley, in his 1989 study of the flora, considered that the mosses, liverworts, club mosses, ferns and orchids – with their dust-like seed – are likely to have arrived by wind dispersal. Other species are more likely to have been carried by birds, particularly by petrels, skuas, gulls and colonising land birds. Fragments of algae and lichen, spores, seeds or fruits can travel on birds' feet, feathers or beaks, and many seeds remain viable after passing through their guts. Eric found no plants that could have arrived by seeds floating on the sea. He considered it debatable whether the long-established aliens – *Poa annua, Stellaria media* and sow thistles – were brought in by early sealers and established on ground disturbed by seabirds, or whether seabirds carried them to the islands. However, for the three aliens arriving within the last 15 years there is no doubt that people were responsible.

Bounty Islands

Until very recently it was thought that these islands had no vascular plants, but in November 2004 a few specimens of Cook's scurvy grass *Lepidium oleraceum* were found growing on ledges and in rock crevices high up on both Funnel Island and Molly Cap.[6] The only other land plants at the Bounties are green algae (at least two species) in and around "freshwater" pools, and four species of crustose lichens clinging to vertical or overhanging rock walls, at altitudes of over 20 metres. Rain and spray sweeps bare most of the islands' granite terrain. Where some guano accumulates between rock slabs, it is trampled by thousands of birds and seals or annually scraped up for nest building.

A sample of Bounty Island guano and bird-nest material analysed in 1985 showed that spores of mosses, liverworts and ferns were reaching the islands on the prevailing westerly winds.[7] It seems obvious that, for millennia, seeds of many plant species must have been taken to the Bounty Islands by birds – as they have to the Antipodes – but that the islands fail to provide an adequate seedbed.

TABLE 4: Native Vascular Plants of Antipodes Islands

Name	Scientific Name
Lycopods (Club mosses) 3	*Lycopodium fastigatum, L. scariosum, L. varium.*
Filices (Ferns) 17	*Asplenium obstusatum, A. terrestre.*
	Blechum durum, B.fluviatile, B. penna-marina, B. sp. ("mountain").
	Histiopteris incisa.
	Hypolepis millefolium.
	Pteridium esculentum.
	Polystichum vestitum.
	Grammitis billardierei, G. magellanica, G. givenii.
	Hymenophyllum flabellatum, H. minimum, H. multifidum.
	Phymatosorus diversifolius.
Flowering Plants: Dicotyledons 31	
Apiaceae 2	*Anisotome antipoda.*
	Apium prostratum denticulatum.
Araliaceae 1	*Stilbocarpa polaris.*
Asteraceae 7	*Helichrysum bellidiodes.*
	Lagenifera petiolata.
	Leptinella plumosa.
	Pleurophyllum criniferum.
	Pseudognaphalium luteoalbum.
	Senecio radiolatus antipodus.
	Taraxacum magellanicum.

Name	Scientific Name
Brassicaceae 2	*Cardamine corymbosa.*
	Lepidium oleraceum.
Callitrichaceae 1	*Callitriche antarctica.*
Caryophyllaceae 4	*Colobanthus apetalis, C. muscoides.*
	Stellaria decipiens decipens, S. decipens angustata.
Crassulaceae 1	*Crassula moschata.*
Gentianaceae (Gentians) 1	*Gentiana antipoda.*
Geraniaceae (Geraniums) 1	*Geranium microphyllum.*
Lobeliaceae (Lobelias) 1	*Pratia arenaria.*
Ongraceae (Willowherbs) 2	*Epilobium alsinoides, E. pedunculare.*
Polygonaceae (Docks) 1	*Rumex neglectus.*
Portlucaceae 1	*Montia fontana.*
Rosaceae (Bidibids) 1	*Acaena minor.*
Rubiaceae (Coprosmas) 4	*Coprosma ciliata, C. perpusilla subantarctica, C. rugosa antipoda, C. r. antipoda x ciliata (hybrid).*
Urticaceae (Nettles) 1	*Urtica australis.*
Flowering Plants: Monocotyledons 19	
Cyperaceae (Sedges) 6	*Carex appressa, C.sectoides, C. ternaria, C. trifida.*
	Isolepis cernua.
	Uncinia hookeri.
Juncaceae (Rushes) 2	*Juncus scheuchzerioides.*
	Luzula crinita.
Orchidaceae (Orchids) 4	*Aporostylis bifolia.*
	Chiloglottis cornuta.
	Corybas trilobus.
	Prasophyllum colensoi.
Poaceae (Grasses) 7	*Agrostis magellanica.*
	Lachnagrostis leptostachys.
	Poa antipoda, P. breviglumis, P. foliosa, P. litorosa.
	Puccinella antipoda.

TABLE 5: Alien Vascular Plants of Antipodes Islands

Name	Scientific name	Status	Date first found
Annual poa	*Poa annua*	Widespread	1890
Sow thistle	*Sonchus asper*	Widespread	1890
Chickweed	*Stellaria media*	Restricted	1890
*Wild turnip	*Brassica rapa*	Restricted	1990
*Pennywort	*Hydrocotyle heteromeria*	Restricted	1997
*Yorkshire fog	*Holcus lanatus*	Restricted	1998

(* = now eradicated)

INSECTS AND OTHER INVERTEBRATES

A lot more research is needed before a listing of resident invertebrates of the Antipodes and Bounty Islands can be anywhere near complete. The only systematic collecting at the Bounty Islands was in 1978; and entomologists are discovering new species with every visit to the Antipodes. In October 1990, a visiting specialist added six moth species to the Antipodes Island fauna during only four days on the main island. Similarly, a species of cave weta (Orthoptera) previously thought to be extinct at the Antipodes – due to mice – has recently been sighted on Bollons Island, and in the year 2000 a previously undescribed carabid beetle was collected there.[8]

About 100 species of insects and 17 spiders are known from the Antipodes Island group. Many of these are also found on Auckland and Campbell Islands, but five are shared only with the Bounties, and about 17 per cent are endemic to the Antipodes. Lower invertebrate life such as mites, collembola, amphipods, aphids, nematodes, earthworms and land snails also occur. The island's invertebrates are found in all habitats, living and feeding in rotting kelp, in rock crevices, soil, leaf litter, and birds' nests; on the roots and leaves of grasses, herbs and shrubs; and in and near fresh water. The caterpillars of the Magpie Moth (*Nyctemera annulata*) feed extensively on the leaves, flowers and stems of the endemic *Senecio*.[9]

In the absence of any soil or land vegetation other than lichens and algae, most of the surprisingly diverse invertebrate fauna of the Bounty Islands depends directly or indirectly on the sea, being sustained by rotting seaweed, bird corpses, other invertebrates and general detritus around the seal and seabird colonies. One exception is a tiny insect (a psocopteran *Sandrapsocus clarki* – named after its collector, Sandra King, and expedition leader, Gerry Clark) found living on vertical rock walls among lichen growth. As far as is known the genus is restricted to the Bounty Islands.[10]

The invertebrate fauna of the Bounties includes 24 insects, three spiders, ringed worms, mites, collembola, amphipods, isopods and a land snail. About 30 per cent of the terrestrial insects are endemic, and include flies, moths, a weta (*Ischyroplectron isolatum*), a tiny flightless parasitic wasp (*Antarctopria diomediae*) and a flightless beetle (*Bountya insularis*). This beetle is remarkable in being from a group found nowhere else in New Zealand – its nearest relatives live in Australia and South America.[11]

In addition, at both island groups, there are many species of parasitic fleas, ticks, mites and lice living on the various seabirds. A very notable feature of all subantarctic insect faunas is a high proportion of flightless species belonging to groups that usually have functional wings. There is evidence – such as the non-use of wings by winged species – that these evolutionary changes do not necessarily result from long isolation, but are due to intense natural selection: to fly is to risk being lost at sea in the severe subantarctic environment.

Invertebrates will have originally reached the islands by much the same mechanisms as the land plants, mainly birds and wind, and a few by humans. But perhaps the Bounty Island spiders and flightless beetle date from a time when the Campbell Plateau was dry land. An example of wind dispersal is a solitary Monarch Butterfly that I observed flying near Dougall Stream, Antipodes, on 8 March 1985, whereas the Brown House Moth (*Hofmannophila pseudospretella*), a cosmopolitan species first found in 1969 among castaway clothing in the Antipodes depot, was obviously introduced by man.[12]

FRESHWATER FISH, AMPHIBIANS AND REPTILES

Although one species of freshwater fish, the koaro (*Galaxias brevipinnis*), lives in streams on the Auckland and Campbell Islands, none has been found at the Antipodes. Perhaps this is not surprising as many of the watercourses there sometimes run dry, and all have waterfalls near the coast.

No amphibians or reptiles have been found on any of New Zealand's subantarctic islands. The nearest lizard populations to the Antipodes and Bounties are skinks living among seabird colonies on Pyramid Rock to the south of Pitt Island, Chatham Islands, and New Zealand's southernmost lizards, both geckos and skinks, are on Stewart Island. Introduced Australian Brown Tree Frogs (*Litoria ewingi*) have spread as far south as Stewart Island, and recently have also reached the Chathams.

BIRDS

Antipodes Islands

Fifty-seven species of birds are known from the Antipodes Islands. Twenty-one are breeding seabirds, comprising two penguins, four albatrosses, 12 other petrels, one skua, one gull and one tern. In addition four species of penguins, four albatrosses, three other petrels, two shags, one skua and one tern are known to visit the islands. There are four endemic land birds (one snipe, two parrots, and one pipit), four resident introduced land birds (one duck and three passerines), and 12 vagrant land birds (two ducks, two waders and one pigeon).[13]

At the Antipodes, Erect-crested and Rockhopper Penguins occur in over 80 mixed colonies around the main island's coastline and on Bollons, Archway and East Windward. Over 5000 pairs of Antipodean Wandering Albatross breed on the main island, and about 115 pairs of Black-browed Mollymawk and 20 pairs of White-capped Mollymawk on Bollons Island.[14] Between 200 and 300 pairs of Light-mantled Sooty Albatross nest on the steep coastal cliffs and cliff ledges of most islands in the group. Several hundred pairs of Northern Giant Petrels nest in small, scattered colonies above the cliffs of the main island. The numbers of Giant Petrels breeding, and their colony sites, vary between years and they are absent from the offshore islets.

Of the burrow-nesting petrels, the White-headed Petrel is the most abundant (up to 300,000 pairs); the White-chinned Petrel (about 100,000 pairs) and the winter breeding Grey Petrel (about 56,000 pairs) are also common. The Subantarctic Little Shearwater nests on the offshore islets in large numbers. The Antipodes Group possibly has the largest population of this species in the South Pacific, up to 100,000 pairs. Other petrels breeding in smaller numbers are the Subantarctic Diving Petrel, Grey-backed Storm Petrel, Black-bellied Storm Petrel, Snares Cape Pigeon (about 300 pairs), Fairy Prion, Soft-plumaged Petrel (1000–5000 pairs) and Sooty Shearwater. Other breeding seabirds are the Subantarctic Skua (up to 100 pairs) and small numbers of Southern Black-backed Gulls and Antarctic Terns.

Rather surprisingly, there are no resident shags at the Antipodes, but the surrounding waters are much deeper than at other New Zealand subantarctic islands where each archipelago has its own endemic species of shag. Very occasionally Campbell Island and Bounty Island Shags have occurred as vagrants, but it seems that no suitable feeding niche exists for these relatively shallow-water bottom-feeders at the Antipodes Islands.

The endemic land birds consist of the Antipodes Island Snipe, Antipodes Island Parakeet, Reischek's Parakeet and the Antipodes Island Pipit. The snipe is found throughout the main island and on Bollons, Archway, East Windward and, almost certainly, on Leeward Island. Its numbers have been roughly estimated at about 8000. Antipodes Island Parakeets occur all over the islands, but are most common in tall dense tussocks and sedges, especially on steeper slopes and along watercourses on the main island. The population remains stable at between 2000 and 3000. Reischek's Parakeet – a subspecies of the New Zealand Red-crowned Parakeet – has quite different food habits, behaviour and breeding season from the Antipodes Island Parakeet. Reischek's Parakeets number somewhere between 4000 and 5000, spread over the main island and most islets, greatest densities being reached in the more open areas of the uplands and around the coast. Antipodes Island Pipits are numerous (1000 to 4000) particularly in more open areas and near penguin colonies on the main island, and on Bollons and Archway Islands.

Self-introduced residents are Mallard Duck, Dunnock, Redpoll and Starling, all of which have been recorded breeding. Grey Duck, Paradise Shelduck, Spur-winged Plover, Rock Pigeon and seven species of small passerines have been reported as vagrants – although it is probable that Silvereye, which are regularly recorded, are actually resident and breeding in small numbers.

Bounty Islands

The only breeding species are seven seabirds – the Erect-crested Penguin, Salvin's Mollymawk, Snares Cape Pigeon, Fulmar Prion, Bounty Island Shag, Southern Black-backed Gull, and Antarctic Tern. Northern Giant Petrels and Subantarctic Skuas are regular non-breeding visitors, and many other petrel species have been reported from the rich waters surrounding the islands.[15]

Erect-crested Penguins nest on at least 12 islands in the group. Recent accurate counts of 2774 nests on Proclamation Island suggest that the total number of breeding pairs at the Bounty Islands is around 20,000. This is far less than a previous rough estimate in 1978, but there is no solid evidence of a population decline. Salvin's Mollymawks nest on at least eight islands. The only accurate population figures are my ground census of 218 active nests on Penguin Island on 7 March 1985 (where Gerry Clark counted 298 from *Totorore* on 30 October 1997); and a ground census, by the *Totorore* researchers, of 3062 active nests on Proclamation Island in November 1997. These counts, and a recent inspection of aerial photographs taken between 1978 and 1995, suggest that total breeding pairs at the Bounty Islands have not significantly declined since the 1970s – and could number about 25,000, rather than the 30,750 pairs suggested in two recent publications. Snares Cape Pigeons nest in alcoves or horizontal cracks on coastal cliffs. Gerry estimated the "total Bounty population to be at least 500 birds" and suggested that Cape Pigeons nested on "all islands not completely wave swept in bad weather".

Fulmar Prions build their nests in rock crevices or under slabs or piles of rock on all the larger islands. In December 1997 a careful survey indicated that there were about 1000 pairs nesting on Proclamation Island. Considering the distribution of suitable nesting habitat on the other islands, I guess that the total population of the Bounty Group could be as low as 10,000 pairs

– considerably less than previous estimates of around 80,000.

Bounty Island Shags nest on sheltered cliff ledges on nearly all islands over 25 metres in elevation. The only exception is Castle Island, which may lack suitable terrain. An estimate by the BAAS expedition party in 1978 gave 569 pairs on 11 islands, whereas the *Totorore* expedition in 1997–98 found 120 occupied nests in 42 colonies on 13 different islands. The later nest count is a minimum only, for very many nests are not visible from below. The best method to accurately determine population size would be by aerial census using low-altitude oblique photography of the now-known nesting ledges. Meanwhile, the best estimate is about 500 breeding pairs.

Southern Black-backed Gulls breed in small numbers. In summer 1997–98, the *Totorore* expedition estimated the total population at 80 to 100 birds, including immatures. Since gulls are aggressively mobbed if they enter penguin or prion colonies, they seem to restrict nesting activity to islands like Lion, Castle and North Rock, where disturbance is less. At the Bounty Islands, Antarctic Terns are solitary breeders, with a few pairs at most islands. A total population of 60 to 70 birds was estimated in 1997–98.

Vagrants found ashore include Rockhopper penguin, Spur-winged Plover, Chaffinch, Redpoll and Starling. Of these, Starlings are the most regularly reported. They are probably better adapted than other vagrant land birds for survival on the Bounties, but a lack of fruiting plants makes it doubtful that they could successfully breed there.

TABLE 6: Birds recorded from the Antipodes Islands

Breeding species	Name	Scientific name
Spheniscidae (Penguins) 2	Erect-crested Penguin	*Eudyptes sclateri*
	Rockhopper Penguin	*Eudyptes chrysocome*
Diomedeidae (Albatrosses) 4	Antipodean Wandering Albatross	*Diomedea antipodensis*
	Black-browed Mollymawk	*Thalassarche melanophris melanophris*
	White-capped Mollymawk	*Thalassarche cauta steadi*
	Light-mantled Sooty Albatross	*Phoebetria palpebrata*

Procellariidea (Petrels, prions) 12	Sooty Shearwater	*Puffinus griseus*
	Subantarctic Little Shearwater	*Puffinus assimilis elegans*
	Subantarctic Diving Petrel	*Pelecanoides urinatrix exsul*
	Grey Petrel	*Procellaria cinerea*
	White-chinned Petrel	*Procellaria aequinoctialis*
	Snares Cape Pigeon	*Daption capense australe*
	Northern Giant Petrel	*Macronectes halli*
	Fairy Prion	*Pachyptila turtur*
	White-headed Petrel	*Pterodroma lessonii*
	Soft-plumaged Petrel	*Pterodroma mollis*
	Grey-backed Storm Petrel	*Garrodia nereis*
	Black-bellied Storm Petrel	*Fregetta tropica*
Anatidae (Water fowl) 1	* Mallard	*Anas platyrhynchos*
Scolopacidae (Snipe) 1	Antipodes Island Snipe	*Coenocorypha aucklandica meinertzhagenae*
Stercorariidae (Skuas) 1	Subantarctic Skua	*Catharacta skua lonnbergi*
Laridae (Gulls and terns) 2	Southern Black-backed Gull	*Larus dominicanus*
	Antarctic Tern	*Sterna vittata bethunei*
Psittacidae (Parrots) 2	Antipodes Island Parakeet	*Cyanoramphus unicolor*
	Reischek's Parakeet	*Cyanorhampus novaezelandiae hochstetteri*
Motacillidae (Pipits) 1	Antipodes Island Pipit	*Anthus novaeseelandiae steindachneri*
Prunellidae (Accentors) 1	* Dunnock	*Prunella modularis*
Fringillidae (Finches) 1	* Redpoll	*Carduelis flammea*
Sturnidae (Starlings) 1	* Starling	*Sturnus vulgaris*

(* = resident self-introduced)

Vagrant species	**Name**	**Scientific name**
Spheniscidae (Penguins) 4	King Penguin	*Aptenodytes patagonicus*
	Gentoo Penguin	*Pygoscelis papua*
	Chinstrap Penguin	*Pygoscelis antarctica*
	Snares Crested Penguin	*Eudyptes robustus*

Diomedeidae (Albatrosses) 5	Sooty Albatross	*Phoebetria fusca*
	Northern Royal Albatross	*Diomedea epomophora sanfordi*
	Campbell Island Mollymawk	*Thalassarche melanophrys impavida*
	Salvin's Mollymawk	*Thalassarche cauta salvini*
	Grey-headed Mollymawk	*Thalassarche chrysostoma*
Procellariidea (Petrels, prions) 3	Blue Petrel	*Halobaena caerulea*
	Mottled Petrel	*Pterodroma inexpectata*
	Antarctic Prion	*Pachyptila desolata*
Phalacrocoracidae (Shags) 2	Bounty Island Shag	*Leucocarbo campbelli ranfurlyi*
	Campbell Island Shag	*Leucocarbo campbelli campbelli*
Anatidae (Water fowl) 2	Grey Duck	*Anas superciliosa*
	Paradise Shelduck	*Tadorna variegata*
Charadriidae (Plovers, etc) 2	Spur-winged Plover	*Vanellus miles*
	Turnstone	*Arenaria interpres*
Stercorariidae (Skuas) 1	Arctic Skua	*Stercorarius parasiticus*
Laridae (Gulls and terns) 1	Arctic tern	*Sterna paradisaea*
Columbidae (Pigeons and doves) 1	Rock pigeon	*Columba livia*
Alaudidae (Larks) 1	Skylark	*Alauda arvensis*
Muscicapidae (Thrushes) 2	Blackbird	*Turdus merula*
	Song thrush	*Turdus philomelos*
Zosteropidae (White-eyes) 1	+ Silvereye	*Zosterops lateralis*
Fringillidae (Finches) 2	Chaffinch	*Fringilla coelebs*
	Goldfinch	*Carduelis carduelis*
Ploceidae (Sparrows) 1	House Sparrow	*Passer domesticus*

(+ = Possibly breeding in small numbers)

TABLE 7: Birds recorded from the Bounty Islands

Species	Name	Scientific Name
Breeding species: 7		
Spheniscidae (Penguins) 1	Erect-crested Penguin	*Eudyptes sclateri*
Diomedeidae (Albatrosses) 1	Salvin's Mollymawk	*Diomedea cauta salvini*
Procellariidea (Petrels, prions) 2	Snares Cape Pigeon	*Daption capense australe*
	Fulmar Prion	*Pachyptila crassirostris*
Phalacrocoracidae (Shags) 1	Bounty Island Shag	*Leucocarbo campbelli ranfurlyi*
Laridae (Gulls and terns) 2	Southern Black-backed Gull	*Larus dominicanus*
	Antarctic Tern	*Sterna vittata bethunei*
Regular visitors: 2		
Procellariidea (Petrels, prions) 1	Northern Giant Petrel	*Macronectes halli*
Stercorariidae (Skuas) 1	Subantarctic Skua	*Catharacta skua lonnbergi*
Vagrant species: 5		
Spheniscidae (Penguins) 1	Rockhopper Penguin	*Eudyptes chrysocome*
Charadriidae (Plovers, etc) 1	Spur-winged Plover	*Vanellus miles*
Fringillidae (Finches) 2	Chaffinch	*Fringilla coelebs*
	Redpoll	*Carduelis flammea*
Sturnidae (Starlings) 1	Starling	*Sturnus vulgaris*

RODENTS

House Mice (*Mus musculus*) – perhaps the most cosmopolitan of all mammals – were accidentally introduced to the main island of the Antipodes sometime before 1907. They now occur widely in all vegetation types from the shoreline to the highest summits. Mouse numbers seem to fluctuate widely with season, breeding probably being correlated with the seeding of tussocks and sedges such as *Poa litorosa* and *Carex appressa*. Fortunately, mice have not reached any of the offshore islets. Comparable sampling and collecting of invertebrates on both Antipodes and Bollons Islands in 1995 revealed that mice have had, and continue to have, a major impact on both the abundance and composition of the Antipodes Island invertebrate fauna.[16]

MICE REACH THE ANTIPODES

Rats and mice are the most expert colonisers of the mammalian world, mainly through their commensal relationship with man. Today, rats inhabit well over 80 per cent of the world's major island groups, and the house mouse has spread virtually everywhere. Both, in their different ways, devastate island faunas that evolved without predatory mammals.

Mice reached Ruapuke Island, Foveaux Strait, when the trading brig *Elizabeth Henrietta* was wrecked in 1824, the Bay of Islands by 1830, the Auckland Islands before 1840, and were common in all New Zealand mainland ports by the 1860s. Since then, they are known to have hitchhiked as stowaways to all of the outlying island groups except the Bounty Islands, although they have not always become established. Even if rats or mice did get ashore at the Bounties it is extremely unlikely that either species would survive due to exposure and a complete lack of dry nest sites on these barren, spray-swept rocks.

Considering the long history of visits by sealers and Government steamers restocking castaway depots, it was perhaps inevitable that mice would reach the Antipodes. Just when colonisation occurred is uncertain, but in 1907 Captain Bollons reported for the first time that they were very numerous in the castaway depot. The tall tussock vegetation is an ideal habitat, and all recent expeditions have found large numbers. Fortunately, rats never arrived at the Antipodes, but there may have been many close shaves. In 1806, sealing gangs then on the island refused to load skins onto the *Governor King*, arguing that the ship was rat-infested and a risk to their work contract which required that the furs be delivered to Sydney in good order and fit for market.

Another incident involved Captain Robert Scott's Antarctic expedition 1910–13 and the support ship *Terra Nova* which made three voyages from New Zealand to the Ross Sea. Over the winter of 1912 she was laid up and refitted at Lyttelton, where rats apparently sneaked aboard. On 14 December 1912 the *Terra Nova* sailed under command of Lieutenant Edward Evans. The scientific programme for the voyage included the running of a line of soundings from Bank's Peninsula to latitude 60° S, longitude 170° W, and then due south to the pack ice. The first leg was thus directly via the Antipodes Islands. The cruise report notes that "on 17 December the Antipodes Islands were passed, the ship labouring in the heavy sea and occasionally rolling her bulwarks under; it was not considered advisable to attempt a landing". Perhaps it was just as well that there was no physical contact with the land, for by this time the Lyttelton rats had bred and the *Terra Nova* was heavily infested. Many ingenious trapping methods were tried and the sailors even used mousetraps to catch the young. Eventually Cheetham, the boatswain, "showed himself an adept at rat-catching and soon freed the ship from the pest". Evans recalled that "he used to throw the rats over the side, and the albatrosses and mollymawks would swoop down and devour the vermin in an incredibly short time".

SEALS

Four species of seal are found at the two island groups – the New Zealand Fur Seal (*Arctocephalus forsteri*), the Subantarctic Fur Seal (*Arctocephalus tropicalis*), the Southern Elephant Seal (*Mirounga leonina*) and the Leopard Seal (*Hydrurga leptonyx*). Hooker's Sea Lion (*Phocarctos hookeri*) – also known as the New Zealand Sea Lion – has never been reported from the Antipodes or Bounty Islands.

New Zealand Fur Seals belong to the group Otariinae, or "eared" seals. This group, which includes the fur seals and sea lions, is distinguished by having prominent external ears and hind flippers that can be drawn forward, and turned outward, to assist in walking on land. The breeding range of the New Zealand Fur Seal includes New Zealand and its southern islands, and also the south and south-west coasts of Australia. Both sexes are dark grey-brown

Subantarctic Fur Seal (male), Antipodes Island.

on the back merging to a lighter shade ventrally. Males reach up to 2.5 metres in length and 185 kg in weight. Females are smaller, with maximum measurements of about 1.5 metres and 50 kg.

From historical records it is clear that New Zealand Fur Seals once occurred in vast numbers on both the Antipodes and Bounty Islands, but the biological status of the two populations was very different. The Bounty Islands are a breeding station which at itspeak had a total population in excess of 56,000 animals. The Antipodes appear to have supported far fewer breeders, but were a seasonal haunt of vast numbers of immature seals migrating from breeding rookeries elsewhere. More than 330,000 fur seals were killed on the Antipodes during the first onslaught of sealing – about one third of the total taken in all of New Zealand and its southern islands. Antipodes sealing thus removed within three years most of the New Zealand Fur Seal's juvenile population, and seriously accelerated the collapse of the species throughout its entire range.

The recovery of the two island populations, following many years of protection, has also differed markedly. At the Bounty Islands fur seals have been breeding for well over 100 years and have steadily increased. Nowadays, about 4500 pups are born there each year and the total population is over 26,000 – nearly half its original size. By contrast, at Antipodes Island, only 220 kilometres to the south, most seals are visiting juveniles from New Zealand and other subantarctic islands and still number less than two per cent of the original vast herds.

An old male New Zealand Fur Seal seen at Antipodes Island in 1950 was the first recorded there in over 120 years. By 1969 about 1000 were visiting, and nowadays numbers build up to over 5000 each March. There are few in winter. The first new-born pups found on the Antipodes since the sealing days were seven at Reef Point in 1985. Since then, breeding at this small rookery has slowly increased and 21 pups were found there in January 2000. Breeding adults are still rare. No evidence of active harems or new-born pups have yet been seen elsewhere during tourist cruises of the shoreline in December or January.

It has been calculated that just over one million sealskins were harvested from New Zealand and the southern islands before 1830. The last full survey of fur seals in New Zealand waters was almost 30 years ago, when the total population was estimated at 30,000. However, they have increased rapidly since and recent published estimates vary between 50,000 and 100,000. Judging from the expansion I have seen at fur seal rookeries on the subantarctic islands and in southern New Zealand in the last 30 years, my guess is that the total population could now number anywhere between 100,000 and 200,000 individuals. But this is still a long way short of the original stock of about one million harvested by the early sealers.[17]

The **Subantarctic Fur Seal** has a circumpolar distribution and is adapted to colder waters than the New Zealand Fur Seal. It breeds mainly on islands in the South Atlantic and Indian Oceans immediately to the north of the Antarctic convergence (Polar Front). Like most other southern fur seals, the Subantarctic Fur Seal is rapidly recovering from previous exploitation and new locations, such as Macquarie Island, are being colonised. Stragglers are now regularly seen well away from the breeding islands, turning up in southern Brazil, Juan Fernandez Archipelago, South Georgia, South Africa, south-western Australia and southern New Zealand – including its subantarctic islands. Both sexes are easily distinguished from the New Zealand Fur Seal by a characteristic white facial "mask" and creamy white chest. Adult males also have a prominent crest of hair at the front of the crown, and their voice is much higher-pitched than that of the New Zealand species.

Most New Zealand records are from the eastern shoreline of Antipodes

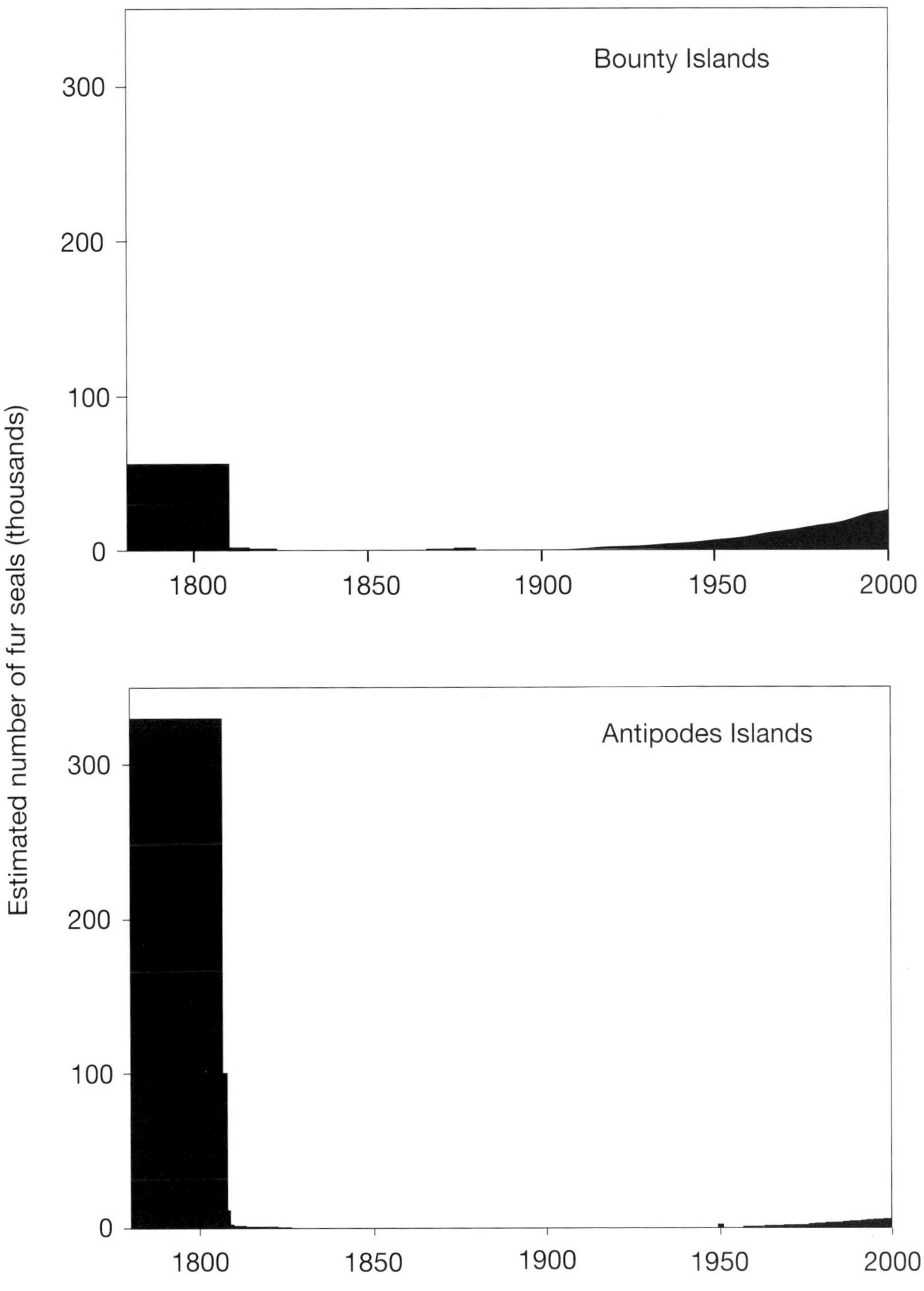

Changes in apparent abundance of New Zealand Fur Seals at the Bounty and Antipodes Islands from discovery to the year 2000.

Island, where the species has been seen in 1978, 1989, 1993, 1994 (two individuals), 1997 and 2000; other records are from the Snares in 1977 and Enderby Island in 1993. None has ever been seen at the Bounty Islands, but there is an unconfirmed report from Big Solander Island, Foveaux Strait.[18]

The status of the mythical "**Upland Seal**" has received some attention from zoologists and historians over the last 50 years. The French naturalist Lesson reported in 1828 that the fur seals previously slaughtered in thousands at the Antipodes and Macquarie Islands had a superior fur and were known as the Upland Seal. This, and the very slow recovery of fur seal populations on these two islands, led to speculation in 1948 by Robert Falla, and later by others, that the species involved may not have been the New Zealand Fur Seal but another, perhaps undescribed and now extinct species.[19] My studies of New Zealand Fur Seals, both at the Antipodes Islands and elsewhere, convinced me that this was not the case, and in 1992 I suggested that the Antipodes and Macquarie Islands may never have supported large breeding populations of fur seals of any species. Rather, they were once hauling grounds for hundreds of thousands of juvenile New Zealand Fur Seals migrating there each summer from breeding rookeries in southern New Zealand, and at the Bounty, Chatham, Auckland and Campbell Islands.[20] Observations supporting this hypothesis include: just such a summer migration of young, non-breeding New Zealand fur seals has occurred at both the Antipodes and Macquarie Islands in recent years; fur seals marked as pups on the West Coast of the South Island of New Zealand have later been recorded at the Antipodes; juvenile seals are more inclined than adults to roam inland; and traditionally the best fur seal pelts came from an age class known to the fur traders as "prime middling pups". In other words, the Antipodes and Macquarie Island fur seal populations were seen by the early sealers as different from those of southern New Zealand simply because they were made up predominantly of small yearling and immature seals. Research by sealing and whaling historian Rhys Richards has found no "evidence whatever for the existence of the 'upland' seal other than the original single reference".[21]

Southern Elephant Seals are in the group of "earless", or "true", seals that lack external ears and do not walk on their hind flippers. They are by far the largest of all Southern Hemisphere seals. Males can grow to over five metres in length and weigh well over 3600 kg; females are only half this length and a quarter the weight. The most prominent feature of the male is an inflatable proboscis, which is not fully developed until about age eight. The species has a circumpolar distribution; in the New Zealand region they haul out to breed mainly on Macquarie Island, but also in much smaller numbers at Campbell and Antipodes Islands.

On Antipodes Island the paucity of suitable breeding beaches mean that numbers would always have been small, even in pre-sealing days. There has been a major reduction over the last 50 years in the breeding populations over much of this seal's range. At Macquarie Island the total population has declined from an estimated 110,000 in the 1950s to about half that figure. At Campbell Island pupping success has dropped over 95 per cent. These changes are most likely due to changing oceanographic conditions and food availability. However, as far as can be judged from occasional incomplete counts, the population at the Antipodes appears to have remained steady – although the only accurate census at the island, when small boats were used to seek out and count pups in all coves and bays, was in November 1978, when total pup production was estimated as 113.[22]

One female Elephant Seal was reported swimming in Bucket Cove, Bounty Islands, in November 1997 – but they have never been seen ashore on that group.[23]

Leopard Seals are also "true" seals. The females are larger than the males, and can reach up to 3.6 metres in length. This species breeds in the Antarctic pack ice, and solitary vagrants occasionally visit the Antipodes Islands, particularly in spring and early summer. The few that I have seen ashore on boulder beaches in Anchorage and Ringdove Bays have been juveniles in poor condition. At the Bounty Islands, one was reported as swimming just outside Bucket Cove in January 1998, but the steep exposed nature of the shoreline makes it unlikely that they would ever haul out there.

CHAPTER TWENTY-ONE

Conclusion

HISTORICAL SUMMARY

> When the whole interior of Australia was as little known as the other side of the moon, the remote subantarctic islands, set in one of the stormiest seas in the globe, were better known and far more frequented than they are today. – Thomas Dunbabin.[1]

We have seen that soon after their discovery the Bounty and Antipodes Islands were populated by American and British sealers working out of Sydney Cove (Port Jackson). In 1805–06 there were at least 14 voyages to Antipodes Island, and at any one time between 31 and 86 sealers were ashore. All these men stayed at least four months, most more than a year, and a few up to two. It is little wonder that the local fur seal population was quickly exterminated. In these first two years of sealing, there were more people ashore, and for longer (over 32,000 people/days), than the total occupancy by sealers, castaways, visitors and scientists ever since (around 29,000 people/days).

Human occupation of Antipodes Island declined rapidly after 1806 along with the remaining fur and Elephant Seals. By mid-1810 only one gang of six sealers was working the island. Similarly, at the Bounty Islands the flush of sealing was over by 1809. Thereafter, sealing activity at both groups was fleeting and spasmodic with a minor resurgence in the 1820s and again in the 1880s. Early in 1830 three deserters from an unsuccessful American sealing vessel opted to spend an extra seven weeks on the Antipodes, not because they were catching seals but because there was more to eat ashore than on board.

The impact of seal harvesting is well documented. Without allowing for wastage, at least 330,000 fur seal skins were shipped from the Antipodes and 56,700 from the Bounties. This is well over a third of the total take for the entire New Zealand region. But otherwise the sealers seem to have had little lasting effect on the islands' ecology. Once the seals were gone, the Antipodes and Bounty Islands had little to offer exploiters – and were largely ignored.

About the middle of the 19th century, New Zealand's subantarctic islands became a hazard to navigation, for along with their neighbours – the Snares, Auckland and Campbell Islands – the Antipodes and Bounties sat astride the busy sea routes plied by sailing ships between Australian ports and Europe. Depots for shipwrecked sailors were established on the islands in the 1880s, and checked by Government steamer or visiting British warship at least annually for over 40 years. In 1893 and 1908, two wrecks at the Antipodes resulted in resident castaways, and brought the islands once again into the public gaze.

With sail giving way to steam, and the opening of the Panama Canal in 1916, the islands were soon remote from the new Pacific trading routes. The depots were abandoned in 1927 and the islands again fell into obscurity. Then followed a period of little human contact. In 1948 Robert Falla wrote: "Speaking generally, the outlying islands receive today less official and popular notice than at any time in the history of settlement in New Zealand."[2] This particularly applied to the Bounty and Antipodes Islands. However, in the second half of the 20th century, scientific and official interest increased, the islands achieved Reserve status and several major expeditions visited.

Since 1990 the Antipodes have seen annual tourist cruises, frequent scientific visits and their third recorded shipwreck. Over the same period, tourist viewing at the Bounty Islands has also increased, though scientific visits there have remained few and far between. In fact, during the 75 years from 1926 to 2000, only 21 visiting parties actually landed on the Bounties and only three camped ashore – one in 1978 and the others in 1997–98.

THE NEW MILLENNIUM

What lies ahead? No historian can successfully predict far into the future. In 1936, Fergus McLaren in his pioneer book on the history of the Auckland Islands concluded that "as far as can be seen, the islands will have no future history. The bleak climate, the unproductive soil, and the isolation

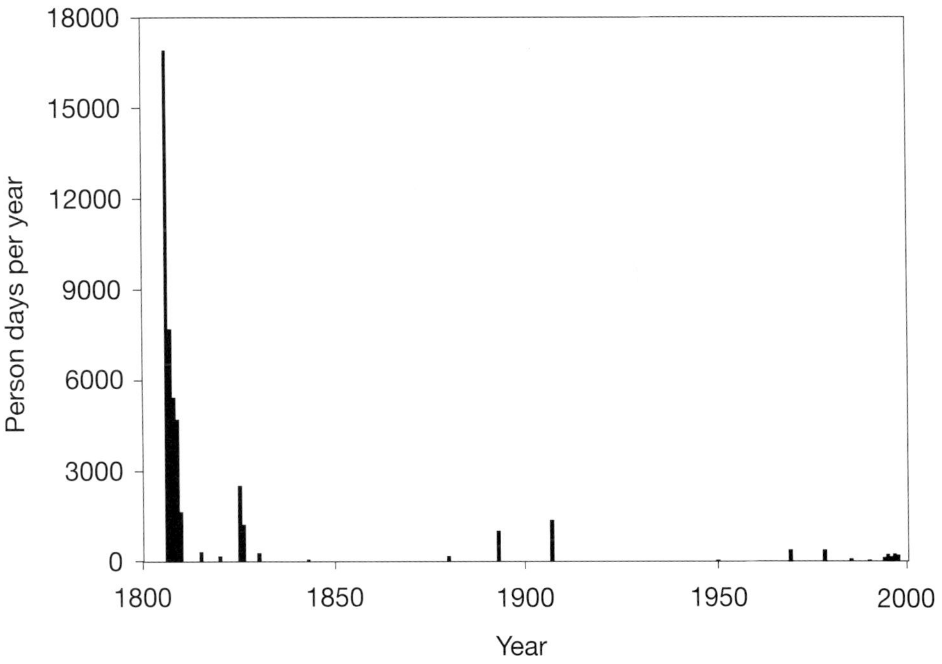

Human occupation of Antipodes Island (person/days per year) from discovery to the year 2000.

of the Auckland Islands under the changed conditions of a modern world, suggest that, in the loneliness of the Sub-Antarctic Ocean, they will be 'world forgetting, by the world forgot'."[3]

How could he have foreseen, 70 years ago, the now world-wide interest in heritage and nature conservation, and the active research and management that is taking place on these unique subantarctic islands? Likewise, Ian Kerr, a meteorologist and Campbell Island's historian,[4] was unable to predict, in 1976, the closing of the island's manned weather station and its replacement with automated equipment in less than 20 years. I doubt that I could be any more successful.

One can anticipate with confidence that monitoring of the islands' ecosystems, and research to detect unexpected threats, will continue. Progress should soon be made at the Antipodes Islands with the eradication of mice, and more slowly with eliminating the few long-standing introduced weeds. Conservation problems for seabirds, seals and other marine life caused by fishing fleets are currently being investigated, along with certain mitigation measures; but with time, new, now-unrecognised problems will arise.

I would like to think that the Royal New Zealand Navy may again become more involved in transporting managers and scientists to the Antipodes and Bounty Islands, as they did during the tenure of the Outlying Islands Reserves Committee in the 1960s, 70s and 80s. A specific management plan for the castaway depot at the Antipodes should also be a high priority, for all of its historic contents and fittings, apart from graffiti, have thoughtlessly been removed in the last 30 years. Also, hopefully, this book will arouse the interest of trained archaeologists, for there is much waiting to be learned of the ways of the early sealers from careful excavation and study of their ancient campsites.

All this must be done with the utmost care. The Antipodes are notable for their lack of introduced weeds and animal pests. In 1985 only three introduced plant species were known, but another three have been found growing there since – though quickly eradicated. Nowadays all stores taken to the islands have to undergo inspection for pests and seeds in a dedicated "quarantine store". Clothing is carefully checked for hitchhiking seeds before embarkation, and team members on the island are on "weed alert".

With the level of legal protection now in place, and active surveillance, perhaps only a pessimist would worry about the long-term future of the islands. Surely, the combination of National Nature Reserve status and World Heritage listing is impregnable. However, these legal conventions could be simply repealed by a majority in the New Zealand Parliament. Human populations are burgeoning, and who knows what new pressures may arise in a rapidly changing world? There are already ever-increasing demands for continuous increased economic growth, which is promoted as the answer to most problems in all levels of society. For instance, strident political calls are currently being made for the sacrifice of part of Fiordland National Park for a commercial gondola route to Milford Sound. Could an even worse nightmare happen – a "tourist concession" on Antipodes Island to counter New Zealand's balance of payments deficit, a development involving an airport, hotel and overland safaris to see the wildlife? The demand for tourist expeditions to see such wild places will continue to grow as individual wealth increases in the developed nations, and as the world's natural habitats continue to shrink at an alarming rate. But with tourists, travellers and wildlife enthusiasts presently limited to viewing from the sea, environmental risks are minimised. Perhaps the real hope for New Zealand's subantarctic islands is that tourism and publicity will raise their public profile so that these last remnants of a natural bygone world will be treasured and protected even more. If ever this becomes of secondary importance, they will forever be lost.

Another human problem in the subantarctic is the trend of "developing" and exploiting new fisheries as old ones are depleted – just as the sealers did. There were proposals in 1989 and 1991 to harvest Yellow-foot paua (abalone) from the subtidal zone of the Bounty and Antipodes Islands. Opposition at the time led to permits being denied, but with increased commercial demand the idea could re-emerge. Any such fishery would seriously compromise the chances of establishing an inshore marine reserve around each island group similar to that recently created at the Auckland Islands.

Couple these sorts of pressures with the known presence of hydrocarbons in the Great South Basin, directly upwind from the Antipodes and Bounty

Islands, and New Zealand's interest in, and political attitudes towards, subantarctic nature reserves could well change in a few generations. Clearly, economic demands and man's inventiveness will in time overcome the difficulties of working a deepwater gas and oil field in the Roaring Forties. There is also the ongoing search for sub-marine mineral deposits. Manganese nodules occur on the seabed near the Antipodes Islands, but are not presently of commercial interest. Fortunately for the Antipodes and Bounties, the islands' rocky shores and often-violent seas make the impact of possible oil spills less threatening – though one serious spill near the Bounties could quickly lead to the extinction of the Bounty Island Shag.

Wider long-term global changes may also increasingly effect the islands. Present-day decreases in Rockhopper Penguins at Antipodes and Campbell Islands, and Southern Elephant Seals at Campbell, demonstrate the now lower productivity of the surrounding seas – perhaps due to a shifting southward of oceanic convergence zones. But the reasons behind such changes in seabird populations are complex. Black-browed and White-capped Mollymawks have colonised the Antipodes in recent times, for they did not nest there in the days of the Government steamers. Future global warming may also lead to changing rainfall and wind patterns, allowing new plants to colonise or dominate the islands.

The Antipodes Nature Reserve is fortunate to have several small offshore islands, notably Bollons Island where – in the absence of mice – indigenous invertebrates, plants and land birds have survived in a completely natural state. However, one other island is very special and its significance often overlooked. The 11-hectare summit of Leeward Island has more than legal protection. It is also guarded by sheer 70-metre cliffs, and fortuitously has never felt the foot of man. Neither sealer, scientist, tourist or helicopter has been there. The little sheltered hollow is a miniature "Lost World" – but with this realisation, why hurry to explore it? What better way to fly the flag of World Heritage Conservation than to give it a special designation, completely off-limits to managers, scientists and tourists alike, as an ecological time capsule – disturbed only by the wind, until such time as the future of the Antipodes Group depends on its desecration.

TABLE 8 Tourist voyages to the Antipodes and Bounty Islands, 1968–2000

Year	Ship	Captain	Expedition Leader	Bounty I.	Antipodes I.
1968	*Magga Dan*	F.E. Bang	Lars Lindblad	12 Jan	—
1982	*Lindblad Explorer*	Chris Coy	Tom Ritchie	1 Feb	1 Feb
1990	*World Discoverer*	Olaf Hartmann	Jack Grove	11 Dec	12 Dec
1992	*Pacific Ruby*	Gerry Clark	Rodney Russ	26 Dec	24–25 Dec
1993	*Pacific Ruby*	Gerry Clark	Rodney Russ	1 Jan	2 Jan
	Pacific Ruby	Gerry Clark	Brian Bell	15 Feb	14 Feb
1994	*Pacific Ruby*	Gerry Clark	Rodney Russ	12 Feb	11 Feb
	Akademik Shokalskiy	Nikolay Vinogradov	Rodney Russ	11 Dec	10 Dec
1995	*Akademik Shokalskiy*	Nikolay Vinogradov	Rodney Russ	15 Nov	16 Nov
1996	*Akademik Shokalskiy*	Sergey Glushkov	Rodney Russ	7 Dec	6 Dec
1997	*Akademik Shokalskiy*	Sergey Glushkov	Rodney Russ	—	3 Jan
1999	*Akademik Shokalskiy*	Nikolay Vinogradov	Rodney Russ	17 Dec	16 Dec
2000	*Akademik Shokalskiy*	Nikolay Vinogradov	Rodney Russ	3 Jan	4 Jan
	Akademik Shokalskiy	Nikolay Vinogradov	Rodney Russ	8 Jan	9 Jan
	Akademik Shokalskiy	Igor Kiselev	Rodney Russ	6 Dec	5 Dec

TABLE 9 Landings on the Bounty Islands, 1926–2000

Year	Month	Ship	Mission
1926	Feb.	*France*	Whitney South Sea expedition
1927	April	*Tutanekai*	NZ Government Steamer patrol
1950	Nov	*Alert*	Falla/Black Antipodes expedition
1961	Feb	*Argo*	Scripps Institute "Monsoon" expedition
1962	Nov	*Taranui*	NZ Oceanographic Institute (NZOI) cruise
1965	Jan	HMNZS *Endeavour*	NZOI research cruise
1968	Jan	*Magga Dan*	Lindblad Expeditions (tourism)
1974	May	HMNZS *Canterbury*	Royal NZ Navy (RNZN) patrol
1976	2 Nov	*Tangaroa*	NZOI (biology cruise)
	18 Nov	*Tangaroa*	NZOI (geophysics cruise).
1978	Sept	*Tangaroa*	NZOI research cruise
	Nov	HMNZS *Waikato*	NZ Wildlife Service BAAS expedition (party of three camped ashore for 13 days)
1983	April	HMNZS *Otago*	RNZN patrol

Year	Month	Ship	Mission
1985	March	HMNZS *Monowai*	Survey, filming and scientific expedition
1989	Dec	*Southern Cross*	TVNZ Natural History Unit filming
1990	Dec	*World Discoverer*	International Ornithological Congress cruise
1992	Dec	*Pacific Ruby*	Heritage Expeditions (tourism)
1997	7 Oct	*Totorore*	Gerry Clark Bounty Islands expedition (establishing camp)
	26 Oct	*Totorore*	(two people camped ashore for 25 days)
	9 Dec	*Totorore*	(2nd party of two camped ashore for 29 days)
1998	23 Jan	*Totorore*	(disestablishing camp)

Gazetteer of Place Names

ANTIPODES ISLAND GROUP

Albatross Point 49° 43′ 05″ S 178° 47′ 35″ E

Easternmost cape south of Ringdove Bay on Antipodes Island. Named Albatross Peak during *Ringdove*'s sketch survey of the Antipodes Island Group in 1896, probably for the Light-mantled Sooty Albatrosses that nest there.

Alert Bay 49° 41′ 15″ S 178° 48′ 40″ E

Bay on the eastern coast of Antipodes Island immediately south of Crater Bay. Named by the University of Canterbury Antipodes Island Expedition (UCAIE) 1969, after Alex Black's 1950 expedition vessel MV *Alert* which used this area as one of its anchorages. The name relates to the bay as far south as Leeward Island, and not just to its extreme northern corner as suggested on NZMS 272/4. This northern corner was a common landing place for passengers from the Government steamers and was known as Penguin Landing (Guthrie-Smith 1927).

Antipodes Island 49° 41′ 35″ S 178° 46′ 26″ E

The main Island of the Antipodes Island Group. Spelling confirmed by New Zealand Geographic Board (NZGB) in 1987. Originally named Isle Penantipode ("from its approach to the antipodes of London") by its discoverer, Captain Henry Waterhouse, commanding *Reliance* in 1800.

Antipodes Island Group 49° 41′ 05″ S 178° 46′ 26″ E

Antipodes Island and its adjacent smaller islands and islets. Name assigned by NZGB in 1987. Not: Antipodes Islands.

Anchorage Bay 49° 40′ 15″ S 178° 48′ 10″ E

Named by New Zealand Oceanographic Institute (NZOI) in 1969. Traditionally the main anchorage at the group. Originally named Depot Anchorage in *The New Zealand Pilot* 1901, and on early charts. The eastern end of this bay (as distinct from Hut Cove) is marked "Landing place" on the 1896 *Ringdove* chart of "Depot Anchorage", and is the most commonly used landing for small boats at the island.

Archway Island 49° 38′ 50″ S 178° 49′ 02″ E

Small island close to the northern end of Bollons Island. Named during the Bounty-Antipodes-Auckland-Snares (BAAS) Expedition, 1978. An archway at its eastern end was labelled "Remarkable Arch" on Captain John Fairchild's 1886 sketch map of the islands, on the 1896 *Ringdove* chart, and on the 1952 British Admiralty chart.

Bollons Island 49° 39′ 15″ S 178° 49′ 20″ E

Second largest island in the Antipodes Island Group, 2 km north of Reef Point. Named by the Officers of the Government Steamer *Hinemoa* after Captain John Bollons, who is the first person known to have climbed it, in January 1901. Originally named "Horseshoe Island" after its shape.

Cave Point 49° 41′ 30″ S 178° 43′ 50″ E

Westernmost point on Antipodes Island. Named by the NZOI in 1969. A huge sea cave nearby was named "Remarkable Cave" on Captain Fairchild's 1886 sketch map.

Central Plateau 49° 41′ 42″ S 178° 46′ 38″ E

Central, raised area of Antipodes Island between Mount Galloway and Mount Waterhouse. Named by UCAIE 1969, which established a field camp there.

Clark Hill 49° 41′ 15″ S 178° 48′ 15″ E

Isolated hill 191 m high behind Alert Bay and north of Dougall Stream. Name not official, but has been used by albatross researchers since 1995. Named after Gerry Clark owner/skipper of the yacht *Totorore*. This peak was directly above his preferred anchorage during the 1994 and 1995 expeditions.

Conical Hill 49° 40′ 35″ S 178° 47′ 58″ E

Distinctively shaped hill 135 m high at the northern edge of the North Plains. Clearly marked ("500" feet) but not named on Captain Fairchild's 1886 sketch map. Named by *Ringdove* in 1896 for its distinctive shape. Confused on some early 20th-century maps with Mount Galloway. Position corrected in 1969 by UCAIE.

Crater Bay 49° 40′ 50″ S 178° 48′ 55″ E

Bay on the eastern coast of Antipodes Island between Alert Bay and Stella Bay. Named by UCAIE 1969. It is the remnant of a series of volcanoes.

Dougall Stream 49° 41′ 41″ S 178° 47′ 42″ E

Stream draining from the Central Plateau and eastern slopes of Mount Galloway to Alert Bay. Named by UCAIE 1969 for William Dougall, photographer of Invercargill, who visited the island in 1888 and described a (mythical) lake on the top of Mount Galloway.

East Windward Island 49° 40′ 50″ S 178° 44′ 10″ E

Small steep rocky island situated about 1 km north east of Cave Point. Name assigned by NZGB, 1980. Not: Inner Windward Island. See: Windward Islands.

Horseshoe Island

Original name for Bollons Island. Still given as an alternative name in *New Zealand Pilot* up until 1946.

Hut Cove 49° 40′ 28″ S 178° 48′ 45″ E

The small, narrow bay just to the west of Reef Point and immediately below the castaway hut (depot) on Antipodes Island. Named by UCAIE 1969. Marked "landing place" on Fairchild's 1886 sketch map, as this is where the *Hinemoa* off-loaded the materials to build the depot.

Hut Stream 49° 40′ 35″ S 178° 48′ 20″ E

The stream draining the North Plains and entering the sea near the Castaway depot. It flows into Hut Cove and not into the eastern end of Anchorage Bay as shown on NZMS 272/4. Name used by Albatross researchers since 1997.

Leeward Island 49° 41′ 40″ S 178° 48′ 50′ E

Small tabular, cliffed island 200 m off the eastern shore of Antipodes Island, midway between Reef Point and Ringdove Bay. Named during *Ringdove*'s 1896 survey on account of its sheltered position in the lee of Antipodes Island.

Mirounga Bay 49° 40′ 45″ S 178° 46′ 25″ E

Wide bay on the north-west coast of Antipodes Island, east of Orde Lees Island. Named during the BAAS Expedition, 1978, after the Southern Elephant Seals (*Mirounga leonina*) that haul out and breed there.

Mount Galloway 49° 41′ 30″S 178° 47′ 02″ E

Highest peak (366 m) on Antipodes Island, situated immediately south of the North Plains. Named by Captain Fairchild of the *Hinemoa* after his chief engineer who accompanied him on a climb to the summit in March 1886.

Mount Melville 49° 42′ 00″ S 178° 47′ 38″ E

Prominent hill (294 m) on east coast of Antipodes Island, north of Ringdove Bay. Name not official, but given by albatross researchers for Brian Melville Walker who was their base radio operator and safety link between 1996 and 2003, and who died on the first day of the 2004 expedition.

Mount Waterhouse 49° 42′ 01″ S 178° 46′ 35″ E

Second-highest peak (356 m) on Antipodes Island, situated 1.15 km south of Mount Galloway. Named by UCAIE 1969, commemorating Captain Henry Waterhouse who discovered the islands.

North Cape 49° 39′ 50″ S 178° 47′ 50″ E

The northernmost point on Antipodes Island. Named by *Ringdove* in 1896 for its geographical position.

North Plains 49° 40′ 40″ S 178° 47′ 40″ E

The generally flat, open area behind Crater and Alert Bays and below the northern slopes of Mount Galloway. Named by UCAIE, 1969.

Orde Lees Islet 49° 40′ 40″ S 178° 45′ 35″ E

Small islet close inshore about halfway along the north west coast of Antipodes Island. Named after Thomas Orde Lees, a member of Sir Ernest Shackleton's *Endurance* expedition, following a sketch survey in March 1947 by the *Northwind*. The name first appeared on a 1947 US Navy Chart, "Islands and Anchorages to the Southward of New Zealand", and a year later on British Admiralty Chart 1022.

Perpendicular Head 49° 39′ 50″ S 178° 47′ 55″ E

Bold headland over 160 m high, immediately east of North Cape on Antipodes Island. Originally named "Perpendicular Cliffs" on Captain Fairchild's 1886 sketch map. Present name first used by F.R. Chapman in 1891 and appeared on *Ringdove's* chart in 1896.

Pipit Peak 49° 41′ 22″ S 178° 47′ 37″ E

Peak (about 190 m high) on low ridge leading down from Mount Galloway, situated midway between that mountain and Clark Hill. Name not official but used by albatross researchers since 1998. The Antipodes Island Pipit is an endemic land bird of the islands.

Point Felix Faure 49° 39′ 14″ S 178° 48′ 50″ E

Westernmost headland on Bollons Island. Name not official, but given here after the French four-masted barque *Président Félix Faure* wrecked beneath these cliffs on 13 March 1908.

Reef Point 49° 40′ 25″ S 178° 48′ 55″ E

North-eastern point of Antipodes Island between Hut Cove and Stella Bay. Named by Captain Fairchild on his 1886 map for its low aspect and offshore rocks.

Reliance Ridge 49° 42′ 45″ S 178° 45′ 55″ E

The ridge feature forming an arc above South Bay on Antipodes Island. Named by UCAIE, 1969, for *Reliance*, Captain Waterhouse's ship.

Ringdove Bay 49° 42′ 40″ S 178° 47′ 10″ E

Large bay on the eastern coast of Antipodes Island, north of Albatross Point. The most secure anchorage for large vessels during prevailing westerly weather. Named for *Ringdove* during surveys by that ship in 1896.

Ringdove Stream 49° 42′ 16″ S 178° 46′ 34″ E

The stream draining into Ringdove Bay, Antipodes Island. Named by UCAIE, 1969.

Sectoides Stream 49° 40′ 51″ S 178° 46′ 35″ E

This stream drains the north-west slopes of Mt. Galloway and the western end of North Plain before entering the sea near the middle of Mirounga Bay. Name not official, but used by albatross researchers since 1997. The stream's lower reaches traverse a swampy depression where the very large native sedge *Carex sectoides* reaches its greatest abundance on the island.

South Bay 49° 43′ 02″ S 178° 45′ 30″ E

Bay on the south coast of Antipodes Island, below Reliance Ridge and NNW of South Islet. Named by UCAIE, 1969. The name originally referred to what was described as a "large open bay" (NZGB 1972; Warham and Johns 1975) encompassing a low peninsula; but the name is now more appropriately applied to the smaller enclosed bay to the east of this peninsula, as on NZMS 272/4 (1978).

South Islet 49° 43′ 30″ S 178° 45′ 40″ E

Small wave swept rock bearing SSE from South Bay and lying about 500 m off the southernmost point of Antipodes Island. First charted and named by *Ringdove* in 1896.

Southern Valley 49° 42′ 20″ S 178° 45′ 45″ E

A prominent depression between Mt. Waterhouse and the northern end of Reliance Ridge, which includes the headwaters of streams flowing into both Ringdove and Stack Bays. Name not official, but used by Dr E.J. Godley (UCAIE, 1969) on a map published in his 1989 paper on the flora of the island.

Southwest Plain 49° 41′ 47″ S 178° 45′ 15″ E

The generally flat, elevated area behind Stack Bay and west of the Central Plateau and Mt. Waterhouse. Name not official, but used by Godley on his 1989 map (see above).

Spirit of the Dawn Rock 49° 42′ 50″ S 178° 43′ 50″ E

Rock (often awash) 2.5 km due south of Cave Point. Marked on Chart NZ 3111 and on NZMS 272/4 as "1.5m high rock". Name not official, but given here after the Liverpool barque *Spirit of the Dawn* wrecked on this reef, with the loss of five lives, on 4 September 1893.

Stack Bay 49° 42′ 00″ S 178° 44′ 30″ E

Large bay immediately SE of Cave Point. Named by NZOI in 1969 for its numerous rock stacks and reefs.

Stella Bay 49° 40′ 35″ S 178° 48′ 57″ E

Bay on the eastern coast of Antipodes Island just to the south of Reef Point. Named by UCAIE, 1969, for the *Stella*, the first Government steamer to search for castaways at the islands.

Totorore Shoal 49° 43′ 24″ S 178° 45′ 40″ E

Line of underwater reefs and turbulent water between South Islet and Antipodes Island. Name not official, but given here after the *Totorore*, lost in this area, with her two crew, on 12 June 1999.

West Windward Island 49° 40′ 50″ S 178° 43′ 20″ E

Small, high rocky island, cleft in two by a chasm, situated about 1 km north west of Cave Point. It is the most westerly of the Antipodes Island Group. Name assigned by NZGB, 1980. Not: Outer Windward Island. See: Windward Islands.

Windward Islands 49° 40′ 50″ S 178° 43′ 45″ E

This group comprising West Windward Island and East Windward Island was named by *Ringdove* in 1896 for their position on the "weather" side of Antipodes Island.

BOUNTY ISLANDS

Bounty Islands 47° 45′ 24″ S 179° 02′ 44″ E

The Bounty Islands are in three clusters, nowadays called the Main Group, the Centre Group and the East Group (NZMS 272/5). Originally named "The Bounty Isles" in 1788 by their discoverer, Lieutenant William Bligh, after his ship HMS *Bounty*. On Captain Fairchild's 1886 map and on the 1952 British Admiralty chart, the Main group was named "Western Group" and the East Group was "Eastern Group". There are also two named rocks – Norman Rocks and Rosario Rock – both submerged, lying several nautical miles westward of the islands (Chart: NZ 3111).

Main Group

Blackfish Shoal 47° 45′ 01″ S 179° 02′ 24″ E

A dangerous underwater reef between Ranfurly and Lion islands. Named during the BAAS expedition, 1978. In rough weather rocks are exposed which resemble the "schools of black fish" seen nearby by *Rosario* in 1870. Name first used on sketch surveys by *Waikato* in 1978, and on RNZN Hydrographic Chart 3111 (1992).

Bradley Cove 47° 44′ 45″ S 179° 01′ 50″ E

The northern end of the channel between Proclamation and Spider islands. Named during the BAAS expedition, 1978, for Captain Ian Bradley, who commanded the support vessel *Waikato* and led the diving team which carried out the expedition's first dive in this area. Originally the name referred specifically to the small cove between Spider Island and Seal Rock.

Bucket Cove 47° 44′ 53″ S 179° 02′ 03″ E

Channel between Proclamation and Tunnel islands. Named in 1978 by the BAAS expedition. A plastic bucket with a short rope attached, was lost here during an extensive subtidal flora and fauna survey of the area and later sighted during a dive at a depth of 39 metres.

Depot Island 47° 44′ 55″ S 179° 01′ 50″ E

The largest of the Bounty Islands, and former site of two castaway depots. The first, built by Captain Fairchild in 1886, was totally destroyed within a year by wind or lightning. A second was built in a more sheltered location in 1891, and of this only a few traces remain. Called "the largest island" or "the principal island" until referred to as "the Depot-island" by *Ringdove* in 1896. Given its present name by members of the BAAS expedition in 1978.

Dog Rock 47° 45′ 04″ S 179° 01′ 45″ E

Small islet lying between Penguin and Ruatara islands. Named during the BAAS expedition, 1978, for its shape as seen from the north-east. Name was first published on Lands and Survey Aerial Plan 1036/5 in 1979, and has been used in scientific publications since 1982.

Lion Island 47° 45′ 00″ S 179° 02′ 40″ E

Easternmost island of the Main Group. Named during the BAAS expedition, 1978. From the expedition's campsite on Proclamation Island, this island had the aspect of a reclining lion with the highest part at the eastern end being the head.

Penguin Island 47° 45′ 05″ S 179° 01′ 20″ E

Westernmost island in the Bounties. Named during the BAAS expedition, 1978, for the Erect-crested Penguins that are a notable feature of the islands.

Proclamation Island 47° 44′ 50″ S 179° 02′ 00″ E

Largest island east of, and separated by a narrow gut from, Depot Island. The original proclamation of possession of the Bounty Islands in 1870 was by Captain George Palmer from *Rosario* anchored nearby. Captain Ian Bradley of *Waikato* performed the exercise again ashore on this island on 7 November 1978.

Ranfurly Island 47° 45′ 00″ S 179° 02′ 10″ E

Island lying between Tunnel and Lion islands. Named during the BAAS expedition, 1978, for the substantial number of endemic Bounty Island Shags (*Leucocarbo campbelli ranfurlyi*) nesting there. The trinomial of the shag's scientific name derives from the Earl of Ranfurly, Governor of New Zealand, who collected the first specimens for the British Museum in 1901.

Ruatara Island 47° 45′ 10″ S 179° 01′ 45″ E

Southernmost island of the Main Group. Named by the NZGB in 1980 for the Maori chief Ruatara (later a friend of the Reverend Samuel Marsden) who with 13 other sealers was stranded on the Bounty Islands by the whaler *Santa Anna* for about nine months in 1808.

Seal Rock 47° 44′ 43″ S 179° 01′ 46″ E

Small islet immediately south east of Spider Island. Named during the BAAS expedition, 1978, for the numerous fur seals that are its only vertebrate fauna. Name in use in scientific publications since 1982.

Skua Rock 47° 44′ 45″ S 179° 01′ 30″ E

Small islet immediately south west of Spider Island. Named during the BAAS expedition, 1978. It is a main roosting area for Southern Skuas at the islands.

Spider Island 47° 44′ 40″ S 179° 01′ 45″ E

The largest of the group of five small islands to the north of Depot Island. Named during the BAAS expedition, 1978. Spider crabs were collected during a dive there. The fact that terrestrial spiders are one of the more prominent invertebrates on the Bounty Islands and the combined shape of this small group as seen on the map, appear to have also influenced the choice of name.

Tunnel Island 47° 44′ 55″ S 179° 02′ 05″ E

Island lying immediately north from the eastern point of Depot Island. Named during the BAAS expedition, 1978, for a tunnel that completely bisects it.

Centre Group

Castle Island 47° 45′ 50″ S 179° 02′ 45″ E

Southernmost island of the Centre Group. Named during the BAAS expedition, 1978. The top of the island is stepped like a castle.

Coronet Island 47° 45′ 47″ S 179° 02′ 32″ E

Westernmost island of the Centre Group. Named during the BAAS expedition, 1978, after the island's shape with three small projections on top, as seen from the north-west. Name first published on the 1979 Aerial Plan, and used in scientific publications since 1982.

Funnel Island 47° 45′ 40″ S 179° 02′ 45″ E

Largest island in the Centre Group and the highest (73 m) in the Bounty Islands. Named during the BAAS expedition, 1978. In moderate to rough seas, a cave that runs through the island collects enough water to funnel a substantial waterspout up through a blowhole high on the island's north-west slopes.

Prion Island 47° 45′ 45″ S 179° 02′ 45″ E

Island immediately south of Funnel Island. Named during the BAAS expedition, 1978, after large flocks of the local Fulmar Prion seen over this island.

East Group

Con Island 47° 45′ 44″ S 179° 04′ 05″ E

Rock immediately south-west from North Rock. Named during the BAAS expedition, 1978, for its resemblance to the conning tower of a partly submerged submarine. Name first published on the 1979 Aerial Plan, and used in scientific publications since 1982.

Molly Cap 47° 46′ 05″ S 179° 03′ 55″ E

High, southernmost island in the East Group. Named during the BAAS expedition, 1978, for the distinctive patch of nesting Salvin's Mollymawks on its summit.

North Rock 47° 45′ 40″ S 179° 04′ 15″ E

Northernmost island in the East Group. Named during the BAAS expedition, 1978, for its position in this group.

Outlying submerged rocks

Norman Rocks 47° 43′ 15″ S 178° 56′ 30″E

Submerged rocks, breaking occasionally, approximately 3.5 nautical miles north-west of Main Group. Named after Captain W.H. Norman, of the *Victoria,* who found these "outlying sunken rocks, very dangerous to approach" in November 1865.

Rosario Rock 47° 49″15″ S 178° 58′ 10″ E

Submerged rock about 4 nautical miles south-west of the Centre Group. First reported by *Rosario* in July 1870. According to the *New Zealand Pilot,* 1883, it sometimes does not break for five or 10 minutes and is "exceedingly dangerous".

Technical and Nautical Terms used in this book

CURRENCY

Pounds, shillings and pence: British units of currency, "Sterling", now obsolete. One pound (£1) was divided into 20 shillings. One shilling (1s) contained 12 pence (12d). One penny (1d) was further divided into two halfpennies, or four farthings. For example: "five pounds, four shillings and three pence ha'penny" was encrypted as £5 4s 3½d. Sometimes prices were given in shillings and pence only, eg "49s 6d".

Dollars: Nineteenth-century references are to Spanish or United States dollars. Ongoing inflation makes it hard to compare historical with modern-day values, but an ordinary seaman in the British Royal Navy earned £16 8s 0d per year in 1800 and about £20 in 1806, £24 in 1853, and £38 in 1880.

AREA

Acre: 0.404 hectares.

Rood: a quarter of an acre, 0.101 ha.

DISTANCE

Chain: 22 yards, 20.117 m.

Mile: a statute mile, 1.61 km.

Nautical mile: one minute of latitude, 1.15 statute miles, 1.85 km

League: a distance of three nautical miles, 5.55 km.

Fathom: unit of depth, 6 feet, 1.83 metres.

SPEED:

Knot: 1 nautical mile per hour, 1.61 mph, 1.85 km/h.

WEIGHT:

Pound: 1 pound (1 lb) equals 454 grams.

Hundredweight: 1 hundredweight (1 cwt) equals 112 lb, 50.8 kg.

Ton: 20 cwt, 1016 kg.

BAROMETRIC PRESSURE

Historically given as inches of mercury: 30″mercury = 1016 millibars.

VOLUME

Sack: a large jute bag used for sealskins, penguin feathers etc.

Barrel of whale or seal oil: approximately 165 litres.

Bundle: a small number of dried sealskins.

Cask of sealskins: about 40 skins.

Gallon: 4.55 litres

Sugar bag: small sack, capable of holding 25 lb of sugar.

Ton or tun of whale or seal oil: six barrels, approximately 1000 litres.

Tonnage of vessel: the tonnage of a trading vessel is calculated on internal volume. Register tonnage is used internationally for assessing dues and charges. It is derived from gross tonnage after deducting space used for crew accommodation, etc. One ton register equals 100 cubic feet or 2.83 cubic metres.

TIME

New Zealand Standard Time (NZST) is exactly 12 hours ahead of Greenwich Mean Time (GMT). Times given in the text are as quoted in the various records consulted. No attempt has been made to convert them to any one system, or allow for the many modes of daylight saving that New Zealand politicians have experimented with since 1868.

SAILING SHIPS

Sailing ships were classified mainly by the pattern of their masts and sails (rig). Most had up to four masts called – in order from bow to stern – foremast, mainmast, mizzen and jigger.

On square-rigged ships the oblong mainsails were carried on cross spars known as "yards", which were angled around to catch the wind by hauling on rope or wire "braces". In addition, square-riggers had many fore-and-aft sails in the form of triangular staysails (on all masts); at least three foresails (staysails and jibs) at the bow; and a gaff-rigged "spanker" at the stern.

On fore-and-aft rigged ships, the mainsails were set between two fore-and-aft spars, hinged to the mast, called the boom (lower) and the gaff (upper). Topsails were triangular and set above the gaff. On these vessels, staysails and jibs were confined to the bow.

Barque (American **Bark**): Sailing ship with three (or four) masts. Square-rigged on the fore and main masts and fore-and-aft rigged on the mizzen (or jigger) mast.

Barquentine: Similar to barque but square-rigged on the foremast only.

Brig: Two-masted vessel square-rigged on both fore and main masts, and also fore-and-aft rigged on the main.

Brigantine: Similar to a brig but square-rigged on the foremast only, and fore-and-aft rigged on the main.

Cutter: Originally a small decked ship with one mast, a bowsprit, a mainsail, a gaff-topsail and at least two jibs. Nowadays the name is also applied to US Coast Guard icebreakers and some other patrol vessels.

Full-rigged ship: Sailing ship with three or more masts, with square sails on all masts, and the aftermast also having a fore-and-aft sail.

Ketch: A two-masted vessel with both masts rigged fore-and-aft, having the foremast taller than the mainmast.

Schooner: A vessel with two or more masts, all rigged fore-and-aft, having the foremast shorter than the mainmast.

Sloop: Originally the name for a flush-decked sailing vessel, regardless of rig. The Royal Navy classified *Reliance* as a "barque-rigged sloop of war". Today the name is used for a small one-masted fore-and-aft rigged vessel, with mainsail and jib.

Snow: A modification of the brig. A snow had its for-and-aft spanker on a separate, short mast sited close behind the main mast. This made for easier working of the sails.

Whaler or **whaleship**: A sailing ship with facilities on deck for flensing and trying down whale blubber.

Bibliography

"Acheron", research vessel. 1972. Log entry. Alex Black, Dunedin.

Adams, C.J. 1985. *Geology of the Antipodes and Bounty Islands, Southwest Pacific.* Institute of Nuclear Sciences, DSIR, Report 300.

"Alaska", bark. 1886. Log entry. *PMB microfilm 278.* Pacific Manuscripts Bureau, Canberra.

"Alert", ship. 1845. Log entry. *PMB microfilm 720.* Pacific Manuscripts Bureau, Canberra.

"Alert", motor launch. 1950. Log entry. Alex Black, Dunedin.

Alexander, D. 1900–1904. New Zealand Journals. Alexander Turnbull Library. MSY-4600. Ranfurly family papers.

Allen, J.A. 1899. Fur-seal hunting in the southern hemisphere. In Jordan, D.S. (Ed): *The fur seals and fur-seal islands of the north Pacific Ocean*, part 3: pp. 307–19. Government Printing Office, Washington.

Amey, J., McAllister, G., Clark, G. 1994. *Antipodes Island Expedition 1994.* Unpubl. Report to NZ Department of Conservation.

Amey, J., McAllister, G., Hanel, C., Clark,G. 1995. *Antipodes Island Expedition 1995.* Unpubl. Report for NZ Department of Conservation.

"Amokura", NZS. 1913. Log entry. Archives New Zealand, Wellington.

Anon. 1876. Bread-fruit. In: *Encyclopaedia Britannica* (9th edition), vol. 4, pp. 241–42. Adam & Charles Black, Edinburgh.

Anon. 1894. Spirit of the Dawn. *Mercantile Marine Service Association Reporter* 19, p. 244 & 288. Lee & Nightingale, Liverpool.

Anon. 1950. Shipping, Wellington. *New Zealand Marine News* 2, p. 106.

Anon. 1967. Eltanin Cruise 27. *Antarctic Journal of the United States* 2, pp. 150–52.

Anon. 1978 a. Subantarctic Islands Expedition. *OSNZ news* 9, p. 5.

Anon. 1978 b. BAAS Expedition. Survey of Antipodes and Bounty Islands. *Antarctic* 8, pp. 279–82.

Anon. 1997. *Nomination of the New Zealand Subantarctic Islands by the Government of New Zealand for inclusion in the World Heritage List.* Department of Conservation, Wellington.

Antipodes Island Expedition. 1969. *Daily Log, 8 January–14 March 1969.* University of Canterbury, Christchurch.

Archey, G. 1923. Notes on Birds of the Sub-Antarctic Islands of New Zealand. *Records of the Canterbury Museum* 2: pp. 117–20.

Armstrong, H. 1868. *Cruise of the brig Amherst. Official Report.* New Zealand Government Gazette, Province of Southland 6 (9), pp. 51–6.

Armstrong, H. 1889. In search of Lost Sailors. *The Leisure Hour*, pp. 379–85; 463–467.

Aston, B.C. 1909. The soil and soil-formers of the Subantarctic Islands, pp. 745–77. In: C. Chilton (Ed). *The Subantarctic Islands of New Zealand.* Philosophical Institute of Canterbury, Wellington.

Atkins, J. 1830. New Zealand, in 1829. *United Service Journal and Naval and Military Magazine.* 1830 (Part 1), pp. 649–58.

Auckland Star. 1927. "The last call": 16 May.

Baker, Alan. 2002–03. Personal communications.

Barrow, J. 1886. *The Mutiny of the Bounty and the Pitcairn Islanders.* George Routledge & Sons. London.

Bartle, J.A. 1976. *Report on a visit to the Bounty Islands.* National Museum of New Zealand, Wellington.

Bastock, J. 1988. *Ships on the Australia Station.* Child & Associates, Frenchs Forest, NSW, Australia.

Beck, R.H. 1926. Letter to Secretary of Marine, dated 1 April. Archives New Zealand: M 14/3/6.

Beck, R.H. 1928. *Beck's Letters and Journal, December 1923–February 1928.* Whitney South Sea Expedition of the American Museum of Natural History. Unpublished volume in Ornithology Library, AMNH, New York.

Begg, A.C., Begg, N.C. 1979. *The World of John Boultbee.* Whitcoulls, Christchurch.

Belgrave, V. 1995. *Report on Subantarctic Islands GPS Survey Project, 3February–3 March.* Unpublished report for NZ Department of Conservation.

Bell, B.D. 1969. *Antipodes Island Expedition. General summary of work carried out and significant observations made.* Unpublished Wildlife Service report.

Bell, B.D. 1979. The Southern Islands of New Zealand. *Wildlife – a review* 10: pp. 5–10.

Bell, B.D., Taylor, R.H. 1970. The wild sheep of Campbell Island. *Forest and Bird* 178: pp. 6–10.

Bell, Brian D. 2001–04. Personal communications.

Black, A. 1950. *Antipodes and Bounty Islands Expedition, Nov.1950.* Movie film and monochrome photographs. Alex Black, Dunedin.

Black, Alex. 2002–03. Personal communications.

Blainey, G. 1994. *A Shorter History of Australia.* William Heinemann, Melbourne.

Bligh, W. 1792. *A Voyage to the South Sea, undertaken by command of His Majesty, for the purpose of conveying the Bread-Fruit tree to the West Indies, in His Majesty's Ship The Bounty.* (First published by George Nicol, London). Facsimile Edition, 1979. Hutchison, Melbourne.

Bollons, J. 1923. Letter to Secretary of Marine, dated 14 April. Archives New Zealand: M 14/3/6.

Bollons, J. 1927. Letter to Secretary of Marine, dated 7 April. Archives New Zealand: M 14/3/6.

Bowden, K.M. 1952. *George Bass 1771–1803.* Oxford University Press, Melbourne.

Bowen, G.F. 1871. Letters with Enclosures. *Appendix to the Journals of the House of Representatives* of *NZ* A-1: pp. 26–28.

Brodie, J.W.; Dawson, E.W. 1971. Antarctic icebergs near New Zealand. *New Zealand Journal of Marine and Freshwater Research* 5: pp. 80–85.

Brown, Grainger. 2003. Personal communications.

Buller, W.L. 1888. *A History of the Birds of New Zealand* (Second Edition). London.

Burrows, A.L. 1976. *Report on subantarctic island cruise of the GMV 'Tangaroa' 16–30 November 1976.* Geophysical Observatory, DSIR, Christchurch.

Burrows, C.J. 1976. Icebergs in the Southern Ocean. *New Zealand Geographer* 32: pp. 127–38.

Callan, L. 2000. *Shipwreck: Tales of survival, courage & calamity at sea.* Hodder Moa Beckett, Auckland.

Carrick, R. 1892. *New Zealand's Lone Lands.* Government Printer, Wellington.

Carrick, R. 1903. *Historical Records of New Zealand South, prior to 1840.* Otago Daily Times & Witness, Dunedin.

Chapman, F.R. 1891. The Outlying Islands south of New Zealand. *Transactions and Proceedings of the New Zealand Institute* 23: pp. 491–522.

Chapman, F.R. 1893. Notes on the Depletion of the Fur-Seal in the Southern Seas. *Canadian Record of Science,* October, 1893: pp. 446–59.

Chapman, F.R. 1895. *Illustrations from sub-arctic New Zealand. Otago Daily Times and Witness,* Christmas Number 1895. 19 December, p. 6.

Chilton, C. 1909. *The Subantarctic Islands of New Zealand.* (2 vols.) Canterbury Philosophical Institute, Wellington: Government Printer.

Chown, S.L., Rodriguez, A.S.L., Gremmen, N.J.M., Gaston, K.J. 2001. World heritage status and conservation of southern ocean islands. *Conservation Biology* 15: pp. 550–557.

Christchurch Press. 1899. "Shipping Intelligence": 3 November.

Christchurch Press. 1908. "Wreck on the Antipodes": 16 May.

Christchurch Press. 1958. "Fishermen looking for new grounds": 19 February.

Christchurch Press. 1963. "Stores, buildings damaged on Auckland Islands": 18 January.

Clark, G. 1995. *The 'Totorore' expedition to the Auckland and Antipodes Islands, New Zealand. December 1994 to April 1995.* Unpublished report for NZ Department of Conservation.

Clark, G. 2000. *The Totorore Voyage* (3rd Edition). Homelands Publications, Kerikeri, New Zealand.

Clark, G,, Amey, J., McAllister, G. 1995. Unexpectedly large numbers of Wandering Albatross (*Diomedia exulans*) breeding on Antipodes Island, New Zealand. *Notornis* 42: pp. 42–46.

Clark, G., Booth, A., Amey, J. 1998. *The Totorore Expedition to the Bounty Islands, New*

Zealand. October 1997 to January 1998. G. Clark, Kerikeri. p. 64.

Clark, G., Robertson, C.J.R. 1996. New Zealand White-capped Mollymawks (*Diomedea cauta cauta*) breeding with Black-browed *Mollymawks (D. melanophrys melanophrys*) at Antipodes Islands, New Zealand. *Notornis* 43: pp. 1–6.

Clausen, V. 1999. "Search fails to turn up missing boat". *Christchurch Press,* 21 June.

Clay, J.O. 1985. *Sub Antarctic Islands Expedition 1985.* Unpublished report to Lands & Survey Department.

Climo, F.M. 1972. *Report – Antipodes Island Expedition. 17–27 Nov., 1972.* Dominion Museum, Wellington.

Cockayne, L. 1904. A Botanical Excursion during Midwinter to the Southern Islands of New Zealand. *Transactions of the New Zealand Institute* 36: pp. 225–333.

Coleman-Cooke, J. 1963. *Discovery II in the Antarctic.* Odhams Press Ltd., London.

Collins, D. 1804. *An Account of the English Colony of New South Wales.* Vol.2. (First published by T. Cadell and W. Davies, London). Australian Edition, 1975. A.H. & A.W. Reed, Terrey Hills, Sydney.

Cooper, Sean. 2005. Personal communication.

Correia, J.G. 1926. *Letters and Journal of Jose G Correia from June 4, 1925 to October 18, 1926.* Whitney South Sea Expedition of the American Museum of Natural History. Unpublished volume in Ornithology Library, AMNH, New York.

Cotter, R.N. 2001. Meteorological observations at Antipodes Island. 30 October–26 November 1995. pp. 62–3. In: P. McClelland et al. 2001. *Antipodes Island Expedition, October–November 1995.* Department of Conservation, Southland.

Crowther, W.L. 1839. *Journal kept from Van Diemen's Land to England on board the barque "Emu", from February 24th to June 22nd 1839.* W.L. Crowther Library, State Library of Tasmania, Hobart.

Crowther, W.E.L.H. 1937. A Naturalist's Voyage from Van Diemen's Land to England. *The Emu* 37: pp. 19–27.

Croxall, J.P., Prince, P.A., Rothery, P., Wood, A.G. 1997. Population changes in albatrosses at South Georgia. In: G. Robertson & R. Gales (Eds). *Albatross Biology and Conservation.* Beaty & Sons, Chipping Norton.

Csordas, S.E. 1962. The Kerguelen fur seal on Macquarie Island. *The Victorian Naturalist* 79: pp. 226–29.

Cullen, D.J. 1969. Quaternary Volcanism at the Antipodes Islands: Its Bearing on Structural Interpretation of the Southwest Pacific. *Journal of Geophysical Research* 74: pp. 4213–20.

Cullen, D.J. 1975. Autochthonous rocks of the Bounty Islands region, South-West Pacific Ocean. *New Zealand Journal of Geology and Geophysics* 18: pp. 767–85.

Cullen, D.J. 1988. Mineralogy of nitrogenous guano on the Bounty Islands, SW Pacific Ocean. *Sedimentology* 93: pp. 421–28.

Cumpston, J.S. 1955. *Sub-Antarctic By-ways: The history of Macquarie Island. A Dependency of Tasmania.* Unpublished Manuscript. Australian Antarctic Division.

Cumpston, J. S. 1968. *Macquarie Island.* Antarctic Division, Department of External Affairs, Melbourne.

Cumpston, J. S. 1977. *Shipping Arrivals & Departures Sydney, 1788–1825*. Roebuck Society, Canberra.

Cunningham, D.M., Moors, P.J. 1994. The decline of Rockhopper Penguins *Eudyptes chrysocome* at Campbell Island, Southern Ocean and the influence of rising sea temperatures. *The Emu* 94: pp. 27–36.

Darby, M. 1970 a. The Natural History of the Bounty Islands. *Animals* 13: pp. 171–77.

Darby, M. 1970 b. Summer seabirds between New Zealand and McMurdo Sound. *Notornis* 17: pp. 28–55.

Darley, B. 1859. Antipodes Island – Incorrect position on Charts. *Nautical Magazine and Naval Chronicle*. June 1859: pp. 332–33.

Davis, L.S. 1998. *University of Otago Antipodes Island Expedition, September – November 1998*. Unpublished Report for the Department of Conservation.

Davis, L.S. 2001. A Superlative Penguin. *Natural History* 2001/11: pp. 46–55.

Dawson, E.W. 1963. New Zealand Oceanographic Institute. Some recent cruises. The marine biogeography of the Bounty–Antipodes region. *NZ Marine Sciences Newsletter* No. 3: pp. 28–29.

Dawson, Elliot. 2002–03. Personal communications.

Delano, A. 1973. *A Narrative of a Voyage to New Holland and Van Diemen's Land*. (Facsimile extract from Delano's "Narrative of Voyages and Travels . . . ", 1817) Cat & Fiddle Press, Hobart.

De Roy, Tui, Amey, Jacinda. 2005. *Mahalia Bounties/Antipodes Expeditions, November 2004*. Unpublished report for Department of Conservation.

Dorman, P. 1991. Subantarctic Islands Bird Cruise. *OSNZ news* 60: 1 September.

Dougall, W. 1888. *Far South*. Southland Times, Invercargill.

Dunbabin, T. 1925. Whalers, Sealers, and Buccaneers. *The Royal Australian Historical Society Journal and Proceedings* 11 (1): pp. 13–21.

Duthie, A. L. 1991. *CAPE Expedition Oral History*. Interview with Alistair Duthie recorded by Fergus Sutherland. Nelson, 3 July 1991.

Eden, A.W. 1955. *Islands of Despair*. Andrew Melrose, London.

Elder, J.R. (Ed.) 1932. *The Letters and Journals of Samuel Marsden 1765–1838*. Coulls Somerville Wilkie & A. H. Reed, Dunedin.

Elliott, J.M. 1950. A memorable visit to the Antipodes. *The Weekly News*: 22 November, p. 5.

Enderby, S. 1809. Letter to Sir Joseph Banks, 21 July 1809. Banks series 23.21, State Library of NSW, Sydney.

Estcourt, I.N. 1965. Oceanography on the Campbell Plateau. *NZDSIR Newsletter* April 1965: pp. 1–2.

Eunson, K. 1974. *The Wreck of the General Grant*. A.H. & A.W. Reed, Wellington.

Evans, E.R., Pennell, H.L. 1913. *Voyages of the Terra Nova*. pp. 281–318. In: Scott's Last Expedition. Vol. 2. MacMillan & Co., London.

Evening Post (Wellington). 1893. "The wreck of the *Spirit of the Dawn*": 12 December.

Evening Post (Wellington). 1927. "Ships and sailors": 25 July.

Evening Post (Wellington). 1947. US Navy to Wellington from Antarctica: 7, 8, 14, 15 March.

Evening Star (Dunedin). 1950. "Party completed detailed survey of outlying islands": 13 November.

Evening Star (Dunedin). 1975. *Veronica* search: 4 October.

Fairchild, J. 1886. Inspection of Antipodes and Bounty Islands and erection of castaway depot huts at both groups. *Appendix to the Journals of the House of Representatives of NZ 1886*. H-24: p. 6.

Falla, R.A. 1948. The outlying Islands of New Zealand. *New Zealand Geographer* 4 (2), pp. 127–54.

Falla, R.A. 1950. Straight through from London. *New Zealand Listener*. 1 December: p. 6.

Falla, R.A. 1953. Change and adjustment in plant and animal communities. *Proceedings of the New Zealand Ecological Society 2*: pp. 3–4.

Falla, R.A. 1962. Exploitation of seals, whales and penguins in New Zealand. *Proceedings of the New Zealand Ecological Society 9*: pp. 34–38.

Falla, R.A. 1975. Report on the 1962–63 Auckland Islands Expedition. pp.339–42, In: J.C. Yaldwyn (Ed). *Preliminary Results of the Auckland Island Expedition 1972–1973*. Department of Lands and Survey, Wellington.

Falla, R.A. (no date). *Cruises of "Amokura"*. MS papers 2366 (Folder 354). Alexander Turnbull Library, Wellington.

Fanning, E. 1924. *Voyages and Discoveries in the South Seas, 1798–1832*. Marine Research Society, Salem, USA.

Findlay, A.G. 1863. *A Directory for Navigation of the South Pacific Ocean; with description of its coasts, islands, etc.* (Second Edition). R.H. Laurie, London.

Fisher, R.L. (Ed.). 1964. *A preliminary Report on Expeditions MONSOON and LUSIAD, 1960–1963. Scripps Institute of Oceanography cruises to the Indian Ocean*. La Jolla: University of California, San Diego.

Fowler, R.M. 1980. *The Furneaux Group, Bass Strait: A Histo*ry. Roebuck Society, Canberra.

Fraser, C. 1985. *Civilian expedition leader's report on the objectives and results of HMNZS Monowai's deployment to New Zealand's subantarctic islands, 7 February–13 March, 1985*. National Film Unit, Wellington.

Fraser, C. 1986. *Beyond the Roaring Forties*. Government Printer, Wellington.

Fraser, M. 1906. The fragments of a lost continent. *The Red Funnel* 1 May 1906: pp. 333–41.

Gabby, J. 1927. *Away aloft and furl*. Manuscript on microfilm 694021. Alexander Turnbull Library, Wellington.

Gaskin, D.E. 1972. Icebergs south-east of New Zealand in 1967. *New Zealand Journal of Marine and Freshwater Research* 6: pp. 387–89.

Glasgow, Lord. 1895. Letter to the Secretary of State for the Colonies. *Appendix to the Journals of the House of Representatives of NZ*, Vol.1, A-1: pp. 10–15.

Godfrey, G.C. 1927. Notice to Mariners No.10 of 1927. *N.Z. Gazette No.11, 3rd March, 1927.*

Godley, E.J. 1979. *Notes on the flora and vegetation of Antipodes Island*. Unpublished report, Botany Division, DSIR. Christchurch.

Godley, E.J. 1989. The flora of Antipodes Island. *New Zealand Journal of Botany* 27: pp. 531–63.

Gordon, J. 1894. Letter and report to Minister of Lands, 2 June 1894. Norman Judd collection, Auckland.

Gordon, J. 1895. "The Campbell Island Sheep and Cattle Grazing Firm." Articles of Agreement, 1895. Norman Judd collection, Auckland.

Gregory, M.R. 1987. Plastics and other seaborne litter on the shores of New Zealand's subantarctic islands. *New Zealand Antarctic Record* 7: pp. 32–47.

Grey, W.J. 1885. *Report on trip to the Auckland, Campbell, Antipodes and Bounty Islands in search of castaways.* Archives NZ. M1 1866/1608.

Guthrie-Smith, H. 1936. *Sorrows and Joys of a New Zealand Naturalist.* Coulls Somerville Wilkie, Dunedin.

Haazen, Henk. 2003. Personal communication.

Hainsworth, D.R. 1967. Exploiting the Pacific Frontier. *Journal of Pacific History*, 2: pp. 59–75.

Hainsworth, D.R. 1972. *The Sydney Traders.* Cassell Australia, Melbourne.

Hall-Jones, F.G. 1945. *Historical Southland.* H & J Smith, Invercargill.

Hamilton, S., Wiltshire, A. 2000 a. *Albatross research trips to Antipodes Island and Adams Island, January/February 2000.* Unpublished report for the Department of Conservation.

Hamilton, S., Wiltshire, A. 2000 b. *Albatross Research Log, 2000.* Unpublished.

Hawkes Bay Herald. 1891. "The Quest for the Kakanui". 12 March.

Hay, C.H., Adams, N.M., Parsons, M.J. 1985. *The marine algae of the subantarctic islands of New Zealand.* Misc. Series No.11. National Museum of New Zealand, Wellington.

Heaphy, C. 1863. A Chapter on Sealing. *Southern Monthly Magazine* 1 (4): pp. 172–75.

Hector, J. 1870. Notes on the Geology of the Outlying Islands of New Zealand with extracts from Official Reports. *Transactions of the New Zealand Institute 2*: pp. 176–86.

Hector, J. 1896. Note on the Geology of the Outlying Islands of New Zealand. *Transactions of the New Zealand Institute* 28: pp. 736–43.

Herdman, H.F.P. 1953. Soundings taken during the Discovery Investigations, 1932–1939. *Discovery Reports* 25: pp. 41–107. Cambridge University Press.

Higham, T. 1991. Jewel in a Cruel Sea. *Listener & TV Times*, September 2: pp. 22–25.

"Hinemoa" SS. 1897. Log entry. Archives New Zealand, Wellington.

Hocking, C. 1969. *Dictionary of disasters at sea, during the age of steam, including sailing ships and ships of war lost in action, 1824–1962.* Vol. 2. M-Z. Lloyds Register of shipping, London.

Hollins, John (Captain). 2000. Personal communication.

Hooper, G. 1910. Report of Voyage of Amokura. Archives New Zealand: M17/3/18.

Hooper, G. 1914. Report on Depot for shipwrecked sailors – Bounty Islands. Archives New Zealand: M1 14/3/2.

Horning, D.S. 1979. Fourteen days on Bligh's islands. *Antarctic* 8: pp. 327–28.

Horning, D.S. 1986. *1978 Expedition to the Bounty and Antipodes Islands,*

New Zealand. Unpublished report, submitted to Wildlife Service, Wellington.
Horning, D.S. (Woody). 2003. Personal communication.
Howard, B. 1940. *Rakiura.* A. H. & A. W. Reed, Dunedin.
Hutton, F.W. 1894. On a new species of Weta *(Locustiae)* from Bounty Island. *Transactions and Proceedings of the New Zealand Institute* 27: pp. 174–76.
Hutton, F.W. 1897. The *Stenopelmatidae* of New Zealand. *Transactions and Proceedings of the New Zealand Institute* 29: pp. 208–42.
Hutton, F.W. 1902. On a small collection of *Diptera* from the southern islands of New Zealand. *Transactions and Proceedings of the New Zealand Institute* 34: pp. 169–75.
Imber, M.J. 1979. Petrels of the Antipodes Islands. *Wildlife – A Review* 10: pp. 11–15.
Imber, M.J. 1983. The lesser petrels of Antipodes Islands, with notes from Prince Edward and Gough islands. *Notornis* 30: pp. 283–98.
Ingram, C.W.N. 1972. *New Zealand Shipwrecks.* A.H. & A.W. Reed, Wellington.
Ingram, C.W.N., Wheatley, P.O. 1936. *Shipwrecks. New Zealand disasters. 1795–1936.* Dunedin Book Publishing Association, Dunedin.
Jackson, R. (Ed). 1886. *The Mercantile Navy list and maritime directory for 1886.* Spottiswoode & Co., London.
Johnston, T.A. 1967. Eltanin Cruise No. 27. *DSIR Newsletter,* June 1967: pp. 13–14.
Jones, A.G.E. 1986. *Ships Employed in the South Seas Trade, 1775–1861. Parts I, II & III.* Roebuck Society, Canberra.
Joyce, J.P. 1894. *Auckland, Campbell and other islands (Report on), and on their seals and Seal-Rookeries.* Report to New Zealand Parliament, Government Printer, Wellington.
Keen, R.J. 1985. Surveying during *Monowai* cruise. Unpublished report of Technical Division, Department of Lands & Survey.
Kerr, I.S. 1976. *Campbell Island – A History.* A. H. & A. W. Reed, Wellington.
Kerr, I.S. 1978. *Sealers in Southern New Zealand.* Manuscript papers 1685, Folder 2, in Alexander Turnbull Library, Wellington.
Kerr, I.S., Judd, N. 1978. *Marlborough Whalers at Campbell Island 1909–1916.* Department of Lands & Survey, Wellington.
Keys, J.R. 1990. Ice. pp. 95–123. In: Glasby, G. P. (Ed.). *Antarctic Sector of the Pacific.* Elsevier, Amsterdam.
King, C.M. 1990. *The Handbook of New Zealand Mammals.* Oxford University Press, Auckland.
Kirk, A.A. 1975. *Fair Winds and Rough Seas.* A.H. & A.W. Reed Ltd., Wellington.
Kirk, T. 1891. On the Botany of Antipodes Island. *Transactions of the New Zealand Institute* 23: pp. 436–41.
Lands & Survey Department, 1890. Map: The Colony of New Zealand. 829a / ca1890 / Acc.398. Alexander Turnbull Library, Wellington.
Lands & Survey Department, 1978. *Establishment of a Presence on Outlying Islands Reserves.* Letter to Minister from Director-General, Department of Lands & Survey. Copy filed G-5-5000, Department of Conservation, Invercargill.
Lands and Survey Department, 1979. *Antipodes Island Management Plan (Draft).* Head Office, Wellington.

Lands and Survey Department, 1982. *Bounty Islands Management Plan.* Head Office, Wellington.

Lindblad Expeditions, 1982. *M.S. Lindblad Explorer Voyage #6249, "In the Wake of the H.M.S. Bounty" (January 31–February 13, 1982). Expedition Log.* Lindblad Expeditions, New York.

Ling, J.K. 1999. Exploitation of fur seals and sea lions from Australia, New Zealand and adjacent subantarctic islands during the eighteenth, nineteenth and twentieth centuries. *Australian Zoologist,* 31 (3): pp. 323–50.

Ling, J.K. 2002. Impact of colonial sealing on seal stocks around Australia, New Zealand and Subantarctic islands between 150 and 170 degrees east. *Australian Mammalogy* 24: pp. 117–26.

Litt, R. 1951. Antipodean Adventure. *Tararua* 5: pp. 39–41.

Little, F., Park, G. 1999. *Overdue Totorore 15/06/1999 Antipodes Islands.* Final report. Maritime Safety Authority of New Zealand, Wellington.

Lloyds. 1893a. *Lloyds Register. British and foreign shipping, 1892–93.* Committee of Lloyds Register, London.

Lloyds. 1893b. Spirit of the Dawn. *Lloyds weekly shipping index.* No. 728, Vol. 28. 8 December 1893, London.

Lloyds. 1906. *Lloyds Register. British and foreign shipping, 1905–06.* Committee of Lloyds Register, London.

Lloyds. 1908a. President Felix Faure. *Lloyds weekly shipping index.* No.1469, Vol. 57. 20 February 1908, London.

Lloyds. 1908b. President Felix Faure. *Lloyds weekly shipping index.* No.1482, Vol. 57. 21 May 1908, London.

Lukins, E. 1896. *Round Southern Isles.* Bond, Finney, and Co., Nelson.

Lyttelton Times, 1908. "Wreck at the Antipodes": 16 May.

Macarthur, D.M.M. 1975. Personal account of the 1962–63 Auckland Islands Expedition. pp. 343–48, In: J.C. Yaldwyn (Ed.). *Preliminary Results of the Auckland Islands Expedition 1972–1973.* Department of Lands and Survey, Wellington.

Mack, J.D. 1966. *Matthew Flinders 1774–1814.* Thomas Nelson, Melbourne.

McAllister, G. & Amey, J. 1999. *Gus McAllister and Jacinda Amey's account of the "Totorore" search, 20 June–2 July 1999.* Unpublished statement to Search and Rescue, Wellington.

McClelland, P., Imber, M., Tennyson,A., Taylor, G., Grant, A., Greene, T., Marris, J., McIntosh, A., Cotter, R. 2001. *Antipodes Island Expedition, October–November 1995.* Southland Conservancy, Department of Conservation.

McCraw, J. 1999. *Coastmaster. The story of Captain James B. Greig.* Silverdale Publications, Hamilton.

McCredie, A. 1945. Letter to Controller of Fisheries, Wellington. Archives New Zealand, M1 2/6/1 pt 6.

McDougall, J.C. 1976. *Visit to Bounty Islands – Permit 1976/6.* NZ Oceanographic Institute, DSIR.

McDougall, R.J. 1978. The Sinking of SS "Hinemoa". *New Zealand Marine News* 29: pp. 83–86.

McLaren, F.B. 1948. *The Auckland Islands: Their Eventful History.* A.H. & A.W. Reed, Wellington.

McNab, R. (no date). *Cases against sealing Vessels, 1811–1834.* Typscript: qms – 0457 in Alexander Turnbull Library, Wellington.

McNab, R. 1907. *Murihiku and the Southern Islands.* William Smith, Invercargill.

McNab, R. 1908. *Historical Records of New Zealand.* (Vols.1 & 2) Government Printer, Wellington.

McNab, R. 1914. *From Tasman to Marsden.* J.Wilkie & Co. Ltd., Dunedin.

Macpherson, J. 1889. Report to Minister of Lands, Wellington, 7 February 1889. Norman Judd collection, Auckland.

Marine Department. 1887. Annual Report. *Appendix to the Journals of the House of Representatives of NZ,* H-4: p. 4.

Marine Department. 1894. Annual Report. *Appendix to the Journals of the House of Representatives of NZ,* H-18: p. 3.

Marine Department. 1895. Annual Report. *Appendix to the Journals of the House of Representatives of NZ,* H-29: p. 5.

Marshall, P. 1909. The Meteorology of Campbell Island, pp.789–92 In: Chilton, C. (Ed.). *The Subantarctic Islands of New Zealand.* Philosophical Institute of Canterbury.

Marris, J. 2001. *7.0 Terrestrial Arthropods.* In: McClelland & others, 2001.

Martin, E.R. 1969. *Marine Department Centennial History.* Marine Department, Wellington.

Mayo, J.J. (Ed.) 1872. *The Mercantile Navy list and Maritime Directory for 1872.* Sir William Mitchell, London.

Melbourne Argus. 1888. Antipodes Islands incorrectly placed on charts: 24 June.

Meurk, C.D. 1985. *Report on the 1985 Southern Islands (New Zealand) Expedition.* Unpublished report, Botany Division, DSIR, Christchurch.

Miskelly, C.M., Cary, P.W., Wass, J.R. 1989. *Research Proposal, Antipodes Island: September 1989–February 1990.* Department of Zoology, University of Canterbury.

Miskelly, C.M., Carey, P. W. & Pollard, S. D. 1990. *Antipodes Island Expedition, 12–16 October 1990. Report.* Department of Zoology, University of Canterbury.

Moore, G. 1968. To Antarctica by Sea. *Pacific Discovery* 2 (4): pp. 10–15.

Moors, P.J. 1980. Southern Great Skuas on Antipodes Island, New Zealand: Observations on foods, breeding, and growth of chicks. *Notornis* 27: pp. 133–46.

Moors, P.J. 1986. Decline in numbers of Rockhopper Penguins at Campbell Island. *Polar Record* 23: pp. 69–73.

Moriarty, H.A. 1886. Seamanship. *Encyclopaedia Britannica* (9th edition). Vol. 21: pp. 589–605. A. & C. Black, Edinburgh.

Munro, C.T. 1923. Copy of dairy kept on a trip round the Southern Islands. March 1923. G-5–6000 in Subantarctic Database, Department of Conservation, Invercargill.

Musgrave, T. 1866. *Castaway on the Auckland Isles.* Lockwood and Co., London.

National Film Unit, 1986. *Beyond the Roaring Forties.* (Documentary, 58 minutes).

"Navy", ship. 1846. Log entry. *PMB microfilm 676.* Pacific Manuscript Bureau, Canberra.

New Zealand Pilot, 1875. (Fourth Edition). Hydrographic Office, Admiralty, London.

New Zealand Pilot, 1883. (Fifth Edition). Hydrographic Office, Admiralty, London.

New Zealand Pilot, 1958. (Twelfth Edition). Hydrographic Office, Admiralty, London.

Newton, J.R. 1979. *BAAS expedition '78.* Unpublished report to Department of Lands & Survey, Wellington.

Newton, J.R. 1980. *Antipodes Island Nature Reserve.* Dissertation for Diploma in Parks & Recreation, Lincoln University, New Zealand.

Nicholson, I.H. 1983. *Shipping Arrivals and Departures Tasmania, 1803–1833.* Roebuck Society, Canberra.

Norman, F.M. (Ed.) 1918. *Memoirs of the life of the Right Hon. David, Seventh Earl of Glasgow, 1833–1915.* T. & A. Constable, Edinburgh.

Norman, W.H., and Musgrave, T. 1866. *Journals of the voyage and proceedings of H.M.C.S. Victoria in search of ship-wrecked people at the Auckland and other islands.* Government Printer, Melbourne.

"Northwind", USCGC. 1947. Log entry. *13 E-2 Logbooks (Northwind).* Boxes 97–98. 6/4/1. U.S. National Archives and Records Administration, Washington.

O'Connor, T. (Ed.) 1999. *New Zealand's Subantarctic Islands.* Reed, Auckland.

Ogilvie-Grant, W.R. 1905. On the birds procured by the Earl of Ranfurly in New Zealand and the adjacent islands. *The Ibis* 8: pp. 543–602.

Oliver, W.R.B. 1927. *New Zealand's Subantarctic Isles.* (Unpublished manuscript). Museum of New Zealand, Wellington. [Printed with modifications as: "Solitary Isles", in *Evening Post*, Wellington, 16 April 1927].

Oliver, W.R.B. 1955. *New Zealand Birds.* A.H. & A.W. Reed, Wellington.

Ollerenshaw, H.J. 1951. *Report on inspection of Antipodes Island and Bounty Islands. 2.11.50–13.11.50.* Wildlife Branch, Department of Internal Affairs. [Archives New Zealand, Dunedin].

OSNZ. 1999. Erect-crested Penguin. *OSNZ news* 92: p. 14.

Otago Daily Times. 1893. "Rescue of castaways": 5 December.

Otago Daily Times. 1908. "The wreck at the Antipodes": 18 & 19 May.

Otago Daily Times. 1913. "Castaways. Sea Captain's experiences": 8 September.

Otago Daily Times. 1975a. Items on "Global Hitch hikers" – 14, 18, 19, & 24 March.

Otago Daily Times. 1975b. Items on *Veronica* search – 22 & 24 September.; 3 October.

Otago Witness. 1893. "Rescue of castaways": 7 December.

Outlying Islands Reserves Committee. 1972. Minutes of meeting on 31 October.

Outlying Islands Reserves Committee. 1973. Minutes of meeting on 27 March.

Outlying Islands Reserves Committee. 1987. *Submission by OIRC on review of Conservation Quangos, 27 November 1987.* Department of Conservation, Head Office, Wellington.

Palmer, G. 1871. Report and Proclamation. *Appendix to the Journals of the House of Representatives of NZ,* A-1: pp. 28–29.

Patrick, B. 1994. Antipodes Island Lepidoptera. *Journal of the Royal Society of New Zealand,* 24: pp. 91–116.

Peat, N. 2003. *Subantarctic New Zealand – A Rare Heritage.* Department of Conservation, Invercargill.

Phelps, W.D. 1871. *Fore and Aft; or, Leaves from the Life of an Old Sailor.* Nichols & Hall, Boston.

Plunket, Lord. 1912. The Outlying Islands of New Zealand. *United Empire.* London, January 1912: pp. 18–28.

Pollard, S.D. 1995. A World Apart. *Natural History,* 11: pp. 54–58.

Poverty Bay Herald. 1902. S.S. *Rimu* for Campbell Island: 13 March.

Pullman, M. 1973. Single-handed around New Zealand. *Sea Spray,* April: pp. 50–53.

Quartermain, L.B. 1967. *South to the Pole: The early history of the Ross Sea Sector, Antarctica.* Oxford University Press, London.

Reay, A., Forsyth, P.J., Turnbull, I.M. 1990. *Geological Investigations on the Antipodes Islands, 8th–18th October 1990.* DSIR Geo immediate field report. File: QM483/710.

Reischek, A. 1889. Notes on the Islands to the South of New Zealand. *Transactions of the New Zealand Institute* 2: pp. 378–89.

Renner, M. & Schulze, A. 1999 (Unpubl.) *Antipodes Island Daily Log: 30 May–2 July 1999.*

Richards, R. 1982. *Whaling and Sealing at the Chatham Islands.* Roebuck Society, Canberra.

Richards, R. 1992. An American Sealing Explorer Captain Isaac Percival's Search for the Nimrod Islands,1828–1830. *The Log of Mystic Seaport,* 44 (3): pp. 59–63.

Richards, R. 1994. "The upland seal" of the Antipodes and Macquarie Islands: a historian's perspective. *Journal of the Royal Society of New Zealand,* 24(3): pp. 289–95.

Richards, R. 1995. *Murihiku Re-viewed.* Lithographic Services, Wellington.

Richards, R. 2003. New market evidence on the depletion of southern fur seals: 1788–1833. *New Zealand Journal of Zoology* 30: pp. 1–9.

Richards, R., Knight, L. 1996. *Jorgen Jorgenson's Observations on Pacific Trade: and Sealing and Whaling in Australian and New Zealand Waters before 1805.* Paramata Press, Wellington.

Ricketts, L.S. 1973. *Antipodes Island. Report to Surveyor-General.* Archives New Zealand, DAFU/D311/151, 13/51.

Ridgeway, N.M. 1975. Hydrology of the Bounty Islands Region. *Memoir New Zealand Oceanographic Institute 75.*

Robertson, C.J.R. 1979. Subantarctic Islands Expedition. *OSNZ news* 10: p. 2.

Robertson, C.J.R., van Tets, G.F. 1982. The status of birds at the Bounty Islands. *Notornis* 29: pp. 311–36.

"Rob Roy", brig. 1830. *Logbook kept on board the brig Rob Roy of Boston, Mass., Isaac Percival, master, for a voyage to the Atlantic, Indian and Pacific Ocean sealing and sea elephant grounds. Olog 29.* G.W. Blunt White Library, Mystic Seaport Museum, Mystic, Connecticut.

Ross, J.O.C. 1987. *William Stewart. Sealing captain, trader and speculator.* Roebuck Society, Canberra.

Russ, Rodney. 2003. Personal communication.

Russell, H.C. 1895. Icebergs in the Southern Ocean. *Journal & Proceedings of the Royal Society of New South Wales,* September 29: pp. 286–315 and Plate 12.

Russell, H.C. 1897. Icebergs in the Southern Ocean, No.2. *Journal & Proceedings of the Royal Society of New South Wales* 31: pp. 221–51.

Sadleir, R.M.F.S., Taylor, R.H., Taylor, G.A. 1986. Breeding of Antarctic Terns (*Sterna vittata bethuni*). *Notornis* 33: pp. 264–65.

Sale, C. 1999 a. *Totorore search by the Yacht Snow Cloud.* Unpublished report to the Maritime Safety Authority of New Zealand.

Sale, C. 1999 b. Letter dated 9/11/99 to the Department of Conservation, Invercargill.

Sale, Chris. 2003. Personal communication.

Schmechel, F. 1998. Expedition to the Bounties. *OSNZ News* 45 (2): pp. 1–3.

Scott, A.W. 1873. *Mammalia, Recent and Extinct.* T. Richards, Government Printer, Sydney.

"Seine", ship. 1844. Log entry. *PMB microfilm 257.* Pacific Manuscripts Bureau, Canberra.

Shand, A. 1894. Notes regarding icebergs at the Chatham Islands. *Transactions and Proceedings of the New Zealand Institute* 25: pp. 516–17.

Shaughnessy, P.D., Fletcher, L. 1987. Fur seals, *Arctocephalus* spp., at Macquarie Island. *NOAA Technical Reports NMFS* 51: pp. 177–88.

Shaw, Lance. 2005. Personal communication.

Sherrin, R.A.A. 1886. *Handbook of the fishes of New Zealand.* Wilson and Horton, Auckland.

Sherrin, R.A.A., Wallace, J.H. 1890. *Early History of New Zealand.* H. Brett, Auckland.

Smith, S.P. 1916. *Reminiscences of a Pioneer Surveyor.* MS 281, Box 1, p. 88. Auckland War Memorial Museum Library.

Smithers, C.N. 1999. *Sandrapsocus clarki*, an unusual new genus and species of Elipsocidae (Insecta: Psocoptera) from the Bounty Islands. *Journal of the Royal Society of New Zealand* 29: pp. 159–64.

Sobel, D., Andrewes, W.J.H. 1999. *The Illustrated Longitude.* Fourth Estate, London

Society Expeditions, 1990. *Project Sub-Antarctic Islands of Australia and New Zealand aboard M/S World Discoverer, December 8–22, 1990. Expedition Log.* Society Expeditions, Inc. Seattle.

Sorensen, J. 1969. New Zealand fur seals with special reference to the 1946 open season. *New Zealand Marine Department, fisheries technical report 42.*

Southland Daily News. 1880: *Shipping* – 11 August, 2 October, 5 October, 20 November.

Southland Daily News. 1893. "The Spirit of the Dawn": 5 December.

Southland Daily News. 1908. "Robbery at island depots – despicable crime": 27 May.

Southland Times. 1880. *Shipping* – 30 June, 26 July, 5 August, 2 October, 9 October, 22 November.

Southland Times. 1881. *Shipping* – 27 August.

Southland Times. 1891. *Shipping* – 7 July, 8 July, 29 August, 7 September, 18 September, 28 September, 29 September.

Spence, A. 1968. A Story of the Campbell Islands. *Tussock Grasslands and Mountain Lands Institute Review* 15: pp. 63–75.

Stackpole, E.A. 1972. *Whales and Destiny.* The University of Massachusetts Press.

Stanley, R.J. 1969. *Castaway Depot.* Unpublished report to the Canterbury Museum from the University of Canterbury Antipodes Island Expedition, 1969.

Stanley, Rob. 1997. Personal communication.

Stevenson, W.P. 1859. Antipodes Island. – Incorrect position on charts. *Nautical Magazine.* June 1859: pp. 333–34.

Stoneham, A. (Ed). 1877. *The Mercantile Navy List and Maritime Directory for 1877.* Sir William Mitchell, London.

Taylor, G.A. 2000. *Action plan for seabird conservation in New Zealand. Parts A and B.* Threatened Species Occasional Publication Nos. 16 &17. Department of Conservation, Wellington.

Taylor, R.H. 1969. *Summary of studies carried out on Campbell and Antipodes Island while with the University of Canterbury Antipodes Island Expedition, 1969.* Unpublished report, Animal Ecology Division, DSIR, Lower Hutt.

Taylor, R.H. 1975 a. What limits kiore (*Rattus exulans*) distribution in New Zealand? *New Zealand Journal of Zoology* 2: pp. 473–77.

Taylor, R.H. 1975 b. Some Ideas on Speciation in New Zealand Parakeets. *Notornis,* 22: pp. 110–21.

Taylor, R.H. 1978. Distribution and interactions of rodent species in New Zealand, pp. 135–43. In: Dingwall, P.R., Atkinson, I.A.E., Hay, C. (Eds.), *The ecology and control of rodents in New Zealand Nature Reserves.* Information Series No.4. Department of Lands and Survey, Wellington.

Taylor, R.H. 1979 a. *Meteorological Observations at Antipodes Island, 9 November–5 December 1978.* Unpublished report, Ecology Division, DSIR, Lower Hutt.

Taylor, R.H. 1979 b. How the Macquarie Island Parakeet became Extinct. *New Zealand Journal of Ecology,* 2: pp. 42–45.

Taylor, R.H. 1982. New Zealand fur seals at the Bounty Islands. *New Zealand Journal of Marine and Freshwater Research,* 16: pp. 1–9.

Taylor, R.H. 1985. Status, Habits and Conservation of *Cyanoramphus* Parakeets in the New Zealand Region, pp. 195–211, In*:* P.J. Moors (Ed.) Conservation of Island Birds. *ICBP Technical Publication No. 3.* Cambridge.

Taylor, R.H. 1990. Records of subantarctic fur seals in New Zealand (Note). *New Zealand Journal of Marine and Freshwater Research* 24: pp. 499–502.

Taylor, R.H. 1992. New Zealand fur seals at the Antipodes Islands. *Journal of the Royal Society of New Zealand,* 22: pp. 107–22.

Taylor, R.H. 1996. *Distribution, abundance and pup production of the New Zealand fur seal (Arctocephalus forsteri Lesson) at the Bounty Islands.* Science for Conservation 32: Department of Conservation, Wellington.

Taylor, R.H., Bell, B.D., Wilson, P.R. 1970. Royal albatross, feral sheep and cattle on Campbell Island. *New Zealand Journal of Science* 13: pp. 78–88.

Taylor, R.H., Taylor, G.A. 1989. Re-assessment of the status of Southern Elephant Seals (*Mirounga leonina*) in New Zealand. *New Zealand Journal of Marine and Freshwater Research* 23: pp. 202–13.

Tennyson, A., Imber, M., Taylor, R. 1998. Numbers of Black-browed Mollymawks (*Diomedea m. melanophrys*) and White-capped Mollymawks (*D. cauta steadi*) at the Antipodes Islands in 1994–95 and their population trends in the New Zealand region. *Notornis* 45: pp. 157–66.

Tennyson, A., Taylor, G. 2001. *4.0 Penguins.* In: McClelland & others, 2001.

Tennyson, A., Taylor, R., Taylor, G., Imber, M., Greene, T. 2002. Unusual bird records from Antipodes Islands in 1978–1995, with a summary of other species recorded at the island group. *Notornis* 49: pp. 241–45.

Thomas, C.W. 1947 a. U.S.C.G.C. Northwind. Annex One (i). In: *Report of Operation Highjump – U.S. Navy Antarctic Development Project 1947.* National Archives and Records Administration, Maryland, U.S.A.

Thomas, C.W. 1947 b. The Coast Guard in Operation Highjump. *Coast Guard Academy Alumni Association Bulletin* (September): pp. 293–98.

Thomas, C.W. 1972. Personal communication.

Thompson, G.M. 1922. *The Naturalisation of animals and plants in New Zealand.* Cambridge University Press.

Thompson, D., Sagar, P. 2002. Declining rockhopper penguin populations in New Zealand. *Water & Atmosphere* 10 (3): pp. 10–12.

Thomson, J.B. 2003. *Elephant Island and Beyond: The life and diaries of Thomas Orde Lees.* The Erskine Press, Norwich.

Tilly, T.C. (Ed.) 1887. *Brett's New Zealand and South Pacific Pilot for the years 1887–88.* H. Brett, Auckland.

Turbott, E.G. 1950. Unpublished field notes.

Turbott, E.G. 1951. Antipodes penguins were not amused. *The Weekly News*: 24 January, p. 22.

Turner, G.M. 1930. *The Sub-Antarctic Islands of New Zealand.* Unpublished. Copy filed G-5-1031. Department of Conservation, Invercargill.

Waite, E.R. 1909. Vertebrata of the Subantarctic Islands of New Zealand, pp. 542–600. In: C. Chilton (Ed). *The Subantarctic Islands of New Zealand.* Philosophical Institute of Canterbury, Wellington.

Walker, Kath. 2003–04. Personal communications.

Walker, K., Elliott, G. 1996. *Monitoring Antipodean Wandering Albatross: 1996 field season.* Unpublished report to Department of Conservation.

Walker, K., Elliott, G. 1997. *Wandering Albatross Research and Monitoring, Auckland and Antipodes Islands 1997.* Unpublished report to Department of Conservation.

Walker, K., Elliott, G. 1998. *The impact of fisheries bycatch on Antipodean Wandering Albatross. Report on the 1997/98 field season.* Unpublished report.

Walker, Kath, Elliott, Graeme. 2001–04. Personal communications.

Walker, K., Elliott, G., Hamilton, S., Wiltshire, A. 1999. *The impact of fisheries bycatch on Antipodean Wandering Albatross. Report on the 1998/99 field season.* Unpublished report.

Warham, J. 1968 (Unpublished). *Antipodes Island Expedition 1969.* Outline proposal for the Expedition. Department of Zoology, University of Canterbury, September 1968.

Warham, J. 1969 (Unpublished). *A Preliminary Report on University of Canterbury Antipodes Island Expedition, 1969.* Department of Zoology, University of Canterbury, August 1969.

Warham, J. 1976 (Unpublished). *South to the Real Antipodes.* Unpublished manuscript,

Department of Zoology, University of Canterbury.

Warham, J., Johns, P.M. 1975. The University of Canterbury Antipodes Island Expedition. *Journal of the Royal Society of New Zealand* 5: pp. 103–31.

Warham, J., Bell, B. D. 1979. The birds of Antipodes Island, New Zealand. *Notornis* 26: pp. 121–69.

Wasserburg, G.J., Craig, H., Menard, H.W., Engel, A.E.J., Engel, C.G. 1963. Age and composition of a Bounty Island granite and age of a Seychelles Islands granite. *Journal of Geology* 71: pp. 785–89.

Waterhouse, H. 1800. HMS *Reliance,* Captain's Log. Entry for 26 March 1800. Public Record Office, London. ADM 51/1312. 76498.

Waterhouse, H. 1800. Chart of Isle Penantipode. National Maritime Museum, Greenwich. FLI/15/9 (Image ID: C1714).

Weimerskirch, H., Jouventin, P. 1997. Changes in population sizes and demographic parameters of six albatross species breeding on the French sub-antarctic islands. In: G. Robertson & R. Gales (Eds.) *Albatross Biology and Conservation.* Beatty & Sons, Chipping Norton.

Westerskov, K. 1991. Off the beaten track . . . The Bounty Islands. Phantom reefs and twenty foot sharks! *New Zealand Underwater,* October/November. 2–3: p. 17.

Williams, Murray. 2004. Personal communication.

Wilson, G.J. 1983. *Distribution and Abundance of Antarctic and Sub-Antarctic Penguins. A synthesis of current knowledge.* BIOMASS Scientific Series Cambridge, SCAR and SCOR.

Wilson, O.H. 1840. Antipodes Island. *The Nautical Magazine and Naval Chronicle.* March 1840: p. 145.

Wilson, P.R., Gaze P.D. 1983. *Report to Lands and Survey Department on short visit to Campbell Island, 1–10 April 1983.* Ecology Division, NZDSIR.

Wilson, R.A. 1891. *Diary of first voyage to Milford Sound and the Sub-Antarctic Islands. 1 October–November 1891.* Alexander Turnbull Library, MS- Papers- 1338.

Wright, M. 2001. *Blue Water Kiwis – New Zealand's Naval Story.* Reed Publishing NZ Ltd.

Notes

1 INTRODUCTION

1 Lands & Survey Department, 1979, 1982.
2 Anon., 1997; O'Connor, 1999; Chown, 2001.
3 Reay, et al., 1990; O'Connor, 1999.
4 Adams, 1985.
5 Cullen, 1988.
6 De Roy & Amey, 2005.
7 Hay et al., 1985.
8 Warham & Johns, 1975; Taylor, 1979 a; Meurk, 1985; Cotter, 2001.

2 DISCOVERY

1 Anon., 1876.
2 Bligh, 1792.
3 Barrow, 1886.
4 Bligh, 1792.
5 Sobel & Andrewes, 1999.
6 Hall-Jones, 1945.
7 Collins, 1804.
8 McNab, 1907.
9 Waterhouse, Log 1800.
10 Waterhouse, Chart 1800.
11 Collins, 1804.

3 THE EARLY SEALERS

1 Mack, 1966.
2 Bowden, 1952.
3 McNab, 1907.
4 McNab, 1907; Sherrin & Wallace, 1890.
5 Fanning, 1924; Fowler, 1980; Ross,1987.
6 Fowler, 1980; Kerr, 1978; Ross, 1987.
7 Stackpole, 1972.
8 Ross, 1987.
9 Howard, 1940.
10 Ross, 1987; Richards & Knight, 1996.
11 Richards & Knight, 1996.
12 Ross, 1987.
13 Fowler, 1980; Ross, 1987.
14 Fowler, 1980; Ross, 1987.
15 Fowler, 1980.
16 Hainsworth, 1967, 1972.
17 Fowler, 1980.
18 Hainsworth, 1967, 1972.
19 Fowler, 1980.
20 Hainsworth, 1972.
21 Fowler, 1980.
22 Ross, 1987.
23 Fowler, 1980; Ross 1987.
24 Stackpole, 1972.
25 Cumpston, 1977; Ross, 1987.
26 Hainsworth, 1972; Fowler, 1980.
27 Delano, 1973.
28 Richards, 1982.
29 Elder, 1932.
30 Carrick, 1903; McNab, 1914.

31 Cumpston, 1977.
32 Enderby, 1809; Cumpston, 1977; Nicholson, 1983; Jones, 1986.
33 Richards, 1982.

4 THE END OF THE SEALING BONANZA

1 Richards, 1982.
2 Ross, 1987.
3 McNab, 1907; Richards, 1982.
4 Hainsworth, 1972; Ross, 1987; Richards, 1994, 1995.
5 Cumpston, 1977; Richards, 1982.
6 Smith, 1916.
7 Richards, 1982.
8 Ross, 1987.
9 McNab, 1907; Cumpston, 1968; Fowler, 1980.
10 Ross, 1987; Cumpston, 1977.
11 McNab, 1907; Nicholson, 1983; Begg & Begg, 1979.
12 McNab, n.d.
13 Cumpston, 1977; Ross, 1987.
14 McNab, n.d.
15 Atkins, 1830; McNab, 1908.
16 *Rob Roy* Log, 1830; Richards, 1992.
17 McNab, 1914.
18 Richards, 1982.
19 This vessel was probably American, as she is missing from all contemporary British, Australian and New Zealand shipping lists. She is not to be confused with the brig *Lord Rodney*, of Chatham Island notoriety, which was reported wrecked at Whangaroa Harbour, New Zealand, in 1836.
20 Heaphy, 1863.
21 *Seine* Log, 1844.
22 *Alert* Log, 1845.
23 *Navy* Log, 1846.
24 Findlay, 1863.
25 *Southland Times*, 5 August 1880.
26 *Southland Times*, 1880.
27 *Southland Daily News*, 1880.
28 *Southland Times*, 1880.
29 Fraser, 1986.
30 Cumpston, 1955.
31 *Southland Times*, 1881.
32 Lukins, 1896.
33 *Southland Times*, 1891.
34 Chapman, 1893.
35 *Alaska* Log, 1886.
36 Archives NZ. M1 2/6/1. Seals 1912–22; Kerr, 1976; Ling, 1999.
37 Sorensen, 1969.
38 Richards, 2003.
39 Ling, 1999, 2002.

5 HAZARDS TO SHIPPING

1 Crowther, 1937.
2 Crowther, 1839; Crowther 1937.
3 Blainey, 1994; Eunson, 1974.
4 Stevenson, 1859.
5 Musgrave, 1866.
6 Norman & Musgrave, 1866.
7 Eunson, 1974.
8 Armstrong, 1868, 1889.
9 Hector, 1870.
10 Armstrong, 1889.
11 Armstrong, 1868.
12 Bowen, 1871.
13 Ingram, 1972.
14 Darby, 1970 a.
15 Bowen, 1871.
16 Palmer, 1871.
17 Bowen, 1871.
18 McLaren, 1948; Kerr, 1976.
19 Carrick, 1903; Cumpston, 1968.
20 *NZ Pilot*, 1883; Kerr, 1976; McCraw, 1999.
21 *NZ Pilot*, 1875.

6 NEW ZEALAND GOVERNMENT STEAMERS

1 Martin, 1969.
2 McCraw, 1999.
3 Archives NZ. M1 1886/1608.

4 *Hinemoa* Log, 1897; Martin, 1969; Kerr, 1976.
5 *Hawkes Bay Herald*, 1891.
6 Kerr, 1976.
7 McDougall, 1978.
8 Gabby, 1927; Wright, 2001.
9 Archives NZ. M1 14/3/6.
10 Archives NZ. Marine Dept. Letterbook, 1880.
11 Martin, 1969.
12 Quartermain, 1967.

7 SUCCOUR FOR CASTAWAYS — DEPOTS, LIVESTOCK AND PLANTS

1 Fairchild, 1886.
2 Newton, 1979, 1980.
3 Glasgow, 1895.
4 Ollerenshaw, 1951.
5 Falla, 1950.
6 *Christchurch Press*, 19 Feb. 1958 & 18 Jan 1963; Falla 1975; Macarthur, 1975.
7 Stanley, 1969.
8 *Otago Daily Times*, 3 Oct 1975.
9 Fairchild, 1886.
10 Marine Department, 1887.
11 Chapman, 1891.
12 Lukins, 1896.
13 Wilson, 1891.
14 Lukins, 1896.
15 Hooper, 1910.
16 Hooper, 1914.
17 Bollons, 1923.
18 Correia, 1926.
19 Beck, 1928.
20 Beck, 1926.
21 Godfrey, 1927.
22 Oliver, 1927; Bollons, 1927.
23 Darby, 1970a.
24 Canterbury Museum records.
25 Carrick, 1892; Joyce, 1894.
26 Kirk, 1891.
27 Carrick, 1892; Wilson, 1891.
28 Thomson, 1922.
29 Cockayne, 1904.
30 Waite, 1909.

8 THE *SPIRIT OF THE DAWN*

1 Mayo, 1872; Stoneham, 1877; Jackson, 1886; Lloyds, 1893a.
2 Lloyds, 1893b.
3 *Otago Daily Times*, 1893; *Southland Daily News*, 1893; *Otago Witness*, 1893.
4 *Otago Daily Times*, 1893.
5 Tilly, 1887.
6 *Evening Post*, 1927.
7 *Otago Daily Times*, 1893.
8 *Otago Daily Times*, 1913.
9 *Otago Daily Times*, 1893.
10 *Otago Witness*, 1893.
11 *Otago Daily Times*, 1913.
12 *Otago Daily Times*, 1893.
13 *Otago Witness*, 1893; Hocking, 1969.
14 *Otago Daily Times*, 1893; Marine Dept., 1894, 1895.
15 *Evening Post*, 1893; Anon., 1894.
16 *Southland Daily News*, 1893.
17 *Otago Daily Times*, 1913.

9 ASK THE NAVY

1 Archives NZ, G 12 no.3, 1894–98.
2 Archives NZ, G 17/10, 119.
3 Archives NZ, RNAS 1, 1889–97.
4 *Christchurch Press*, 1899; Ogilvie-Grant, 1905.
5 Archives NZ, G 12 no.5, 1903–04.

10 THE *PRÉSIDENT FÉLIX FAURE*

1 Lloyds, 1906; Ingram & Wheatley, 1936.
2 *Christchurch Press*, 1908.
3 Lloyds, 1908 a&b; *Otago Daily Times*, 1908.
4 *Otago Daily Times*, 1908.
5 *Otago Daily Times*, 1908.
6 *Christchurch Press*, 1908.
7 *Lyttelton Times*, 1908.

8 *Christchurch Press*, 1908.
9 *Lyttelton Times*, 1908; *Christchurch Press*, 1908.
10 *Otago Daily Times*, 1908.
11 *Otago Daily Times*, 1908.

11 AN ATTEMPT TO PROMOTE PASTORAL FARMING

1 Bowen, 1871.
2 Armstrong, 1868.
3 Fairchild, 1886.
4 Macpherson, 1889.
5 Lands & Survey Department, 1890.
6 Joyce, 1894.
7 Gordon, 1894.
8 McLaren, 1948; Kerr, 1976.
9 Gordon, 1895.
10 Archives NZ, Dunedin. LS 13/51.
11 Kerr, 1976.
12 Archives NZ. M1 1901/2204.
13 Alexander, 1900–04.
14 *Poverty Bay Herald*, 1902; Kerr, 1976.
15 Archives NZ, Dunedin. LS 13/51.

12 TRAVELLERS, NATURALISTS AND SCIENTISTS, 1886–1927

1 Archives NZ, M1 17/4/34.
2 Reischek, 1889.
3 Buller, 1888.
4 Reischek, 1889.
5 Dougall, 1888.
6 Chapman, 1891, 1895; Kirk, 1891.
7 Chapman, 1895.
8 Wilson, 1891; Carrick, 1892.
9 Glasgow, 1895; Hector, 1896; Norman, 1918; Godley, 1989.
10 Lukins, 1896.
11 Alexander, 1900–04.
12 Ogilvie-Grant, 1905.
13 Alexander, 1900–04; Ogilvie-Grant, 1905.
14 Hutton, 1902.
15 Hutton, 1894, 1897.
16 Alexander, 1900–04.
17 www.matapihi.org.nz
18 Cockayne, 1904.
19 Aston, 1909.
20 Archey, 1923; Munro, 1923.
21 Oliver, 1955.
22 Turner, 1930.
23 Guthrie-Smith, 1936.
24 Oliver, 1927; Hay et al.,1985; Godley, 1989.

13 EXPEDITIONS AND VISITS, 1926–1969

1 Beck, 1928.
2 Correria, 1926.
3 Falla, 1948, 1950; Herdman, 1953; Coleman-Cooke, 1963.
4 Duthie, 1991.
5 McCredie, 1945.
6 Sorensen, 1969; Archives NZ, M1 2/6/1 part 6.
7 Thomas, 1947a.
8 *Northwind* Log, 1947.
9 Thomas, 1947 b.
10 Thomas, pers. comm. 1972.
11 Thomas, 1947 a & b; *Northwind* Log, 1947.
12 *Evening Post*, 1947; Thompson, 2003.
13 *Evening Star*, 1950; Falla, 1950; Elliott, 1950; *Alert* log, 1950; Turbott, 1950, 1951.
14 Anon., 1950.
15 Black, 2002–03
16 *Alert* log, 1950.
17 Ollerenshaw, 1951.
18 Litt, 1951.
19 *Christchurch Press*, 1958; Kerr, 1976.
20 Fisher, 1964; Wasserburg et al., 1963.
21 Dawson, 1963; 2002–03.
22 Cullen, 1975.
23 Cullen, 1969.
24 Dawson, 2002–03.

25 Estcourt, 1965; Cullen, 1969; Warham & Johns, 1975, Ridgeway, 1975.
26 Anon.,1967; Johnston, 1967; Godley, 1989; Taylor, 1992.
27 Kirk, 1975.
28 Darby, 1970 a.
29 Moore, 1968.
30 Darby, 1970 a.
31 Moore, 1968.
32 Darby, 1970 b.

14 UNIVERSITY OF CANTERBURY EXPEDITION, 1969

1 Warham, 1968, 1969.
2 Warham & Johns, 1975.
3 Taylor et al., 1970.
4 Warham, 1976.
5 Stanley, 1997.
6 Bell, 1969.
7 Warham & Bell, 1979.
8 Taylor, 1975 b, 1979 b.
9 Taylor, 1969.
10 *Antipodes* Log, 1969.
11 *Antipodes* Log, 1969.
12 *Antipodes* Log, 1969.

15 EXPEDITIONS AND VISITS, 1970–1978

1 Bell & Taylor, 1970.
2 OIRC, 1972,1973.
3 Baker, 2002–03; Black, 2002–03.
4 *Acheron* Log, 1972; Climo, 1972.
5 Baker, 2002–03.
6 *Acheron* Log, 1972; Baker, 2002–03; Black, 2002–03.
7 Ricketts, 1973.
8 Pullman, 1973.
9 Taylor, 1982, 1996.
10 Taylor, 1982.
11 Russ, pers. comm., 2003.
12 *Otago Daily Times*, 1975a.
13 *Otago Daily Times*, 1975b; *Evening Star*, 1975.
14 Bartle, 1976; McDougall, 1976.
15 Burrows, A.L.,1976; Dawson, 2002–03.
16 Hay et al., 1985.

16 BAAS WILDLIFE SERVICE EXPEDITION, 1978

1 Anon, 1978 a & b; Robertson, 1979; Bell, 1979.
2 Horning, 1986.
3 Taylor, 1982.
4 Horning, 1979; Robertson & Van Tets, 1982.
5 Horning, pers. comm. 2003.
6 Horning, 1986.
7 Horning, pers. comm. 2003.
8 Moors, 1980.
9 Horning, 1986.
10 Taylor, 1985.
11 Imber, 1979, 1983.
12 Lands & Survey, 1978.
13 Newton, 1979.
14 Taylor, 1992.
15 Imber, 1983.
16 Taylor, 1990.

17 EXPEDITIONS AND VISITS, 1979–1990

1 Lindblad Expeditions, 1982.
2 Wilson & Gaze, 1983; Taylor, 1992.
3 Fraser, 1985.
4 Williams, 2004.
5 National Film Unit, 1986.
6 Keen, 1985.
7 Peat, 2003; Williams, 2004.
8 Fraser, 1986.
9 Clay, 1985.
10 Meurk, 1985.
11 Gregory, 1987.
12 Westerskov, 1991.
13 Fraser, 1986; Sadleir, et al., 1986; Taylor, 1992, 1996.
14 TVNZ series "*Islands*": Part 1, *Islands – Splendid Isolation.*

15 Miskelly, et al., 1989.
16 Miskelly, et al., 1990.
17 Reay, et al., 1990.
18 Patrick, 1994.
19 Pollard, 1995.
20 Higham, 1991.

18 CHANGING TIMES

1 Dorman, 1991.
2 Society Expeditions, 1990.
3 Brown, pers. comm., 2003.
4 Heritage Expedition Logs. Dec. 1992–Feb.1994.
5 Heritage Expedition Logs. Dec. 1994–Feb. 1996.
6 Amey et al., 1994; Clark et al., 1995; Clark & Roberston, 1996.
7 Clark, 1995.
8 Amey et al., 1995.
9 Belgrave, 1995.
10 McClelland, et al., 2001.
11 Walker, pers. comm., 2003–04.
12 Walker & Elliott, 1996; Shaw, 2005.
13 Clark et al., 1998.
14 Schmechel, 1998.
15 Walker & Elliott, 1998, 2001–04.
16 Davis, 1998, 2001; Shaw, 2005.
17 Walker, et al., 1999.

19 THE WRECK OF THE *TOTORORE*

1 Little & Park, 1999.
2 Renner & Schulze, 1999.
3 Renner & Schulze, 1999.
4 Renner & Schulze, 1999.
5 Clausen, 1999.
6 Howard, 1940.
7 Eden, 1955.
8 McAllister & Amey, 1999.
9 McAllister & Amey, 1999.
10 Renner & Schulze, 1999.
11 McAllister & Amey, 1999.
12 Sale, 1999a.
13 Sale, 1999b.
14 Sale, 1999a, 2003; Little & Park, 1999.
15 Haazen, 2003.
16 Russ, 2003.
17 Hamilton & Wiltshire, 2000a.
18 Hamilton & Wiltshire, 2000b.
19 Little & Park, 1999.
20 Sale, 1999a.

20 NATURAL HISTORY

1 Horning, 1986.
2 Westerskov, 1991; Cooper, 2005.
3 Hay et. al., 1985.
4 Godley, 1979.
5 Godley, 1989.
6 DeRoy & Amey, 2005.
7 Meurk, 1985.
8 Hamilton & Wiltshire, 2000 a.
9 Horning, 1986; Anon., 1997.
10 Smithers, 1999.
11 Horning, 1986; Anon., 1997.
12 Patrick, 1994.
13 Taylor, 2000; Tennyson et al., 2002.
14 Tennyson et al., 1998.
15 Robertson & Van Tets, 1982; Clark et al., 1998; Taylor, 2000.
16 Taylor, 1969; Marris, 2001.
17 Taylor, 1982, 1990, 1992, 1996; Ling, 2002; Richards, 2003.
18 Taylor, 1990, & unpublished.
19 Csordas, 1962; Falla, 1962; Shaughnessy & Fletcher, 1987.
20 Taylor, 1992.
21 Richards, 1994.
22 Taylor & Taylor, 1989.
23 Clark et al., 1998.

21 CONCLUSION

1 Dunbabin, 1925.
2 Falla, 1948.
3 McLaren, 1948.
4 Kerr, 1976.

Index

Page numbers in bold refer to illustrations